the sandman
companion

the sandman
companion

hy bender

TITAN BOOKS
LONDON

Vertigo, all characters, their distinctive likenesses, and related
indicia featured in this publication are trademarks of DC Comics.

ISBN 1 84023 150 5 (hardcover)
ISBN 1 84023 164 5 (softcover)

Published by Titan Books, a division of
Titan Publishing Group Ltd., 144 Southwark Street,
London SE1 0UP, under license from DC Comics.

A CIP catalogue record for this title is available
from the British Library.

Other comics reference titles and graphic novels
can be ordered from Titan Books Mail Order, Bowden House,
36 Northampton Road, Market Harbourough, Leics, LE16 9HE.
Or you can call 01858 4333169 with your credit card details.

Designed by Murphy Fogelnest
Title-page art by Stan Woch and Dick Giordano
First hardcover edition: January 2000

10 9 8 7 6 5 4 3 2 1

Printed in Canada

To

NEIL GAIMAN

AND

ALAN MOORE,

FOR THEIR

WIT

AND

KINDNESS

The quintessential Morpheus, Lord of Dreams, from the early years of *The Sandman*.

contents

Acknowledgments   ix

Introduction   xi

PART ONE: **overview**

1   Getting Started with *Sandman*   2

2   A Dream Is Born   12

PART TWO: **the *sandman* collections**

3   Preludes & Nocturnes   28

4   The Doll's House   41

5   Dream Country   62

6   Season of Mists   89

7   A Game of You   110

8   Fables and Reflections   131

9   Brief Lives   159

10 Worlds' End   176

11 The Kindly Ones   186

12 The Wake   203

PART THREE: **backstory**

13 Secret Origins   232

14 Music, Poetry, and Patterns   250

15 Struggles and Triumphs   258

appendixes

A   *Sandman* Credits   264

B   Additional *Sandman* Tales   271

C   For More Information...   272

16 pages of color illustrations follow page 114.

acknowledgments

My heartfelt thanks go to Neil Gaiman
for all his time and help; to my editor Karen
Berger for her sharp suggestions; and to
Murphy Fogelnest for designing and laying
out this book so beautifully.

My thanks also go to the more than
two dozen people who generously gave of
their time by letting me interview them.
This book is much richer for the information
and wisdom they provided.

In addition, I want to thank Tracey M. Siesser,
Lorraine Garland, Ken Houghton, Joy Levine,
Elizabeth McIntyre, Thom Carnell, Joe Fulgham,
Professor Alan Levitan, Professor Joe Sanders,
Professor Edward James, and Michael Zulli for
their help above and beyond the call.

Finally, I'd like to thank the wonderful people
in my monthly reading group—including
Loretta Brady, Ron Bruno, Tiffany Haick, Mikki
Morrissette, Henri Rosen, Raphael Rothstein,
Linda Scott, Ranbir Sidhu, Mona Temchin,
Katherine Turok, and Mary Vandivier—for all
the lively discussions we've had about literature,
which ultimately contributed to this book

introduction

The next century's task will be to rediscover its gods.
—ANDRÉ MALRAUX

We have the right, and the obligation, to tell old stories in our own ways, because they are *our* stories.
—NEIL GAIMAN

Welcome to a world of gods, myths and dreams. Welcome to the world of *Sandman*. If you aren't already a fan, you may be surprised to find topics such as the soul and the subconscious being sensitively handled in *comic books*, which are commonly perceived as shallow entertainment. But the reason that the medium, like Rodney Dangerfield, "don't get no respect" is mostly the result of a series of historical accidents—such as U.S. comics publishers traditionally targeting children and teens as their primary audience—not as a result of any aesthetic problem with the marriage of words and pictures.

The truth is that spectacular, mind-blowing comics have been produced since the modern comic book was born in the 1930s. Further, the field reached high levels of sophistication in the 1980s, thanks to such groundbreaking works as Frank Miller's gritty futuristic miniseries *The Dark Knight Returns*, Alan Moore's literate horror series *Swamp Thing* and super-hero epic *Watchmen*, and Art Spiegelman's insightful portrayal of the Holocaust and its aftermath in *Maus: A Survivor's Tale*.

Carefully taking in these developments at the time was a young British writer named Neil Gaiman, who started producing a few notable stories of his own. Industry giant DC Comics was sufficiently impressed with Gaiman's initial efforts to ask him to create a monthly title. The result was an unusual series that debuted in 1989 starring a pale-skinned, dour sovereign whose royal titles include "the Sandman."

The Sandman violates all the rules about what makes a character popular in the super-hero-dominated comics industry. Instead of fighting criminals or saving lives, his sole concern is to maintain "The Dreaming," which is the infinite, ever-changing psychic landscape we visit every night while asleep. Rather than being muscular, cheery, and colorful, he's thin, humorless, and perpetually dressed in black. In lieu of maintaining a secret identity to fit in with normal people, he prefers to avoid people (but nonetheless loves taking on scores of different names, including Morpheus, Oneiros, Lord Shaper, Nightmare King, Prince of Stories, and—most frequently—Dream). And instead of battling for his life against monsters and mad scientists, he seldom encounters situations that place him in any physical jeopardy . . . because his powers rival those of gods.

To further make reader identification difficult, the Sandman isn't even human. He's a ten-billion-year-old member of the Endless, a family of anthropomorphic personifications of such universal forces as Destiny (the blind caretaker of a book that contains all past, present, and future events), Desire (a sexy, androgynous Patrick Nagel print come to life), and Death (an ankh-wearing Goth girl so appealing that you almost look forward to ultimately meeting her). They're called the Endless because, as projections of fundamental ideas, they're immortal—but that doesn't stop them from occasionally trying to kill one another.

There are many other players in *Sandman*, as well. Over the course of the series, we meet mythic figures such as Lucifer, Kali, and Orpheus; historical figures such as Augustus Caesar, Marco Polo, Geoffrey Chaucer, and (in one particularly surreal tale) an aging John Belushi; bizarre figures such as a librarian who preserves books that were dreamt of but never written, a woman who keeps house with the ghost of the man who impregnated her, and a nightmare who uses his teeth-filled eye sockets to munch on the eyeballs of his victims; and scores of others culled from our collective unconscious. But the real star of the series wasn't Dream or any of his supporting cast; it was Gaiman's playful, brilliant writing and imagery, which weave an intricate metamyth around the very subject of myth.

Readers of *Sandman* are treated to an annual convention for serial killers; a lost universe where cats hunt people like mice; a dance bar that's blasted to smithereens by the sexual power of a goddess; and a beach where a vacationing Lucifer grudgingly compliments God on the beauty of his sunsets. These and scores of comparable inventive scenes provide a journey you're unlikely to forget.

To bolster the reality of his creations, Gaiman employed a quiet writing style that invites you to fill in the silences with your own imagination. His complex story, often pushed forward with little more than carefully dropped hints, culminates in something akin to a religious experience.

Sandman has garnered critical acclaim from some of the best writers in the world, including Norman Mailer, Stephen King, Clive Barker, Gene Wolfe, and Ramsey Campbell. Best-selling novelist Peter Straub recently told me:

> When I started reading *Sandman*, the first thing that struck me was its maturity. Gaiman was telling this ambitious, complex story, and at the same time communicating very deep emotions and very interesting ideas.

As I continued to follow *Sandman*, I was repeatedly impressed by Gaiman's originality and imagination; and by his ability to tie diverse story elements together. Some of his tales fold back in on themselves, others depart for completely foreign realms—and yet everything rhymes, everything connects towards a meaningful resolution. It takes a real gift to travel in as many directions as Gaiman does and still keep moving forward.

Sandman is one of the most intelligent and accomplished works of fantasy I've ever encountered.

Harlan Ellison, who has won scores of writing awards and has influenced generations of fantasy and SF authors with such anthologies as *Dangerous Visions*, is another *Sandman* fan. He told me:

Neil's *Sandman* work is on a par with great literature. I remember finishing issues of *Sandman* and just sitting there trying to catch my breath, saying, "What a ride this guy has taken me on."

And I'd add, "how brilliantly clever." I'm a fairly clever guy, and I knew that I was catching maybe a *third* of the cultural references in each issue that Neil would just casually drop in. Neil has a cornucopial mind that's able to draw on references from any period in history.

In each generation there are a small number of talents who do the seminal work that influences everyone else. Neil is one of those talents.

Of course, *Sandman*'s impact goes beyond an appreciation for its craftsmanship. Here's how rock star Tori Amos once explained the appeal of the series:

We don't remember our myths anymore. And what is myth? It's just truth that has happened and that we've forgotten, but that's still happening now. . . .

Neil helps us get in touch with our own memories; he opens a window for us to go in and find ourselves.

Comics are a collaborative medium, so many superb pencillers, inkers, and colorists helped *Sandman* achieve its critical success. In fact, because of the quality of Gaiman's scripts, *Sandman* attracted some of the finest artists in the industry. Karen Berger, the savvy editor who encouraged Gaiman's experimentation, signed up the people needed to make the series go, and coordinated the whole process to ensure *Sandman* came out on schedule every month.

As word spread, the series became a hit with comics fans; and just as important, it built up a loyal audience of book readers who normally don't look at comics at all. Instead of the cancellation Gaiman initially expected, his series ended up enjoying a spectacular seven-year run . . . and DC would have happily allowed it to go on for seven more, if the author hadn't decided that the story had reached its natural conclusion and pulled the plug.

Along the way, Gaiman and his talented collaborators produced seventy-six issues that have won just about every industry award available. A tale starring William Shakespeare even landed the 1991 World Fantasy Award for Best Short Story, making *Sandman* the first monthly comic to ever receive a literary prize.

Most comics disappear after their initial publication, but here again *Sandman* broke the rules. Since it was such an enduring and popular series, DC collected the two-thousand-page saga into ten volumes sold through both comics shops and bookstores; and it's in this format that the series has found its largest audience. Rather than fade away, *Sandman* becomes more popular each year with book readers. To date, the *Sandman* collections have sold more than one million copies internationally.

THE PURPOSE OF THIS BOOK

If you're an avid fan of *Sandman* or have read only a few stories, you know the series can, of course, be read without the aid of a guide. But what makes *Sandman* so intriguing is that this compelling, readable saga is both wonderfully complex yet subtle, operating on multiple levels. As with any significant work of literature, there's a lot more to *Sandman* than what appears on the surface; and to unearth those extra layers requires some effort..

Why bother to make that effort? One reason is simply curiosity—the fun derived from peeking beneath the covers. Another is to better understand the unforgettable characters you encounter in the series. A third reason is that by exploring any major work of art, you come to better understand the world you live in and to better understand yourself.

But perhaps the most straightforward reason is to achieve, in the words of Vladimir Nabokov, "aesthetic bliss." The more in touch you are with how a work of art electrifies your emotions and imagination, the more pleasure you're likely to derive from it. To fully delight in a work's beauty, you must read actively and passionately; and you must have enough information to appreciate what the author is doing.

To help with the latter, this book includes edited transcripts of interviews I conducted with Neil Gaiman over a five-day period in New York. The book also contains excerpts of conversations I had with over two dozen other talents who contributed to the series. These interviews reveal the origins of *Sandman's* primary characters, discuss the series' themes, identify critical recurring images, and provide lots of other behind-the-scenes information, giving you the keys you need to unlock Gaiman's mammoth saga.

You can also read *The Sandman Companion* simply for the fun of it. Neil Gaiman is a witty and charming talker, and the conversations with him allow you to peek into the mind of one of the most interesting writers of our time.

overview

getting started with *sandman*

1

The most beautiful thing we can experience is the mysterious.
It is the source of all true art and science.

—ALBERT EINSTEIN

Mysteries are vital to both our lives and the stories that sustain our lives. But, just as it's sensible to study a guidebook or map before traveling to an intriguing new place, you may find it helpful to pick up some background information before journeying to the complex world of *Sandman*. You can do so by reading this chapter, which answers some of the most common questions about the series.

WHAT IS *SANDMAN* ABOUT?

The flippant answer is, of course, "About two thousand pages."

And there's actually some wisdom behind that facile response: if the series could be neatly summed up in a few paragraphs, its creators wouldn't have had to take two thousand pages to tell it.

But briefly (and *very* roughly): *Sandman* is about a being who's the personification of dreams and rules the place where we spend a third of our lives. The series tells about how this godlike being comes to question his past actions, and the consequences of that questioning; and the memorable characters he encounters along the way.

Sandman is also about peering beneath the surface of things, and recognizing the importance of dream, myth and the transcendent in our lives.

And *Sandman* is about stories—where they come from and how they shape us.

HOW ARE THE *SANDMAN* COLLECTIONS ORGANIZED?

Sandman was originally published as a twenty-four-page monthly comic book. Following the conventions of the comics industry, each issue was numbered sequentially, starting with #1 (published in December 1988) and ending with #75 (published in March 1996). In addition, a forty-eight-page issue titled *The Sandman Special* was published in September 1991, so there are a total of seventy-six issues in the series.

Because of *Sandman*'s popularity with mainstream readers, DC Comics eventually decided to collect the issues in book form, starting in May 1990. This didn't impose any artificial structure on the *Sandman* tales, however, because Neil Gaiman was writing long story arcs that extended across multiple issues anyway. For example, Gaiman's first storyline ran for eight issues, so the first collection, *Preludes & Nocturnes*, contains #1–8; the second storyline ran from issues 9 through 16, so the second collection, *The Doll's House*, contains #9–16; and so on.

One complication is that Gaiman occasionally produced several single-issue stories following a long story arc, so the collections don't always follow the sequential numbering of the series. For example, the short story collection *Fables and Reflections* contains issues #29–31, #38–40, #50, and *The Sandman Special*.

One other complication is that *The Doll's House* should begin with #9, but most editions of it actually begin with #8—that is, with a reprint of the final issue in *Preludes & Nocturnes*. There's no significance to this duplication, though; it's simply the result of a marketing decision that's since become obsolete. (For the full explanation, see chapter 4.)

Otherwise, the organization of the original *Sandman* issues into book collections is pretty straightforward. Here are the ten collections and their contents:

I. *Preludes & Nocturnes* (#1–8; introduction by F. Paul Wilson/ Karen Berger)

II. *The Doll's House* (#8–16; introduction by Clive Barker)

III. *Dream Country* (#17–20; introduction by Steve Erickson)

IV. *Season of Mists* (#21–28; introduction by Harlan Ellison)

V. *A Game of You* (#32–37; introduction by Samuel R. Delany)

VI. *Fables and Reflections* (#29–31, #38–40, #50, and *The Sandman Special*, plus a ten-page story titled "Fear of Falling" from *Vertigo Preview*; introduction by Gene Wolfe)

VII. *Brief Lives* (#41–49; introduction by Peter Straub)

VIII. *Worlds' End* (#51–56; introduction by Stephen King)

IX. *The Kindly Ones* (#57–69, plus an eight-page story titled "The Castle" from *Vertigo Jam 1*; introduction by Frank McConnell)

X. *The Wake* (#70–75; introduction by Mikal Gilmore)

In this book, an issue may be referred to by either its issue number (*Sandman 42*) or its position in a collection (chapter 2 of *Brief Lives*). You can use the list above to translate one reference to the other.

WHY SHOULD I READ A COMIC BOOK?

If someone asked, "Why should I read books?" or "Why should I watch movies?" the question would seem patently absurd. But despite the fact that great work has been done in comics form for years, comic books have not yet achieved the acceptance enjoyed by other media. Neil Gaiman illustrates the point with this anecdote:

Once, while at a party in London, the editor of the literary reviews page of a major newspaper struck up a conversation with me, and we chatted pleasantly until he asked what I did for a living. "I write comics," I said; and I watched the editor's interest instantly drain away, as if he suddenly realized he was speaking to someone beneath his nose.

Just to be polite, he followed up by inquiring, "Oh, yes? Which comics have you written?" So I mentioned a few titles, which he nodded at perfunctorily; and I concluded, "I also did this thing called *Sandman*." At that point he became excited and said, "Hang on, I know who you are. You're Neil Gaiman!" I admitted that I was. "My God, man, you don't write comics," he said. "You write graphic novels!"

He meant it as a compliment, I suppose. But all of a sudden I felt like someone who'd been informed that she wasn't actually a hooker; that in fact she was a lady of the evening.

This editor had obviously heard positive things about *Sandman*; but he was so stuck on the idea that comics are juvenile he couldn't deal with something good being done as a comic book. He needed to put *Sandman* in a box to make it respectable.

If you don't normally read comics, you may feel empathy for that editor. Comic books are relatively young, having existed for less than a century; and like most new media, they've often been stigmatized as a lesser entertainment, suitable primarily for children and the lower classes.

Movies went through a similar difficult period. It took decades for film to be taken seriously as an art form and to be acknowledged as a medium with unique strengths that can speak as powerfully as any other to the human heart.

Comic books are just as legitimate a medium for expression. After all, the term "comics" simply refers to the combination of words and pictures, set within sequential panels. If we can be deeply moved by words alone (as in novels) or pictures alone (via paintings), why not by the marriage of the two?

Samuel R. Delany, author of *Dhalgren*, *The Einstein Intersection*, and *Babel-17*, agrees. "Each medium does things the others can't," says Delany, "and one medium isn't replaceable by another. What you can do in comics you can't do in movies. What you can do on the stage you can't do in a novel. It's not the content one should look at. It's the intensity and the vividness with which the form of a medium disseminates the experience of the medium itself.

"For example," continues Delany, "comics handles time in ways that verbal narrative and movies can't match. In a comic, you can have three panels in a row where the actions are half a second apart, followed by a fourth, the same size and on the same row, set a century later; and the transition will feel perfectly natural. A comic can also slip into slow motion or fast motion seamlessly. And a comic can ramp up the impact by going back and forth, panel by panel, between close-ups and far shots, building tremendous energy by their alternation. The same effects in a novel or film would come off as terribly awkward."

Comics can actually be seen as falling somewhere between novels and films. The visuals of a comic tend to make it more accessible than straight prose, easing you into a narrative by giving you a foundation of images to play with. At the same time, a comic is static and can provide only selected details of a scene, so it forces you to fill in an enormous amount of information with your imagination. The latter process gives you a more introspective and intimate experience than you'd have watching a movie.

Groundbreaking comics writer Alan Moore is especially taken by the combination of words and images, which he says has a biological component. "Our brains are divided into right and left halves," explains Moore. "The right brain is the pre-verbal, subconscious half, which deals with images; and the left brain is the verbal, reasoning half, which is concerned with language. Comics is a medium that, almost uniquely, brings both halves of the brain into play at once. That is, when you look at a comics panel, the right brain decodes the pictures at the same time the left brain decodes the words. There are many ways to exploit this process as an artist; for example, by creating an image that shows one thing and accompanying it by text that says something quite different, you can achieve a sort of flash in a reader's mind. The range of subtle effects possible is extraordinary and, so far, has been almost unexplored. It's this kind of potential that makes comics exciting for me."

Artist and comics philosopher Scott McCloud emphasizes a different juxtaposition: the one between two sequential panels. In his landmark book *Understanding Comics*, McCloud notes that when we see only part of something, we automatically complete the missing pieces with our imagination. To demonstrate, McCloud's book shows one panel in which an ax is being raised behind a man and a second panel in which an "EEYAA!" sound effect floats over a moonlit city. As McCloud puts it, "I may have drawn an ax being raised in this example, but I'm not the one who let it drop or decided how hard the blow, or who screamed, or why. That, dear reader, was your special crime, each of you committing it in your own style. All of you participated in the murder. All of you held the ax and chose your spot. To kill a man between panels is to condemn him to a thousand deaths."

McCloud expands on this notion to cover *any* sequence in comics: "Several times on every page, the reader is released—like a trapeze artist—into the open air of imagination, then caught by the outstretched arms of the ever-present next panel. [Within a panel,] the artist can only convey information visually. But between panels, none of our senses are required at all. Which is why all of our senses are engaged."

According to McCloud, this mental filling-in of action between panels "fosters an intimacy surpassed only by the written word; a silent, secret contract between creator and audience [in which] we take two static, unmoving images and give them life and motion and the illusion of time. . . . The comics creators ask us to join a dance of the seen and the unseen, the visible and the invisible. This dance is unique to comics. No other art form gives so much to its audience while asking so much from them as well."

Have writers and artists realized the full potential of comics? Arguably, not yet. For example, readers are still waiting for a comics work of such power that it virtually defines the art form in the way that, say, Leo Tolstoy's *War and Peace* defines the novel, or that Orson Welles's *Citizen Kane* defines film.

But the field is getting there. During the past fifteen years, breathtaking comics have been produced by such luminaries as Alan Moore (writer of *V for Vendetta, Swamp Thing, Watchmen, Miracleman,* and *From Hell*), Frank Miller (writer/artist of *The Dark Knight Returns*), and Art Spiegelman (writer/artist of *Maus*, which was the first dramatic comic to win a Pulitzer Prize). And the artistic precedents created by these talents opened the door for Neil Gaiman to come in and create *Sandman*.

HOW WAS AN ISSUE OF *SANDMAN* CREATED?

An issue began with writer Neil Gaiman dreaming up a tale he wanted to tell. Gaiman discussed the story with his editor, Karen Berger, and then wrote a script. After Berger reviewed it, the script was sent to a penciller who Gaiman and Berger had agreed would be stylistically suitable for the story. A penciller is an illustrator who, as the title indicates, works in pencil, transforming the written characters and art descriptions into dynamic imagery.

Choosing a penciller was a key step, in two ways. First, Gaiman always strove to match up a story with a penciller whose style was appropriate for bringing a particular tale to life. Second, Gaiman insisted on tailoring his writing to a penciller's personal strengths; in fact, he felt so strongly about this that he wouldn't start script-

KELLI BICKMAN

Neil Gaiman, writer and creative vision behind *The Sandman*.

ing a story until he knew who was going to be drawing it. Gaiman also made a point of asking pencillers what they most and least liked to draw, because he wanted to provide material that each artist was genuinely enthusiastic about illustrating. He felt such enthusiasm would inevitably shine through in the finished work.

Once a penciller was signed up, Gaiman fleshed out his original idea in the form of a script that functioned as a blueprint for the story. He broke his story down into pages, and into the individual units on each page called panels (which can be thought of as windows into the world of the story). Gaiman wrote very detailed scripts that described the arrangement of the panels on each page, the imagery in each panel, and subtleties such as the mood he was striving for. He also included all the title text, captions, dialogue, and other verbiage that would appear on the printed pages, along with occasional suggestions to the letterer and colorist.

After Gaiman was through, his script went to editor Berger for her edits and approval, and was then passed along to the penciller Gaiman and Berger had agreed upon. Berger reviewed the artwork as it came in to make sure that the storytelling was reflective of the script and the characters and scenes were accurately represented. She then prepared the artwork for lettering, by positioning or "balloon placing," the word balloons and captions on photocopies of the pencilled pages. These served as guides for calligrapher Todd Klein, who did a spectacular job of hand-lettering the series' entire seven-year run. (The only exceptions were issues 11 and 12, which Klein skipped because he was on his honeymoon.)

After the pages were lettered, they were sent to an inker who Berger and Gaiman felt would best match the penciller's style. An inker is an artist who translates the graphite drawings of the penciller into reproducible black lines by adding a variety of textures, shading, and depth.

The pages then went to a colorist: specifically, Robbie Busch for issues 1–18, Steve Oliff for #19–22, Danny Vozzo for #23–49 and #51–75, and Lovern Kindzierski for the jewel-like #50. (For more information on the latter, see "Illustrating 'Ramadan,'" p. 156.) Busch and Vozzo physically painted reproductions of the artwork with watercolors; these "color guides" then went to separators, who translated the colors into combinations of red, yellow, blue, and black film. Oliff and Kindzierski both owned studios set up to perform color separations and so handled the "seps" themselves, which gave them much tighter control over how the coloring turned out. (Nowadays, virtually all comics coloring is done directly on computer, eliminating the need for color guides and providing full creative control to the colorist.)

While all this was taking place, artist Dave McKean was creating a mind-blowing cover for the story fated to put most other comics covers to shame—a feat he managed to pull off for each of *Sandman*'s seventy-six issues.

Finally, after all the necessary pages were proofed and assembled by Berger, her assistant editor, and DC's production staff, the issue of *Sandman* was sent out to be printed . . . and work on the next month's issue began.

WHY IS THE SERIES SO LONG?

Two thousand pages may seem like an inordinate amount of space to devote to one tale. But *Sandman*'s primary story, which focuses on the title character, isn't told in a linear way; and more important, Neil Gaiman constructed his series to operate as a kind of story machine. "I made the Sandman as old as the universe," Gaiman says, "because that gave me all of time and all of space to play with. And I made him the incarnation of dreams and stories because that gave me a framework for telling virtually any kind of tale."

Gaiman took full advantage of that framework. The series includes such diverse fare as a ten-thousand-year-old African folk story about forbidden love; a day with Augustus Caesar that reveals the true reason Rome fell; a look at the role a singing head played in the French Revolution; and dozens of other bizarre and wondrous events that are jumbled around, leaping back and forth in time and space—as if you were dreaming them.

On one level, the various stories work as independent units. They had to as a practical matter, because *Sandman* originally appeared in monthly twenty-four-page installments, and new readers were coming into the series with every issue. On another level, though, the diverse stories can be seen as pieces of a vast jigsaw puzzle that help shape the series' primary tale about the Sandman himself.

If you're used to a more straightforward approach to storytelling, consider these words penned years ago by world-famous novelist Milan Kundera: "Dramatic tension is the real curse of the novel, because it transforms everything, even the most beautiful pages, even the most surprising scenes and observations, merely into steps leading to the final resolution, in which the meaning of everything that preceded is concentrated. A novel shouldn't be like a bicycle race but a feast of many courses."

Sandman is a feast of many courses.

WHAT LITERARY INFLUENCES LED TO *SANDMAN*?

Neil Gaiman is exceptionally well-read, so it's a safe bet that an entire library of books and comics went into *Sandman*. Gaiman is reluctant to name all the volumes he drew upon, but he's pointed to the writings of science fiction authors Roger Zelazny and Samuel R. Delany as being especially influential; and in the comics field, to the work of his friend and mentor Alan Moore.

Moore confirms and expands on those sources: "Neil and I were both very, very impressed by the New Wave science fiction scene in the mid-1960s. Samuel R. Delany was, and still is, an incredible writer. The late Roger Zelazny's novels, such as *Lord of Light* and *Isle of the Dead*, were also extraordinary, bringing an emotionally credible touch to tales of high fantasy.

"The New Wave movement gave us amazing visions from other writers too," Moore adds, "including J. G. Ballard, M. John Harrison, and John Sladek. Their worldview was so different that, at first exposure, it was almost incomprehensible. But it quickly became addictive, like a drug.

"The New Wave generated a massive burst of energy that revitalized the imaginations of a number of people, certainly including mine," says Moore. "It was progressive, taking the hidebound science fiction reader of the time and shaking him by the scruff of the neck, doing things with the genre that nobody had ever thought of doing before. Just to see one could write that way," Moore says, "that you could take an old form and create something completely unanticipated with it, was highly inspiring. And it was a notion I carried into my own line of work. I imagine that Neil got a certain amount of rocket fuel from that, as well."

In fact, Moore went on to virtually reinvent comics by infusing old, tired situations and genres with a sharp, witty, and contemporary point of view. Moore's work was so remarkable that it inspired Gaiman, who had ignored comics for years, to start reading them again . . . and eventually to write comics himself, employing a similar pioneering approach.

Moore's influence didn't end there, either. Gaiman is famous for writing very long comics scripts that carefully describe what happens in every panel. There's only one person in the industry who writes scripts that are even longer.

A previously unpublished sketch of the Sandman, originally intended for use as a trading card.

"Yes," admits Moore (whose script for the twenty-six-page first issue of his classic *Watchmen* comic ran over a hundred pages), "that bad habit came from me.

"You've got to remember," Moore quickly adds, "that in my day comics weren't regarded as being of much importance and publishers weren't particularly supportive about your work. So when you wrote a script, you'd have no idea who'd be drawing it, or lettering it, or coloring it; which meant there were all sorts of things that could go wrong. My solution was to put into a script every nuance of the images in my head, so it was crystal clear what I was aiming for, down to the finest detail.

"As it happened," continues Moore, "that approach got the best results. Artists didn't feel crushed or restricted by all the description; most of them seemed to enjoy it. Also, I found that by trying to think of every angle of a story from the standpoint of my collaborators, I'd come up with effects that I wouldn't have otherwise.

"So when Neil asked me, 'How does one write a comic script?' I showed him how I write a comic script. And that's what doomed Neil, and everybody who works with him, to these huge, mammoth wedges of paper for each story he does.

"I'd like to think my main influence was the understanding that it's quite all right to trust your own ideas and to consider your own perspective valid.

"In other words," Moore concludes, "if Neil got anything from me, I hope it was a respect for one's individual voice; and an insistence on the right to bring that voice to whatever material you're handling."

WHAT'S THE CONNECTION BETWEEN *SANDMAN* AND THE GOTH MOVEMENT?

In the late 1970s, an offshoot of the punk scene developed called Goth (named after the medieval Gothic era). Goth has since developed into an umbrella term that covers a number of diverse interests, including dark music, vampirism, paganism, and a "look" centered around pale faces and black clothing. Goth styles and sensibilities have been popping up throughout mainstream culture, ranging from *The X-Files* to Stephen King's *Gerald's Game* to Madonna's music video *Frozen*.

Caitlín R. Kiernan, who happens to be both a goth and the writer of the *Sandman* spin-off series *The Dreaming*, explains that "Goth, unlike punk, is not about anarchy or thumbing your nose at authority; it's about being completely introspective. Goth attracts people whose sight has turned deeply inward."

Neil Gaiman isn't a Goth, and neither are any of the other people who worked on the series; but various aesthetic decisions made by Gaiman and artist Mike Dringenberg led to the series' characters eventually becoming part of Goth culture.

Gaiman first became aware of *Sandman*'s popularity with Goths when he was guest of honor at the 1994 World Horror Convention and observed a number of fans, as he put it, "clad in black from head to foot." Gaiman is famous for wearing black himself, but for different motives: "It's a sensible color, it goes with anything black; and I have no dress sense or imagination with clothes. To try to decide between two different shirts renders me paralyzed. So I own twenty identical black Armani T-shirts, which makes life simple."

Despite the fact it wasn't intentional, the Sandman and his sister Death were created with all the elements needed to become Goth icons. Both have the pale skin and black clothing that are standards in Goth fashion. In addition, the characters represent two very recognizable Goth personality types: Dream as the lonely, Byronic, moping goth, and Death as the perky, friendly, sensible goth.

Elizabeth McIntyre, who runs the popular Goth Web site Rosa Mvndi, says Death is especially embraced by the movement because "she's an image that goths wish would be projected about us more often; someone who's beautiful, intelligent, and has a great attitude."

Death's look incorporates ancient Egyptian symbols—her facial makeup includes the Eye of Horus, and she wears an ankh around her neck, which were both images popular with rock music fans when Mike Dringenberg was drawing the character. As Caitlín R. Kiernan explains, "The Eye of Horus goes straight back to Siouxsie Sioux, who was doing it in the early 1980s; and Death's look in general owes something to Patricia Morrison. As for the ankh, it originally made its way into Goth culture via Tony Scott's 1983 film *The Hunger*—which also features Eye of Horus makeup in a brief flashback scene."

After artist Dringenberg linked those symbols with Death, however, their visibility and popularity increased exponentially. McIntyre gives much of the credit to the Internet: "A lot of people who wouldn't have considered going into a comic shop would see scanned pictures of Death and Dream on the Web and be very attracted to those images; and they'd then follow up by buying the monthly *Sandman* issues or the book collections."

She adds, "There are goths who haven't even read *Sandman* but will have Death posters up everywhere; and they'll have their enshrined copy of *Death: The High Cost of Living*."

In a 1998 interview with Thom Carnell, editor of the Goth magazine *Carpe Noctem*, Gaiman delightedly noted how Death is triggering fashion trends: "You'll run into young ladies dressed as Death because they've seen other young ladies dressed as Death, and they haven't got a clue as to who Death is. They like the style. They like the look. [For example,] I love the fact that the fashion of wearing a top hat seems to be slowly spreading because these Death/Goth girls are wearing top hats. It seems to have started off just from people reading the Death comic *The High Cost of Living* and putting on the hat, and from there it's drifted out into society. How cool is that?"

Despite the fact Gaiman never wrote with goths in mind, his use of such story elements as fantastic romanticism and the dysfunctional Endless family strike a chord. As Kiernan puts it, "The stories touch on, and in fact often revolve around, things that deeply concern goths, and so had a powerful resonance within the Goth community."

—

a dream is born

2

Nothing happens unless first a dream.

—CARL SANDBURG

Neil Gaiman was born above his father's small grocery store in Portchester, England, on November 10, 1960. Gaiman's mother loved stories and enthusiastically exposed her son to the written word; one of Gaiman's clearest memories is of wooden alphabet letters his mom bought him when he was two. "We painted the vowels red with nail varnish," he recalls, "and so vowels have always smelled to me of varnish."

Gaiman's mother also made a point of reading books to him. By age three, however, he became impatient with having a go-between and made the effort to read to himself. It was the start of a lifelong addiction.

"I'd always carry books around with me," says Gaiman. "My parents would frisk me before we went to a family gathering, like a wedding or bar mitzvah, because they assumed I had a book on me somewhere. And they were right; I'd usually spend the day under a table reading."

Gaiman tackled books indiscriminately. When he was old enough to visit his local children's library, he quickly devoured the entire collection. He then turned his attention to the adult stacks, starting at A and working his way through the volumes alphabetically.

Although he cheerfully read everything, Gaiman especially loved stories involving magic and fantasy by such authors as James Branch Cabell, C. S. Lewis, and J. R. R. Tolkien. "My great daydream when I was ten," says Gaiman, "was to travel to a parallel universe exactly like ours—except in that other universe, no one had ever written *Lord of the Rings*. I would bring along my copy, get someone to type it out for me in manuscript, send the pages off to a publisher, and then be celebrated as the author of *Lord of the Rings* without doing any of the work."

Gaiman began composing poems at age three, and he started writing stories with continuing characters at eight. But it would take him a long time to develop confidence as a fiction writer.

Another form of fantasy attracted Gaiman's attention in the summer of 1967, when a friend of his father lent him a cardboard box filled with comic books. The box included Marvel's *The Mighty Thor*, which fascinated Gaiman and led him to actively seek out books on mythology. "I was disappointed to learn the real Thor of Norse legends was big and bearded," says Gaiman, "as opposed to Marvel's blond Fabio lookalike with winged helmet. But I liked the fact that Loki was pretty much the same in both versions." Gaiman later drew heavily on his knowledge of mythology to create such storylines as *Season of Mists*.

The box of comics also contained *Justice League of America* 47, which provided Gaiman with his first glimpse of DC's original Sandman—a detective costumed with a gas mask and wielding a gun that dispensed sleeping gas. (In tribute, Gaiman ultimately used the odd mask's design as the basis of the helmet worn by his own version of the Sandman.)

Gaiman was hooked. As he eventually wrote on the letters page of *Sandman* 4, the issues were returned to their owner a few weeks later, "but I continued to hunt down and read American comics. The damage had been done.... It wasn't just a box of comics, it was a Box of Dreams."

By age eleven, Gaiman had become so enchanted with comics that he decided he wanted to write them for a living. He kept this plan to himself, however, until he was fifteen and a special counselor came to his school to provide career guidance.

"When the advisor asked me what I wanted to do, I didn't hesitate, because I'd been waiting to tell the appropriate person for years," says Gaiman. "So I answered, 'I want to write American comic books.' And what I wanted *him* to say was, 'Okay, that is a commendable ambition. You should go to the School of Visual Arts in New York, and you should work on your craft, and these are the people with whom you should talk to get you on your way.'

"Instead, he just replied, 'Oh, you can't do that. Have you ever considered accountancy?'"

Gaiman laughs about it now, but he says that at the time "it really, weirdly hurt. This counselor was the first person to flatly ask me what I wanted to do; and after I finally answered the question out loud, he told me my goal was unreachable. And it made me give up; I quit reading comics for nine years."

Of course, such discouraging moments are a routine part of virtually any artist's development, but obviously Gaiman overcame this early rejection of his dream. How he did so, and what zigs and zags in his writing career led to his creating *Sandman*, are revealed in the interview that follows.

THE JOURNALISM YEARS

HB: What did you do after you swore off comics in 1975?

NG: I still read lots of books, of course. And I'd begun trying to write professionally in 1980. I completed a number of short stories, and a draft of a children's book, but no one would buy my fiction.

After about 18 months of rejection slips—nice rejection slips, but rejections nonetheless—I abruptly decided one day, "Either I have no talent—which I do not choose to believe—or I'm simply not going about this the right way. I'm going to switch to journalism, and in the process I'm going to figure out how the world works—how magazine articles get assigned, how books get published, how television scripts get sold."

I bought a copy of the *Writer's and Artist's Yearbook*, which lists contact information for magazines, and I started phoning editors cold. When asked who I'd previously written for, I lied. I knew that no editor was likely to check on me, because all that really mattered was the quality of the idea I was pitching and, after I got the assignment, the quality of my writing.

HB: So even when starting a nonfiction career, you resorted to storytelling. Which magazines did you claim to have worked for?

NG: *Time Out, City Limits, The Observer, The Sunday Times of London Magazine*—in other words, U.K. publications I respected. And over the next five years, I actually did write for every magazine I'd mentioned during that first week of cold calls. So I wasn't really lying, I was merely being anachronistic. [*Laughter.*]

HB: Which magazine was wise enough to hand you your first assignment?

NG: *Penthouse.* [*Laughter.*] Robert Silverberg was in town for an SF convention, and I pitched an interview idea to another magazine using the line, "Bob Silverberg is the guy who put sex in science fiction." The editor wasn't interested, but he said, "Why don't you try *Penthouse*? They like anything arty with a sex twist." So I did, and they went for it. I ended up doing quite a few articles for that publication, because it turned out one of its editors was a big SF fan. When a features editor left, *Penthouse* even offered me the job; but I decided to stick to freelancing.

HB: *Penthouse* wasn't the only men's magazine you worked for.

NG: Correct; my steadiest gig was for *Knave*. By sheer coincidence, I phoned *Knave's* editor, Ian Pemble, shortly after he'd had a sort of "road to Damascus" experience. He'd apparently said to himself, "I'm the editor of a magazine that readers buy exclusively because it's got photographs of naked ladies and a lewd letters section. Nobody cares about the articles, but we need them to fill the pages between the ads. So I might as well publish the kind of articles that I'd like to read." Therefore, he hired me, Kim Newman, Dave Langford, John Grant, and a bunch of other good writers who were part of the English SF scene, and we did regular features for *Knave* that had no sex content whatsoever. For a couple of years, *Knave* became my most dependable source of income, as Ian allowed me to do monthly interviews with anyone I thought was cool—people such as Harry Harrison, Terry Jones, and Douglas Adams.

HB: So you met a lot of people whose work you loved, and you got a lot of professional writing experience. It sounds like your plan to learn about the world worked out fine.

NG: It did. And the oddest part is, within a few months of being a journalist, I landed contracts for two books—a quickie rock book about Duran Duran that I did for money, and a collection of silly excerpts from science fiction novels and genre movies titled *Ghastly Beyond Belief* that I and my coauthor Kim Newman did for the sheer fun of it.

FALLING IN LOVE AGAIN

HB: Eventually, comics came back into your life. How did that happen?

NG: Through Alan Moore's amazing work on *Swamp Thing*. In 1984, while waiting for a train at Victoria Station, I noticed a newsstand with piles of comics, and *Swamp Thing* 25, "The Sleep of Reason," caught my eye. I was dead set against buying it, but I read it just standing there and flipping. As I did so, I started thinking, "This is really good. But it can't be, because comics are no good."

HB: You actually thought that?

NG: Oh, yeah; I'd made my decision. And I put the *Swamp Thing* issue back on one of the piles.

The next month I was at Victoria Station again, and I picked up *Swamp Thing* 26, "A Time of Running," once again reading it while standing at the newsstand, again thinking, "This is really well written, but I don't know," and again putting it back.

A couple of months went by until I returned to that newsstand, but a process of erosion must have quietly taken place on my mental barriers, because when I spotted *Swamp Thing* 28, "The Burial," I simply bought it and read it on the train, carefully.

LEIGH BAULCH

The inhuman aspect of Sandman is clear in this proposal sketch.

A proposal sketch touching on the magical and somewhat surreal aspects of *The Sandman*.

SANDMAN
MODEL SHEET NO 10
11-10-87

THIS IS THE FIRST NON-BOWIE VERSION AND, WHILST IT HAS A HARDER EDGE TO IT I THINK IT PROVES TO BE TOO MASCULINE. IT ALSO INTRODUCES THE CONCEPT OF IMAGERY APPEARING AMONGST THE 'FLAMES' OF HIS ROBE.

The Sandman's nature as a being encompassing many tales is first hinted at in this proposal sketch.

And that was the final straw; what was left of my resistance crumbled. I proceeded to make regular and frequent visits to London's Forbidden Planet shop to buy comics.

HB: Were you mostly buying Alan's work? Or did Alan's artistry simply give you an excuse to fall in love with comics again?

NG: The latter; I fell in love with comics again. It was like returning to an old flame and discovering that she was still beautiful. But Alan's stuff was impressive. He showed what one can really do with comics, that they can be as powerful a vehicle for art as any other medium.

HB: You had a professional basis for making that conclusion, because you were working as a film critic at the time.

NG: In fact, I saw just about every movie that was released between 1984 and 1986, mostly while sitting in little preview theaters.

HB: Why did you stop doing it after 1986?

NG: One day I figured out that over the course of two years, I'd watched more than seven hundred films. So I asked myself, "Just how many of these movies have made my life *cooler*?" In other words, of which of these films can I say, "I really would not have been the same person if I hadn't seen this?" And I came up with Terry Gilliam's *Brazil*; Mark Romanek and Keith Gordon's *Static*; and *Pumping Iron II: The Women*, for which I had a bizarre fondness. [*Laughter.*]

HB: So, not a large percentage.

NG: No. And it just hit me that the time I'd spent watching and reviewing, say, Chuck Norris's *The Delta Force* was time I'd never get back. It made me realize I should move on to a more fulfilling line of work.

MOORE, MCKEAN, AND MAGIC

HB: During that same period, you became friends with Alan Moore, who—present company excluded—is arguably the finest comics writer in the history of the medium. How did you and Alan first hook up with each other?

NG: When my book *Ghastly Beyond Belief,* which I wrote with Kim Newman, was published in 1985, I sent Alan a copy accompanied by a note that basically said, "You've given me enormous amounts of pleasure, I think you're terrific, and this is something I've done. Hope you like it." Alan called me a week later and went [*doing an uncannily accurate impersonation*]: "You bastard. I lost an entire afternoon's work reading your book!" [*Laughter.*] From then on, we were phone pals.

HB: You've since met Alan many times. How would you describe him?

NG: Hairy, like a yeti. [*Laughter.*] And huge—Alan looms at you, like a lion. But he's also very gentle; incredibly funny; and utterly brilliant.

HB: I know that Alan is the one who taught you about writing a comics script. Do you recall how that happened?

I WILL
show you
TERROR
in a
handful
of dust

SANDMAN™

HE CONTROLS YOUR DREAMS

A horror-edged fantasy,
set in the DC Universe.
Available monthly in
DC's New Format.
Beginning in November

Written by Neil Gaiman,
writer of Black Orchid
Art by Sam Kieth and
Mike Dringenberg
Covers by Dave McKean

Suggested For Mature Readers

® TM DC Comics Inc • 1988

The original advertisement for *The Sandman*, including a quote inspired by T. S. Eliot.

NG: Oh, certainly. About eight months after we first chatted, I mentioned to Alan that two of his favorite writers, Clive Barker and Ramsey Campbell, were going to be at the British Fantasy Convention at Birmingham. As a result of my journalism work, I knew both Clive and Ramsey, so I told Alan, "Come on down; I'll look after you and make sure you don't feel out of place." And he did, and I did, and we had a great time.

Toward the end of the day, we were talking about comics, and I said, "I don't understand what a comics script looks like. How do you tell the artist what to draw?" So he showed me a script's format, step by step, on a sheet of paper: "Put down 'Page 1 panel 1' like this, then describe what happens in the panel, then write the name of the first character who talks, then put down his dialogue," and so on.

After receiving that tutorial, I went home and wrote a short comics script titled "The Day My Pad Went Mad" based on Alan's wonderful John Constantine character. In retrospect, the story wasn't very good, and the ending was wrong. But I sent the script to Alan, and he told me, "Yeah, it's all right. The ending's a bit off." And then he actually used a few lines of my story in *Swamp Thing* 51, "Home Free," which was very encouraging to me.

I next wrote a sixteenth-century *Swamp Thing* script titled "Jack in the Green" and sent it to Alan. When I asked him if it was okay, he said "Yeah, I would've been proud to write that." That made me very happy.

And then—proving the driven nature of my ambition to begin a fiction career—I wrote absolutely no other scripts. I went, "Okay, now I know how to write a comic book" and left it at that.

HB: So what gave you the push you needed?

NG: A few months later, while in a pub near Forbidden Planet, I bumped into a guy who said he was going to create a comic book produced by "untried, new talent only." In retrospect, I should've asked, "Is that because anyone who's been around the block would know enough to not get involved with this project?" But I was young, so I sent him the two scripts I'd written, he told me that they were "brilliant," and I agreed to sign on.

Things didn't work out with him, as you might have guessed; but among the other untried new talents he found was a young lad who liked to draw named Dave McKean. And that's how Dave and I met.

HB: How did you and Dave become such close friends and collaborators? Did you just naturally hit it off?

NG: Basically. We admired each other enormously—I thought he was a genius. And we liked each other enormously.

HB: How would you describe your and Dave's artistic tastes?

NG: Like huge Venn diagrams—they overlap, but they're focused in different directions. Dave exposes me to art, music, and theater people like Russell Mills, and I expose Dave to people like Stephen Sondheim. These differences are very useful for both of us, because he sees things that I don't, and I point out things that he wouldn't have thought of.

HB: What led to you and Dave first collaborating?

NG: Shortly after Dave and I met, Paul Gravette from *Escape* magazine came by to do an article about the comic book project we were working on. Paul liked what Dave was drawing, and he liked what I was writing, and he asked if we'd do a five-page strip for *Escape*. Dave and I talked it over, and about a week later I rang Paul and asked, "Is it okay if, instead of a five-page strip, we do a forty-four-page graphic novel called *Violent Cases*?" And Paul, bless him, said yes. So we did.

HB: How did you and Dave go from working on your critically acclaimed *Violent Cases* to working for DC Comics?

NG: Sporadically. Dave took the first stab at it in August 1986, when he paid out of his own pocket to travel to New York and visit every comics publisher in the area—Marvel, DC, Neal Adams's Continuity Studios, and so on. It seemed to me one would have to be blind to not recognize his talent, but he came back with no work. He hadn't run into the right people.

The following month, September 1986, was the annual U.K. Comic Art Convention, and Karen Berger was attending it as DC Comics' liaison to British writers and artists. I walked up to Karen and introduced myself, and she responded, "Oh yes, Alan Moore's mentioned you." Taking that as a good sign, I immediately mailed her my *Swamp Thing* script, "Jack in the Green."

Five months later, after seeing that Alan Moore, Brian Bolland, Dave Gibbons, and other Britishers had worked out really well, DC decided that it wanted the rest of us. In February 1987, Alan called to tell me that Karen was returning to town on a U.K. talent-hunting expedition. And accompanying her this time would be Dick Giordano, who was DC's vice president—

HB: Let me interrupt your personal tale a moment to note that DC's perception was on the money—there was, as it turned out, a great deal of comics talent in the U.K. just waiting to be tapped by a shrewd publisher. Why do you think that was the case?

NG: Part of it was simply that no one had bothered to come after us before. But a more important reason, in my opinion, is that there was a generation in the U.K. who'd grown up reading DC comics from a bizarre perspective. In America, those comics were perceived without irony; in England, they were like postcards from another world. The idea of a place that looked like New York, the idea of fire hydrants and pizzerias, was just as strange to us as the idea that anyone would wear a cape and fly over them.

Also, these comics were being read by bright, rebellious kids, and we perceived them as part of a dynamic cultural movement—along with David Bowie and punk rock, Roger Zelazny and the New Wave in science fiction, and stories by William Burroughs.

HB: How did you place yourself and Dave in the sights of DC's talent hunt?

NG: Quite simply, I asked a U.K. comics friend to give me the name of the hotel where they were staying. I rang them, Dick answered, and I said, "An English comics writer and English comics artist want to come and see you." And Dick said, "Okay. Thursday, two o'clock."

I then called Dave to tell him we were going to see Dick and Karen, and Dave responded, "They don't want to see us. He was just being polite." [*Laughter.*] I said, "Dave, we're going." And to prepare, I wrote a Phantom Stranger plot overnight.

THE SANDMAN COMPANION

Sample artwork by Sam Kieth and Mike Dringenberg, the series' first illustrators.

HB: I'd like to point out that the attitude you're now describing is about 180 degrees from that of the boy whose spirit was crushed by a guidance counselor. It sounds like your years spent as a journalist really paid off, if only in building your self-confidence.

NG: This is true. So Thursday came, and off we went—Dave still protesting that they'll just send us away, as people did during his trip to New York. We opened the door, and Karen looked up and said, "Neil! I didn't know it was you we were meeting. I wanted to get in touch anyway, because I read your 'Jack in the Green' story on the plane coming over and really liked it." Again, a good sign.

Dave showed his stuff to Dick, and Dick loved it, because Dick is a skilled artist with a trained eye. I then pitched my Phantom Stranger story—and they said "No, Paul Kupperberg is handling Phantom Stranger. What else would you like to do?"

So I proceeded to list character after character, and they said no, no, no, because all those characters had already been promised to other writers.

Finally, I suggested Black Orchid, and Karen responded "Black Hawk Kid? Who's he?" [*Laughter.*]

HB: In other words, you worked your way down to a character so obscure that no other person had even considered using her.

NG: Pretty much. Dick recognized the reference, though, and he said, "Yeah, Black Orchid, I remember her. Great character. Sure, do Black Orchid."

On the train home, I'd already started plotting. The next morning, I phoned Dave and spent literally a half hour telling him the entire story. He loved it, and he went off and did four paintings. Meanwhile, I sat down and wrote a long outline. And we dropped off our completed work at Karen and Dick's hotel just before they left on Sunday afternoon. Years later, Karen told me that the most important thing for them was the fact that on Thursday they told us to do Black Orchid, and on Sunday they walked away with a detailed outline and these four huge, gorgeous paintings.

So that was how Dave and I came to work for DC Comics.

A DREAM COMES TRUE

HB: Because of the fine work you and Dave turned in for the three-issue *Black Orchid* miniseries, DC decided to publish it in a glossy, Prestige format, which remains in print to this day. How did you move from that to *Sandman*?

NG: Again, sporadically. The next step occurred in September 1987, when DC people were again attending the U.K. Comic Art Convention. Dave and I were talking to Karen Berger and Jenette Kahn over dinner. Karen asked me what I wanted to write after the *Black Orchid* issues were completed. I'd found that character to be a fairly rigid one with limited story possibilities, so I said, "I'd like to write a series that can go anywhere. Maybe I could do something with DC's version of the *Sandman* from the 1970s." And they nodded politely but noncommittally.

The next significant event was a phone call from Karen, about a month later, in which she said, "Neil, there's a problem; we're worried about *Black Orchid*. We're publishing it as a pricey Prestige format book, but it's being done by two guys who no one's ever heard of, and it's about a character who nobody remembers. On top of that, Black Orchid is female, and female characters don't sell." That was the received wisdom at the time. Perceptions about the financial viability of women leads in comics have since changed, but this was October 1987.

So I said, "What do you propose?" And Karen said, "Grant Morrison is writing a Batman story called *Arkham Asylum*, and we like it a lot and will be heavily promoting it. We're going to assign Dave McKean to draw it, and that will make people know who Dave is. And we're going to give you a monthly comic, which will allow you to build up your own name recognition. After you and Dave have both achieved some prominence, we'll release *Black Orchid*."

HB: So *Sandman* resulted from an effort to promote *Black Orchid*?

NG: Ultimately, yes. I wasn't happy about it at the time, because Dave and I naturally wanted our work to see print as soon as possible. We also didn't like the idea of having older material published after newer material, because we were young artists just beginning to build a body of work and were concerned about being perceived as retrograde. And in the end, DC decided against sitting on *Black Orchid* for eighteen months, so the series was published before *Arkham Asylum* anyway—and it sold just fine, proving all the worries to be groundless.

HB: Going back to when Karen had offered you a monthly series—what happened next?

NG: Karen asked me what character I wanted to do a series about. And I said, "Phantom Stranger." [*Laughter.*]

HB: That's funny now partly because of the many wonderful non–super-hero characters that have since been created by writers like you and Alan Moore. At the time, though, Phantom Stranger was one of the few horror/mystery characters DC had who was open-ended—that is, whose shtick was to wear a cool-looking hat and trench coat, and basically drift from one weird event to another.

NG: And that turned out to be what axed him. When I proposed Phantom Stranger, Karen actually said okay, and I thought that was that. The next day, however, Karen rang me again and reported, "Dick says you can't do Phantom Stranger because he's not a heroic character. He's too passive, he's all about other people's stories. What else would you like to do?"

So I said, "I dunno, how about the Demon?" And Karen said, "No, Matt Wagner's doing a revival of the Demon. What else would you like to do?" And I may have mentioned some other characters, I don't remember now.

And Karen finally said, "Look, what about that Sandman idea you were pitching a month ago? Why don't you use him for your monthly book? Only don't use the 1970s Sandman, because Roy Thomas is already using him for *Infinity, Inc.*" What had fascinated me wasn't anything about that character per se, but the notion of someone who lived in dreams. So Karen, God bless her, said, "Create a new charac-ter with the same name." And I said, "Oh. Okay." And it was a wonderful solution, because it freed me from the baggage of DC continuity.

HB: So you started writing.

NG: I started writing a couple of pages of an outline. And shortly afterward, we had a hurricane, in late October 1987. It was the first English hurricane in over three hundred years. And the trees came down, and the power went out.

HB: An auspicious start for a horror series.

NG: Definitely. We were without electricity for a week, and I couldn't write be-cause I was working entirely on computer at that point. Therefore, while DC was tapping its foot waiting for me to pound out an outline, I instead wandered around the house in darkness and experienced seven days of enforced "not being able to write." And, looking back, I think that was so good for me.

When the electricity finally came back on, I remember going from room to room, turning the lights on and off, exulting in the power. And then, having had the time and the proper environment to reflect on the series, I quickly completed my *Sandman* outline and sent it off to DC. And, after some back-and-forth questions and answers, it was approved.

CREATIVE BATTLES

HB: Regarding the back-and-forth, were there any important aspects of the book you had to fight for?

NG: There was only one critical battle, which both Dave and I had to fight, and that was for our decision to keep the Sandman off the cover after issue 1. DC kept ask-ing, "But how will readers know that it's a Sandman comic if he's not on the cover?" And we kept answering, "Because it will say 'Sandman' in big letters at the top." We finally won that battle, and it was an extremely important victory.

HB: Why was it so important?

NG: Because it meant we were operating outside the paradigm of comics. Until that point, it was an absolute rule that a monthly comic always features its lead character on the cover. Hero-less covers had been done for miniseries, such as Alan Moore and Dave Gibbons's *Watchmen*, but never for a monthly book. So Dave McKean's *Sandman* covers made a strong statement that helped free me to experiment with what appeared inside the comic. For example, it made it easy to do entire issues in which the Sandman never appeared.

HB: There's at least one other battle I can think of that you also won, albeit late in the series, involving language.

NG: Oh yes; in *Sandman* 64, we finally got permission to use the word *fuck*. That was a first for Vertigo, the DC Comics fantasy/horror imprint which at that point was publishing *Sandman*. I'd included *fuck* in some of my previous scripts, but it never made it onto the published page; which was unfortunate, because I only put it in when I felt it was important to the story. So I started a little campaign, saying, "This is ridiculous, there are scenes where I need to use that kind of language." It took a while, but eventually I and other Vertigo writers got the right to use the *f*-word.

HB: Any repercussions?

NG: Absolutely none. [*Laughter.*] That's the other point—all the things that people worry about never, ever repercuss.

EARLY THOUGHTS ABOUT THE SANDMAN

Here are Gaiman's original notes on using the 1970s version of DC's Sandman in a series:

What I find fascinating about the Sandman is the idea of someone who travels in dreams. That's interesting. I'd like to junk most of the rest of it, though. Or rather, take it one step further. The Sandman inhabits the Dream Stream. His method of transportation is walking through dreams. If he's hungry, he'll eat in a dream with food in it. If he wants to meet someone, he'll meet in a dream at a specific time.

His Dream Dome was something he "created" when he first entered the Dream Stream. It was held together fairly stably at first from his concentrated ability to hold it in position. As he became more accustomed to the Dream Stream, became less rigid about it, his place began to change. Bits of it still exist, but in the midst of an ever-changing place, fragments of rooms he's known and places he's dreamed that run together into a whole.

The costume was Jeb's,—the kid, who perceived him like that. He does dress in red and gold, but the clothes shift and modulate according to who is perceiving him, or how he perceives himself.

It might be fun to strip back to mythological/classical roots—say, Gates of Horn and Gates of Ivory through which true dreams and false dreams come. Also to decide to what extent dreams are internal or external.

There are a number of inhabitants of the Dream Stream, most of whom are coagulated lumps of dream essence, basic archetypes and such: Cain and Abel, keepers of Mysteries and Secrets, the first murderer and first victim; possibly the other DC horror hosts (with the exception of Elvira), Eve, the Witching Hour witches, and so forth; the Brute and Blob, who are clots of dream, of intellect and pure emotion. Other things as well intrude on dreams: things from darker dimensions, etc. But nowhere nearly as much as people would think.

The Sandman could take an active role in dreams on occasion—summon dreaming people to the Dream Dome, and so forth. I would like to draw parallels between this Sandman and the e1arlier ones—at least so far as the Simon & Kirby Sandman seemed to pursue criminals into dreams. You had that rhyme:

There is no land
beyond the law
Where tyrants rule
with unshakable power.
It's a dream from which
the evil wake
To face their fate...
Their terrifying hour.

HB: So despite the numerous zigs and zags along the way, everything worked out. Do you feel your life would have been different if DC had initially given you the nod to do, say, Phantom Stranger, or the Demon, or the 1970s Sandman?

NG: I don't think so. Regardless of the character I was handed, I probably would've ended up doing most of the things that I ultimately did. If I'd started with an existing DC character, though, I'm not sure I would've brought to it the extra commitment that I gave to *Sandman*.

HB: What do you mean by "extra commitment"?

NG: There were periods near the end of the series where *Sandman* seemed larger, deeper, more important than my whole life was. These days, you can ask me a *Sandman* question and my answer might well be, "I don't remember," and I'd need to check the pertinent issue to respond. While I was working on *Sandman*, however, I remembered all of it, at all times—panel for panel, line for line, word for word. I also remembered where everything came from, who everyone was, what stories I'd told about every character and what stories I intended to tell—I was keeping all of that stuff in my head, loaded in the RAM of my brain. It was an enormous relief when the series was completed, because that allowed me to "unload it from memory."

HB: You clearly still recall a great deal, though. Which makes we wonder: now that *Sandman* is over, do you ever miss the characters?

NG: No, for the simple reason that they haven't gone away. I've let go of the minutiae, but the characters continue to live inside my head. They'll always be a part of me.

—

the sandman collections
PART TWO

preludes & nocturnes

3

reludes & Nocturnes is the eight-issue story arc that kicks off the *Sandman* saga. These early issues feature a linear narrative that leans heavily on plot development. Also, as with any new venture, there are occasional moments of awkwardness resulting from the creative team's struggles to find the best approach. The storytelling is consistently inventive and compelling, however, and some of the tales in this collection number among the best in the series.

The saga begins in 1916 with an English magician named Roderick Burgess attempting to capture Death. Burgess's spell goes awry, and the mage instead snares Death's younger brother Dream—or, as the series title refers to him, the Sandman. The Sandman is one of the Endless, an immortal being created by the universe to embody and protect the realm of dreams.

Burgess strips the unconscious Sandman of his pouch, helmet, ruby, and clothing, and places him naked in a glass cage surrounded by a mystic circle. When the prisoner awakens, Burgess demands immortality, power, and a pledge against revenge as the conditions for the Sandman's release; but Dream refuses to even acknowledge Burgess's existence. Instead, the Sandman maintains a stoic silence for the duration of his imprisonment in Burgess's basement . . . which lasts seventy-two years.

Shortly after the Sandman's capture on June 11, 1916, people worldwide fall prey to an ailment that baffled doctors refer to as the "sleepy sickness." In 1932, one of the victims, named Unity Kinkaid is raped and nine months later gives birth to a girl—without ever waking up.

In 1930, the Sandman's tools are stolen by Burgess's mistress Ethel Cripps, and his second-in-command, Ruthven Sykes. (This is subtly foreshadowed on page 15 when Sykes stares lovingly at a photo of Ethel as someone else refers to the Endless named "Desire.") To obtain an amulet of protection against Burgess's vengeance, Sykes trades away the helmet to a demon from hell. In 1936, however, Cripps steals both the amulet and the Sandman's ruby from Sykes, sealing the man's doom.

Roderick Burgess dies of old age in 1947, but his son Alex takes his place as Magus and maintains the Sandman's imprisonment. This situation continues until (judging by the newspaper date on page 26) September 14, 1988, when Alex accidentally erases part of the magic circle with his wheelchair. The Sandman quickly takes advantage of the mistake and, after seven decades, escapes.

Dream's freedom causes the people with sleepy sickness to finally regain consciousness. As for Alex, the Sandman curses him with "eternal waking," which is a nightmare that makes Alex perpetually believe he's woken up . . . only to discover a moment later that he's still dreaming. Issue 1 ends with Alex's nurse and his lover Paul McGuire frantically trying to awaken him, but not succeeding.

A very weak Sandman proceeds to return to The Dreaming, which is the infinite, ever-changing place we all go to when asleep. He's shaken by the deterioration his realm has suffered during the years of his absence; this doubles his determination to restore his power, much of which resides in the three stolen tools, and he embarks on a heroic quest to reclaim his pouch, helmet, and ruby.

The Sandman pursues the pouch, which holds the sands of dream, with the help of a perpetually smoking and joking English magician named John Constantine. The forces released by the pouch turn out to have destroyed several lives, including a man whose body has been horrifically transformed into living wallpaper; but the Sandman manages to bluff his way through the dangerous dreams and get his first tool back.

The Sandman's retrieval of his helm of office proves a more formidable challenge, because it resides in hell. After battling his way into the infernal realm, Dream is led to a woman named Nada, whom he apparently loves—but whom he has nonetheless condemned to be tortured for the past ten thousand years.

Lucifer eventually summons all the demons of hell, and the Sandman uses his pouch to identify Choronzon as the one who possesses his helmet. Dream then calls on ancient rules to challenge Choronzon to a battle of clashing realities; and he wins with "hope," a concept the demon can't counter.

After Choronzon gives up the helmet, Lucifer demands a reason for why he should now let the Sandman leave, asking, "What power have dreams in hell?" The Sandman replies, "You say that dreams have no power here? Tell me, Lucifer Morningstar—ask yourselves, all of you—what power would hell have if those here imprisoned were not able to dream of heaven?" The demons part to let the Sandman pass; but as they do so, Lucifer vows, "One day I shall destroy him."

Dream's winning back his helmet also has a consequence that's implied rather than stated—it results in breaking the spell over Choronzon's amulet of protection, which in turns results in the death of the by-now-ancient Ethel Cripps.

With pouch and helmet in tow, all that's left for the Sandman to retrieve is his ruby. This is a tool that normally carries out the Sandman's wishes so he doesn't have to think about how to perform every task himself; that is, it functions as a kind of genie's genie. But the ruby is posthumously passed on by Ethel Cripps to her son, the psychotic Doctor John Dee; and Dee alters the ruby so drastically that when the Sandman tries to retrieve it, it absorbs much of his power and knocks him unconscious.

For twenty-four hours, Dee turns a diner into a horror-filled hell on earth, and he begins to exert the same insane forces on the rest of the world.

The Sandman tries to stop Dee, but he's outmatched by his own tool. Dee ends up defeating himself, however, by destroying the ruby in an effort to kill Dream. This action frees all the power stored in the jewel, restoring the Sandman to full strength. A surprisingly grateful Dream returns the favor by taking Dee back home . . . to his padded cell at the Arkham Asylum for the Criminally Insane.

Having both reclaimed his tools and attained more power than he's had in eons, the Sandman repairs the damage done by Dee. Unlike a conventional triumphant hero, however, the Sandman celebrates the completion of his quest by going to Washington Square Park in Greenwich Village to feed pigeons, and to brood about how unsatisfied and empty he feels with no death-defying feats left to accomplish.

It's at this point that a vibrant new character enters the picture—Dream's older sister, Death. Beautiful, perky, and utterly sensible, Death begins by expounding upon the charms of the film *Mary Poppins*, and uttering the immortal phrases "supercalifragilisticexpialidocious" and "peachy keen." When this fails to get a rise out of her brother, Death throws a loaf of bread at him and instructs him to, in effect, get a life. She then suggests he accompany her on her rounds . . . which consists of helping people make the transition from their death in one plane of existence to a life in another.

After watching Death carry out her duties with perpetual grace, wit, and compassion, the Sandman realizes that "my sister has a function to perform, even as I do. The Endless have their responsibilities. I have responsibilities." He determines to return to The Dreaming and begin the repair of his realm.

Issue 8 is the aesthetic turning point in the series, because it shifts the storytelling emphasis from plot development to mood and character development. Much of the "action" in this story consists merely of two characters walking around New York; but it's easily the most gripping tale in *Preludes & Nocturnes*. Issue 8 also sets the tone for what follows in future collections.

SOME THINGS WORTH NOTICING

Neil Gaiman is a writer who loves to overturn expectations, and there are ample examples of this in *Preludes & Nocturnes*.

In a standard epic quest, the hero starts out in ordinary surroundings, and then experiences some kind of shock that sends him into a shadow realm where he does battle with primal forces.

In the Sandman's case, however, his ordinary surroundings *are* the shadow realm, because he's the personification of myths and dreams. Therefore, the shock he experiences is being dragged from his realm of mystery and nightmare to some penny-ante magician's basement. And instead of doing battle with epic forces, he remains a still and silent prisoner in that basement for seventy-two years.

Nonetheless, this quiet experience has a profound effect on the Sandman. The extent to which it changes him isn't apparent until later in the series . . . and isn't something he even realizes himself. But we can deduce that a metamorphosis is occurring from visual clues, such as the Sandman looking like a fetus after he's captured; his being kept naked in a womblike glass bowl; and his feigning death to get his cage opened, after which he springs to life.

It's also notable that Neil Gaiman's summary of *Preludes & Nocturnes*— which appears at the front of *The Doll's House* collection—states that right before Burgess cast his spell, the Sandman had been "tried almost beyond endurance" and was "near-lifeless" at the time of his capture (a statement echoed in *Brief Lives*). We can assume it was his exhaustion that allowed Dream to be captured by a paltry spell. It's possible this exhaustion also made him more open to gaining a new perspective.

After his escape, the Sandman returns to his realm (through the fabled Gates of Horn and Ivory referred to by Homer in *The Odyssey* and Virgil in *The Aeneid*), and that gives him the opportunity to become reacquainted with some of the regular inhabitants of The Dreaming. These include the brothers Cain and Abel; a woman named Eve who lives with a raven; a librarian named Lucien; and (as visitors) the Three Witches, or the Hecateae. Each of these characters was a host of his or her own DC Comics horror title in the 1970s, and so including them added an extra level of resonance and interest for old-time comics readers. (More information about these characters appears in chapter 13, "Secret Origins.")

After getting his bearings, the Sandman undertakes something approaching a standard heroic journey by pursuing his pouch, helmet, and ruby. Arguably the most interesting aspect of this journey isn't its effect on him, however, but on the facets of his personality that it reveals to us, the readers.

For example, we're shown by contrast that the Sandman resists the temptation of becoming addicted to his dreams; abusing his subjects; and allowing dreams to run wild and turn people insane. We also see the Sandman show remarkable calm, courage, and intelligence in facing down his pouch's rogue dreams with a bluff; battling his way in and out of hell using little more than his wits; and selflessly confronting an opponent who has the ability to drain his life. In addition, we learn that the Sandman honors his debts (for example, when he helps John Constantine, and even John Dee), and that he takes rules and responsibilities very seriously.

At the same time, however, the Sandman admits to condemning Nada, a woman he loves, to be tortured in hell for the past ten thousand years. Further, Dream almost never demonstrates warmth, compassion, or humor. Even his laid-back sister Death loses her temper over his stuffy, mopey attitude, tossing a loaf of bread at his head—a not insignificant act, since grain is traditionally a symbol of life, and of wisdom. And, as is noted by the quotation from the Book of Job that appears on the first page of *Preludes & Nocturnes*, "the price of wisdom is above rubies."

The Sandman therefore comes across as someone who is very conscientious, capable and even self-sacrificing when performing his job; but he's markedly deficient when it comes to handling people and relationships. In this first storyline, the Sandman learns that he's better off without his ruby, because one can become subtly trapped by one's tools. It remains to be seen whether he will learn a similar lesson about rules.

SPELLS AND CAGES

HB: I've read some comments that indicate you didn't take *Sandman* very seriously initially—that is, not until you'd found your voice in the series and made it your own. For example, your longtime collaborator Dave McKean has portrayed your early attitude as, "I'm doing this thing for this huge company, and this is the sort of thing they usually do, and you can only go so far."

NG: Well, I always took *Sandman* seriously. In many ways, I worked *harder* on the series' first eight issues than I did on any of the others. As I mentioned before, I spent nearly six months writing *Sandman* 1. It was very, very hard work.

But at the same time, *Sandman* was initially my "throwing mud at the wall" comic. For everything else I was doing, I had an aesthetic justification, or at least rationalization, and a bunch of rules that would be important, with the hope of changing the face of comics in some positive way. *Sandman* was simply my monthly comic. And I was going to do whatever worked, and I was going to have fun, and I was going to experiment.

HB: What was your approach for these initial stories?

NG: I started off by exploring genres. For example, the first issue was patterned after classical English horror stories like the ones written by Dennis Wheatley.

HB: It shows. For example, I really liked the Roderick Burgess incantation that trapped the Sandman. Did you make that up out of whole cloth?

NG: Thanks; and yes. The words are mine, at least; I took the rhythm from a Henry Treece poem titled "The Magic Wood," which goes, in part, "The wood is full of shining eyes, the wood is full of creeping feet, the wood is full of tiny cries, you must not go in the wood at night!"

HB: The spell casting makes me think of the famous English occultist Aleister Crowley. Was Roderick based on Crowley?

NG: Not really. When researching the story, I was pleased and excited about having an excuse to finally read Crowley's books. Unfortunately, I found his prose style about as appealing as chewing tin foil, and I ultimately gave up on him.

I did draw a feeling from Dennis Wheatley's novel *The Devil Rides Out*, however,

The cast of *The Sandman* began to expand with the introduction of characters including the Hecateae, also known as the Three Witches.

and Wheatley based his evil magician on Crowley; so you might say Burgess partly comes from Crowley, twice removed.

HB: Speaking of things you're often asked, I know another one is, "When Burgess died, wasn't Death there to meet him? And if so, wouldn't she have found out at that point about the Sandman being imprisoned by Burgess?"

NG: Right, with the implication that this is a huge hole in the plot. But to my mind, Death knew about the Sandman being trapped as soon as it happened. Everyone in his family did.

The reason the Endless didn't free him isn't because they weren't aware of the situation, but because they aren't a superteam; rushing to the rescue isn't what they're about. The Endless stick to hoeing their own farms. As personifications of things, they're not causative. They're barely reactive.

Besides, even if the Endless had acted to break the Sandman out, he probably would've been angry at them for doing so. He definitely wouldn't have been anything approaching appreciative.

HB: Why?

NG: Mostly because he felt it was his responsibility to take care of himself.

Also, the Sandman was a very stuffy character at the time of his capture. Just how stuffy becomes clear with subsequent stories that show his behavior in earlier eras.

WHAT? You wanted DEATH? Then count yourself lucky for the sake of your species and your petty planet that you did NOT succeed...

...that instead you snared Death's younger BROTHER...

SAM KIETH / MIKE DRINGENBERG

Dream confronts his captor, the mystic Roderick Burgess.

HORROR AND SUPER HEROES

HB: What genre was issue 2 patterned after?

NG: Partly 1950s E.C. comics, but mostly 1970s DC horror comics. I've always had a deep and peculiar fondness for Cain and Abel, the Three Witches, and all those other odd DC mystery characters.

HB: There was more going on than homage, though. In that story, you provide a lot of information to help us understand the Sandman's realm.

In addition, you use the Three Witches to foreshadow events that occur much later. The maiden, mother, and crone who comprise the Witches appear periodically throughout *Sandman* under numerous names, including the Hecateae, the Fates, the Weird Sisters, and the Kindly Ones. When the Sandman thanks them for answering his questions, they respond: "'Thank you,' he says! You don't thank the Fates, Dreamkin! Ahahahahahaha! HEEEE! We haven't helped you!" That unsettling laughter resonates throughout the series.

NG: They're a cheery bunch.

HB: Yep. [*Laughter.*] What genres were you tackling in the following two issues?

NG: Issue 3 was meant to be my Ramsey Campbell/Clive Barker British urban horror tale. It also let me work with Alan Moore's wonderful character John Constantine. Unfortunately, my favorite image for that story is something that didn't really materialize visually—a human body turned inside out, still alive and spread all over the walls of a room. Due to a variety of problems, what appeared on the printed page looked like little more than gunky brown wallpaper. [*Laughter.*]

Issue 4 was based on the work of fantasists such as John W. Campbell writing for the

THE SANDMAN COMPANION

1940s pulp magazine *Unknown*. It was by far the most popular issue of *Sandman* until issue 8, where Death made her debut. The double-page spread on pages 12 and 13, by the way, is a direct steal from Robert Heinlein's novel *Magic Incorporated*.

HB: What about issue 5, where you had the Sandman interact with DC super heroes?

NG: At the time, I thought it would be a good idea to show where the Sandman fit into the DC Universe. I was walking a tightrope, really. I wanted the series to look enough like a super-hero comic to get people who liked super heroes to read it; and I wanted it to look enough like a horror comic to allow me to write the sort of fantasy stories I was interested in writing.

HB: Karen Berger told me she felt that was clever of you, because it eased existing comics readers into the series.

NG: There's truth to that. On another level, though, these early stories were essentially five-finger exercises to help me find out what my voice sounds like. That was why I titled the book collecting these stories *Preludes & Nocturnes*. They're preludes to my figuring out my approach to the series.

THE AUTHOR FINDS HIS VOICE

HB: When do you feel you actually found your voice?

NG: *Sandman* 6 was the first time I tried to break all the rules of what had been done in comics to date, to go as far as I could go. In that story, a small bunch of people are essentially tortured to death over a twenty-four-hour period. A lot of readers said they stopped buying *Sandman* after issue 6 and didn't come back for ages, until they were told it was safe.

I also toyed with some ideas for that story that didn't make it into the script. For example, when I looked at its title, "24 Hours," I thought—inspired by Peter Greenaway's 1988 film *Drowning by Numbers*—"Hey, I've got twenty-four pages. I'll

KAREN BERGER ON STORYTELLING STRATEGIES

Vertigo Executive Editor Karen Berger learned about comics editing such titles as *The Legion of Super-Heroes*, *House of Mystery*, and Alan Moore's *Swamp Thing*.

Berger's sharpness, comfort with non-super-hero titles, and excellent working relationship with Brits such as Moore snared her the position of DC's liaison to the U.K. That appointment, in turn, led to Berger meeting and hiring Neil Gaiman, and then editing *Sandman* for its entire seven-year run.

"When Neil began Sandman," says Berger,

"everyone reading comics was primarily buying super-hero titles. Neil created the trappings of a super-hero comic, in terms of the structure, the uses of conflict, and the pacing—albeit with cooler clothes and, arguably, cooler concepts. So he got existing comics readers into a territory they were familiar with, but which was in key ways a very different territory; and then he slowly moved them further and further out to the range of the unfamiliar. Timing is important; and Neil is very, very good with timing."

do an hour a page." But I gave up on that when I realized that the first few pages had to be devoted to introducing the characters properly.

Issue 6 was also important for me because it was the first time I realized on a gut level, not just an intellectual one, that I was writing a story about stories.

HB: How so?

NG: In many ways, *Sandman* 6 is about storytelling. It begins with an essay about a waitress who wants to be a writer and about the kinds of stories she tells—and that essay is the nearest I came early on to giving away the overall plot of *Sandman*. There are lots of hints in issues 1 and 2, but the captions about the waitress are pretty explicit. Page 4 begins "All Bette's stories have happy endings. That's because she knows where to stop. She's realized the real problem with stories—if you keep them going long enough, they always end in death." That's a major theme in *Sandman*—you get happy endings only by stopping at a certain point.

HB: It sounds like you'd already sketched out plot points that wouldn't occur until years later in the series. That also means you knew you'd wrap up the saga at a certain point, even though ending a monthly series solely for aesthetic reasons was—and still is—practically unheard of in comics.

NG: You're quite right. I felt like I was taking on the role of a Columbus, saying "I believe there is a land—over there—to the west of us! I'm going to head out and see if I can find that land."

The fallen Lord of Dreams, with his mystical accoutrements in the splash page of *Sandman* 1.

THE SANDMAN COMPANION

Sam Kieth was the first penciller on *Sandman*, illustrating issues 1 through 5. Kieth designed the Sandman (based on Neil Gaiman's initial sketches), and churned out numerous visual ideas that Gaiman ended up using as story elements (for example, the wall of faces in issue 3). But Kieth increasingly felt that he and Gaiman were tugging in different directions, making the artist feel "like Jimi Hendrix in the Beatles," and so Kieth opted to leave the series.

Mike Dringenberg, whom Kieth had brought in as his inker, took over as penciller with issue 6; and Dringenberg in turn brought in as inker the talented Malcolm Jones III (who has since passed away). Dringenberg ultimately pencilled eleven spectacular issues of *Sandman*, with ten of them inked by Jones.

Sam Kieth went on to write and draw the popular comic book *The Maxx*—which became an animated miniseries on MTV.

Mind you, that doesn't mean I thought I'd actually be allowed to make the voyage. Critical success and financial success are not at all synonymous, and I thought the series would probably be canceled within the year.

In fact, that's why the first story arc is eight issues long. At the time, a monthly comic would run at least one year and have a four-month lead time, so issue 8 was the point at which a publisher would phone you and say "We're really sorry. We like it, it's achieved some minor critical acclaim, but it's not selling. Please start resolving the loose ends so we can gracefully close everything down by issue 12."

HB: If you'd received that dreaded phone call, would you have moved up your timetable and tried to resolve everything during the subsequent four issues?

NG: Oh, no. I would've done four issues of short stories or something. And I would've hoped that, a few years down the line, someone would say to me, "Remember that *Sandman* thing you did? We really liked it. Why don't you come back and pick it up again?"

When I reached issue 8, however, *Sandman* was selling better than any horror comic since the 1970s. At that point, instead of being a Columbus with somewhat vague ideas about a new land, I was able to take a close look at what I was trying to do and make very specific plans. By issue 10, I knew in great detail where I was going and how I was going to get there.

HB: Though you ended up making a number of unexpected side trips.

NG: True, which caused the journey to take about twice as long as I'd expected. I'd originally planned the series to last for about forty issues, and it ran for seventy-five—or seventy-six, counting *The Sandman Special*.

HB: Yep. What can you say about issue 7, "Sound and Fury"?

NG: It wrapped up the Sandman's quest for his tools of office, and it restored him to full power by having Doctor Dee destroy his ruby—demonstrating that tools can be the subtlest of traps.

Sandman Editor Karen Berger on issue 8, "The Sound of Her Wings":

I knew that Neil was very talented, but it didn't become obvious to me that *Sandman* would take off until issue 8. It wasn't just the introduction of Death as a character, but an emotional core that Neil got into the story.

Neil's earlier work was technically very good, but I felt that he was keeping us at a distance emotionally, to the point where he was almost cold at times. With issue 8, it all came together. And he then just kept on surprising me as the series went on.

By the way, panel 4 on page 4 was meant to be a clue to help readers begin understanding the whole *Sandman* package; it was supposed to show how the Sandman looked long ago when he was creating the ruby. My script described the Sandman's skin, hair, and clothing as all white, the implication being that that's how a manifestation of Dream starts out. But none of that information made it to the printed page.

HB: Is there anything you'd care to mention about the layout of issue 7, which concludes the three-part Doctor Dee story?

NG: I like that the last page, which ties up the Doctor Dee story, uses Arkham Asylum as a frame for three panels showing order restored; and that this is a mirror image of the first page of issue 5, which begins the Doctor Dee story, and which uses Arkham Asylum as a frame for three panels that indicate impending chaos. Also, there's no hint of the Sandman on the first page of issue 5, but his image encompasses Arkham on the last page of issue 7. I thought it was a nice way of visually emphasizing the Sandman's success in regaining control of The Dreaming.

My favorite image in issue 7, however, is the last one on page 22, which is a silhouette of Dream on one end, the villain named Scarecrow on the other, and a Dorothy-like Doctor Dee in the middle.

HB: With Doctor Dee saying "There's no place like home" as he's being returned to his padded cell in the asylum. That's definitely a charmer.

Following the bizarre and horrific Dee saga, you do an issue that's utterly gentle and sweet—and infused with a very different *D*, named Death. You begin your script for issue 8 by noting, "This is a really quiet issue. Slow paced. Not particularly exciting either visually or in terms of story. But if they've stuck with us this far, they'll stay with us for this one, too. It'll be a change of pace, but it's a one-off; and it's the one I've been looking forward to writing since we began." At the end, you conclude, "I had more fun on this script than I've had on anything for a long while—one of the few times I've actually been irritated if anything took me away from the keyboard." In retrospect, your instincts were dead on. Most people point to issue 8 as *Sandman*'s turning point, the story where your true voice entirely breaks through.

TITLES AND COVERS

HB: For *Sandman*'s first year or so, you ended each issue with a blurb announcing the title of the next issue. The funny thing is, what you put down never turned out to be the actual title. For example, issue 8, which debuts the Sandman's sister, is called "The Sound of Her Wings"; but issue 7 ends with: "Next: A Death in the Family." [*Laughter.*] Was all this misdirection intentional?

NG: Oh, yes; that was me having some extra fun. For example, for issue 5—which is actually titled "Passengers"—I ended issue 4 with "Next: Monsters & Miracles," which is based on a line in an Ogden Nash poem that goes "Where there's a monster, there's a miracle." It fits because issue 5 features the first *Sandman* appearances of both the monstrous Doctor Dee and the super hero Mister Miracle.

To give just one other example, my alternative title for issue 6, "Waiting for the End of the World," was taken from the title of an Elvis Costello song. I thought that was appropriate because—aside from the fact it's a fairly accurate description of what happens in issue 6—the title of issue 1, "Sleep of the Just," also came from an Elvis Costello song.

HB: You obviously enjoyed playing these word games. Why did you stop?

NG: Despite my repeatedly trying to explain what I was doing, the "mistitled" blurbs were causing too much confusion in the editorial and production departments. The last straw for me was when a key "Next" blurb was lost for issue 13.

HB: Do you have any comments to offer about *Sandman*'s first eight covers?

NG: Simply that Dave and I wanted to do a portrait gallery. Therefore, the first cover features the Sandman, and subsequent covers portray the Three Witches, John Constantine, Lucifer, Mister Miracle, an innocent bystander, Doctor Dee, and Death.

After that, I began a new story arc, and so Dave created a new visual approach to suit it. He did the same thing for each new story arc; Dave was always looking for ways to be innovative.

Another proposal sketch of the Sandman by Dave McKean.

Dave McKean has illustrated numerous book covers and CD covers; publications ranging from *The New Yorker* to his comic book *Cages*; and several graphic novels in collaboration with Neil Gaiman, including *Violent Cases*, *Black Orchid*, *Signal to Noise*, and *Mr. Punch*.

The *Detroit Free Press* has called McKean's drawings "often surreal, sometimes obscure, but always alluring." That assessment certainly applies to McKean's seventy-six astonishing covers for *Sandman*.

"The concept for each issue's cover came from the story," says McKean, "but the execution came mostly from whatever I happened to be playing around with at the time. There was no great master plan other than, as much as possible, to not repeat myself, to not do what was expected, and to not play by the rules. Most of the rules were so ancient that nobody even remembered the reasons behind them, so they could be easily discarded."

The composition of his famous cover for *Sandman* 1, recalls McKean, "was inspired by a beautiful poster for Peter Greenaway's 1987 film *The Belly of an Architect*. Putting shelving on the sides and stocking little objects on them was my way of getting across that the Sandman was more of an idea than a standardized character. Comics publishers typically create style sheets that show how a character looks from the front, from the side, and so forth. My thought was that any artist who came to the Sandman could recreate him, making him that artist's idea of Dream."

McKean concedes that a main character who looked radically different every few issues might have created confusion for readers trying to follow the storylines. "But I was doing illustrations, not storytelling," he says, "and I felt it was the job of the covers to bend and stretch things as much as possible."

As a result, McKean consciously stayed away from the literal. "My approach was to try and symbolize the feeling of each story, rather than represent specific events from it. After the first few issues, I didn't even read Neil's scripts; I just had him describe each story to me because he would, almost subconsciously, mention the key elements I needed in the process. These often weren't tied to the big events in the issue, which had to do with narrative, but odd little images that captured the mood and concepts of the story.

"In addition," continues McKean, "I wanted each cover to function as a filter, in that you could read the story inside—which was usually drawn in a conventional, realistic style—and then skew your perspective of what you've read through the image that appeared on the front, as if the cover were tinted glass."

"I did each cover in about a day," he says, "not to get the job over with as quickly as possible, but to capture the 'rush' of creation. I was always doodling and jotting down ideas, though, so there was a fair amount of mental preparation behind each execution.

"Every cover was an experiment," concludes McKean. "That involved taking a lot of risks, of course, and sometimes the experiment didn't turn out very well; but I think more successes resulted overall than would've had I played it safe."

—

the doll's house

4

**It is an anxious, sometimes a dangerous thing to be a doll.
Dolls cannot choose, they can only be chosen; they cannot "do,"
they can only be done by.**

—RUMER GODDEN, FROM HER BOOK *THE DOLL'S HOUSE*

U nlike the relatively linear storyline of *Preludes & Nocturnes*, *The Doll's House* jumps between time and space with a kind of dream logic: its subject matter ranges from a ten-thousand-year-old African love affair to the Faustian bargain made by an unpromising young writer named William Shakespeare to a convention in modern-day Georgia held for serial killers. As Neil Gaiman wrote in his script for issue 14, the stories are "about women, and men's attitudes to women; about the houses and walls that people build around themselves and each other, for protection, or for imprisonment, or both; and about the tearing down of those walls." As a result, the title of *The Doll's House* is a nod to the classic Henrik Ibsen play about a woman liberating herself from traditional roles; and it was especially inspired by the children's book of the same name by Rumer Godden.

The storyline begins with a folk tale that's been passed down from generation to generation by the men of an African tribe. According to a grandfather telling the tale to his grandson, these tribesmen are the direct descendants of the first people on earth.

Long, long ago (says the grandfather), the original members of the tribe lived in a vast glass city ruled by a wise and beautiful queen named Nada. Their only problem was that Nada had no husband, and she could never find a man who suited her. One day a stranger appeared, however, and a single glance at him stole Nada's heart. Through determination and courage, the great queen tracked the stranger down to his castle and declared her love for him. He accepted and returned her statement of love; but he also revealed himself to be no man, but the Lord of Dreams. This filled Nada with terror, because it's forbidden for a mortal to love a member of the Endless.

Nada tried to flee her beloved, first by returning to the waking world, and then by taking the form of a gazelle; but each time the Sandman chased and caught her. Nada then used a sharp rock to break her maidenhead, reasoning Dream's ardor would dissipate if she was no longer a virgin; but the Sandman merely said, "I am no mortal man, and I love you as no mortal man could love. What matters your body to me?" And with that, he drew her into his black robe, and the two of them spent the night making love.

The next morning, Nada's fears were realized. When the sun saw her and Dream together, it threw down a blazing fireball that razed her glass city to the ground, leaving behind nothing but sand . . . and glass shards in the shape of hearts. Horrified, and determined to prevent even worse catastrophes, Nada flung herself from a mountaintop to a bloody death; but even this didn't stop Dream's pursuit of her. Following Nada to the border of the realm of death, the Sandman issued his lover an ultimatum: agree to be his bride, or suffer eternal torment. Nada pointed out that only disaster would result from their staying together, and she begged Dream to simply let her go. But in his pride, the Sandman demanded that Nada provide an answer. With no other option, Nada refused to be Dream's bride . . . and, true to his word, he condemned her to hell.

After the grandfather concludes the ancient tale, a caption informs us that the generations of women in the tribe tell their own version of the story . . . the implication being that there are certain details that would make the Sandman's actions seem even worse. (We also know there's at least some truth to the tale, because we've already seen a modern-day Dream encounter Nada in issue 4, when his quest for his helmet takes him to hell. Upon seeing him, Nada begs to be released from her torture; but the Sandman just says, "It has been 10,000 years, Nada. Yes, I still love you; but I have not yet forgiven you.")

Following this distressing prologue, two more members of the Endless are briefly introduced. One is Despair, who's in the habit of cutting up her face with a hook-ring. The other is the androgynous Desire, who lives in a giant replica of his-her body—in other words (reversing the collection's title), in a house that's a doll. Desire reveals that it was behind the intense attraction between the Sandman and Nada, but the affair didn't work out as planned. Desire is now involved in another scheme to ensnare the Sandman, however, involving something called a "vortex" that brings dreams together.

In this era, the vortex is a young woman with multicolored hair named Rose Walker. We first see her traveling to England to meet Unity Kinkaid—who turns out to be a biological grandmother Rose never knew existed. Readers with sharp memories will recognize Unity as the woman suffering from "sleepy sickness" in issue 1 who was raped and later gave birth (to Rose's mother) without ever waking up. With the Sandman freed, Unity has rejoined the living; and she now asks Rose to reunite the family by locating Jed, Rose's missing brother.

Meanwhile, we learn another consequence of the Sandman's imprisonment is that it allowed four dream beings to escape his realm: Brute and Glob, Fiddler's Green, and the Corinthian. Although Rose is oblivious of her special powers,

Dream knows about them, and—by keeping an eye on her via a talking raven named Matthew—the Sandman uses Rose's natural ability as a "dream magnet" to locate his missing creations.

Rose first leads the Sandman to Brute and Glob, who have constructed their own dream realm within Jed's mind. The thoroughly amoral duo accomplished this by making Jed's waking world so unendurable that he was impelled to escape it by creating more and more elaborate dreams (resembling *Little Nemo in Slumberland* comic strips). To reinforce these fantasies, Brute and Glob even made their own "kid-friendly" version of the Sandman via the ghost of deceased super hero Hector Hall—accompanied by Hector's dazed wife Lyta, who has been six months pregnant in this dream world for the past two years.

Brute and Glob, Jed, and the gaudy version of the Sandman all originally appeared—and were played straight—in a short-lived 1970s DC comic titled *The Sandman*. Issue 12's "Playing House" therefore works as a parody of that comic; and it also serves to make crystal clear how little that earlier version of the Sandman has to do with the current one. When the two versions meet, Dream bursts into uncontrollable laughter. Dream then dissipates Hector's ghost with a wave of his hand.

As for Lyta Hall, Dream treats her almost as shabbily as he once did Nada. Sobbing, she says, "You killed Hector. You destroyed our home. You've ruined my life." The Sandman coldly responds, "You are free to go. Build yourself a new life, Hippolyta Hall. Oh, I almost forgot. The child—the child you have carried so long in dreams. That child is mine. Take good care of it. One day I will come for it." And Dream disappears, leaving Lyta replying to the empty room, "You take my child over my dead body, you spooky bastard. Over my dead body."

Nor does Jed fare much better. Although the Sandman makes a point of punishing Brute and Glob, he doesn't lift a finger to help their young victim, imprisoned for years in a basement (a situation that Dream should empathize with). Instead, Jed is simply left to wander away from the wreckage—and to be picked up shortly by the third escaped dream, the Corinthian.

The latter is a personification of nightmare who, in place of eyes, has mouths with teeth; and whose favorite pastime is to feed those mouths the eyeballs of young boys. The Corinthian puts Jed in the trunk of his car, planning to use the child later for a snack.

He delays his fun because he's on his way to a major event: the first annual convention for serial killers. As one of the attendees comments, "You know what's so great about something like this? We're all so different. United by our common interests." The juxtaposition of this murderous obsession with the usual trappings of an SF or comic book convention—complete with speeches (including a guest of honor talk by the Corinthian), a film program (screening such fare as *The Collector, Compulsion,* and *In Cold Blood*) and panel discussions (on such topics as "Make It Pay," "Women in Serial Killing," and "We Are What We Are")—paints a picture of utterly banal evil.

Thanks to yet another vortex-generated coincidence, Rose is staying in the hotel in which the convention is taking place; and with her is the fourth missing dream, Fiddler's Green. The latter isn't actually a person but a place—in The Dreaming, he appears as an especially lovely and peaceful stretch of trees, mountains, springs, meadows, and green glades. In the waking world, however, he's taken the name of Gilbert and the appearance of the late author G. K. Chesterton.

Gilbert tells Rose an early version of the Little Red Riding Hood legend that is charged with twisted sexuality and violence. The tale proves prophetic when the red-and-blond-haired Rose is attacked a little later by Funland, a serial killer wearing a wolf T-shirt and a wolf-ears cap. Fortunately, Gilbert sensed trouble coming and provided Rose with Morpheus's name on a slip of paper. When Rose reads out the name, the Sandman appears, and he quickly disposes of Funland by putting him in a dream inspired by Oscar Wilde's tale "The Selfish Giant."

The Sandman then moves to the convention area, where he finds the Corinthian making his guest of honor speech. Dream credits the Corinthian for inspiring the modern phenomenon of serial killing, and then chastises him—not for being evil, but for demonstrating such small vision! "You were my masterpiece, or so I thought," says the Sandman. "A nightmare created to be the darkness, and the fear of darkness in every human heart. . . . But look at you. Forty years walking the earth, honing yourself, infecting others with your joy of death and what have you given them? . . . Nothing. Just something else for people to be scared of, that's all." Dream then proceeds to uncreate his creation, until all that's left of the Corinthian is a small, toothy skull; and the Sandman promises the skull, "The next time I make you, you shall not be so flawed and petty, little dream."

The Sandman works a different kind of disintegration on the rest of the serial killers—he strips away their fantasies of being noble warriors and maltreated heroes, removing all the justifications they cling to for their actions. All that's left to them is the realization of (in Dream's words) "just how little that means."

Afterward, Gilbert hears Jed sobbing in the Corinthian's car trunk, and he and Rose get the boy to a hospital. Rose returns to her room in Florida to await Jed's recovery and, exhausted, goes to sleep.

While Rose sleeps, her powers as a vortex kick in and she begins sensing the dreams of everyone in her house; and she realizes "how thin and fragile the walls that divide them truly are." She downs the barriers, allowing the dreams to crash together; and then her mind begins to do the same thing to millions of other dreams.

Before more damage can be done, however, the Sandman takes Rose to The Dreaming and tells her that aeons ago, and half a universe away, a vortex was allowed to run its full course—and the inhabitants of an entire world lost their minds and perished. The Sandman vows that he'll never allow that to happen again; and the only solution is to kill the vortex.

But Rose's grandmother Unity Kinkaid comes to the rescue. Unity is almost ninety and dying, but nonetheless musters the strength to enter The Dreaming where she tells the Sandman that it was she, not Rose, who was supposed to have been the vortex (which some sharp readers may have already guessed because of her unusual name), and it was only the Sandman's imprisonment and Unity's subsequent sleepy sickness that caused Rose to become the vortex instead. A confused Dream says, "I do not understand." Unity replies, "Of course you don't. You're obviously not very bright, but I shouldn't let it bother you."

Unity then instructs Rose to give her what makes Rose the vortex; and as anything is possible in The Dreaming, Rose reaches into her chest and extracts a jewel-like heart (which resembles the glass shard in the prologue story, "Tales in the Sand"). Rose then hands her heart over to Unity (an image that recurs throughout the series), who proclaims that she is now the vortex; Unity then dies, taking the threat of the vortex with her.

With Rose no longer a threat, the Sandman lets her resume her life. Rose isn't sure how to cope with all she's seen, however, because "it means that we're just dolls. We don't have a clue what's really going down, we just kid ourselves that we're in control of our lives while a paper's thickness away things that would drive us mad if we thought about them for too long play with us, and move us around from room to room, and put us away at night when they're tired, or bored." And so Rose decides that everything she saw in The Dreaming was just a dream . . . and that it's time for her to wake up.

The Sandman, on the other hand, isn't prepared to close his eyes to what happened and so pays a call on Desire. His androgynous sibling admits to being the mysterious rapist of Unity Kinkaid who, fifty years before, fathered Unity's daughter—and therefore is Rose's grandfather. "Was I to take the life of one of our blood," asks Dream, "with all that that would entail?" "Does it matter?" says Desire. "It didn't work."

The Sandman responds with words that are effectively the answer to Rose's lament: "We of the Endless are the servants of the living—we are *not* their masters. We exist because they know, deep in their hearts, that we exist. When the last living thing has left this universe, then our task will be done. And we do not manipulate them. If anything, they manipulate us. We are *their* toys."

The interplay between humans and Endless is explored in a story placed in the middle of *The Doll's House*: "Men of Good Fortune." This tale begins with Death dragging her brother Dream to a pub in 1389 so that he can learn to better understand people. "At least *I* get out and meet them," she says. "I just think maybe it would be good for you to see them on *their* terms instead of yours."

The tavern is full of the usual chatter: complaints about taxes, crime, and high prices, and predictions about the end of the world. At one table sits Geoffrey Chaucer, who's listening to a friend criticize his book *Canterbury Tales*, which appeared just a year before in 1388, as "filthy tales in rhyme about pilgrims." (Chaucer's work is, of course, now considered a classic; and *The Canterbury Tales* was later used as the foundation of the collection *Worlds' End*.) What most catches the attention of the two Endless, however, is a man named Hob Gadling who tells his drinking mates that he doesn't intend to die: "It's rubbish, death is. I mean, there's so much to do. So many things to see. People to drink with. Women to swive. You lot may die. I expect you will, 'cos you're stupid. Not me, though."

Amused by Gadling's bluster, Dream asks Death to make the man's absurd claim come true. Death, who takes the matter more seriously, agrees; and she leaves to let her brother get to know Gadling. When Hob repeats that dying "is a mug's game; I won't have any part of it," the Sandman responds, "Then you must tell me what it's like [not to die]. Let us meet here again, Robert Gadling. In this tavern of the White Horse. In a hundred years." Hob's drinking companions find this hilarious; but a hundred years later, both Hob and Dream show up for the appointment.

Hob asks if he's inadvertently made a bargain with the devil. "No," says Dream, "I am merely . . . interested." After quizzing Hob about what he's done since their first meeting (which turns out to include working a new trade called "printing"), the Sandman asks Hob if he still wants to live. "Oh yes," replies Gadling. And so they agree to continue meeting once every century.

In 1589, Hob reports that he's delighted with the good fortune he's found— a wife, a son, riches, and a high place in society. While they talk, the Sandman's attention is caught by an eager but unpromising writer at another table named William Shakespeare—and Dream, who numbers among his skills the ability to open doors, agrees to open one in Shakespeare's mind in exchange for some favors. The results of this encounter are followed up in subsequent collections.

In 1689, Hob arrives in the opposite condition of the last meeting. The wife he loved so much died in childbirth; and his only son died at twenty in a brawl, plunging Hob into a deep depression. Then his neighbors, noticing he didn't age, tried to drown Gadling as a witch; and after that, things got even worse. "I've hated every second of the last eighty years," says Hob. *"Every bloody second."* Dream asks Gadling if he's now ready to die. "Are you crazy?" Hob answers. "Death is a mug's game. I got so much to live for."

In 1789, Gadling's fortunes have reversed again, thanks largely to his investments in the slave trade. The Sandman advises Hob to reconsider the way he's making a living: "It is a poor thing to enslave another. I would suggest you find yourself a different line of business." The irony of this sound advice considered against his treatment of Nada (whom he keeps imprisoned in Hell) appears lost on Dream.

By 1889, Hob has decided that he'll fundamentally be the same man no matter how long he lives; and he tells the Sandman that the reason he meets with Hob isn't to observe what changes immortality will bring, but because Dream is lonely and enjoys Hob's friendship.

The Sandman is incensed and as he walks away in a huff, Hob says, "Tell you what. I'll be here in a hundred years' time. If you're here then too, it'll be because we're friends. No other reason."

And in 1989, directly following his telling Lyta Hall he had to leave because of "a prior engagement," the Sandman travels to the pub and says to an anxious Hob, "I have always heard it was impolite to keep one's friends waiting."

SOME THINGS WORTH NOTICING

At first blush, you might expect someone who rules over dreams and stories to display flexibility, openness, sensitivity, and even a certain amount of flightiness. But *The Doll's House* shows the Sandman to be inflexible (he almost kills Rose without considering other options), insular (Death has to drag him to a pub because he has no friends), closed off to people's feelings (he destroys the world of Lyta Hall, tells her he's going to steal her baby, and then disappears), and entirely devoted to his duties and responsibilities.

This incongruity may be at least partly understood by considering the nature of the Sandman. As demonstrated by such scholars as Carl Jung and Joseph Campbell, there are certain primal images and myths that crop up in every culture because they're built into our collective unconsciousness and are as fundamental to us as air and water. People rely on these archetypes to have dreams and to create stories; but the Sandman *is* dream and story. In other words, his very being is composed of dream-stuff that, by definition, is universal and eternal . . . and very, very slow to change.

Of course, myths take on different forms in different cultures . . . and so the Sandman takes on different forms based on who he's talking to. For example, although we normally see him as pale and white skinned, Nada sees him as an African man with black skin; and in "Men of Good Fortune," the Sandman is equally as comfortable wearing the fashions of the fourteenth century as he is wearing the fashions of the twentieth. These different forms are merely surface alterations, however. As Hob observes after he's lived for more than five hundred years, "I've seen people, and they don't change. Not in the important things." Similarly, no matter how much he alters his appearance, the Sandman remains fundamentally the same.

All this doesn't excuse the Sandman's behavior, as there's nothing in Dream's job description that requires him to be prideful, or act without compassion, or treat people like mayflies whose most notable characteristic is a relatively brief life. It also doesn't mean that the Sandman, who has a personality independent of his job, *can't* change. But by understanding Dream's nature, we can at least empathize with how truly difficult it is for him to change.

Some additional insights regarding the Sandman can be obtained by considering the characters who mirror him. In "Playing House," the modern face of the Corinthian is finally revealed to us. He treats people as little more than vehicles for eyeballs, and as a means to the thrill of the kill. The Corinthian's extravagant abuse of people helps call attention to the Sandman's more subtle crimes—treating people as little more than vehicles for dreams.

Penciller Mike Dringenberg, who illustrated "Collectors," says, "The Corinthian is someone who devours everything he sees. I'd say that makes him an unsettling symbol for *artists*. Everything I see, for example, becomes visual reference. And everything a writer like Neil hears and sees becomes reference; Neil once described his brain as a tape recorder that's switched on at all times. Neil even posed as the Corinthian for the cover of the 'Collectors' issue." When looked at this way, the Corinthian becomes a dark mirror not only for Dream, but for William Shakespeare, whose obsession with stories is explored in later collections.

The Doll's House gives us a clearer picture of the Sandman's realm, The Dreaming. We learn that it's a large community, with over eleven thousand creatures plucked from our collective unconscious. Among them are beings who look human, creatures such as Matthew, a talking raven, and Gilbert, a wise land mass. This wide variety of beings living in accord with one another jibes with the ancient mythological concept that everything in the universe—animal, plant, even land—is in some manner sentient . . . and has at least as much worth as people do.

The richness and complexity of The Dreaming demonstrates that although the Sandman may be too obsessive about his duties, he does genuinely fine work—and genuinely cares about his realm.

LEADING VERSUS FOLLOWING AN AUDIENCE

HG: Your first story arc, *Preludes & Nocturnes*, was about the Sandman heroically battling to reclaim his kingdom, and it was very successful. Why did you follow it with something as different as *The Doll's House*?

NG: At the time I'd finished scripting *Preludes & Nocturnes*, the most popular issue by far was number 4, in which the Sandman journeys to hell. Everybody loved that, and they wanted him to go back to hell as soon as possible. I considered accommodating them, because I'd already sketched out most of what would happen in the series, and I knew that one of the storylines I wanted to do was *Season of Mists*. However, my fear was that if *Season of Mists* was the very next story arc, *Sandman* could turn into *X-Men*.

HB: Since *X-Men* titles have topped comic book sales charts for the past decade, a lot of writers wouldn't consider that a bad thing.

NG: But my goal wasn't to be a crowd pleaser. Gene Wolfe once defined good literature as that which can be read with pleasure by an educated audience, and reread with increased pleasure. I wanted to produce good literature.

I saw *The Doll's House* as an opportunity to begin training my audience to accept a broader range of material than they may have been used to seeing in comics. *The Doll's House* isn't focused on the Sandman at all but on a girl named Rose Walker. Dream pops up periodically in the story, but his participation is scaled way back.

ECHOES OF PRELUDES

HB: Before we discuss the comics section of *The Doll's House*, I want to ask about the rather thorough text synopsis you provided of the previous storyline—the only time you did so in a *Sandman* collection. Was there a special reason for including that summary?

NG: There was, but it will take a little explaining.

Sandman started as just another comic book—that is, a twenty-four-page periodical. Each issue was supposed to go on sale for a month and then vanish. By the time the series entered its second year, however, it had gotten a lot of praise and press attention, which culminated in a big write-up by Mikal Gilmore for *Rolling Stone* magazine. DC's marketing department decided to take advantage of the publicity by putting together a collection of *Sandman* stories. The general feeling was that I'd found my voice by the start of the second storyline, and also that Mike Dringenberg's realistic artwork would be more accessible to mainstream readers than Sam Kieth's fantasy-oriented style, so the marketing folks chose *The Doll's House* to be published as a book. Since the first storyline wasn't available in book form, a synopsis was required for new readers. Also, I already had one available, because I'd written it for *Sandman* 8, for which DC had previously created a big campaign to hook more people on the series.

HB: Your text provided more than just a recap, though; you described events that never actually made it to the printed page.

NG: My feeling was that if regular *Sandman* readers happened to go to the trouble of reading the synopsis, they should be rewarded for their trouble with some extra chunks of information that I didn't have enough room to include in the printed story.

HB: I guess the unique circumstances behind this collection also account for why it's the only one to include an issue from a previous storyline—my copy begins with issue 8, "The Sound of Her Wings," which is actually the end of the first story arc.

NG: Yes, and I wasn't happy about that. But issue 8, which introduces Death, was my most popular at the time, so the marketing folks insisted on including it.

After DC saw that sales of *The Doll's House* were healthy, the first storyline was collected as *Preludes & Nocturnes*, and the first set of short stories was simultaneously collected as *Dream Country*; those two books came out in the same month. When *Preludes & Nocturnes* and *Dream Country* also did well, the decision was made to publish every *Sandman* storyline as a book.

As for the issue 8 redundancy, new editions of *The Doll's House* now skip it and begin properly with issue 9.

GLASS HEARTS

HB: The first story proper, "Tales in the Sand," reads like a true African fairy tale. Given its authentic feel, I was surprised to learn that you didn't do any research for it.

NG: I didn't do research specifically for the story. However, I'd been reading African myths and folk tales for years—like the ones about Anansi, the trickster spider god—and lots of them stuck in my mind.

HB: What about the intriguing tales you allude to on page 1: "The Lizard Who Lost His Male Member" and "The Trickster Who Sold Ape Dung to King Lion Telling Him It Was the Soul of the Moon"?

NG: I made those up, too. [*Laughter.*] Among the joys of this issue was that it was my first attempt in the series at pure pastiche—that is, openly imitating an established style of storytelling. I'd played around with pastiche previously in terms of mood, but this was my first try at wholly imitating the voice and spirit of an anthropological and ethnographical folk tale.

I was also excited about tackling something from an oral tradition, because I love the rhythm and language of such stories.

HB: I thought your wording choices made the rhythm come through beautifully. Another contributing factor, though, was the way you structured the panels. What was your thinking behind the page layout?

NG: I wanted a simple "beat, beat, beat, beat" of four panels on top and a long panel on the bottom of each page. That gave me lots of space to tell the Nada story but also allowed me to periodically return to the framing sequence with the grandfather and grandson. And the repetition of the layout on every page simulated the singsong quality of folk tales.

HB: According to the grandfather, each tribesman hears the folk story only once and tells it only once; and the story's been passed down through many, many generations. Quite a few details must have been lost or altered after so many retellings.

NG: In fact, I actively tried to present a story you could sense had decayed a bit over the years, so you'd know you weren't getting the events quite as they happened, just something close to the truth. That's why, for example, the tale about Nada is suddenly intruded upon by a "Why the Weaver Bird Is Brown" fable. It's obvious that the latter isn't literally true but that over time it worked its way into the Nada story.

HB: "Tales in the Sand" is pretty primal. Were there any censorship issues?

NG: The bottom panel of page 15 had to be slightly redrawn. When Nada uses a rock to take away her virginity, I had the young tribesman cradle his penis in sympathy; but DC felt that image might have been misconstrued. [Laughter.]

HB: Can you talk a little about the rule that says a human can't mate with one of the Endless? For example, is that rule in conflict with Desire making Unity Kinkaid pregnant in issue 1?

NG: It's not a conflict, because what the story says is, "It is not given to mortals to love the Endless." For one of the Endless to rape a sleeping woman is an entirely different matter.

As a plot device, this rule of the universe helps set up the Desire versus Dream conflict. And it helps generate a story in which the idea of men's tales versus women's tales is introduced.

HB: Which jibes with *Sandman* alternating between male- and female-oriented storylines.

I'd say this story confirms your unique voice and perspective. How long did you take to script it?

NG: Only a few days, which was exceptionally fast for me. It was the first time I wrote a *Sandman* issue as a story first, so I could concentrate on the rhythm of the language. After I finished the story, I broke it down panel by panel.

HB: That approach clearly works for you when crafting stories centered around language. You used it again years later for the lyrical *Sandman* 50, "Ramadan"— which was the highest-selling issue of the series.

THE THRESHOLD AND THE DREAMING

HB: Following the prologue story, we meet the androgynous Desire for the first time; and we learn Desire lives in a giant replica of its body called The Threshold. Where did that come from?

NG: I stole the name from a story Clive Barker planned to do that included me as a character, but that he never wound up writing. The story featured a realm of pain called "The Threshold," which I thought was a nice name for a place because *threshold* contains *hold*, meaning a home or fortress. And I came up with the idea of Desire residing in its body because I decided desire lives under the skin.

HB: A few pages later, we meet Rose Walker. How would you describe her as a character?

NG: She's sensible, kind of cool, and kind of damaged. And a heroine.

HB: It's not until Rose's dream that we get a good look around the Sandman's castle.

NG: Rose's dream provides more information about the inhabitants of The

---

TIPPING OVER THE PAGE

Artist Mike Dringenberg on illustrating a dream:

When Rose Walker falls asleep on page 9, I decided to twist the page around to visually express her mental perspective. By page 10, all the panels are tipped over on their sides, reflecting Rose's world tipping over as she enters a state of mind she's never experienced before. The panels don't "right" themselves until page 15, when she leaves the Sandman's castle . . . and wakes up.

---

the doll's house

Dreaming. It introduces the Corinthian and Fiddler's Green; and through Lucien's census, the fact that there are thousands of other assorted characters.

HB: Are all those beings really needed by the Sandman to maintain The Dreaming?

NG: Oh, not at all. He could actually run the whole place by himself.

HB: So why did he create all those servants to help out?

NG: Fundamentally, he likes the company. I always assumed the Sandman spent millions of years in a version of The Dreaming completely on his own; and I think he quite enjoys the alternative of having others around—though he'd never admit it.

HB: If that's the case, would the Sandman ever consider making a woman for himself that he could get along with?

NG: Given how long Dream's been around, it's perfectly possible that he tried to at some point; and that he eventually got bored with her, or she eventually left him. At any rate, there's no rule against it; the only rule is that no mortal may love the Endless.

I should add that the Sandman didn't create *all* the beings in The Dreaming. Some of them were fleeing from other places and took refuge there; others wound up there by accident and decided to stay; and, given the nature of the place, some of them were spontaneously born there.

HB: And some of them occasionally decide to leave, like Fiddler's Green. What made you think of modeling him after one of your favorite authors, G. K. Chesterton?

NG: Fiddler's Green is a disembodied place, not a person; so in order for it to go walkies, it had to make itself a body. I liked the idea that an escaping dream would copy a person who it liked, rather than necessarily having the originality to make a person in its own right.

HB: While we're on the subject of the Sandman's realm, here's something a bit silly that I've wondered about: What language is spoken in The Dreaming?

NG: I've always assumed it's the language that you hear in the back of your head.

HB: Glad I asked. [*Laughter.*]

THE SANDMAN LAUGHS

HB: Following Rose's exploration of The Dreaming, she meets her grandmother Unity Kinkaid; and she then leaves to try to locate her brother Jed. The scene then shifts to Jed, who is imprisoned in a basement, his only relief fantastic dreams that resemble Winsor McCay's *Little Nemo in Slumberland* comic strips. As a McCay fan, I enormously enjoyed those takeoffs of his work.

NG: Thank you; but I wish we'd been allowed to mimic the look and feel of *Little Nemo* more closely. The "In the Land of Marvelous Dreams" pages were supposed to have been lettered in McCay's style, but some people at DC got worried about copyright infringement—even though *Little Nemo* was published in 1905!

A page in which dreams (featuring a more heroic Sandman) collide with real-world horror, in an homage to another dream-fantasy, Winsor McCay's classic comic strip *Little Nemo in Slumberland*.

On the plus side, we numbered the panels the way McCay did, and we used McCay-like shapes and forms. I also really liked including McCay's standard "Mother! Save me! I am falling to the ground! Oh! Oh!"; and then, instead of the final panel where Nemo normally says, "Mama! Mama!" and his mother reassures him, putting in, "Shut up, you little bastard, or I'll *really* give you something to scream about!" [*Laughter.*]

HB: It's a delicious moment of parody, and also makes for a remarkable delineation between a child's charming fantasy life and his horrible real life.

Another thing you parody is the 1970s version of the Sandman, which was written by Joe Simon and pencilled by Jack Kirby. You clearly had fun with Hector Hall's lines.

NG: Oh, sure. Totally manipulated and trapped in a dream, with his wife, Lyta, pregnant for years, Hector reassures her by saying, "Honey, you're talking to the man who rescued the Tooth Fairy from the Jovian Fish-Men. Who stopped the Big Bad Wolf from huffing down the Chrysler Building. Nobody ever beats the Sandman. Everything is going to be just fine." I also liked his reaction to Dream: "Hold, foul nightmare creature! Or I will disperse your fabric with my ultrasonic whistle. Tweeeep!" [*Laughter.*]

And then he says, "Monster, you shall never get past me." Dream asks, "And who are you?" And Hector answers, "I am the Sandman, Guardian of the dreams of men, protector against wicked nightmares, lord of the Dream Dome, and friend of children everywhere!" [*Laughter.*]

And then the Sandman goes, "You are *what?* Hrrr. Hrr. Hrrraahh." And that's the point where you realize that Dream is actually laughing—the only time he does so in the series. Then he says, "This has been amusing, little ghost, and that was not something I expected. But every playtime must come to an end. This dream is over." A few people complained that I'd killed Hector Hall. But I really didn't; he was killed long before in the DC comic *Infinity, Inc.* I just put his ghost to rest.

DRINKING WITH IMMORTALS

HB: Many readers don't immediately understand why part 4, "Men of Good Fortune," is even in *The Doll's House,* because the story doesn't seem to flow from the preceding narrative.

NG: In the previous tale, "Playing House," the Sandman destroys the dream Lyta Hall has been living in for the past two years, tells her that he'll be coming by one day to take her then-unborn child, and then excuses himself by saying, "I have a prior engagement, I am afraid. I can discuss this no further." Beneath the last panel of that story, I had asked for a blurb that said: "Next: The Prior Engagement." Unfortunately, someone must have decided the blurb was incorrect because it didn't match the next issue's title and took it on themselves to remove it. As a result, all you see beneath the last panel is some mysterious white space. The prior engagement referred to, of course, was the Sandman's centennial appointment with Hob Gadling in 1989; and it was genuinely important for Dream not to miss it, because it was the meeting in which he affirmed their friendship.

HB: The production error helps explain why "Men of Good Fortune" seems to appear abrupt. However, another reason is that this story is meant to stand apart and sum up the main themes of the surrounding storyline—which concern how people build up and tear down the walls they construct around themselves. Is there a scene that you'd say encapsulates this theme?

NG: It's hard to choose one scene, because the point of "Men of Good Fortune" is that it's progressive. If you press me, though, I suppose Hob's big speech at the end comes close. He tells the Sandman: "Y'know, I think I know why we meet here, century after century. It's not because you want to see what happens when a man don't die. You've seen what happens. I doubt I'm any wiser than I was five hundred years back.... [People] don't change. Not in the important things. I doubt I'll ever seek death. You've observed all that. But you knew it from the start. I think you're here for something else."

The Sandman asks, "And what might that be?" And Hob answers, "Friendship. I think you're lonely." Dream angrily responds, "You dare? You dare imply that I might befriend a mortal? That one of my kind might need companionship? You dare to call me lonely?" And Hob says, "Yes. Yes, I do. Tell you what. I'll be here in a hundred years' time. If you're here then, too—it'll be because we're friends. No other reason."

On the last page, we see Hob sitting at the table by himself, nervously waiting; and then looking up, with a wry smile, and saying, "I ... I wasn't sure you were coming." And the Sandman, smiling—

Hob Gadling, contemporary of Geoffrey Chaucer, a man who achieves immortality through the Sandman.

for him, anyway—replies: "Really? I have always heard it was impolite to keep one's friends waiting." That, to me, is thematically the heart of *The Doll's House*.

HB: Hob isn't the only important character who debuts here; the issue is also notable for introducing an aspiring playwright named William Shakespeare. How did that come about?

NG: Very circuitously. All I had in mind originally was to write a story about Hob Gadling. It was 1989 when I started plotting, so I set the story to begin six hundred years earlier, in 1389. I then researched what events occurred in 1489, 1589, 1689, and so on, to ensure that the story would be historically accurate in each of these '89 years.

When I reached 1589, I saw it was the era of both William Shakespeare and Christopher Marlowe, so I looked up what they'd done to that point. I learned Marlowe had just written *Faustus*, one of the greatest plays in the English language. Shakespeare, on the other hand, had so far written only one play, *Henry VI*. I sat down and read *Henry VI*, and it was awful. [*Laughter.*]

While reading it, I got a vision of Shakespeare being sort of like I was early on—that is, someone who desperately wants to be a good writer more than anything else in the world. And that interested me.

Had I happened to pick a later year—say 1594, when Shakespeare was at the height of his powers—I wouldn't have bothered to even place him in the pub. But I loved the idea of having Marlowe, who in 1589 was the finest playwright in the English language, talking to this little wannabe writer, this fanboy, named William Shakespeare. And Marlowe telling Shakespeare that as far as writing goes, he should stick to acting.

So I wrote the scene which ends with Shakespeare saying, "I would give anything to have your gifts. Or more than anything to give men dreams that would live on long after I am dead. I'd bargain, like your Faustus, for that boon." I looked at the line I'd just written, and it was suddenly obvious to me what needed to happen next. The Sandman overhears Shakespeare's remark, and he asks Hob Gadling who the young fella is. And Hob replies, "Acts a bit. Wrote a play." [*Laughter.*] That, of course, is a nod to the infamous early Hollywood critique given Fred Astaire: "Can't act. Slightly bald. Can dance a little."

The Sandman wanders over and says, "I heard your talk, Will. Would you write great plays? Create new dreams to spur the minds of men? Is that your will?" I should note, by the way, that I wrote all of the dialogue between Shakespeare and the Sandman, and Shakespeare and Marlowe, in iambic pentameter.

Shakespeare replies, "It is." And the Sandman says, "Then let us talk." And off they go.

When I'd gotten to that point, I knew immediately what the deal was going to be: Shakespeare writing two magical plays for Dream. And I knew which of his plays they'd be—the only two that are original, as opposed to being based on historical events or other people's stories. Those two fantasies also happen to be my favorites, which made the decision easy. And they worked well chronologically, because one is arguably the first of Shakespeare's truly great plays, and the other is the last play he wrote by himself.

HB: What can you say about the artwork?

NG: Michael Zulli was terrific. He'd previously done *Puma Blues*, which is a comic book about animals, and I'd hear other writers say, "I want to get Michael Zulli to do this story, it has animals." But what I noticed is that he's really good at drawing environments that are well thought out.

I knew that for "Men of Good Fortune" to work, it needed to make readers feel that they were moving forward through time, century by century, and the way to do that was to get all the costuming, architecture, and other period details right visually—in other words, to recreate an environment in the pub that would be appropriate for each century being represented. It called for someone meticulous about details, and Michael struck me as the person for the job.

HB: You clearly had fun with "Men of Good Fortune." Near the end of your script, you wrote, "Last page . . . It's funny. Normally when I reach the end, I'm jubilant. Whereas with this one, I'm sort of sad, like it's a pity it has to be over. I'd love to just carry it on indefinitely. There's all this neat stuff I found out about the past I never got to put in. Sigh . . ."

NG: "Men of Good Fortune" is definitely one of my favorite stories.

THE CORINTHIAN AND THE CEREAL CONVENTION

HB: After the Endless, the most memorable character in *Sandman* may be the Corinthian, the nightmare with teeth for eyes. What led you to create him?

NG: I wanted someone who was the embodiment of, for want of a better phrase, the romantic spirit of serial killing. [*Laughter.*]

Serial killing had not yet been depicted as hip and groovy, but I could see that coming; for example, I'd begun noticing serial killer fanzines, complete with prison interviews. And I wanted to say, "This isn't hip, this isn't cool."

HB: Where did his name come from?

NG: It's a seventeenth-century slang word for a licentious rake who does things like frequent brothels. But *Sandman*'s Corinthian doesn't have sex; he eats eyeballs. And he's homosexual, in the sense that he prefers to eat the eyeballs of boys.

The name can also be traced to Corinth; and the letters of Paul; and Corinthian columns; and even to the advertising firm that made it part of a car's sales slogan simply because it sounded good: "upholstered in fine Corinthian leather." I wanted the character to appear very cool and charismatic, in a way that the Sandman doesn't.

At the same time, one of my favorite moments in the series is when the Sandman uncreates the Corinthian because, at the end of the day, he was nowhere near as bad and huge and awful as he should have been. Dream uncreates him out of irritation, because the Corinthian was petty; he'd missed the whole point of what he was made for.

HB: How'd you come up with the "teeth for eyes" imagery?

NG: Just from random doodling. Where the eyes should be, I found myself drawing

TRIGGERING MEMORIES OF REALITY

Artist Michael Zulli on drawing *Sandman* 13:

What first drew me to "Men of Good Fortune" was the title, because I'm a big Lou Reed fan. I'm also a history buff, so I liked the idea of representing all the different periods in the story, and I did my best to be historically accurate—though had I been scrupulous about it, I would've made the pub a lot dirtier and smokier, at least up until the period of that amazing new invention, "the chimney."

Unlike a movie director, I don't have the ability to physically gather all the elements of a scene and then simply film them. Instead, I have to remember how people tend to arrange themselves in a room, what furniture is likely to be there, where the light should be coming from, and so on, and then combine those elements in a way that triggers a memory of reality in the reader's mind.

Comics are often compared to film, but I see them as being much more like theater, another medium that can't physically show everything and so must rely on suggestion supported by a few perfectly chosen details. I try to render characters and their environments with enough fidelity to maintain the illusion of reality—and avoid having my audience want to throw tomatoes at me.

TRADING CARD ART BY DAVE GIBBONS

The Corinthian, created by the Sandman to be the ultimate nightmare, ended up a disappointment to his creator.

mouths with little teeth and I stepped back and thought, "This is really disturbing. I should use this."

I also liked what could be done with dark glasses and viewpoint. In *The Doll's House*, the panels from the Corinthian's point of view are tinted blue when his glasses are on and not tinted when he takes them off. Because we start off seeing things from his point of view, it takes a while before we discover what his eyes look like.

HB: The Corinthian goes to a serial killer convention. How was that wonderful idea born?

NG: It came to me during the World Fantasy Convention in London in October 1988, two months before the publication of *Sandman* 1. WFC isn't a fan gathering; it's mostly attended by writers and editors. So at 2 a.m., I looked around the bar and—in a strange, glistening moment of clarity—realized a convention is just a bunch of disparate people getting together for a long weekend to feel special. These people have nothing in common except for the one shared interest that unites them—be it Barbie dolls, or a 1960s TV show, or comic books. And I thought, "What if serial killers had conventions too?"

As soon as the idea struck me, I realized it was likely to come to other writers as well. I had the strong feeling that the idea had come to me first; but because of the stories I'd already worked up, I knew that it was going to be about fourteen months until I could get to it—if *Sandman* was even being published by issue 14. That was scary, because I was worried somebody would get to it before I could; but no one did.

THE SANDMAN COMPANION

HB: How much research did you do for the "Collectors" issue?

NG: I read everything I could find from November 1988 through most of 1989 on serial killing—which, thankfully, is a lot less than what's around now—to the point where I felt that I understood the urge, the fantasies, the justifications, and could sort of think like a serial killer. When I felt that I "got it," I stopped reading and started writing.

HB: Where did you find the early version of "Little Red Riding Hood"?

NG: I first read it in the 1985 book *The Great Cat Massacre and Other Episodes in French Cultural History* by Robert Darnton. Until then, I'd seen only the famous cleaned-up version by Charles Perrault; but even in that one, Red Riding Hood is eaten by the wolf. There's clearly bizarre psychosexual things going on in the early version, in which the girl consumes the blood and flesh of her grandmother, and has such exchanges with the wolf as: "Where shall I put my skirt?" "Throw it on the fire; you won't need it anymore." She finally goes naked into the bed with the "grandmother" who is the wolf—who then eats her. I thought it was an appropriate start for a story about serial killers.

HB: There's quite a bit of horror in the issue, but there's also some very funny dark humor. On page 12, for example, Nimrod tells a story about a woman who says, "Help—I've been reaped!" The policeman says, "Don't you mean raped?" And she replies, "No, he used a scythe." The caption lets us know that Nimrod is thinking, "Laugh you bastards laugh at my joke or I'll . . ." [*Laughter.*] The joke is questionable, but Nimrod's thoughts are hysterical.

NG: Thanks. I also got a kick out of the panel on religion on page 18.

HB: Oh, all the panels are great fun. Do you have anything to say about Philip Sitz, the journalist who tries to attend the gathering undercover?

NG: I felt every convention should have at least one fan, if only for contrast. Philip's cover was instantly blown for comics fans, by the way, because The Bogeyman was a serial killer who'd previously died in an Alan Moore–scripted issue of *Swamp Thing*.

HB: Given the gruesome nature of "Collectors," did you run into any censorship problems?

NG: Just a few. The main change was on page 27, where I wanted the guy to talk very clinically, coldly, and uncaringly about things like masturbation, and then get more and more euphemistic as he talked about killing people. So he began by saying, "I used to masturbate compulsively"; and then he started to talk about the urge building up and his "doing it," until you realized he'd shifted to talking about murder. After I handed in the script, though, I got a phone message from Karen saying, "People don't masturbate in the DC Universe." Taking that as a formal policy statement, I rewrote the page.

HB: I also noticed that your script refers to the character who likes amusement parks as "Disneyland," but in the issue he's named "Funland."

NG: That change was made just before we went to press, because some people got a bit worried about our upsetting Disney. Similarly, the character originally wore mouse ears, and they were changed at the last minute to wolf ears. I didn't strongly object, because I didn't feel either of those changes hurt the story; in fact, the wolf ears relate nicely to the Little Red Riding Hood tale.

HB: Toward the end, you connect Funland to another famous fairy tale.

NG: Yes; on page 31, when the children gather around him in his dream and say, "Of course we forgive you. Now, let us play some more in these gardens, which are paradise." That's a paraphrase of a line from the end of Oscar Wilde's fairy tale "The Selfish Giant." I thought it was the sort of fantasy Funland would appreciate.

HB: Actually, all the serial killers in your story appear to maintain weirdly rich fantasy lives.

NG: That's probably the most significant thing I picked up from my reading. That's why the Sandman comes in and says, "Until now, you have all sustained fantasies in which you are the maltreated heroes of your own stories. Comforting daydreams in which, ultimately, you are shown to be in the right. No more. For all of you, the dream is over. I have taken it away. For this is my judgment on you: that you shall know, at all times, and forever, exactly what you are. And you shall know just how *little* that means." In other words, he took away their illusions, so that all they are now are people who kill their fellow human beings.

ALAN MOORE'S FAVORITE NEIL GAIMAN ANECDOTE

Neil and some other friends were visiting me in Northampton, and we all went out to dinner. We hadn't seen each other for a while, so we spent the meal catching up on what each of us had been doing. When it was my turn, I began telling everyone about the story I was doing for *From Hell*, my comic about Jack the Ripper. I'm a man who loves his work, and I do tend to give all I've got when I'm describing a scene.

So I was just describing a ritual disembowelment of a woman in London and the almost supernatural aura surrounding it, and Neil suddenly got up and said, "Excuse me, I'm just going to go outside a minute." And he went outside, overcome by the sheer demonic power of my presentation.

When he came back in, I forget which body organ was being removed at that point in my narrative; but Neil caught a few words, did a complete U-turn, and walked straight back out.

When we went searching for him later, Neil was sitting in the gutter outside the restaurant, head in his hands, looking absolutely wretched. And he was being mothered by a bag lady. It was a very Neil Gaiman moment; the lady almost could've been Mad Hettie from his *Sandman* stories emerged to persecute him.

I remember looking down, with no sympathy for him whatsoever, and just chuckling and saying, "Neil Scary Trousers Gaiman, Master of Modern Terror."

DREAMS AND HEARTS

HB: The next-to-last story, "Into the Night," in some ways mirrors part 2, "Moving In." For example, both stories begin by showing the house Rose is staying in, except part 2 begins in daylight and part 6 begins at night.

NG: That's actually somewhat true throughout. That is, using "Men of Good Fortune" as a divider, the stories in the first half of the collection are more or less reflected by their counterparts in the second half of the collection. The mirroring effect isn't uniform, though; it becomes more noticeable the further out you move from the middle.

HB: What's the main thing you wanted to do in the "Into the Night" story?

NG: To explore what the various people in the house were dreaming, which results in some insights. For example, Barbie dreams about being a princess in a magical fantasy land, which reveals hidden depths. Hal dreams about Judy Garland searching for her real face, which is an idea I got from interviewing a professional drag queen in London who used to dream about his friends' faces becoming scarred or falling apart.

One of the spider women, Zelda, has a weird Gothic dream about her life: "GothicHeroinesSecretBridesOfTheFacelessSlavesOfTheForbiddenHouseOfThe NamelessNightOfTheCastleOfDreadDesireWithMelmothWeWalkTheCorridors OfOtranto." Zelda also dreams about her stammer, which makes you suddenly realize why she's always whispering.

By the way, the paragraph Zelda reads on page 13 is the beginning of M. R. James's story "Lost Hearts"—which, of course, is the title of the next issue. Unfortunately, the quote isn't from the original story but a rewrite done for children; I picked it off my shelf and typed it in without looking closely, and didn't realize my mistake until years later.

HB: Where did you come up with Zelda and the other spider woman, Chantal?

NG: They were inspired partly by a spider-lady couple I met once; I couldn't figure out whether they were sisters, or lovers, or mother and daughter. They were also partly inspired by a lesbian couple I knew, one of whom treated the other one like a sock puppet—she would whisper in her ear, and her lover would speak for her.

HB: What about the final story, where Rose is rescued by Unity in The Dreaming, and the Sandman confronts Desire?

NG: I liked that Rose gives away her heart to her grandmother; and then, when she's reunited with her mother and brother, kind of gets her heart back again. I also like that the ending takes us back to the beginning, with Desire in Desire's heart.

If you leaf through the series, you'll find either an image of a heart or the word *heart* in virtually every issue. Hearts are a major part of what *Sandman* is about.

—

dream country

5

Everything goes by the board: honor, pride, decency . . .
to get the book written. If a writer has to rob his mother, he will not hesitate;
the "Ode on a Grecian Urn" is worth any number of old ladies.

—WILLIAM FAULKNER

The four short stories in *Dream Country* all revolve around ancient and near-forgotten myths. As Death explains in the final tale, "Mythologies take longer to die than people believe. They linger on in a kind of dream country that affects all of you." The lingering legends explored range from a Greek Muse to an Egyptian sun god, and from the land of Faerie to a lost world ruled by cats.

Neil Gaiman was in top form when creating these stories, and two of them—"A Dream of a Thousand Cats" and "A Midsummer Night's Dream"—rank among the best in the series.

Kicking off the book is "Calliope," which begins with author Richard Madoc saying, "I don't have any idea." Madoc's first novel was a best-seller, but he's eight months past the deadline for his second and still hasn't been able to even start it. Desperate, Madoc exploits the good will of one of his fans to obtain a trichinobezoar, which is a grotesque human hairball reputed to have healing powers. Madoc then gives the bezoar to an older writer, Erasmus Fry, in exchange for a much rarer prize: an ancient Muse named Calliope. (In Greek mythology, Calliope is one of nine Muses born of Zeus, the king of the gods, and Mnemosyne, the goddess of memory. Calliope is the Muse of the heroic epic.)

Fry explains that he captured Calliope in 1927 and hasn't treated her gently during her sixty years of imprisonment. When a grief-stricken Calliope reminds Fry that he promised to free her before he died, the old author cynically responds, "Writers are liars, my dear. Surely you have realized that by now?"

Madoc follows Fry's advice by imprisoning Calliope in his attic . . . and raping her. He's rewarded by a flood of inspiration, and writes his novel in five weeks. Madoc continues to periodically rape Calliope, and his career soars as he crafts a string of hit novels, plays, and movie scripts. The disconnection between his work and how he achieves it is highlighted by some party chatter, in which an attractive blond tells him, "I loved your characterization of Aileen. There aren't enough strong women in fiction." Madoc replies, "Actually, I do tend to regard myself as a femi-

THE SANDMAN COMPANION

nist writer." The blond responds, "So tell me—where do you get your ideas?"

Calliope calls for help on a trinity of Muses who, in mythological history, pre-date her sisters: Aiode (song), Mneme (memory), and Melete (meditation). Appearing as the maiden-mother-crone trio who pop up throughout the series, they tell her that "there are few of the old powers willing or able to meddle in mortal affairs these days." They suggest her best hope is her former lover—who, we learn for the first time, is Dream, with whom Calliope had a child. Although the relationship ended badly, Calliope is desperate enough to accept even the help of Oneiros (the Greek name for the Lord of Dreams). As shown in issue 1, the Sandman was imprisoned himself until September 1988; but by March 1990, he's discovered Calliope's plight and (to her surprise and relief) decides to rescue her.

Madoc learns that Erasmus Fry died a few months back by poisoning himself and that night when he falls asleep, the Sandman enters his dreams and demands Calliope's release. Madoc refuses, saying he still needs ideas. As the Prince of Stories, the furious Sandman overwhelms Madoc's mind with ideas, causing the author to try to get them out of his head as quickly as he can—which results in his scrawling them on a wall with the blood of his own fingertips. Undergoing this torture convinces Madoc to finally release Calliope.

Dream asks Calliope what she'll do now. The Muse responds, "I don't know. Return to the minds of humanity, I suspect. My time is over, and this age of the world is not my age." Gratefully, she adds, "You have changed, Oneiros. In the old days, you would have left me to rot forever, without turning a hair." Calliope then asks Dream to release Madoc (in notable contrast to the Sandman's treatment in issue 1 of Alex Burgess, who's still being punished by a curse of eternal waking). The Sandman and Calliope then part, and the memory of the Sandman begins fading from Richard Madoc's mind like a fleeting dream ... until he ends the story by muttering, "It's gone. I've got no idea anymore. No idea at all."

The second story, "A Dream of a Thousand Cats," begins with an excited kitten going to a feline meeting to hear a well-known Siamese cat evangelize about how to change the world. Perched in a cemetery in the dead of night, the Siamese explains that she considered herself in control of her life and a valued member of her human family until she had kittens...and her owners chose to drown them. In her sleep, she prayed for a way to change the subordinate position of her race; and she was told to seek out the dreamscape's ruler, the Cat of Dreams. After many hardships, the brave Siamese reached the Sandman, who appeared to her as a huge black tomcat with glowing red eyes.

Peering into those eyes, the Siamese saw a lost world in which cats were the size of people, and vice versa; and the only function of humans was to bring pleasure to cats, as servants and as prey. It was a paradise on Earth, until one day a visionary arose among the humans. "Dreams shape the world. Dreams create the world anew, every night," he said. "Dream a world in which we are the dominant species, in which we are the kings and the queens, and the gods. Dream a world in which we will no longer be hunted and killed by cats. . . . If enough of us dream it, then it will happen. Dreams shape the world." This visionary traveled all over to preach his message; and one night, when a thousand humans dreamed his dream at the same time, everything changed: "Humans were huge, and cats were tiny. Humans were the dominant species, and we were prey to them, to dogs, to their metal machines. Prey to the world the humans had brought with them."

Returning from the vision, the Siamese asked the Sandman, "So they dreamed the world into the form it is now?" And the Sandman replied, "Not exactly. They dreamed the world so it *always* was the way it is now, little one. There never *was* a world of high cat-ladies and cat-lords. They changed the universe from the beginning of all things, until the end of time."

The Siamese understood what she had to do; and so she now travels everywhere, preaching her revelation: "Dream the world. Not this pallid shadow of reality. Dream the world the way it *truly* is. A world in which all cats are queens and kings of creation. That is my message. And I shall keep moving, keep repeating it, until I die. Or until a thousand cats hear my words, and believe them, and dream . . . and we come again to paradise."

The meeting breaks up, and the rapt kitten asks an alley cat, "Do you think it will happen?" "Little one," says the other, "I would like to see anyone—prophet, king or god—persuade a thousand cats to do *anything* at the same time. No, it will never happen." But the kitten believes in the vision; and that night, while the kitten's humans comment on how cute it looks hunting in its sleep . . . the kitten dreams.

The third tale, "A Midsummer Night's Dream," is about William Shakespeare putting on a play for the Faerie folk and for the Sandman, in half fulfillment of the bargain Dream and Shakespeare made in issue 13. This complex tale, which won the 1991 World Fantasy Award for Best Short Story, is described in detail by Neil Gaiman later in this chapter.

Dream Country concludes with "Facade," which focuses on Urania "Rainie" Blackwell, a former U.S. intelligence agent who was ordered to expose herself to an ancient Egyptian artifact called the Orb of Ra. Doing so made Rainie into a near invulnerable metamorph who can change her body into any element (ranging from helium to iron, and from uranium to gold). In most comic books, Rainie's reaction to having such powers would be to become a super hero and fight evil . . . and, as it happens, she did precisely that during 1967 and 1968 in the DC comic *Metamorpho*. In this story, however, Rainie's apparently had time to ponder the fact that, in many ways, she's no longer human. Her body now contains nothing resembling flesh, blood, or internal organs; and her chalk white skin makes her look like she has a hideous disease. Rainie can grow silicate faces that appear human, but they harden and fall off after a day or so. Rainie keeps these face-masks littered about her apartment, using them as artwork, as ashtrays . . . and as grim reminders of the person she used to be.

Her sense of "otherness" causes Rainie to become a frightened shut-in who spends her days alone in her apartment, hardly moving, with virtually her only joy coming from a brief weekly call she makes to her veteran's benefits contact.

This depressing pattern is broken when an old colleague calls who isn't aware of Rainie's condition. They meet for lunch, and Rainie tries hard to enjoy herself, but everything her friend happily chatters about regarding her normal life reminds Element Girl of her abnormality . . . which culminates in Rainie's face falling into her spaghetti. Running home, Rainie calls her benefits contact—only to be told he's been transferred to another department. Rainie's reaction is an overwhelming desire to kill herself; but since her body is impervious to harm, she doesn't even know how to do that.

At this point, Death happens to pass by (due to the death of someone in the building); and, as usual, she says some sensible things. When Rainie mentions that she can't bring herself to throw away her human-looking faces, Death responds, "You people always hold onto old identities, old faces and masks, long after they've served their purpose. But you've got to learn to throw things away eventually." This can be interpreted to mean Rainie should finally let go of her old life as a human and learn to accept, and even relish, her new one as a metamorph. But Rainie hears it only as an encouragement to commit suicide; and when she figures out who she's talking to, she becomes elated: "Blessed, merciful death. You've come to make it all stop?"

Death explains that she's not blessed or merciful, but just doing her job: "For some folks death is a release, and for others death is an abomination, a terrible thing. But in the end, I'm there for all of them . . . and I'm also here, talking to you. But I'm not your death. At least, not yet."

Death continues, "When the first living thing existed, I was there, waiting. When the last living thing dies, my job will be finished. I'll put the chairs on the tables, turn out the lights and lock the universe behind me when I leave."

There's a lot of information in that speech, but Rainie hears only one thing: "Are you saying that you won't help me? . . . That I've got another two thousand years of being a freak? Two thousand years of hell?"

Death replies, "You make your own hell, Rainie. . . . Your life is your own. So is your death. And oblivion? That's not an option, I'm afraid."

Having presented options for living that Rainie refuses to hear, Death tells Rainie how to achieve her wish—which is by simply asking it of Ra, the sun god who transformed her. All it takes to reach him is to look out a window.

Raising the blinds to finally let sunlight flood into her perpetually dark apartment, Rainie says: "Please, Sir—I don't want to be me. Thank you for making me special, but I don't want to be special. I just want it to stop. Can you make me normal again?" In her mind, Ra tells her to look at him. Rainie does so and exclaims, "I never realized before. The sun. It's just a mask, too. And the face behind it. . . . It's beautiful." And with that, Rainie dies . . . leaving behind a petrified body wearing an expression of beatific joy.

And Death remarks, "Have fun, Rainie. Better luck next time."

SOME THINGS WORTH NOTICING

Myth is not the only thematic element connecting the stories *in*
Another is the exploration of wishes and their consequences. Richar
tally exploits Calliope to fulfill his wish for ideas, and eventually beco
out hack who's abandoned by Dream and left with no ideas at all. Ano
William Shakespeare, is granted his wish for greatness by the Sandman *h*
focuses so intensely on his work and artistic vision that he neglects his *f*
and by failing to see what's happening under his nose, loses his only son.
trast, Urania Blackwell detests the greatness thrust upon her, and wishes *for*
mal human life filled with family and friends. Because she can't let go of *that*
and adjust to her situation, she ultimately wishes herself dead.

In fact, the only ones in *Dream Country* who end up relatively happy *are*
cats . . . and they're the only ones whose wish *isn't* granted. Pursuing the wish *fi*
both the Siamese and the kitten with hope and purpose, however, creating a *jour*
ney for them that's arguably much more important than the destination.

Another element common to all four stories is imprisonment. Echoing the
Sandman's confinement in a basement, his former lover Calliope is imprisoned in
an attic; Urania Blackwell imprisons herself in her apartment; and the cats are
imprisoned by the whims of their human masters. The shackles on Shakespeare are
less visible but just as real: he's imprisoned by his obsession with words and stories,
which builds a wall between him and his son.

The most significant thing that links these tales in the context of the series, however, is that they all highlight aspects of Dream. The cat story is the most straightforward, showing us that the Sandman's duties extend well beyond merely human
dreams; and that, at his best, the Sandman provides dreamers with revelation and
hope.

The other three tales reflect darker sides of Dream. It's not a stretch to guess
that the way Rick Madoc perpetually uses Calliope and then returns to his obsession with career is an exaggerated echo of the way the Sandman himself used to
treat Calliope when they were lovers.

Also notable are the references to the Sandman and Calliope's son. On page
10 of the first story, Melete says, "But she did bear his cub. That boy–child, who
went to Hades for his lady-love, and died in Thrace, torn apart by the sisters of the
frenzy, for his sacrilege." Further, on page 10 of the Shakespeare tale, Titania says, "It
seems to me that I heard this tale sung once, in old Greece, by a boy with a lyre."
And on page 20 of the same story, a line from Shakespeare's actual play mentions
"the riot of the tipsy Bacchanals, tearing the Thracian singer in their rage." (If you
still don't know who the Sandman's son is, another clue appears on the last page of
"Calliope.") The linking of "Calliope" and "A Midsummer Night's Dream" by references to the Sandman's child can be read to imply that Dream created the same
gulfs between himself and his son that Shakespeare creates with Hamnet.

Finally, there's Urania Blackwell, a woman who persists in hanging on to an obsolete identity. Because she refuses to adjust her perception of herself to her new circumstances, Rainie ends up losing her life. "Facade" can therefore be read as a cautionary tale for the Sandman, who (as Calliope pointedly observes) is himself going through changes—and will need to go through more as the series progresses.

A CHANGE OF PACE

HB: Why did you alternate between doing long storylines, such as *Season of Mists* and *Brief Lives*, with writing the single-issue short stories that appear in the collections *Dream Country, Fables and Reflections,* and *Worlds' End*?

NG: Whenever I was working on a long storyline, I'd get several ideas for tales I'd love to write—but wasn't able to because I was in the middle of this bloody long story! So when the story arc was completed, I'd tackle the ideas that I'd put on hold.

HB: You know, that's not the answer I'd expected. I thought you did it because *Sandman* was a monthly comic, and you wanted to periodically give readers a break from having to deal with long stretches between story segments by providing them with complete-in-one-issue tales.

NG: Oh, that was part of it, too. The short stories were also useful as leaping-on points for new readers, since it allowed them to jump in without being caught in the middle of an ongoing story, or having to commit more than the price of one issue to try *Sandman* out and enjoy a complete tale.

But I primarily did it because it felt right. There's an old Hollywood anecdote about Harry Cohn of Columbia Pictures who, after watching a screening, proclaimed that the movie had to be cut by nineteen minutes. When asked how he had come up with nineteen minutes—as opposed to, say, fifteen or twenty-five—he said that nineteen minutes before the credits rolled, his ass started to squirm; and if that was true for him, it would be true for the asses of audiences around the country.

I felt pretty much the same way. I wasn't just the author of *Sandman*, I was also a member of its audience. I simply got to read the scripts five or six months before anyone else—or, when my ability to meet deadlines collapsed toward the end, about two weeks before anyone else ... [*Laughter.*] So whenever I grew tired of a long Sandman story and felt it was time for some short ones, I just assumed that most everyone else felt the same way. It was the equivalent of my bum starting to squirm.

The same principle applied to how often major characters appeared. For example, the Sandman wasn't in the comic terribly much. He'd come in when I'd miss him, when I'd go, "It's been a while since we've had a good Dream story, let's bring him back to center stage." Ditto for Death, and Delirium, and other popular characters.

HB: I believe there was one additional benefit to doing the shorts, which involved artists.

NG: Right; it allowed a penciller and me to get comfortable with each other over the course of a single, enclosed tale. Whenever possible, I'd have an artist new to *Sandman* do a short story with me first, and then have that artist tackle a multipart storyline. In this collection, for example, Kelley Jones pencilled the stories "Calliope" and "A Dream of a Thousand Cats," and he then almost immediately went on to illustrate *Season of Mists*.

WRITER'S BLOCKS

HB: Let's talk about "Calliope." That story wasn't a smooth ride.

NG: No, I had a lot of trouble getting it to work. I began by trying to do a story titled "Sex and Violets," in which the hobgoblin Puck is very, very old and is hanging on to the only youth he has left by consuming flowers native to England. He runs a brothel in London that has one whore: a succubus. Rock stars, writers, artists, and so on come and give Puck native English flowers, and in exchange they're allowed to visit the succubus. And they leave with ideas, but only after the succubus drains away a year or so of their lives.

I wrote two versions of that story, and then threw the whole concept away and wrote "Calliope."

But I still love the idea of first meeting Robin Goodfellow when he's very, very old, and then meeting him two issues later as this wild young creature being released into the world. It's always fun to see things out of sequence, so you can later go, "Oh, that's why he's the way he is."

HB: It's a bit ironic that you had so many problems starting "Calliope," considering the story is about an artist holding a Muse hostage to get over his writing problems.

NG: Well, now that you mention it, there was a strange regularity to the problem early on; I had to back up and restart issues 2, 7, 12, and 17—that is, every five months, like clockwork. After 17, though, things got a little better; I didn't have the "throw away and restart" difficulty again until issue 25, which was in the middle of *Season of Mists*; and then issue 31, "Three Septembers and a January."

HB: Were you at all concerned that writing about writer's block was something of a cliché?

NG: No, because no one had yet done a story about an imprisoned Muse being abused. Strangely enough, the same month Dave Sim in *Cerebus* included some line about "Don't abuse your muse or you'll lose your muse." [*Laughter.*]

HB: "Calliope" as a story is relatively straightforward, but I'd like to chat about some of its details. For example, where did you find a reference to the trichinobezoar?

NG: Dr. Guy Lawley, who's been kind enough to provide me with medical information for stories—and who's the only doctor I know who writes comics—actually found me a photograph of a trichinobezoar. It's just as Kelley Jones depicted it; a weird, matted hairball, shaped like the inside of a stomach.

HB: I also enjoyed the reward the doctor in the story is given: a signature on Madoc's book *The Cabaret of Dr. Caligari*. That's a cute spin on the 1919 German Expressionist film *The Cabinet of Dr. Caligari*, about a magician who uses a hypnotized victim to carry out his bidding.

NG: It's fun playing around with titles. Another example is on page 12; *The Spirit Who Had Half of Everything* was one of James Branch Cabell's original names for a chapter in his book *Figures of Earth*.

HB: There are also several visual in-jokes in the story. Madoc's office is a fairly accurate representation of your office at the time ... aside from it missing your bust of Groucho Marx.

NG: Yep. Kelley had never seen my office, but I sent him a bunch of reference photos. Another fun one for me is that the host of *The Book Nook* TV show is Kim Newman, my coauthor on *Ghastly Beyond Belief* back in 1985. And the images of England—such as the middle panel on page 3—were from photos I took of locations like the London embankment and then mailed to Kelley.

HB: *Dream Country* also includes the script for this story—which is the only time a collection provides such a peek behind the curtains. Was that your idea?

NG: No, it came from DC's marketing staffers. They felt the collection was too thin with just four stories and so wanted to add something. I'd have preferred including the script for "A Midsummer Night's Dream," because there are things I did there that are pretty clever but don't call attention to themselves. But the marketing folks believed the script for issue 17 made for a better straight read.

What ultimately convinced me to include a script at all was that I'd spent a good part of my youth desperately wanting to write comics, but I was stopped by not knowing the mechanics and the format. I never saw what a comics script looks like until Alan Moore showed me a few of his. I therefore thought including a script in a *Sandman* collection might be helpful to anyone else in the same situation—although as I point out in my introduction to it, that script represents only how *I* write comics, not how anyone else should.

HB: I'd say the script is of interest to a broader audience than just comics writers, though.

NG: You're probably right, because I've found lots of people are puzzled about the whole process. You tell someone "I write comics," and they ask if that means you letter in the word balloons. If including the script helps clarify for some readers what a comics writer does, that's definitely a happy bonus.

A DREAM OF A BETTER WORLD . . . FOR CATS

HB: You've described the problems you had starting "Calliope." Did your next story, "A Dream of a Thousand Cats," come easier?

Calliope,
a muse who,
like the Sandman,
was captured
and abused in
the name of
mortal power.

A gathering of cats
attempts to remake
the world in "A Dream
of a Thousand Cats."

THE SANDMAN COMPANION

Penciller Kelley Jones employed his moody, expressionistic style to help create seven issues of *Sandman*: "Calliope," "A Dream of a Thousand Cats," and chapters 1–3 and 5–6 of *Season of Mists*.

For his first assignment, Jones had to draw a young Calliope who was nude through most of issue 17, "but her nakedness was anything but sexual," he says. "In Greek mythology Calliope was an extremely beautiful woman, but after sixty years of imprisonment you can only see hints of that.

"What I mostly had in mind," continues Jones, "were Mathew Brady's photographs of soldiers in the U.S. Civil War. One set of photos shows these noble, idealistic Union soldiers going off to fight a great war to end slavery. Then a second set shows the soldiers in Andersonville, the infamous Georgia prison camp that's been described as hell on earth; and the nobility is still in the Union soldiers' eyes, but they don't look human anymore. Instead, they look haunted, and sad . . . and *forgotten*. The worst thing I think can happen to someone is that he or she is forgotten, and I tried to get that feeling across for Calliope.

"Neil didn't specify all of that," adds Jones, "but as with any character, I method-acted Calliope. I try to let things speak to me when I'm reading a script, and they tell me how they need to be drawn."

NG: More than that; it was the quickest *Sandman* issue I ever wrote. I knocked off the entire ten-thousand-word script in a weekend, and spent just a couple of days on fix-ups.

HB: Was the speed due to your feeling inspired?

NG: Maybe; but the truth is that for years I was suspicious of this story. Even though many readers said they liked it, it came so fast that I didn't think it could be good. When I read the story now, though, I honestly can't see any significant difference between it and the ones surrounding it.

HB: Oh, I'd go a lot further; it ranks among the very best issues of the series. Kelley Jones says people come up to him all the time and tell him it's their favorite. They also tell him that this was the issue they would give their friends to get them hooked on *Sandman*.

NG: Yes, I've heard that from fans, too. Another interesting thing is it's the only issue people give me to sign that's typically suffered cat damage, such as clawing; people come up to me with the most bizarre anecdotes about how "my cat got at this comic." It makes me wonder if I gave away some secret cat knowledge, and the cats resent it.

HB: What gave you the idea for the story?

NG: I wanted to do something about consensual reality; and about dreams being fundamentally superior to reality because they create it and shape it. With that in mind, I was driving one day and saw a huge black cat by the side of the road that looked like a patch of night in the middle of the sunshine; and it just hit me that that's what the Sandman would look like if he was a cat.

Here is a condensed and edited version of an interview with rock star Tori Amos conducted by Brian Hibbs for the October 1993 issue of *Magian Line* (a delightful newsletter published by Sadie MacFarlane):

Neil's "Calliope" story really hit home for me. I understood what it was like for the author, Richard Madoc, not being able to write; and how he would do anything to be able to write again. And yet, what is your work worth when you have no honor as a person anymore?

It's very easy to make excuses, to lie, when fame starts to come, because you can justify it in so many ways; you know, "It upsets me as an artist to do this." I won't mention names, but I've seen it left and right . . . and I've done it myself.

I reread the "Calliope" story a lot, because it makes me remember why I do certain things and where I stand with myself. It puts me in line, because it makes me realize when I'm playing that game.

If you're lying to yourself—and I did that for about ten years straight—you can't be all you are; you become a non-person. Richard Madoc's not an evil guy. He just bought into something, like we all do at times. Understanding what these choices cost, and our being willing to take responsibility for them, is the big thing . . . I think that Neil's work really encourages you to not lie to yourself.

So I thought, why not do a story about cats changing reality, with a light touch—similar to Fritz Leiber's 1958 story "Space-Time for Springers"? I decided it should be based around the idea that cats once ruled the world—and whether that happens to be true or not, it's the story cats tell other cats. [*Laughter.*]

Then it occurred to me that nobody can make even *three* cats do anything . . . except turn up in time for dinner. So getting a thousand to agree on anything would be impossible. At that point, I pretty much had the story; the rest of the details came from just sitting down and writing.

FACES AND MASKS

HB: How did you come up with "Facade"?

NG: It sprang from a set of images that just popped into my head: first of a woman living in a room with faces that would harden and fall off; and then the woman using those faces as ashtrays. I wedded that to an idea I'd had of somebody who was essentially suicidal and immortal; somebody who wanted to die, but couldn't.

HB: Why did you select Element Girl to fill that role?

NG: Element Girl was a DC hero who'd been completely forgotten. She didn't even get an entry in the *Who's Who in the DC Universe* book, which includes the most obscure characters.

Because Urania Blackwell had fallen through the cracks of DC's history, when I phoned Karen and asked, "Can I kill Element Girl?" Karen responded, "Who? Is that someone from the Legion of Super-Heroes?" [*Laughter.*] And then, after quick-ly checking with DC's continuity cops, Karen told me, "Sure, you can kill her if you want to."

HB: So knocking off a more visible character would've required going through a lot more red tape. But I suspect that's not the only reason.

NG: Oh sure; I remembered Element Girl very fondly from the *Metamorpho* comics I read as a kid. Metamorpho himself was always written as a self-pitying freak—he'd constantly be saying things like, "She might love me . . . if only I wasn't so damn ugly." [*Laughter.*] But at the same time, he was always off and about behav-ing like a noble super hero. I thought, what if I took his negative attitude up anoth-er notch . . . and applied it to his former sidekick? What if she had all these amazing superpowers, but her world had shrunk to the size of her apartment; and the fact that she's potentially one of the most powerful beings in the universe is not some-thing that she regards as in any way a blessing, but as an awful thing that she'd undo if she could. And so her only link with life is this guy on the end of the phone who arranges her monthly compensation check; and she'd happily kill herself, if she could just figure out how.

HOW TO DRAW CATS

Kelley Jones did a fabulous job on "Calliope," but editor Karen Berger wanted variety, so she wasn't planning to use him for the next issue. However, Jones ended up getting the assignment by de-fault. "Nobody else wanted to touch the script," he recalls, "for the simple reason that all the charac-ters in it were *cats*. Even the Sandman wasn't in it, except as a tomcat. But I had no experience drawing cats, and I relished the challenges doing the story would provide.

"I felt it was important to give each cat his or her own look and body language," he says, "so they would be perceived as individuals, not just animals. But all the cats were actually modeled after my orange tabby Knuckles. I put Knuckles through hell, making him stand still and hold dif-ferent poses. Photos I took of him when he was young were also helpful, for the scenes involving kittens.

"I drew everything at ground level," Jones says, "because I wanted the reader to see every-thing from a cat's perspective. For example, the few times people appear, you only see their feet. The world the cats live in is a secret one in which we play a very secondary role, and that's the atti-tude I brought to my drawings."

Considerable thought also went into the nuts and bolts of the artwork. "I used some washes," Jones recalls, "and generally worked in a heavy, chunky black style to better get across the motion of cats. I also spoke with the inker, Malcolm Jones III, about avoiding the ruler and doing as much as possible by eyeball to produce a rough, organic texture. I didn't want this issue to come across looking like something new but like one of fifty ti-tles DC was publishing that month starring cats, so we strove to give it a real worn, comfortable feel.

"I loved it," says Jones, "because it wasn't just about kitty-cats but about an oppressed group. And because it shows that any creature who dreams is in the Sandman's realm—which helps to extend our perceptions of the world well beyond the arrogance of humanity."

HOW TO MAKE CATS TALK

Todd Klein on lettering the dialogue for *Sandman* 18:

In comics, we normally show people communicating with each other by using word balloons and people thinking to themselves by using thought balloons. In issue 18, however, the characters weren't people, but cats. If I'd used word balloons, they would have looked like supernatural talking cats; and if I'd used thought balloons, they would have looked like alien telepathic cats.

I decided a good compromise was to combine the two. So I used the tail of a word balloon at the beginning and end, but I put thought balloon bubbles in between the tails. Combining those verbal and nonverbal comics icons seemed right for the cats, who I figured communicate on a more primal level than we do.

HB: How did you choose Colleen Doran to be the penciller?

NG: I'd been looking at Colleen's work and noticed she had many different styles, but I thought she had an awful lot of potential and was being underused. Also, she was really good at facial expressions and could draw real women, so I thought she'd be perfect for this story about, basically, a woman alone in a room. I should add that Malcolm Jones III was a consistently great inker, but he did an exceptional job with Colleen's work—he brought out everything that she put into her pencilling and then added a grungy, raggedy quality that was just right for the story.

HB: I'd agree. I've spoken to some people who actively *dislike* what happens in the story, though. On at least a surface level, "Facade" can be read as being about a woman who kills herself because she's no longer pretty.

NG: Oh, but the story isn't about feminine beauty. It could just as easily have been about a male character.

What it's really about is someone whose life has just *shrunk*. You want to say to that person, "But you're amazingly cool and powerful. You can do anything. And yet you're living in a one-room flat, scared to go out." But from Rainie's perspective, she's stuck in a body that's no longer even remotely human; and she's facing the prospect of spending the next ten thousand years smoking cigarettes in a room full of empty faces. She doesn't see how to get free of that . . . except by dying.

Is the suicide ending problematic? Quite possibly. Do I as a person think Rainie's solution was the correct one? No, I don't. But none of that bothers me, because I feel the ending works in the context of the story; I feel it's true to itself.

SHAKESPEARE'S DREAM, PAGE BY PAGE

HB: *Sandman 19*, "A Midsummer Night's Dream," is the only monthly comic in history to win a literary award: the 1991 World Fantasy Award for Best Short Story. I'd therefore like to give it special attention by having you guide us through it page by page. Besides shedding light on this particular story, I think such a tour will help make clear just how much research and thought you put into virtually every issue. To begin, how did you choose Charles Vess to do the pencilling and inking?

NG: Charles had already illustrated the play *A Midsummer Night's Dream* for Donning/Starblaze, so it was clear he could handle the Shakespeare side of the story. When I met Charles at the 1989 San Diego Comics Convention, he showed me some other work that included these amazing fairies, which convinced me he'd do a great job on the Faerie folk, as well—and that clinched it. Charles's artwork on this issue was wonderful, and it's a large reason for why the story works.

HB: What choices had you made about the story going in?

NG: I knew I was going to base it around *A Midsummer Night's Dream*; that the play would be performed before an audience of fairies; and that I'd rather not have the performance take place in London.

HB: Why not London?

NG: I was following the lead of Rudyard Kipling, who'd written that the fairies had left our cities a long time ago. That's why I set my stage on the Sussex Downs, which is where Kipling placed his fairies; only instead of Kipling's spot near Burwash, which was his home in the latter years of his life, I picked a spot twenty

---

METHOD DRAWING

Artist Colleen Doran uses the same techniques as an actor trained in the Stanislavsky method—she works from the inside out. "A penciller does more than design a character's look," says Doran. "She has to get inside the character, to figure out the right body language and subtleties of facial expression. Neil and I spent hours on the phone discussing, for every single panel, what Rainie's face would look like, what her hands were doing, what her feet were doing, how her body would be slumped, and so on. I also acted out every scene in front of a big mirror to see what my own body did.

"When the story starts," she says, "we don't see much of Rainie; just a hand, a lump of a body, and an eye. But the whole first page screams of anxiety. Every little detail contributes—the darkened room, the little clock, the cigarettes, the debris on the table . . . and the creepy way she flicks ashes into a hardened, discarded face.

"On page 2, Rainie walks with the telephone, but her body language is directed inward; she's stooped over a bit, and she's clutching herself, clearly not relaxed. Even more disturbing is page 3, where Rainie sits on her couch like a stone, and day turns into night without her moving at all.

"On page 4, she hears the phone ring, and her first reaction is to rear back; but then on the next page, she bursts into a grin when she finds out it's an old friend—and the contrast is so sad, because it shows us that she *is* capable of happiness. Rainie's body language starts to relax and open up during this conversation; but after it's over she starts brooding about meeting with her friend, and she folds back into herself, sitting on her couch like a stone again.

"The way Neil worked it out, those first five pages show a constantly repeating cycle of despair. It's a very unsettling and appropriate opening for a story in which the protagonist ends up killing herself."

---

dream country

miles south of where *I* was living. The latter area had two advantages: I knew it really well, and I knew that it hadn't changed much over the past five hundred years.

HB: What was your next step?

NG: I went out and bought every book I could find on the time period, because I didn't want to include anything that was grossly inaccurate or anachronistic; suspension of disbelief is a fragile balloon. Especially helpful was a book I found on the life of Shakespeare as an actor, which provided me with details about how the plays were produced at the time.

Several other reference books made me feel satisfied that *A Midsummer Night's Dream* was written either in 1593 or within a couple of years of that date. I settled on 1593 for my story because there was a plague in London that year, which provides a reason for Shakespeare's troupe to be outside the city for a while, performing from village to village, and ending up in the South Downs.

Finally, I researched the history of the South Downs and read about the Long Man of Wilmington, a huge chalk outline of a man holding two long sticks, which can be seen on a Downs hillside to this day.

HB: Here. [*Points to the first panel of issue 19.*]

NG: Yep. Only I thought it would be interesting if instead of looking at it as a man with two sticks, I saw it as a man standing in a doorway. "Wilmington" may have been derived from the longer name "Wendel's Mound Town," and the chalked figure Wendel was thought by some to be a god. Further, "Wendel" comes from the old Norse *Venda*, meaning "to change course, to travel, to move forward." So it seemed reasonable to me to refer to the chalked figure as Wendel and to designate him as a gatekeeper.

Therefore, our story begins with a long shot that shows us Wendel's Mound in the background, along with a caption that informs us the date is June 23, 1593. In the foreground is Shakespeare's troupe—about twenty people—traveling in wagons and carts. And leading the pack are Hamnet and William Shakespeare.

Hamnet says, "But father, you said that we would be performing the new play tonight. Where shall we play it if not in an Inn?" And Shakespeare answers, "I have no idea. But we will know soon. Keep your eyes on the road ahead, lad."

Will Kemp then runs up. All the actors' names here are accurate, by the way, as history has preserved information on all of Shakespeare's players. Will Kemp was the chief clown and would certainly have taken the part of Bottom in this play. So Kemp says, "Will, a moment of your time . . . I have an idea! How would it be if I were to be eating a pork pie, in the first scene? And then, I could sit on it, during Bob Armin's speech." Shakespeare gently replies, "I think not." Kemp persists, "But it would make them laugh." And Shakespeare says, "It would also make them laugh if you broke wind loudly, Kemp. Please—just the lines and jests I have writ for you." This was actually based on a famous W. S. Gilbert anecdote, in which George

Grossmith—who was Gilbert's clown—came up to him and said, "Did you see that bit of business I did, Mr. Gilbert?" "Yes," said Gilbert, "I did." "Well, I think I'm going to keep it in." "No," said Gilbert, "you're not." "But it made them laugh." "It would have made them laugh," answered Gilbert sonorously, "if you had sat down on a pork pie."

Which brings us to the final panel. My rule for a last panel—and especially for one on a right-hand page—is that it ought to make you want to turn the page. It's part of the basic rule of storytelling.

HB: What do you mean?

NG: Over my fifteen years as a professional writer, I've evolved the following definition: "A story is anything that will make a reader turn pages—and then come away, when he or she is finished, not feeling cheated." In my opinion, that's the only critical rule for a story; otherwise, anything goes.

Therefore, the job of a last panel is to make the reader sufficiently interested to turn the page and continue reading. In this case, I imagined the equivalent of a little tremulous note on the violins as Hamnet says, "Father! I can see a man on the way, there! ... Will he be our audience?" And Shakespeare replies, "I fear so, lad." Then the panel ends, leaving the reader wondering, "Why is he afraid? What is the problem here?"

So we turn the page, and there's a shadowy figure—who, we'll discover shortly, is the Sandman. Shakespeare says, "Hamnet, go and wait with Condell and the other boys." And then we get one silent panel of Hamnet, alone and looking it, as his father leaves him to conduct his business.

By this point, I realized that I was not just going to be telling Shakespeare's story but also Hamnet's; and that at heart this was going to be a story about the relationship, and the enormous gulfs, between a father and his son.

HB: How much of that relationship was based on historical fact?

NG: Shakespeare definitely spent long periods in London away from his family. It's also fact that Hamnet died in 1596, at age eleven. We don't know whether Hamnet ever went on the road with his father, but it's entirely possible that he did.

As for my take on Shakespeare, I'm basing a lot of it on what I personally find scary about being a storyteller. When something terrible is happening, 99 percent of you is feeling terrible, but 1 percent is standing off to the side—like a little cartoon devil on your shoulder—and saying, "I can use this. Let's see, I'm so upset that I'm actually crying. Are my eyes just tearing, or are they stinging? Yes, they're stinging, and I can feel the tears rolling down my cheeks. How do they feel? Hot. Good, what else?" That's the kind of disconnectedness I wanted to explore.

So, we now have the Sandman asking Shakespeare if everything is ready, and telling him that "Wendel's Mound was a theatre before your race came to this island." Shakespeare asks, "Before the Normans?" Dream, amused as only someone who regards five hundred years ago as recent history might be, replies, "Before the humans."

Notice that I placed the setup line "Before the Normans?" in one panel and the punchline "Before the humans" in a separate panel. Doing so takes advantage of the "beat" nature of panels; the joke wouldn't have been as effective with both lines in the same panel. One of the mistakes that writers new to comics make is to not exploit this natural rhythm of panels.

HB: This is also one of the rare occasions when the Sandman shows a sense of humor.

NG: Yes, though not the only instance. For example, in *The Doll's House*, he finds the Hector Hall version of Sandman absolutely hilarious. [*Laughter.*] He's not completely humorless; it's more a matter of his sense of humor being not quite human.

Anyway, Richard Burbage, the leading man, goes on about how good he is. I always figured that Burbage was a bit full of himself.

HB: As opposed to any other actor.

NG: "I see that you understand the theatre, messire." [*Laughter.*]

There's some more dialogue, in which it's established that the success of the play is very important to both the Sandman and Shakespeare. Shakespeare next tells his troupe, "Bestir yourselves there, lumpkins! And into your costumes! We perform the play here, on this green, within the hour." We then turn the page—and arrive at one of my favorite scenes.

I've always found it interesting that boys played girls in Shakespeare's plays. I decided that, following the old Japanese tradition, such boys would have lots of male admirers, many of whom wouldn't even consider themselves gay. So Condell says, "I can't wait until we're back in the smoke"—referring to London, which from the thirteenth century until about 1960 often had a thick pool of smoke hanging over it, primarily as a result of coal brought down from the sea. Nash responds, "As soon as the plague season is over, we'll be back at the Curtain, and the Cross Keys, and you can make up to all your admirers again." And Condell answers, "Cow. At least I have admirers."

Condell, who is costumed as Titania, then asks Hamnet, "How do I look?" and receives the reply, "You look very pretty." Condell, pleased, says, "Thank you, Hamnet. For that, you shall have a strawberry." This foreshadows a key scene that occurs later, when the real Titania offers Hamnet some Faerie fruit.

Next, we pull back to get a look at the theater they've prepared; and I put in some behind-the-scenes stage chatter, just because it was fun to write.

Dream then turns to the hill and says, "Wendel! Open your door." Something the Sandman does throughout the series is open doors; it's one of his special skills. In response, the white-chalked figure comes alive, pulls opens a door, and lets the fairies through into our world. In contrast to Shakespeare's people, who are ragtag and dirty from all their traveling, the Faerie folk look regal and perfect.

It's also worth noting that Auberon, the king of Faerie, is horned. This is partly because I wanted to make him look noticeably different from the Sandman, with whom Auberon shares many characteristics—both are tall, pale, thin, regal, and grim. But it's also because ram's horns were then a traditional way of indicating a cuckold. Auberon will be watching a play in which his queen, Titania, is unfaithful; and there are subtle hints throughout the story that the Sandman and Titania were once lovers.

HB: Do you have anything to say about the panel composition on page 5?

NG: I liked having three small panels, running along the top tier, opening up into a much larger panel. It reinforced the concept of a door opening up to let powerful forces through.

HB: How about the credits at the bottom, which begin, "Written by Neil Gaiman, with additional material taken from the play by William Shakespeare"? Was that any sort of homage to the 1983 TV series *Black Adder*, which featured the end credits "Written by Richard Curtis and Rowan Atkinson, with additional dialogue by William Shakespeare"? Or a reverse homage to the infamous opening credit of the 1929 movie *The Taming of the Shrew*, which read: "By William Shakespeare . . . with additional dialogue by Sam Taylor"? [*Laughter.*]

NG: You and I share affection for those credits; but in this case, all I really had in mind was that about half of the story's dialogue was taken from Shakespeare, and I felt it proper to acknowledge that.

By the way, the lines I quoted from the play were of two types: They either conveyed major beats of the plot, helping readers understand what was going on; or they in some way commented on the themes of my story, or of *Sandman* in general.

At the top of page 6, we meet Puck, who is apelike. His first line is "ho ho ho," which is from "The Ballad of Robin Goodfellow"—possibly written by Ben Jonson, but more probably a folk song—which is filled with little verses that describe funny things Puck does and end with "ho ho ho."

Puck continues, "They say the seven Endless are forever, Mighty Dream. You and the other six, until the death of time itself. What say you to that, King of the riddle-realms?" In addition to bringing up the idea of the Sandman dying, this passage is notable because it's the first time in the series someone states flat out that there are *seven* Endless.

Auberon chides Puck for being rude, but the Sandman points out, "It is a fool's prerogative to utter truths that no one else will speak." He gets to make a similar comment in *The Kindly Ones*, by the way, but with a topper: on page 23 of part 4, Dream says, "It is always the prerogative of children and half-wits to point out that the emperor has no clothes. But the half-wit remains a half-wit, and the emperor remains an emperor."

On page 7 of our tale, the play begins. In the actual production, it's probable that the two actors playing Theseus and Hippolyta would also have played Oberon and

Titania. I ignored historical accuracy here, however, because I liked the idea of Shakespeare playing Theseus and Burbage playing Oberon. This let me begin with Shakespeare looking out at his Faerie audience and becoming so startled that he forgets lines that came from his own pen. Todd Klein, our wonderful letterer, gave Shakespeare a word balloon with nothing in it but three dots, which shows that Shakespeare is actively not saying anything, rather than being passively silent.

After several panels of Shakespeare staring and sweating, we cut to a panel where the Sandman looks nervous—for him, at least. What he's thinking is, "Oh no, this is never going to work, why did I ever place my trust in mortals?"

Then Hamnet appears from behind the stage and prompts his father with the first line. We know for certain that prompters were used back then, because most of Shakespeare's plays were preserved via prompter copies. Hamnet's little push gets Shakespeare going, and the play commences ... and even offers a little dig at Dream on the last panel of the page: "The pale companion is not for our pomp."

Starting on page 8, and continuing through most of the rest of the story, are four layers of simultaneous action from which we cut back and forth. One layer is the play being performed onstage; another is the activity taking place backstage; the third is the reaction of the front row of the audience—which consists of the Sandman, Titania, Auberon, and Puck; and the fourth is the reaction of the back row of the audience—for which I created the giant Bevis, the tree spirit Peaseblossom, and the goat-woman Skarrow. The panel layout reflects this; virtually every page both begins and ends with the onstage performance, while the middle section of each page shows us what's going on backstage or in the audience.

HB: The peanut gallery at the back of the audience is especially delightful. How did you come to put in those characters?

NG: First, I simply liked the idea of these terrifying Faerie creatures rabbiting on amongst themselves during the performance.

Also, I couldn't assume all my readers were familiar with the play, so I needed characters who could periodically explain what was going on in Shakespeare's story. I hate the phrase "As you know, ..." as a device for providing exposition, so instead I have exchanges like this one on page 8: "What's this? What means this prancing, chattering mortal flesh? Methinks perhaps the Dream Lord brought us here to feed?" "Nar. Issa wossname. You know. Thingie. A play. They're pretendin' things. That one up there, Lysander, he loves her, Hermia, but her dad wants her to marry the other one, Demetrius, see? ... Issa love story. Not dinner." [*Laughter.*]

Going to the top of page 9, we see Will Kemp holding his pork pie; and next we move backstage for a panel to note the reaction of an actor to the audience—"But Master Will, they are not human!" Then we cut to an interesting shot in which the animal-like Puck is being caressed by the king, showing the almost sexual relationship between people and their pets. It's clear, however, that Puck hungers to go out and play with the mortals.

This never
completed
page of
artwork from
"A Midsummer
Night's Dream"
reveals the
delicate
touch of
Charles Vess's
pencil.

William
Shakespeare,
flanked by
Auberon and
Titania, king
and queen
of the realm
of Faerie.

dream country

Page 9 ends with the Faerie folk laughing uproariously at Will Kemp's lines, which tells us that yes, the play is working.

HB: And we readers feel genuine relief at that point. Thanks to a variety of prior incidents—the Sandman nervously frowning, Shakespeare sweating, actors expressing terror about the audience, the fairies talking about eating the actors—you've hooked us into getting emotionally involved and rooting for the success of the play. But just when we start to relax, you bring the play's version of Puck to the stage.

NG: Right, via the "I am that merry wanderer of the night" line. And Peaseblossom's reaction is "I am that giggling-dangerous-totally-bloody-psychotic-menace-to-life-and-limb, more like it." Bevis doesn't disagree, but instead responds, "Shush, Peaseblossom. The Puck might hear you!" This exchange lets us know that even these formidable creatures fear Puck.

We next see Hamnet perform his part in the play as the Indian boy. Unfortunately, he catches Titania's eye, who comments hungrily, "A beautiful child. Most pleasant. Will I meet him?" And the Sandman says, "I have told Shekespear to call an interval, halfway through the play; and you will meet him then." The fact is, Shakespeare's plays didn't have intermissions. I needed a period when the actors and audience could mingle, though, so I put an intermission in anyway and blamed it on Dream.

Titania then asks the Sandman about his relationship with Shakespeare, and he replies, "We came to an ... arrangement, four years back. I'd give him what he thinks he most desires—and in return he'd write two plays for me. This is the first of them." "I understand," she replies. You might notice this conversation is in iambic pentameter—echoing the conversation the Sandman is referring to, which occurred in issue 13 and was also written in iambic pentameter.

ILLUSTRATING A LEGENDARY ISSUE

Charles Vess on his award-winning artwork for "A Midsummer Night's Dream":

I both pencilled and inked "A Midsummer Night's Dream," and I'm not superfast, so it took me two and a half months. There was a lot of research involved, but it was great fun.

I based Auberon's look, with the giant red armor, on a suit of armor created by Victorian sculptor Alfred Gilbert. Titania was pretty traditional. Many of the other Faeirie folk, such as Beavis, Skarrow, and Peaseblossom, were references to work by British fantasy artists Brian Froud and Alan Lee.

I spent a lot of time getting Sussex Downs right, and especially the Long Man of Wilmington

chalk figure. Later on I got to visit the area and see Wendel, who's about a hundred feet high. The ground is very white there, so people pulled the turf off and burned the exposed area, leaving only whiteness and the green grass around it—like sculpting in earth. I also visited a pub in Wilmington called The Giant's Rift, which had a drawing on its sign of the chalk figure sitting at a table and drinking a beer.

On the other hand, I couldn't find reference pictures of Shakespeare's actors, or of Hamnet, or even of young Shakespeare, so I had to make educated guesses about how to draw them.

Shakespeare's young son Hamnet reflects on his father's devotion to work above all else.

We get more exposition, courtesy of our fairies in the back row; and then a moving passage from the play: "Ay me! For pity! What a dream was here! Lysander, look how I do quake with fear! Methought a serpent ate my heart away, and you stood smiling at his cruel prey." I think if I ever staged the play myself, I'd have Puck costumed as a serpent.

HB: The placement of that passage is especially appropriate, because it's immediately followed by page 13—which is arguably the heart of the story.

NG: Yes; the scene where Hamnet talks about his relationship with his father.

Interestingly, this wasn't in the original story. My scripts were usually approved by my editor, Karen Berger, as a matter of course; but after I handed in my first draft for this issue, Karen said, "What you've written lacks a human center of any kind. It's of interest only to Shakespeare scholars." And she told me to rewrite it, which was a rare event. One of the things that's great about Karen is she almost never makes editorial changes, because I'm usually on track; but when a story needs fixing, she doesn't hesitate to step in.

After some thought, I ended up leaving almost everything in the script the same except the first six panels of page 13, which were originally devoted to some clownish performances onstage. I entirely replaced those panels with a scene that showed us Shakespeare's career from Hamnet's perspective; and that one change gave the story its heart.

HB: Hamnet's dialogue includes some of the most memorable and disturbing lines in the series: "It's like he's somewhere else. Anything that happens, he just makes stories out of it. I'm less real to him than any of the characters in his plays. Mother says he's changed in the last five years, but I don't remember him any other way. Judith—she's my twin sister—she once joked that if I died, he'd just write a play about it. 'Hamnet.'"

NG: And Tommy's reply is, "I would be proud of him, if he were my father"—which is totally unresponsive! One of the things I do again and again in *Sandman*—and in this story—is show two people having a conversation where they're not listening to each other at all; they're really having two monologues. I do this so often, it's practically a signature technique.

I then end the page with Puck making a comment on the play that I really like: "This is magnificent—and it is true! It never happened; yet it is still true. What magic art is this?"

Shakespeare then calls the intermission I mentioned a bit earlier, and during this interval, Burbage asks the king of Faerie for gold, which isn't very wise. Fortunately, Auberon is merely amused, and he gives Burbage a pouch filled with huge gold coins. After the Faerie folk leave, we aren't very surprised to see these turn into yellow leaves.

Also, Puck puts the actor portraying him to sleep so he can take over the role himself, saying, "You played me well, mortal. But I have played me for time out of mind. And I do Robin Goodfellow better than anyone." That's based on a line from the album *Lou Reed Live: Take No Prisoners*; Lou's talking about people copying his act, and he says, "Y'know, I do Lou Reed better than anyone. Watch me turn into Lou Reed before your eyes!"

At the top of page 16, a satisfied Dream has his hand on Shakespeare's shoulder—and echoing this image, in the background, Titania is talking persuasively to young Hamnet. The Sandman says, "They are well pleased, as am I, good Will. It is finely crafted, and it will last." Shakespeare says, "If you are satisfied, then our bargain is half-concluded. One other play then, celebrating dreams, at the end of my career." This spells out for the first time what bargain was struck in issue 13. It also sets up my writing an issue based around a second Shakespeare play.

Shakespeare continues, "Yes, 'The Dream' is the best thing I have written; and it plays well. Not even Kit Marlowe will be able to gainsay that." The Sandman then heartlessly responds, "You have not heard? Marlowe is dead, Will. He died in Deptford, three weeks back, of a knife wound to the head."

HB: In your script, your description of the panel reads: "Close up on the Sandman's face. Totally impassive. He's merely passing on a morsel of inconsequential gossip; after all, humans die all over the place, all the time, don't they? Eyes are dark hollow sockets with tiny flames glittering in them."

NG: Keep in mind this is the pre-imprisonment Sandman, who's not very sensitive to people's feelings. As for the information he conveys, the troupe was on tour and news traveled slowly then, so there's no way Shakespeare could have known. But Marlowe's death hits him hard. "Why did you tell this to me now?" he asks. "This news could have waited. Marlowe was my friend." The Sandman, genuinely surprised, answers, "I did not realize it would hurt you so." And Shakespeare says, "You did not realize? No, your kind care not for human lives. Dark stranger, already I half-regret our bargain." He half-regrets it, of course, because so far he's completed only half the bargain.

And in the same panel that Shakespeare is expressing regret, Titania is giving Hamnet a piece of Faerie fruit. In the next panel, we see Hamnet eat the fruit as Titania quietly tells him, ". . . and bonny dragons that will come when you do call them and fly you through the honeyed amber skies. There is no night in my land, pretty boy, and it is forever summer's twilight." At this point, we pretty much know that Hamnet's doom is sealed.

And we also know that Shakespeare hasn't noticed. If he'd been looking after his son—or if he'd even listened to his own play, stopping to inspect the habits of the Faerie queen he writes about—the outcome might have been different. But he didn't.

The day is now noticeably dark. Among the things I love about this issue are the subtle effects colorist Steve Oliff managed as the story went on. The issue starts with the colors of morning and, panel by panel, the colors grow darker. It's actually one of my favorite coloring jobs in the series, capturing the look of watercolor work.

On page 17, Auberon says, "This must be our last visit to this Earth, Shaper. Things have changed, and will change more; and Gaia no longer welcomes us as once she did." The Sandman replies, "I know, and I regret it much." Titania then chimes in, "But you will always be welcome in our land, Dream Lord. The gates to Faerie are never fully closed. Come when you wish." The Sandman replies, "Perhaps one day I will." And he eventually does, of course—but that's another story.

HB: You then cut to Shakespeare, who is intently watching the uncommonly fine performance of Dick Cowley—not realizing that, as you put it in your script, "We're looking at Puck, playing the actor playing Puck."

COLORING A LEGENDARY ISSUE

Steve Oliff on the exceptional coloring job he did for "A Midsummer Night's Dream":

A colorist brings depth to a book. Colors can help define a time and place, and set the mood and aura of a story. On *Sandman* 19, my team tried to evoke the right feeling for each scene—bright peach schemes for the early part of the day, for example. The play begins in the morning and ends at night, so we keyed our colors to start out sunny and light, and very gradually evolved to darker schemes as the day went on, until night fell on page 23 and we ended with total black.

My favorite aspect of the issue, though, was the interplay among the different layers of the story. We used subtly different color effects for each: relatively bright, comic-bookish colors for the stage performances; a muted blue, fantasy-like color scheme for the audience; and a muted but naturalistic color scheme for the real-world backstage scenes.

As for Neil's comment that it looks like water-colors, all I can say is that we were pretty good fakers. This was among the first computer-aided coloring jobs done for DC, by the way, but it was still long before the days of Adobe Photoshop, so we had to figure out blends mathematically using a cut-color system; such effects are significantly easier to create now.

NG: While Shakespeare watches, Hamnet tugs at his sleeve. "Not now, child," he admonishes, "I must see this." And Hamnet whispers, "She was such a pretty lady, Father, and she said such things to me." And so Shakespeare misses the last chance to hear his son tell him something very important. I then allow the play to comment on both of them with the classic line we've reached at that point: "Lord, what fools these mortals be!"

On page 18, Peaseblossom complains about the way he's being portrayed on stage: "Did you hear that? Peaseblossom! That's meant to be me, that is! Iss nuffink like me! Nuffink! . . . Issa wossname. Travelogue? Nah. Travesty. That's it." That's my one anachronistic, and slightly embarrassing, joke. [*Laughter.*] If I could've come up with a word that was used back then and had the right sound, I would've done; but I figured the fairies exist a bit outside of our timestream anyway, so *travelogue* it was.

At the top of page 19, we reach what always struck me as—while also managing to be comic—the one moment of genuine, moving tragedy in the play, because it's about how the pranks of great and powerful fairies affect small and powerless mortals. Bottom wakes up and says, "I have had a most rare vision. I have had a dream, past the wit of man to say what dream it was. Man is but an ass, if he go about to expound this dream. Methought I was—there is no man can tell what…" The text of the play continues, "The eye of man hath not heard, the ear of man hath not seen, man's hand is not able to taste, his tongue to conceive, nor his heart to report, what my dream was. I will get Peter Quince to write a ballad of this dream: it shall be called Bottom's Dream, because it hath no bottom." And it really doesn't.

Appropriately, the next panel shows a very rare instance of the Sandman questioning his actions out loud: "I wonder, Titania. I wonder if I have done right. And I wonder why I wonder. Will is a willing vehicle for the great stories. Through him they will live for an age of man; and his words will echo down through time. It is what he wanted. But he did not understand the price. Mortals never do. They only see the prize, their heart's desire, their dream. But the price of getting what you want, is getting what you once wanted. And had I told him? Had he understood? What then? It would have made no difference. Have I done right, Titania? Have I done right?" It's a weird, unique little moment of self-knowledge. It's also when I feel it's clearest he and Titania were lovers, because Dream almost never reaches out to someone so openly. Keeping with the theme of the story, however, Titania was too absorbed with what was happening onstage to have listened to a word he said, and so simply responds, "Hm? Oh, it is a wonderful play, Lord Shaper. Most enchanting and fine."

Page 20 demonstrates one of the most powerful features of the comics medium: ironic counterpoint between words and pictures. In panel 2, Shakespeare as Theseus recites the line, "One sees more devils than vast Hell can hold" while he's facing an audience of nightmare Faerie creatures, staring back through the twilight with bright and burning eyes. In panel 3, Shakespeare continues off-panel, "The lover, all as frantic, sees Helen's beauty in a brow of Egypt," and pictured is an eight-year-old Hamnet goofy with love for Titania.

On page 21, I address the one big question left dangling: Why did the Sandman commission this play? He gives Auberon and Titania this answer: "During your stay on this Earth, the Faerie"—that's a typo, by the way; it should be "Faerie folk" or "fair folk" or "fairies," as "Faerie" in *Sandman*, spelled like that, is the name of the place, not the inhabitants—"the Faerie folk have afforded me much diversion and entertainment. Now you have left for your own haunts, and I would repay you all for the amusement. And more: They shall not forget you. That was important to me; that King Auberon and Queen Titania will be remembered by mortals, until this age is gone."

HB: I really like that. In a way, it also foreshadows issue 50, which is probably your most popular *Sandman* story.

NG: Yes; and in addition, it demonstrates that the Sandman pays his debts.

Auberon replies, "We thank you, Shaper. But this diversion, although pleasant, is not true. Things never happened thus." And the Sandman echoes Puck's delighted comment from page 13: "Oh, but it is true. Things need not have happened to be true. Tales and dreams are the shadow-truths that will endure when mere facts are dust and ashes, and forgot."

The last panel on this page shows a peanut gallery Shakespeare himself created within his play, consisting of Theseus and Hippolyta remarking on the action. Hippolyta says, "This is the silliest stuff that ever I heard." And Theseus replies, "The best in this kind are but shadows; and the worst are no worse, if imagination amend them." Which is a commentary on this story and on everybody in it.

On page 22, it's revealed that Auberon knew all along that Puck was onstage, as he gestures with amusement and says, "Come, my Puck, and leave this foolishness, for now the time for our return draws near. Already Wendel opens up his gate." But Puck answers, "What, leave, My Lord? When there are mortals to confusticate and vex? Go you all. Your Puck will stay—the last hobgoblin in a dreary world. Ho ho ho!" The Sandman bids all the Faerie folk farewell except for Puck, who is left alone on page 23 to finish up the play.

HB: Can you talk a bit about the way page 23 is constructed?

NG: It's a six-panel grid that shows Puck progressively letting go of the human guise he wore to become more and more a hobgoblin; and which shows the night grow progressively darker with each panel, so that in panel 5 we see only glittering eyes and teeth—which is a cliché, but nonetheless cool—and in the last panel, total blackness.

In contrast to that utter fall of night, page 24 opens to bright morning again. Shakespeare and his players have fallen asleep on the hill, fully clothed, and are just now stirring—or, as Keats put it, "And I awoke and found me here on the cold hill's side." Burbage discovers Auberon's gold has turned to leaves and complains they were cheated; but Shakespeare replies, "No, for we were paid full well. Which other troupe has played to such an audience?"

Hamnet then runs up and says, "Father! I had such a strange dream. There was a great lady, who wanted me to go with her to a distant land . . ." And Shakespeare, who is much wiser about plays than what's going on under his nose, says, "Foolish fancies, boy. On the cart today, you must practice your handwriting. Perhaps you could write a letter to your mother, or to Judith." And Burbage, recovered and ready to seek gold elsewhere, says, "Come on, you vagabonds! Stir yourselves! We can be in Lewes by late afternoon, and there's an inn I know will be glad of a troupe of actors with a new comedy to show . . ."

Which brings us to the final panel. In my script, I asked for it to appear as white lettering on a black background, but I much prefer the way it was actually done, as black lettering against a tan orange:

"Hamnet Shakespeare died in 1596, aged eleven.

"Robin Goodfellow's present whereabouts are unknown."

HB: You've just demonstrated that a *Sandman* issue is littered with references to literature, history, music, and so on. I'm sure there are additional references in issue 19 alone that you've skipped over for the sake of time and that went completely past me. Are you at all concerned about readers missing such stuff?

NG: It's true that there are references throughout *Sandman* that people will miss. But *Sandman* isn't about that; it's about the big sweep of the story.

I like the fact that these days I'm getting fan mail from people who read *Sandman* when they were seventeen, and now they're going back and rereading it in their late twenties and discovering it's a completely different story, and getting all the stuff they didn't get out of it the first time.

But they enjoyed it that first time too, which for me is the important thing. It means I've created a story that's accessible and interesting, on a number of levels.

Puck delivers the closing lines of "A Midsummer Night's Dream" before returning to the realm of Faerie.

season of mists

6

I sent my Soul through the Invisible,
Some letter of that After-life to spell: And by and by my Soul return'd to me,
And answer'd: "I Myself am Heaven and Hell."

—OMAR KHAYYÁM

In the *Dream Country* story "Facade," Death tells someone who claims her life is hell that "You make your own hell." *Season of Mists* carries that notion a step further . . . it tells us that even after death, you're damned only if you choose to be.

Season of Mists begins with the three Fates visiting Destiny, the oldest of the Endless, to tell him major events will be initiated in his realm. When Destiny protests that "this place is beyond beginnings and endings," the Fates ominously reply, "Everything created has a beginning . . . as everything created has an end." Although Destiny doesn't normally launch actions, he checks his book and reads what he's destined to do—or, from his perspective, what a future version of him has already done—and calls a family meeting.

The resulting reunion shows us six members of the Endless family sitting at a seven-sided table. We learn that the last time they all got together was three hundred years ago, for a meeting in which the missing seventh Endless (referred to only as "The Prodigal") announced that he was leaving both them and his kingdom.

Five of the remaining Endless have already appeared in previous issues. The one Endless at the meeting who we're seeing for the first time is Delirium. A text description tells us that she's the youngest of the family and was once called Delight. Delirium's behavior swings from infantile awkwardness to childlike happiness to adolescent anger; but she also has hidden depths, as indicated when she points to Destiny and says, "I know lots of things, things about us. Things not even *he* knows."

The meeting quickly reveals pent-up anger, personality conflicts, and sibling rivalry among various members of the Endless, demonstrating that despite their enormous powers, they're as dysfunctional as any human family. The tension reaches its zenith when Desire needles Dream about his inability to sustain a romantic relationship, making such comments as, "How's your love life? Killed any girlfriends recently? Or sentenced any more of them to hell?" Barely restraining himself, a fuming Sandman walks out, and is soon followed by the sibling he feels closest to . . . Death.

His older sister tries to comfort him; but as Dream continues to play the part of martyr, she admits that everything Desire said is true. The Sandman is shocked by Death's words, but he nonetheless vows that if he's committed an injustice, he will rectify it by freeing Nada. Death returns to the dining table to resume the meeting, but Destiny says there's no need, as the purpose of the gathering has been achieved—Dream is returning to Hell.

Before going, the Sandman proceeds to tie up some loose ends by visiting Lyta Hall's newborn baby and naming him "Daniel"; visiting his friend Hob Gadling for what may be their last glass of wine together; and making arrangements for The Dreaming to continue running smoothly even if he winds up captured and imprisoned in hell. (Notably, the Sandman doesn't appear as concerned about being killed, telling his subjects, "If I am destroyed, another aspect of Dream will fill my shoes. I trust you will all make my re-assumption of the role an easy one.")

Girding himself for battle, Dream approaches the imposing main gate of hell . . . only to discover it's already open, and unguarded. He immediately heads to where he last saw Nada, but she's no longer there. Dream then notices that no one else seems to be around, either, and calls out for Lucifer. The king of hell appears and does the very last thing the Sandman expects—he cheerfully announces that he's quit his job.

As Dream tries to contain his horror at the idea of someone of Morningstar's stature abandoning his realm, Lucifer explains that after "10 billion years spent providing a place for dead mortals to torture themselves," he's ceased to care about ruling people who "like all masochists . . . called the shots—'burn me,' 'freeze me,' 'eat me,' 'hurt me.'" Lucifer protests he was never to blame for inducing anyone to sin, and that he's never had an interest in owning souls: "They die, and they come here—having transgressed against what they believed to be right—and expect us to fulfill their desire for pain and retribution. I don't *make* them come here. . . . I need no souls. And how can *anyone* own a soul? No, they belong to themselves. They just hate to have to face up to it."

As the fallen angel locks up the various gates of hell, the Sandman asks what he will do without his kingdom. Lucifer replies, "I could lie on a beach, somewhere, perhaps? Listen to music? Build a house? Learn how to dance, or to play the piano? It matters not. I have had my fill of the old life, and that is all I care about."

Dream watches as Lucifer goes about evicting hell's last remaining residents, and once these stragglers are sent away, Lucifer has the Sandman, in a short but agonizing sequence, cut off his wings. The fallen angel then frees himself of his final encumbrance—by handing Dream the key to his infernal kingdom. "It's all yours now, Morpheus. You're the sole monarch of a locked and empty hell," says Lucifer. "Perhaps it will destroy you. And perhaps it won't. But I doubt it will make your life any easier."

As word gets out that the Sandman holds possession of, in Death's words, "The most desirable plot of psychic real estate in the whole order of created things," a number of forces descend on Dream's castle to persuade him to yield ownership of hell to them. As a result, the Sandman must practice a very delicate diplomacy as he plays host to scores of gods and other powers who try to bribe and/or intimidate him.

With the multitude of offers and threats buzzing around in his brain, an overwhelmed Sandman momentarily lets the key to hell fall to the floor. A few seconds later, however, he bends and picks the key up again; and he mutters, "If only it were that easy. If I could just throw it away . . ."

Meanwhile, his guests at the castle aren't the only reason Dream feels pressured to make a quick decision. When the residents of hell were evicted, they had to go somewhere else . . . which means that many who have been long dead are returning to the land of the living. This is reflected in microcosm by the events in an English school that's virtually empty during Christmas break but suddenly fills with evil boys from the past who rise from their graves and, along with the school's headmaster, create a new hell on earth.

Just as things are coming to a boil, however, the Sandman is saved by a deus ex machina (literally!) when the creator of both the Silver City and its reflection decides to reclaim hell, and to place it under the charge of Remiel and Duma, two angels sent from the Silver City to act as observers. This is heartbreaking news for the two angels; as Remiel explains, "Does He not understand what this means? To be exiled into the darkness? To be Banished from our Creator's Light, his grace? We are too pure for our feet to ever touch the base clay—why then should we be forced into the Pit?" But in the end, Duma accepts the key, and Remiel opts to accompany him as coruler of hell.

The angels aren't the only ones upset; so are a number of the beings who sought Hell for themselves. Most notably, Azazel of hell renounces the Sandman's hospitality and, using Nada as bait, tries to destroy him. The demon miscalculates, and the Sandman imprisons the creature within a glass globe (echoing his own imprisonment in Burgess's glass cage). Dream then asks his stunned and now frightened guests, "Does anyone else in this place have a problem with my decision?" Not surprisingly, no one else does, and they all make their peace with him.

With the fate of Hell decided, most of the Sandman's guests clear out from his castle, but a few still require his attention. One is Nuala, whom Queen Titania (from issue 19) sent as a gift from Faerie. Neither the Sandman nor Nuala is anxious for her to stay, but her brother Cluracan warns that if Titania's gift is rejected, "the Queen will *not* be best pleased—and Nuala herself will risk her severest displeasure." In exasperation, Dream gives in, but adds, "I mislike little magics in this realm." With a gesture, he strips Nuala of the Faerie glamour she's been wearing to make her appear as a tall, gorgeous, haughty blond, revealing that she's actually dowdy and a bit mousy: short, pointy-eared, brown-haired, insecure, and rather sweet.

The Sandman must also deal with another guest wearing a glamour: the trickster Loki, who avoided being returned to prison by switching places with Susano, the Japanese storm god, when everyone's attention was diverted by Dream's fight with Azazel. The Sandman says he will liberate Susano but offers to place a dream image in his stead, allowing Loki to remain free. "If I were to do this thing," Dream adds, "you would be in my debt. You understand this?" And Loki replies, "I understand."

Finally, Dream turns his attention to Nada, whom he successfully rescued during his battle with Azazel. He arranges to talk with his former lover over dinner (echoing the dinner at Destiny's table); but given the ten-thousand-year history of pain and torture between them, the conversation is awkward.

Dream tries to say he's sorry, but it's clearly not something he does very often because he's exceptionally bad at it: "Nada. Ten thousand years ago, I . . . I condemned you to hell. I now think . . . I think I might have acted wrongly. I think perhaps I should apologize." Nada quite reasonably responds, "You think you *may* have acted wrongly? You think *perhaps* you'll apologize? You *think?*"—and, after getting a few more things off her chest, she slaps Dream across the face, really hard.

Earlier in the storyline, the Sandman became very angry when Cluracan merely touched his cloak, so we can imagine just how furious Dream is at someone forcefully hitting his bare flesh. He sputters, "You struck me. No one may strike me; and here—here at the heart of the Dreaming . . . I should . . . I . . . I ought to . . ." But Nada, demonstrating the royal qualities that probably attracted the Sandman to her in the first place, counters, "Yes? What will you do to me, Dreamlord? Send me back to hell?"

Recognizing defeat, Dream finally utters the apology he should've given in the first place: "I am sorry, Nada. You are right. What I did was foolish, and heartless, and . . . and unfair; you hurt my pride, and I hurt you. I was wrong. There is nothing else I can say." And with that, they kiss and (as best they can under the circumstances) make up.

The Sandman repeats the offer he first made to Nada after they slept together—stay with him and be his queen. This isn't as reckless as it sounds, because in her current state as a spirit ("I have no true body anymore, after all; I am one of the dead"), Nada wouldn't be violating the rule against a mortal loving one of the Endless. Nonetheless, Nada declines. The former queen then makes a notable counteroffer: "You could give all this up, you know." This alternative wasn't mentioned in the tale told by the men of her tribe in issue 9—but it's presumably part of the women's version of the story. Dream declines in turn, saying, "My answer has not changed. I have my responsibilities. I cannot abandon them."

With neither of them budging, the lovers once again part; but this time with affection. Nada chooses to return to humanity, and so is reincarnated in a Hong Kong hospital as a baby boy. The Sandman holds the newborn child in his arms and says: "I will not forget you, Nada. Live a good life. You will always be welcome in The Dreaming, whatsoever body you wear."

The focus then shifts from the Sandman to the three angels of the story. We first see Lucifer, free of his reign over hell, sunning himself on an Australian beach. An elderly man strolls up to Lucifer and confides that despite hardships he's endured to rival that of Job's, he continues to come out to watch the sun set: "Most every night it's a bloody *beaut*. And every night it's *different*. And I think, well, I've had a shit of a life, all things considered. It wasn't fair. Everyone I've ever loved is dead, and my leg hurts all the bloody time. But I think, any God that can do sunsets like that, a different one every night . . . 'Struth, well, you've got to *respect* the old bastard, haven't you?" After the old man leaves, Lucifer Morningstar—the angel who was once the bringer of the morning light—grins at the sky and says, "All right. I admit it. He's got a point. The sunsets are bloody *marvelous*, you old bastard." Smiling, Lucifer lies back and adds softly, "Satisfied?"

Meanwhile, Remiel and Duma are contemplating their roles as the new custodians of hell. Duma, as usual, remains silent and unreadable; but Remiel is actively trying to put the best light on their situation: "Perhaps it's a blessing. Perhaps it's an opportunity to do good." So saying, Remiel flies to one of the souls and tells him that the torture he's experiencing is a form of love for which one day he'll thank them . . . eerily echoing the lecture given by the school headmaster in chapter 4. As Remiel flies away to repeat his speech to another victim, the tortured soul whispers, "But . . . you don't understand. . . . That makes it worse. That makes it so much worse. . . ."

But Remiel doesn't hear, as he's too busy thinking that perhaps he judged his reassignment too harshly: "After all, this is part of the plan, is it not? Then how could it *not* be for the best, in this, the best of all possible worlds? Perhaps events have ended happily, after all. Happily ever after. In hell." Juxtaposed against these thoughts is an image in the background of the ivory tower Remiel lives in; while in the foreground, a demon with teeth for nipples is busy skewering a pile of naked, emaciated people lying in a pond of icy water. That same demon appeared on the first page of chapter 1, which began, "Once upon a time . . ."

Finally, we return to Destiny's garden, and we see him reading in his book the same ending we just did: "Happily ever after, in hell." As Destiny continues wandering through his realm, we're presented with a passage from a book never written by G. K. Chesterton, taken from Lucien's Library of Dreams: "October knew, of course, that the action of turning a page, of ending a chapter or of shutting a book, did not end a tale. Having admitted that, he would also avow that happy endings were never difficult to find: 'It is simply a matter,' he explained to April, 'of finding a sunny place in a garden, where the light is golden and the grass is soft; somewhere to rest, to stop reading, and to be content.'"

SOME THINGS WORTH NOTICING

One of the marks of a great writer is to do things that are the opposite of what an audience expects and yet feel, by the end of the story, inevitable. Neil Gaiman performs this trick throughout *Sandman*, but the collection most artfully crammed with such twists is *Season of Mists*, in which almost nothing is what it seems.

The tale begins with beings nearly as old as the universe, and with more power than gods, who can't even manage to have a peaceful family meal together. This dichotomy is echoed later by the guests in the Sandman's castle, many of whom are worshiped as gods and yet demonstrate as much greed, treachery, insensitivity, and pettiness as the lowliest human. Even the Sandman himself is shown to have grievously wronged a woman he loves—and for no better reason than pride. In all these cases, the message is clear: power doesn't automatically convey wisdom. And, by the same token, beings of power don't merit our blind trust.

Also notable is Gaiman's portrayal of hell as a place people go to only when, on some level, they choose to do so—and as a place they're free to leave at any time. In other words, what happens to us isn't in the hands of some Higher Power—what happens is ultimately up to us.

This is exemplified by the most surprising and complex character in *Season of Mists*, the fallen angel Lucifer. We expect Lucifer to behave in a purely evil manner, and to engage the Sandman in a brutal battle. But the references at Destiny's dinner to the missing seventh Endless foreshadow Lucifer's actions . . . because, like "the Prodigal," Lucifer chooses to abandon his realm.

A prime example of how Gaiman plays with our expectations is the scene in chapter 2 where Lucifer's subject Mazikeen (who has half a mouth) confesses her love for him and asks to go with him. In response, Lucifer takes her long, jagged knife, tells her he'll be traveling alone, and pulls her body to him, saying, "Come close to me"—making us feel sure he's about to stab Mazikeen to death.

When we turn the page, however, we see Lucifer instead inserting his tongue, knifelike, into Mazikeen's mouth to give her monstrously deformed face a very passionate kiss. He then thanks her and, as he sends her away, tells her she's very beautiful. And he hands the Sandman the knife so that Dream can cut off Morningstar's wings.

When we next see Lucifer, he's lounging on a beach, enjoying the simple pleasure of a sunset . . . and, according to the script for chapter 8, "coming the closest he has since before the Creation to admitting he was wrong. Even the Devil can change his ways and escape damnation."

In contrast, the Sandman has good intentions, but he's virtually a prisoner of his commitment to external responsibilities. Dream takes the key to hell as if he has no choice. In fact, the Sandman always has a choice—not to take the key in the first place, or to get rid of the key at any point after accepting it. The hook that keeps him attached is Dream's strong feelings of duty and obligation.

In *Season of Mists*, the Sandman is saved by (quite literally) an act of God. He can't always be so lucky, however; and several decisions Dream makes in this story will come to haunt him in subsequent collections.

HB: Is it true *Season of Mists* almost didn't happen because someone else had independently come up with a similar idea?

NG: It is. I began plotting *Season of Mists* at the same time I wrote issue 4, in May 1988. I then happened to mention it to my good friend Rick Veitch, and he said, "You can't do a story about Lucifer quitting. I'm doing that for DC myself, in a miniseries called *King Hell*." Rick had planned a giant crossover event, involving most of the DC Universe, in which Lucifer left hell in order to wreak havoc and evil in the world. So I sighed and said, "Oh, all right, I'll forget about my story." But shortly after that, Rick opted to leave DC, which axed the plans for his project; and so I returned to my abandoned plot and eventually wrote *Season of Mists*. Rick later used his title for his own publishing imprint, though: King Hell Press.

HB: What was your inspiration for the idea?

NG: Pierre Teilhard de Chardin's book *The Divine Milieu*, in which he wrote, "You have told me, O God, to believe in Hell. But you have forbidden me to hold with absolute certainty that a single man has been damned." Between that and *Sandman* 4, it occurred to me Lucifer could one day get tired of Hell, of being the Adversary, and of all the crap that goes with it; that he could simply choose to walk away and do something else.

Lucifer turns the key to Hell one last time before giving it to the Sandman.

HB: In your script for chapter 2, you wrote, "Bear in mind that Lucifer is not necessarily a bad person; or at least, that people can change, and repent—that leopards sometimes do change their spots, given enough time. He's had a long time to think things over, after all ... and he used to be an angel."

NG: The most wise and beautiful angel. He was once at God's right hand, which is a lovely place to be. But he loved God too much; he wanted him all to himself, and refused to worship humanity.

Then again, he was fated to take that path. As he says in chapter 2, "I thought I was rebelling. I thought I was defying His rule. No ... I was merely fulfilling another tiny segment of His Great and Powerful Plan. If I had not rebelled, another would have in my stead."

Lucifer is such a wonderful character, he more or less wrote himself. I especially enjoyed his speech near the end of chapter 2: "Why do they blame me for all their little failings? They use my name as if I spend my entire day sitting on their shoulders, forcing them to commit acts they would otherwise find repulsive. 'The Devil Made Me Do It.' I have never made one of them do *anything*. They live their own tiny lives. I do not live their lives for them."

HB: What went into Lucifer's appearance?

NG: My mental picture was of David Bowie, back when he was a nineteen-year-old hippie. A junkie angel with a cruel slyness—but still an angel, soft and beautiful. He has no genitalia, and no navel; he walks on plain bare feet; and he has leathery, batlike wings that grew after his feathery wings were ripped off.

HB: I'd add that your basic strategy for Lucifer was understatement. For example, in your script for page 11 of chapter 1, you describe Lucifer's reaction to the news that the Sandman is returning as follows: "Close up on Lucifer. He's back gazing across his land; only now, for the first time, he's grinning joyously, hilariously. Make this a huge, wide grin, not an evil grin at all. If you make it unpleasant or evil or mad, it'll be a million times less scary than if he's simply happy; because he's Lucifer, and he's scary as hell because he's who he is."

NG: It helped that Lucifer has a history few characters can match; and I reinforced that image in readers' minds three pages earlier, when the Sandman tells Matthew, "Saving only his Creator, he is still perhaps the most powerful being there is." Matthew asks, "More powerful than *you*?" And the Sandman answers, "Oh yes. By far." Previous storylines had established the enormous power Dream has, so that's all that needed to be said.

HB: You've just explained what inspired the story. What about its title?

NG: It came from John Keats's poem "To Autumn," which begins, "Season of mists and mellow fruitfulness"—a line I usually misremember as "Season of mists and mellow frightfulness." It's actually a sweet little poem about how much Keats likes autumn; but it struck me as an appropriate title because I pictured everything taking place over a couple of weeks in November, and because the story is about mists both literal and allegorical—all the way through, alliances shift, power structures change, and nothing is easy to hold on to.

HB: How would you describe your overall approach?

NG: Big and Victorian and baroque; very elaborate and ornate. For example, some readers grumbled about the hardcover edition not having a dustcover; but I wanted something that would look like an old family Bible.

HB: Oh, I think it's a wonderful design. It has a rich brown cover looking like mottled leather, with gold lettering on the spine, and a golden key with a hook on top—the key to hell. Also, bits of ornamentation are etched about the key, including an infinity symbol. Physically, it's my favorite hardcover in the series.

NG: Thanks. Dave McKean, as always, did the design, but it's the hardcover that had the most input from me. I wanted it to be a kind of Victorian object.

I also selected the typeface we used for Harlan Ellison's introduction from a book published over a hundred years ago. Dave then went out and found a typeface that was the modern equivalent. I loved that *st* and *ct* combinations get joined in the typeface via an ornate hook on top.

Even the chapter titles are in a Victorian style—strange, drawn-out things that very intently try to summarize everything. For example, chapter 6's title is "In which the vexing question of the sovereignty of Hell is finally settled, to the satisfaction of some; the finer points of hospitality; and in which it is demonstrated that while some may fall, others are pushed."

NAMES AND DREAMED BOOKS

HB: The story begins with a gathering of the Endless. Right after the various siblings arrive, though, something unique in the series occurs—you break the action to provide six short text essays. What led you to do that?

NG: By page 8, I'd presented the reader with a number of the key characters in the series, and I was about to have them interact, but I hadn't really explained who most of them were yet. It seemed to me a good idea to first stop and provide a little piece on each of them, as if I were writing entries in a very weird encyclopedia. It was one of those strange techniques that shouldn't have worked but somehow did.

HB: One of the descriptions that most struck me was the Sandman's: "Dream accumulates names to himself like others make friends; but he permits himself few friends."

In contrast, the Sandman has a virtual army of names. There are titles, such as King of Dreams, Master of the Realm of Sleep, King of the Nightmare Realms, Monarch of the Sleeping Marches, Lord of the Dreamworld, and Prince of Stories—the latter being a phrase I've read you took from the Velvet Underground song "I'm Set Free." You also created names for Dream used by various cultures, such as Lord L'zoril, which is what the Martians called him, and Kai'ckul, which is what Nada's African subjects called him; and a variety of other names, such as Oneiromancer, Lord Shaper, Shaper of Forms, and His Darkness Dream of the Endless. He's probably the most-named character in comics history.

NG: The fun of that being, he doesn't really *have* a name.

HB: What do you mean?

NG: Any possible name for any dream god will attach itself to Dream, but none of them are really his name. Even "Dream" isn't a name; it's a function, a word that describes his area of responsibility.

HB: By that reasoning, Desire's name isn't actually Desire, Despair's name isn't Despair, and so on.

NG: Right; none of the Endless truly have names, just functions. That's why, by the way, the Endless referred to their missing sibling in issue 10 as "the Prodigal," as opposed to his name as one of the Endless. Since he's abandoned his function, he's also in effect abandoned his name.

HB: Following the text descriptions, we see dinner being served by odd little creatures. What are they?

NG: I'm not entirely sure. In *Brief Lives*, Delirium refers to them as Destiny's "little flappy things" and seems to believe they're his pets; but I think they're just his servants. They're miniature versions of Destiny's robe, about the size of pillows, and with no one inside them. I refer to them as the Destinyettes. [*Laughter.*]

But the main thing I like about the dinner is that it helped clarify the Sandman's code of behavior. As was shown in "Tales in the Sand," Dream is perfectly capable of doing the most awful things; but if it's pointed out that he's done something terrible, and he actually believes it, then he's quite willing to go off and try to fix things—even if the attempt may cause his doom.

HB: Near the beginning of chapter 1, Matthew asks Lucien what's so special about his library. Lucien explains, "Somewhere in here is every story that has ever been dreamed." That's a lovely idea, and you make use of it throughout the series. Did you make it up from whole cloth?

NG: I thought so when I wrote it. Years later, though, I was looking through some books by my favorite fantasy author, James Branch Cabell, and was reminded that *Beyond Life* has a character with a library of ideal books; so I probably nicked the idea for Lucien's library from that.

Much later, a reader gave me a 1986 book I'd never heard of by Steven Millhauser titled *From the Realm of Morpheus*, which has a dream god who's tubby, sleepy and horny—in other words, nothing like the Sandman—but who has a library of dreamed books too. So it's apparently one of those ideas that floated around in the ether and was picked up on by a number of authors.

HB: What process did you go through to create the wonderful imaginary books in the library?

NG: Some of them I just wanted to read—such as *Psmith and Jeeves*, which would've brought together two of P. G. Wodehouse's best characters. Some were books I thought should have been written but weren't, like *The Conscience of Sherlock Holmes*—which is the one thing Holmes didn't have. Some of the books were actually planned by their authors; for example, *The Lost Road* is a story begun and then abandoned by J. R. R. Tolkien.

And some were just made up for fun. For example, in *Brief Lives*, for a section of the library dealing with guidebooks, Jill Thompson stuck in *Alleys and Bradstreets*, which is simply a tip of the hat to Jill's friend Tim Bradstreet.

HB: There are also titles in your scripts that letterer Todd Klein couldn't fit onto the bookshelves. Two I especially liked were *Lord Greystoke of Barsoom* by Edgar Rice Burroughs and *Cthulhu Springtime* by H. P. Lovecraft. [*Laughter.*]

You make clear the library contains all the books that have ever been dreamed. If someone in The Dreaming wanted to read a book that had actually been published, though, would he or she have to seek it out in the waking world?

NG: Oh no; all published books are in a distant annex of Lucien's library. A very *small* annex.

After all, many people dream of books but never become writers. At the beginning of *The Kindly Ones*, for example, Lucien shows a visitor a book the dreamer didn't even realize he'd created: *The Bestselling Romantic Spy Thriller I Used to Think About on the Bus That Would Sell a Billion Copies and Mean I'd Never Have to Work Again.*

Further, even a professional author typically dreams up a hundred books for every one he publishes.

And even a book the author has published is but a sad shadow of the one he dreamed. [*Laughter.*]

HB: There's just one other thing about Lucien's library I'm curious about: behind the area up front filled with books, are there sections for tales told in other media, such as cinema and paintings and music?

NG: Oh, sure. There's definitely, for example, a movie collection that includes all the stories Orson Welles made in his head but could never get the financing to film.

GOING TO HELL

HB: I think chapter 1 works beautifully, so I was surprised when I learned that you'd written it against your will.

NG: Well, I'd wanted to go straight from the meeting of the Endless to the Sandman journeying to Hell. When I mentioned that to my editor, Karen Berger, though, she said "You can't do it, because there'll be some political turmoil going on in hell that month in another DC title, *The Demon*; Lucifer can't quit hell until the following month." This led to the only fight Karen and I had over the seven-year run of the series; and it all took place on paper. I blew my top and sent a fax saying, "Nobody reading *Sandman* is going to be reading *The Demon*, nobody's going to care, you're upsetting the master plan," blah blah blah. And Karen sent me a fax back saying "You really pissed me off, what you said was uncalled for. And y'know what, I'm the editor of this comic, dammit." I thought it over and decided Karen was right; so I sent her an apologetic fax, and I wrote what is now chapter 1.

At the time, I viewed that issue as filler. In retrospect, though, it gave me the opportunity to build up the tension and have those wonderful scenes with Lucifer and Cain, and put in the first appearance of Lyta's son, and do the toast with Hob.

HB: You also use that issue to try and reconcile your version of hell with that of various other DC comics; on page 19, for example, Lucifer discusses some recent political struggles in his realm that had nothing to do with your storyline.

NG: Right; it was my attempt to maintain a semblance of DC continuity. As far as I was concerned, though, those other series weren't even necessarily covering the same infernal realm. I always figured that every author has the right to his own hell. [*Laughter.*]

Continuity has its uses, though. For example, I was quite proud of myself for realizing his mark made Cain the perfect messenger, because he's the one inhabitant of The Dreaming who Lucifer wouldn't hurt. I also loved it when I was rereading the Bible and ran across Genesis 4:16: "And Cain went out from the presence of the Lord and dwelt in the land of Nod." [*Laughter.*] Lucifer cites the passage himself on page 10, and then adds, "Where you still live, eh?"

HB: Another fascinating character in chapter 1 is Lucifer's loyal servant Mazikeen.

NG: She was great fun to write. Half her face is gorgeous, and half's been blown away by some horrible accident. I'd therefore make up her lines, say them out loud using only half my mouth, and then mark down what came out. For example, Mazikeen's first words, "Shut up, scum. Speak when you are spoken to. Get down on your *knees*," ended up phonetically as "Schuck uck, sgun. Shveeg vhen zhu ah schvogen tzu. Ghetch *downg* ong hyouh *hnees.*"

I have no idea how many readers actually follow what she's saying; but I provided hints by having Lucifer occasionally repeat some of her words.

Lucifer Morningstar bids farewell to his faithful servant, the half-deformed Mazikeen.

THE SANDMAN COMPANION

HB: Following that scene, you show the Sandman visiting Lyta Hall's baby. Lyta reentered the waking world, six months pregnant, in issue 12; and yet she doesn't have her baby until ten months later, in issue 22. Was time in *Sandman* supposed to follow time in our world?

NG: Pretty much. The main exception is the one you're pointing to now, the baby's sixteen-month gestation. I had no choice, though, because I couldn't have comfortably fit the baby into an earlier issue; and I needed for him to be virtually newborn in chapter 1 so the Sandman could come and name him. The only excuse I can offer is that time works differently in dreams, which is where the baby resided for a couple of years before being born.

HB: Why did Dream name the boy Daniel?

NG: It begins with *D*, for a start. [*Laughter.*] And it connects to the Daniel in the Bible who has visions and interprets dreams.

HB: And who champions the supremacy of the spiritual world over the physical world. I didn't make the connection until you just explained it, but now it seems obvious.

The Sandman's last detour is a visit to his friend Hob Gadling, who makes this toast: "To absent friends, lost loves, old gods, and the season of mists; and may each and every one of us give the devil his due." Is that original?

NG: It is, although many readers assume otherwise because it's set in quotes and italics. The rhythm of it was inspired by an oath sworn by characters in Hope Mirlees's novel *Lud in the Mist*, but the words are entirely mine.

HB: It occurs to me that Hob's name can itself stand for a kind of devil, as in *hobgoblin*.

NG: That's so, but it's not something I had in mind when creating him. I simply wanted to give him a name that was once a common diminutive but has since died out. "Hob" used to be—along with "Bob" and "Bobby"—short for "Robert." But while "Bob" lives on, "Hob" is now anachronistic, which serves to remind readers just how old he is.

HB: Is there anything else to say about chapter 1?

NG: Just that I really like how Kelley Jones handled the Sandman's helmet. Mike Dringenberg made it look a bit too much like the gas mask of the original DC Sandman character, who was just a guy who fought crime using sleeping gas. Chris Bachalo was the first artist to make the helmet look bony, in issue 12. And under Kelley's pencils, the helmet actually looked like vertebrae, which I thought was wonderful.

HB: And quite appropriate; on page 11 of *Sandman* 49, you reveal that Dream's helm was fashioned from the skull and spine of one of three gods who had, a very long time ago, tried to take over The Dreaming.

I also liked the contrast you created between the last two pages of chapter 1, which show Dream quietly and solemnly preparing to go to battle; and the last two pages of issue 11, in which Dream looks like Arnold Schwarzenegger as he cockily suits up for war and puns "It's my move" against a checkerboard background.

NG: What both of those scenes have in common, though, is that the major battle Dream braces himself for never happens.

HB: You set that up especially nicely at the start of chapter 2, when a tiny Sandman stands before a gate of hell so enormous it has to be spread across two pages.

NG: I love Kelley Jones's and Dick Giordano's work there. That's just the main gate,

ILLUSTRATING SEASON OF MISTS

Kelley Jones enjoyed the challenge he had pencilling *Season of Mists.* "It's very big and grand," he says, "but very small and eccentric at the same time. And both of those facets of the story had to come across visually."

One example of this duality appears in the double-page spread illustrating the main gate of Hell. "I spent days on that gate to make it terrifying in its scope," he says, "because I felt the entrance to Lucifer's realm should be an incredibly intimidating place designed to scare the living hell out of you. And I also tried to get across how small the Sandman was in comparison."

Another example of grandeur appears on pages 4 and 5 of chapter 6, which shows scores of gods awaiting the Sandman's decision in a Great Hall of his castle. "That was a huge amount of work," says Jones. "I filled it with historical images, many of them based on dreams; for example, I remembered reading El Cid dreamt he would defeat the Moors, so I put in a drawing of that; and Columbus dreamt of discovering a new world, so I put that in too. All of those little touches were absolutely useless for the story itself, but they infused the artwork with extra energy.

"Although I wanted the Great Hall to be beautiful, I also wanted it to be sterile," continues Jones, "because I felt Dream had access to all the greatest minds in history but never fully understood the beauty of their thoughts. So I created huge black walls underneath the designs, and black pillars, and stairs that go off into nowhere. It's a fancy baroque room that infuses you with its history and size, but that never lets you feel homey; it doesn't contain a single comfy couch."

Jones visually conveyed attitudes in smaller ways, as well—such as by putting an expressionistic spin on the Sandman's clothing. "Dream mostly just talks in this story, and is usually trying to hide what he's feeling, which could have made him dull visually," says Jones. "My solution was to show the emotional turmoil going on just beneath the surface through the billows and ripples of his flowing cloak, which moves like it's alive."

Jones also put a lot of thought into the look of the various gods and other cosmic beings in the story. "I tried to draw the Japanese god very flat, like an 1850s woodcut," he says, "and to make the Egyptian gods very stiff, the way they appear in ancient wall paintings. I also leaned on the work of great nineteenth-century illustrators: I based the genie carrying Lord Order on drawings by Aubrey Beardsley, and the angels on artwork by Gustave Doré." Quickest to execute were the representatives of Order and Chaos in chapter 3. "For page 11," Jones explains, "Neil told me to draw Order as just a bunch of cubes, like a pop art design from the 1960s; and to draw Chaos the same way, but then smear the cubes around using a copy machine. It was the easiest page I've ever done, but it turned out looking really cool."

Before abandoning Hell, Lucifer has Dream cut off his wings.

though; one of the fun things about chapter 2 was showing Lucifer locking up the various other ones, ranging from a gelatinous gate that no human could walk through, to a charming wooden gate set in a low stone fence, to a door in a modern business office.

HB: You also wrote some memorable scenes about the few stragglers who refuse to leave hell.

NG: My favorite is Breschau, because he's so hugely proud of all the terrible, wicked things he'd done: "I am *Breschau* of *Livonia*. I ripped out the tongues of those who spoke against me, and cut the unborn babes from the wombs of my enemies' women. . . . I took my mother by force, and I strangled my sister when she would not consent to my advances. . . . I am *Breschau*, and *this* is *my punishment*." And Lucifer says simply, "You must go." Breschau answers, "Did you not hear me, fiend? I have killed—" And Lucifer impatiently interrupts, "I heard. You killed a number of people who by now would be long-since dead anyway. So what?" [*Laughter.*]

Livonia actually existed, by the way; it was a part of Russia until 1918, when it was divided between Latvia and Estonia. It was a country famous for its desert and its werewolves.

HB: There's also a nice scene on pages 14 through 16 in which Lucifer stands on top of a rock and gives his version of what led to his fall from heaven and his decision, ten billion years later, to finally abandon hell.

NG: That was partly inspired by the wonderful Peter Cook and Dudley Moore film *Bedazzled*. The best scene in the movie is when the Devil climbs on top of a box and, playacting the role of God, quickly demonstrates that it's more fun to be above it all receiving worship than down below supplying the worship. In homage to that scene, I gave Lucifer a rock to climb up on.

season of mists

HB: After Dream cuts off his wings, Lucifer says, "And what will they do on Earth, I wonder, when the dead start coming back?" Frankly, I thought that would be a major subplot, but you showed only a bit of it, via the schoolboys in chapter 4.

NG: I actually planned that as a major subplot and even wrote the first seven pages of it, but I ended up throwing it all away. It was good material, involving creepy magical types on the run; a young lady named Isolde Bane and her baby Anthony; a group calling themselves the Fashion Satanists; and the return of Daniel Bustamonte from issue 1. It would've been a very cool story, but it also would've taken a lot of space, probably making *Season of Mists* run for four more issues than it actually did; and at the time, I didn't want to strain the patience of my readers with a thirteen-issue storyline.

HB: You eventually did just that, with *The Kindly Ones*.

NG: True, but by then there were so many loose ends to tie up that the story just had to be that long. I also felt that anyone who'd stuck that far wasn't likely to suddenly stop reading. But early on with *Season of Mists*, I felt I needed to create a tight story; and I still believe I made the right choice.

JUGGLING GODS

HB: Once word spreads that the Sandman holds the key to an empty hell, hordes of cosmic beings descend on his palace. This results in Norse gods, Egyptian gods, and Japanese gods rubbing shoulders with one another, along with fairies, demons, angels, and representatives of Order and Chaos. That you managed to get all those clashing belief systems under the same roof and create a workable story was an impressive achievement.

NG: I'm still not sure how I did it. It was largely a balancing trick, like one of those things jugglers do with spinning plates.

HB: You had thousands of gods to choose from. How did you decide which dozen or so deities to concentrate on?

NG: I tended to pick the ones with whom I thought readers would be the most familiar. They aren't the only who arrive at the palace, though; as pages 4 and 5 of chapter 6 indicate, there were many, many gods who came to petition the Sandman for possession of hell.

HB: Most of the pantheons you include are well established in history, but the representatives of Order and Chaos are something else again.

NG: Right; Order and Chaos are part of the DC Universe theology—and, I always assumed, inspired by the work of Michael Moorcock, who first came up with the concept of Order and Chaos gods.

It tickled me to represent Order as a cardboard box. And since I was the father of a six-year-old at the time—my daughter Holly—it didn't seem a stretch to incarnate Chaos as a small girl. Holly had just had her birthday, for which she put on a clown face and wore oversize clothing and wandered around with balloons, and I thought, "There we go, that's what Shivering Jemmy will look like." As for her name, I nicked it from an old English dictionary of slang; it was a term for a type of beggar who stood and shivered at you.

HB: Given all the theologies you were dealing with, did you receive any outraged letters?

NG: I did; but most of them were from comics fans who felt I was creating cruel parodies of the Marvel Comics characters Thor, Loki, and Odin. [*Laughter.*] At the same time, I received quite a few letters from readers in Denmark, Norway, and Sweden who thanked me for portraying the Norse gods accurately.

All I really did was follow the actual legends. In Norse mythology, Thor is enormously strong, bearded, and overmuscled; and he's also quite stupid, and is easily made drunk. And if you rub his hammer, it really *does* get bigger. [*Laughter.*] The legends also strongly imply that Thor's wife is bonking Loki on the side.

HB: Were there any other complaints?

NG: Some people grumbled about the Supreme Being—the creator of the Silver City—coming in at the end and settling the affair by saying, "Right, hell is going back to being run by fallen angels." These readers felt I was portraying the Judeo-Christian god as more powerful than any other.

HB: I thought perhaps you'd done that as a reflection of Judeo-Christian countries being the most militarily powerful in the world at this point in history.

NG: No, not at all. I don't even believe the creator who turns up near the end of *Season of Mists* is necessarily the same as the Judeo-Christian god. That's indicated on page 14 of chapter 3, which says of the home of the angels, "Before the first dawn, the Silver City was. It is not Paradise. It is not Heaven. It is the Silver City, that is not part of the order of created things."

But more to the point, *Sandman* is a comic book that's part of the DC Universe, and the DC Universe has always portrayed hell as having been created by the creator of the angels. From that perspective, the ending seemed to me a comfortable option.

HB: While we're on the subject of gods and belief systems, I wonder if you could talk a little about your personal connections to religion. For example, what effect did religion have on you when you were young?

NG: I'd say the most important factor was my growing up as a Jewish kid in a Church of England school. That had a big impact on me, because it made me feel like an outsider. In a sense, it made me view *everything* as myth.

HB: Your answer reminds me of a passage in your autobiographical prose story "One Life, Furnished in Early Moorcock." It reads: "His head swam with religions. The weekend was now given to the intricate patterns and language of Judaism; each weekday morning to the wood-scented, stained-glass solemnities of the Church of England; and the nights belonged to his own religion, the one he made up for himself, a strange, multicolored pantheon in which the Lords of Chaos (Arioch, Xiombarg, and the rest) rubbed shoulders with the Phantom Stranger from the DC Comics and Sam the trickster-Buddha from Zelazny's *Lord of Light*, and vampires and talking cats and ogres, and all the things from the Lang colored Fairy books: in which all the mythologies existed simultaneously in a magnificent anarchy of belief."

That's lovely. It also jibes with something *I've* long believed, which is that growing up with contrasting cultures provides a solid foundation for becoming an artist, because it creates a distancing effect that prevents you from accepting things, that forces you to look at everything with fresh eyes.

NG: Yes; and I feel that way almost constantly, in any situation. I actually love feeling like an outsider. For example, I really enjoyed the first six years I spent in the U.S. because everything was so alien. I'm starting to get used to America now, which makes me think it may be time to move somewhere else.

HB: What about faith? Do you currently consider yourself religious?

NG: I'm honestly not sure. A few years ago I was on a stage taking written questions from the audience and one of the slips of paper asked, "Do you have any personal religious beliefs?" and my entire response was "Yes." [*Laughter.*]

I've obviously spent a lot of time thinking about myth and religion. I've also spent time with things like *The Skeptical Inquirer* magazine, and Carl Sagan's book *The Demon-Haunted World: Science as a Candle in the Dark*; but while I was reading them, I was thinking, "Yes, yes, yes; but don't you need to maintain a core of solid, rock-hard belief to be an atheist in this world?" [*Laughter.*] I think what I really like is the idea of belief itself.

I'm with J. B. S. Haldane, who said, "The universe is not only stranger than we suppose, but stranger than we can suppose." That's the kind of perspective that makes one unflappable. And it's the kind of attitude that leads one to create fiction.

SCHOOL DAYS AND HELL

HB: When writing *Sandman*, you tended to place a tale in the middle of a storyline that commented on and summed up the themes of the storyline. This collection's chapter 4 is a prime example; you even privately title it "Interlude" in your script. Can you point to a scene where the themes are discussed?

NG: Well, there's the one that starts on page 22. Our main characters Paine and Rowland—two young English schoolboys who happen to be dead—are talking. Paine says, "Rowland. I'm scared." Rowland answers, "Look at it this way: Do you want to be a ghost in an attic all your life?" Paine replies, "Yes. You're right. It's part of growing up, I suppose. You always have to leave something behind you," and so saying, allows himself to drift away from his dead body.

Then Paine continues, "What about all the rest of them? Do you think they'll ever have to go back to hell?" Rowland answers, "Go back? I don't know. I think Hell's something you carry around with you. Not somewhere you go . . . They're doing the same things they always did. They're doing it to themselves. That's hell." And Paine says, "I don't think I agree. I think maybe hell is a place. But you don't have to stay anywhere forever."

HB: You say in your script that you chose to set the story in an English boarding school for two reasons: "One of which is just not feeling in control of the U.S. school system enough, but being certain I could do the U.K.; and the other is simply the sense of time and history we can get out of the U.K., which after all has more of a history of institutionalized sadism, torture, homosexuality, and pain built into its educational system than the U.S. equivalent."

That's a strong statement. Even more unsettling, though, is the next thing you say in the script: "The school itself will be an amalgam of a few that I attended, plus a few fictional schools from literature, plus the sort of nightmare accretion of schools that I've built over the years into what I imagine as 'school.' When I dream, for example, this is the kind of school I'll dream of."

NG: Yes. Many details were taken straight from my memory; for example, on page 4: "The smell of school is a strange, pervasive thing: it's disinfectant, wood polish and ink, chalk dust, pipe tobacco, boiled cabbage, paper, flatulence, and socks." American schools have a different set of smells, but those are definitely the ones from my British childhood.

Edwin Paine and Charles Rowland, ghostly English schoolboys.

And the headmaster's speech on page 15 was easily the most fun for me to write in the whole collection. It's pretty accurate.

In other words, aside from the fact that everything in the story is made up, issue 25 is autobiographical; or, to put it another way, Charles Rowland is largely me.

DIPLOMACY AND RESONANCE

HB: The story's tension escalates in chapter 5, in which the Sandman spends the night meeting privately with various deities who either threaten him or try to bribe him in an attempt to win hell's prime real estate for themselves.

NG: I definitely enjoyed the diplomacy that was going on in that issue. Something else fun we did was subtly change the Sandman's appearance every time he spoke with a different god. When Dream talks to the Japanese god, for example, his face looks Asian; and when Dream chats with Bast on the following page, his face becomes feline.

HB: Chapter 5 is also notable for introducing two important new characters: Cluracan, the ambassador from Faerie, and his sister Nuala.

NG: Cluracan isn't really his name, by the way. It's an Irish word that represents a type of fairy, like *leprechaun*; except instead of pots of gold, a cluracan is primarily interested in wine. According to Katharine Briggs's *Encyclopedia of Fairies*, a cluracan does things like scare dishonest servants who steal from their master's wine cellar; and "sometimes he makes himself so objectionable that the owner decides to move, but the cluracan pops into a cask to move with him." [*Laughter.*]

The Cluracan in this story is definitely a drunk. In chapter 6, we also learn that he's gay, and promiscuous, and too clever for his own good.

HB: Speaking of drunks, you had some fun with Thor as well.

NG: Yep. I especially enjoyed his hangover, which allowed us to put a rain cloud over the head of the Thunder God. Todd took it a step further and put champagne bubbles into one of his word balloons.

HB: Going from the absurd to the sublime: What are the histories of the angels Duma and Remiel, who end up taking over hell? Did you get them from the Bible?

NG: No, the only named angels in the Bible are Michael and Gabriel; but information about the others comes from things like the Apocrypha and the *Book of Enoch*. According to Gustav Davidson's *A Dictionary of Angels*, Duma is "the angel of silence and of the stillness of death. Duma is also a tutelary angel of Egypt, prince of hell, and angel of vindication. *The Zohar* speaks of him as having 'tens of thousands of angels of destruction' under him, and as being 'chief of demons in Gehinnom (i.e., hell) with 12,000 myriads of attendants, all charged with the punishment of the souls of sinners.'" And Remiel is "one of the seven archangels who attend the throne of God, as stated in *Enoch I*, 20. He is called Jeremiel or Uriel in various translations of *IV Esdras*, and described as 'one of the holy angels whom God has set over those who rise (from the dead).'"

HB: Did you know from the start that the Sandman's dilemma would be resolved by the angels reclaiming hell?

NG: Actually, it's one of the few times when I *did* know precisely how a storyline would end. I usually at least pretended to myself that I didn't know how I'd tie things up, so that getting to the end could be a surprise. For this story, though, it was important for me to keep in mind that the ones who get hell are the ones who absolutely don't want it.

HB: Azazel foolishly renounces the protection afforded Dream's guests, and the demon ends up imprisoned in a small glass globe. We then see the Sandman, at the top of page 20, place the globe into a pirate-type treasure chest. Other items in the chest include the Corinthian's skull, which last appeared in issue 14; a bottled city, which we learn more about in issue 50; and an old-fashioned pocket watch, which we learn more about in issue 54. Did you know at the time that other items in the chest would play roles in tales two or three years down the line?

NG: Oh, sure. I didn't yet know every detail of those future stories, of course, but I had a rough idea of what would happen in them. And I liked planting such advance visual clues because I felt they gave the series extra texture, and also because I figured they'd provide a special kick to anyone carefully rereading the series.

HB: Another example of a visual echo is the Sandman's dinner with Nada.

NG: Yes; the page layouts are the same "four panels on top and long panel on the bottom" used in issue 9. Not many readers are likely to notice that, but I feel it creates a nice resonance.

HB: The scene that occurs just a few pages later is very quiet, but is arguably the most powerful one in the storyline: the former Bringer of the Morning Light admiring God's sunset. Can you talk a bit about it?

NG: Well, I set it in Perth because I wanted a beach that faced the setting sun. And also because Australia is about as far as you can get to the end of the world without falling off. [*Laughter.*]

One thing I somewhat regret is having the old man's son die in Vietnam. I put that in because Americans tend to forget Australians fought in the war too; but in retrospect, the line probably just ended up confusing readers. Also, a lot of readers didn't understand that pom is simply an Australian word for an English person.

But yes, I like that scene a lot too. It's as close as we get to a rapprochement between heaven and hell.

HB: Finally, does Lucifer's realm reflect your personal vision of hell?

NG: Oh no; I was just following Milton, and what details had already been established in previous DC comics. My own idea of hell is staring at a blank computer screen without being able to think of a single believable character, a single original story, or a single thing worth saying. Staring at that blank screen, forever—*that's* what hell is for a writer.

—

a game of you

7

**One flew east, one flew west,
One flew over the cuckoo's nest.**

—NURSERY RHYME

In an introduction to the Brazilian edition, Neil Gaiman provided the following summary of *A Game of You*: "It's a story that weaves and ducks through many genres of fiction, from mainstream to fantasy to horror; almost all of its 159 pages take place over a period of less than 24 hours. It weaves together many things I've thought and wondered about—the relationship between people and stories; and the differences between men and women, adults and children, tales and reality. Magical realism perhaps, but neither the magic nor the reality are as easy to separate, or indeed, to identify, as one might perhaps wish."

Gaiman provides some additional insights via these comments in his script for chapter 5: "What I want to do here, without destroying the story as an adventure yarn, is grab the subtext and make it text, grab the metaphor and make it text; allow that we're spinning a metafiction and see how far we can push that fact before it collapses in on itself. Which is going to be hard; good fantasy is as delicate as butterfly wings, and just as liable to crumble if improperly handled, leaving you with something that can no longer fly."

For some readers, *A Game of You* really didn't fly; for them, its unsettling blend of high fantasy and harsh reality have made it the least popular of the *Sandman* collections. At the same time, however, the story is among Gaiman's favorites; it contains a number of unforgettable scenes and images; and it introduces a character who plays a key role later in the series. Therefore, love it or hate it, *A Game of You* demands attention.

The story begins with a three-page sequence that summarizes the arc the plot will take. The first panel is mostly filled with white snow, except for some disturbing blackness along the edges; and the first dialogue caption reads, "What will we do, Prinado? Why, we will perish. We will all die, and the Land will die, and the world will die, and the Cuckoo will reign in bleak dominion over all."

As four unseen characters named Luz, Wilkinson, Prinado, and Martin Tenbones debate the accuracy of that statement, our view progressively zooms in from long shots of the all-white landscape to a horrific closeup of a dark figure, clutching a parchment, who's been gutted and left to rot in the snow. Our view then moves past him, briefly becoming all-white again, and then turning darker and darker as we move toward the cave where our four speakers are hiding out. By the middle panel of page 3, we see nothing but blackness; and in the bottom panel, nothing but a pair of determined eyes shining in that blackness.

Following this mini-prologue, the scene shifts to a young woman who is reminiscent of a Barbie doll. In fact, she's the Barbie we previously met in *The Doll's House*, when she was living in Florida with a man named Ken. At that time, Barbie acted as if she had a plastic personality to match her looks; but in her dreams, she lived a wondrous fantasy life, having adventures as "Princess Barbara" accompanied by a loyal giant dog named Martin Tenbones. The fact that one of the characters on page 3 is also named Martin Tenbones, and that on page 1 Luz refers to a princess, tells us that the land threatened by the Cuckoo and Barbie's dreamworld are one and the same.

The top of page 4 shows that Barbie has moved from her cookie-cutter home in Florida to a run-down apartment in New York; she's sleeping alone, indicating that she's no longer married to yuppie Ken (the original script for issue 36 described her T-shirt as saying "Die, Yuppie Scum"); and hanging on her wall are large photographs of naked people with tattoos, scars, and pierced body parts. We soon also learn that Barbie makes herself up as a different person every day—for example, by drawing a chessboard across half her face with black and white greasepaint.

All these lifestyle changes were sparked by a night two years ago when (unbeknownst to Barbie) Rose Walker manifested her powers as the vortex. A side effect of the events in issue 15 was that Barbie stopped dreaming. This is why Luz says "the Princess [is] gone," Prinado speculates "she mus' be dead, or she 'as forgotten us," and Martin Tenbones declares, "She cannot have forgotten us. But she may be hurt, in her other world."

Encouraging Barbie to live out her fantasies in the waking world—for example, by window-shopping at Tiffany's when she's broke—is her neighbor and best friend, Wanda. Also residing in their Lower East Side building are a lesbian couple named Hazel and Foxglove; a quiet, bookish-looking woman calling herself Thessaly; and a surly man named George. Like Barbie, none of these people are quite what they seem.

Wanda is a preoperative transsexual who was born in Kansas under the name Alvin Mann. Hazel McNamara, although she has no interest in men, is pregnant as a result of an ill-considered one-night stand. Foxglove's given name is Donna Cavanagh, and she used to be the lover of Judy Talbot (the lesbian killed in *Sandman* 6, "24 Hours"). Thessaly (a pseudonym) is a pragmatic, ruthless witch who's at least three thousand years old, and was one of the Thessalian witches of ancient Greece. And George (a.k.a. Gwas-Y-Gog) is a tool of the ominous Cuckoo who threatens to destroy Barbie's dreamworld—and who discovered and enslaved George while he was visiting her land in his dreams, so that he could do her bidding in the waking world.

Just how thin the line is between dreams and reality is demonstrated when Barbie and Wanda encounter a homeless woman on the subway begging for change. Wanda tells the woman to "bug off and die," but Barbie—despite Wanda's frowns, and Barbie being tight for cash herself—drops some coins in the woman's cup. The woman then spots a small puppy and goes into a panic, repeating over and over, "I don't like dogs," until the subway doors open and she frantically flees. Wanda gives Barbie an "I told you so" smile and then adds, "You gotta develop a thicker hide if you're going to be a real New Yorker" (an ironic comment on a number of levels, not the least of which being that Wanda's from Kansas).

As for the homeless woman, her day goes from bad to worse when she emerges from the subway and runs straight into the largest dog in the world: Martin Tenbones. Using a dreamstone called the Porpentine, Tenbones crossed over into the waking world to search for Barbie. Unfortunately, Tenbones knows nothing of our world, so he's quickly struck by a car; and a few minutes later, he's surrounded by policemen with guns. At this tense moment, Barbie appears, and Tenbones joyfully leaps toward her . . . causing the policemen to think he's attacking her and shoot him. With his dying breath, Tenbones gives Barbie the Porpentine and tells her that she's needed. A thoroughly confused but heartbroken Barbie cries, making the greasepaint on her face run together—so that half her face appears normal, and the other half looks like the snow-covered landscape of her dreamworld.

Although what she's just experienced doesn't seem rational, Barbie can't forget her friend's sacrifice, and so honors his last request by using the Porpentine to return to her fantasy land. Once there, she's greeted by the characters whose words we encountered at the beginning of the story: Luz, a green dodo bird; Prinado, an ape wearing the red jacket and cap of an organ grinder's monkey; and Wilkinson, a giant shrew wearing a film noir raincoat, and a fedora with a press card stuck into the hatband. They tell Barbie that to avoid the land's destruction by the Cuckoo, they must make the dangerous journey to the Isle of Thorns, uniting the Porpentine with the land's other object of power, the Hierogram. And that's just what the four of them commence to do.

Meanwhile, George tries to end the quest by sending out nightmare birds to drain the will of Barbie's neighbors as they sleep and then use them to destroy the Porpentine—which now resides not only in the dreamworld but also on Barbie's chest as she lies sleeping in her apartment.

One bird gives Wanda—who's terrified of surgery—a nightmare about her penis being removed by surgeons from the "Weirdzo" (a.k.a. Bizarro) world. Another bird gives Hazel a nightmare about finding a dead baby that devours her and Foxglove's normal child, and that will then turn on them (reflecting Hazel's concerns about her pregnancy . . . as well as the nature of a cuckoo to place her egg

THE SANDMAN COMPANION

in another bird's nest, and for her hatchling to kill the other baby birds by pushing them out of the nest). And a third dream bird makes Foxglove imagine that her former lover Judy has returned to pick up their relationship where it left off—a scary prospect both because Judy used to hit Fox, and because Judy killed herself by shoving skewers into her eyes in *Sandman* 6.

A fourth bird tries to work its dark magic on Thessaly, but the Cuckoo didn't anticipate dealing with an ancient Greek witch. Instead of having a nightmare, Thess simply wakes up, smashes the bird against a wall, and burns the corpse to a crisp. She then calmly gets a knife, walks upstairs, politely asks to come into George's apartment . . . and stabs him in the chest, instantly killing him.

Thessaly next gathers all her other neighbors into George's room, including Barbie's sleeping body (which Wanda carries upstairs). The witch then cuts off George's face, removes his eyes and tongue, and nails them to a nearby wall; and then casts a spell allowing her to converse with his spirit. After some prodding, George explains that he was doing the bidding of the Cuckoo, who wants to destroy the fantasy land so she can be free of it and fly away.

Thessaly, who takes any attack directed at her dead seriously, determines to travel to Barbie's dreamworld because the Cuckoo "needs to be taught a lesson." Telling Foxglove and Hazel that she needs their help, the witch explains that "there are two ways into another's dreams. We can go through the Dream King; or we can go by the moon's road. But the Dream King has little time for women, and even less for my kind; while the moon is ever ours. It's time to draw down the moon."

Thess summons the Three-Who-Are-One (who pop up throughout the series), and with their help literally calls the moon down from the sky for a few moments. This allows lesbian Foxglove, pregnant Hazel, and millennia-old Thessaly (i.e., maiden, mother, and crone) to walk the moon's road into Barbie's dream. In addition, however, it wreaks havoc with the weather, causing a hurricane that was going to blow itself out harmlessly over the ocean to turn and head toward New York.

Wanda doesn't accompany Thessaly, in part so she can guard the still-sleeping Barbie, but mostly (according to George's nailed-up face) because Wanda was born a man, and nothing she can do will ever convince the moon that she's anything other than a man.

Meanwhile, Princess Barbie's quest in the dreamworld is a series of triumphs and tragedies. Prinado is killed in the dark forest by the eerie creatures called Tweeners. Barbie, Wilkinson, and Luz escape down one of the lost paths of "Murphy," until they reach the Brightly Shining Sea. Luz, who volunteers to get help against the Cuckoo, is captured, and the Cuckoo hypnotizes her to betray her friends. Luz leads the Black Guard back to where Barbie is hiding and, while trying to protect his princess, Wilkinson is killed.

Barbie is taken prisoner and led to the Citadel of the Cuckoo . . . which, to her shock, turns out to be her childhood home in Florida. And the Cuckoo turns out to be a gap-toothed, freckle-faced version of Barbie at age six. Barbie says, "You're me." Her captor responds, "Not quite. I'm part of you. Sort of. You created me. Kind of. I'm the Cuckoo."

The pigtailed tyrant notes that Barbie has a dull childhood, and as a result read a lot and developed an active imagination. "Boys and girls are different," explains the Cuckoo. "Little boys have fantasies in which they're faster, or smarter, or able to fly. Where they hide their faces in secret identities, and listen to the people who despise them admiring their remarkable deeds." But little girls, she says, have fantasies that are "much less convoluted. Their parents are not their parents. Their lives are not their lives. They are princesses, lost princesses from distant lands. And one day the king and queen, their *real* parents, will take them back to their land, and then they'll be happy for ever and ever. Little cuckoos."

She continues, "You left yourself wide open for me, really... It's a little like possession. Only I didn't bother with your body. I moved into your dreamworld. Into those parts of your life you weren't using. You were everything I needed." But the Cuckoo is grown up now and ready to fly to other worlds. Her only problem is she's still stuck in Barbie's mind.

The Cuckoo uses her voice to hypnotize Barbie, and leads the princess to the Isle of Thorns for a special ceremony at moonrise in which both the Porpentine and the Hierogram will be destroyed, sealing the death of the land. Just before the appointed hour, the cavalry seems to arrive in the form of Foxglove, Hazel, and Thessaly (who previously did another "George" by temporarily calling back the spirit of Wilkinson for directions). But the quick-thinking Cuckoo, who still looks like an adorable little girl, shouts for help and tells Thessaly that the one she needs to stop is Luz. Thessaly responds by breaking Luz's neck. Then, with everyone's guard down, the Cuckoo uses her voice to take control of Thess, Fox, and Hazel.

With no one left to stop her, the Cuckoo forces Barbie to swing her Porpentine dreamstone at the huge stone encarved with the Hierogram (which says "Dreaming" in Japanese Katakana lettering). When the two objects of power collide, they both explode ... and the dreamworld begins to die.

To the Cuckoo's surprise, however, this triggers the appearance of the creator of the land—the Sandman, a.k.a. Morpheus, a.k.a. "Murphy." We learn that there are thousands of such lands in The Dreaming, but the Sandman created this one for a former lover named Alianora. One by one, the inhabitants of the world, living and dead, proceed to walk into the Sandman's cloak, followed at last by Alianora; and then Dream sends them all to rest, turning the land to dust.

By the terms of a compact he made long ago, the Sandman then offers Barbie, who physically triggered the land's end, a boon. Thessaly wants her to ask for the death of the Cuckoo; but Barbie opts for "the Dorothy option," returning her and her friends to the waking world safe and sound. This allows a delighted Cuckoo to sprout her wings and, finally, fly away.

Unfortunately, back in New York, the hurricane has returned with a

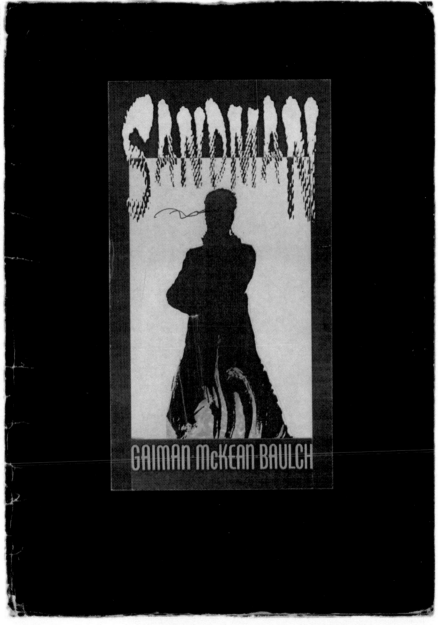

Cover of the original proposal for *The Sandman*.

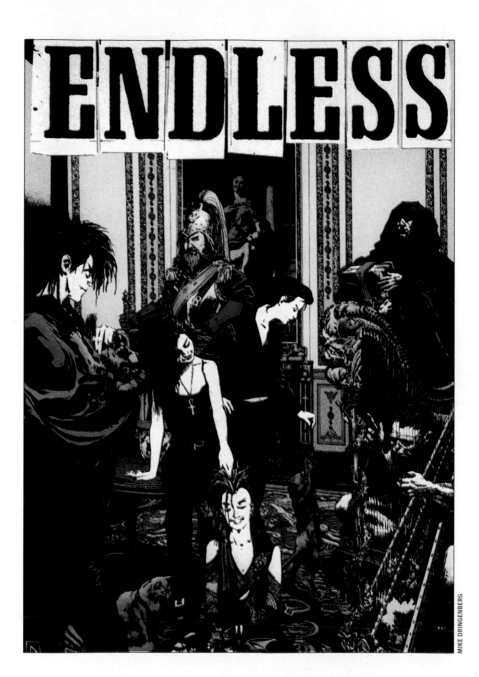

MIKE DRINGENBERG

The rare poster image of the Endless, subtitled "Still Life with Cats"
(also regularly seen on Darlene's door on *Roseanne*).

THIRTEEN

DEATH

DAVE MCKEAN

Death of the Endless, from the Vertigo Tarot Deck.

From the Vertigo Tarot Deck (clockwise, from upper left): Lucifer; Destiny; Morpheus; Delirium.

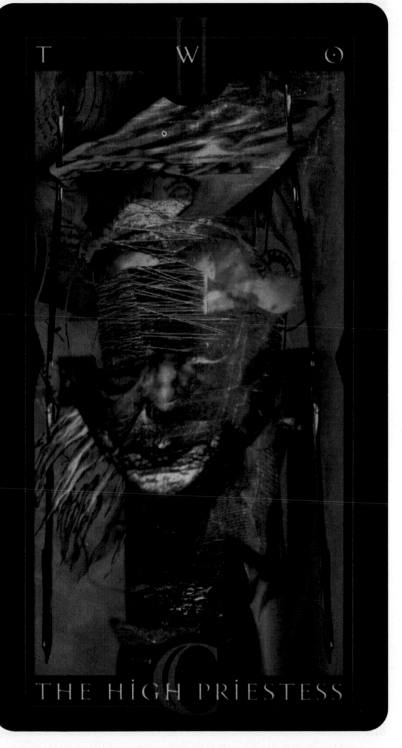

TWO ☉

THE HiGH PRiESTESS

Mad Hettie, a homeless woman who's also an ancient witch, from the Vertigo Tarot Deck.

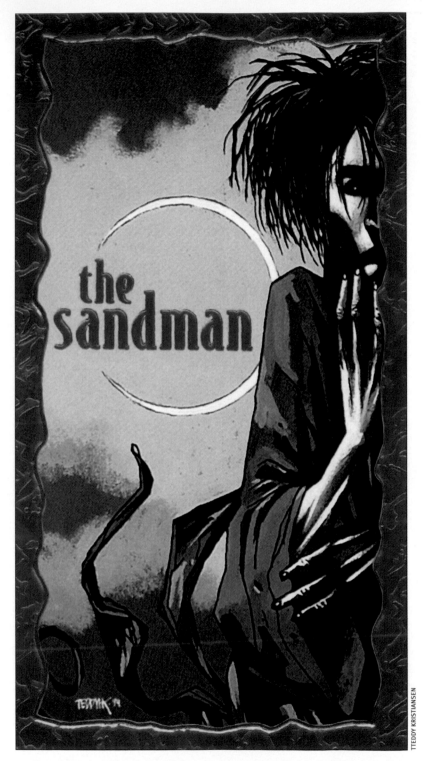

Morpheus, the Prince of Stories, who rules beyond the shores of night, from the Vertigo trading card set.

KENT WILLIAMS

BILL SIENKIEWICZ

A haunting, spectral Destiny and his grimoire, from the Sandman trading card set.

Death, the Goth reaper, as winsome as she is wise, from the Sandman trading card set.

The enigmatic Dream, in his ceremonial helm and cloak, from the Sandman trading card set.

Despair, Desire's bleak twin, from the Sandman trading card set.

Delirium,
who was
once Delight,
from the
Sandman
trading
card set.

JILL THOMPSON

GLENN FABRY

Destruction, the
prodigal brother
and gypsy warrior,
from the Sandman
trading card set.

Desire of the Endless: neither male nor female, or possibly both. This full-body painting was rejected for the Sandman trading card set. This is the first time the original version has been seen.

Cover of *The Sandman* #1, illustrated by Dave McKean, who contributed
cover images for the entire run of the series.

Cover of
The Sandman #8;
illustrator
Dave McKean
consciously
employed different
techniques and
styles for every
new story arc.

Cover of
The Sandman #19,
"A Midsummer's
Night Dream," the
only story in comic
book form to win
the World
Fantasy Award.

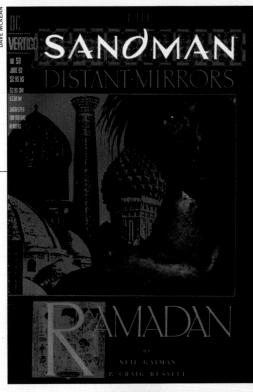

Cover of *The Sandman* #50, "Ramadan," which was many readers' all-time favorite issue of the series.

Cover of *The Sandman* #75, the final issue of the series.

DAVE MCKEAN

The Sandman continues to be published internationally.

A French edition featuring issues 5–8 of *Preludes & Nocturnes*.

A Norwegian editon of *The Doll's House*.

DAVE MCKEAN

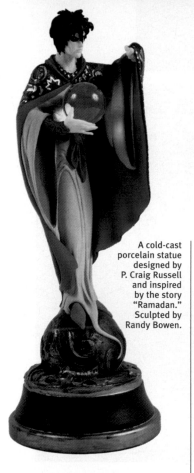

A cold-cast porcelain statue designed by P. Craig Russell and inspired by the story "Ramadan." Sculpted by Randy Bowen.

DAVE MCKEAN

A Japanese edition of *The Doll's House*.

The third
Greek
volume
of *The
Sandman*.

DAVE MCKEAN

A German
edition of
*Fables and
Reflections*.

DAVE MCKEAN

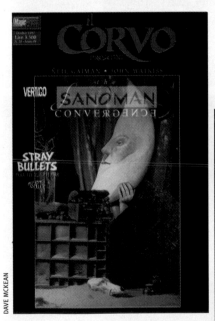

DAVE MCKEAN

Two issues of an Italian comics
anthology featuring the Sandman.

JON J MUTH

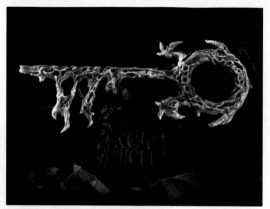

A tenth-anniversary bronze replica of the first Sandman statue from 1988, which was sculpted by Randy Bowen based on designs by Kelley Jones.

Above:
A three-dimensional rendering of the Key to Hell, as first seen in *Season of Mists*. Designed and sculpted by William Pacquet.

Left:
Porcelain statue of Death, designed by Chris Bachalo and sculpted by Randy Bowen.

The Lord of Dreams meets his successor in the Sandman bookend set, designed by Michael Zulli and sculpted by William Pacquet.

vengeance. Wanda takes in a homeless woman who's being battered by the wind, only to discover she's the "I-don't-like-dogs" lady Wanda previously snubbed on the subway. The duo end up getting along well, but their friendship is short-lived . . . the hurricane smashes into the old tenement building, knocking it down and killing them both. The sleeping Barbie escapes injury, however, as the body of the homeless woman she was kind to earlier shields her from the falling bricks.

The story ends with Barbie in Kansas, with a veil drawn on her face, attending Wanda's funeral. Wanda's family feels her death by hurricane was divine retribution for her sinful ways. To set things right, they have the mortician cut off her hair, dress her as a man, and place on her tombstone "Alvin Robert Caleb Mann, 1966–1991/For they have sown the wind, and they shall reap the whirlwind."

Barbie is quiet during the ceremony; but after everyone else has left, she honors her friend by placing a collection of "Weirdzo" comic book stories on the casket. And then, using her friend's favorite garish red lipstick, she crosses out "Alvin" on the tombstone and writes "Wanda."

On the bus ride out of town, Barbie dreams of Wanda dressed like the good witch Glinda, looking utterly feminine and beautiful. Wanda is standing next to Death; and when they spot Barbie watching them, they smile at her and wave.

Barbie realizes that "everybody has a secret world inside of them. I mean *everybody*. All of the people in the whole world—no matter how dull and boring they are on the outside. Inside them they've all got unimaginable, magnificent, wonderful, stupid, amazing worlds. Not just one world. Hundreds of them. Thousands, maybe. Isn't that a weird thought?"

She acknowledges that "we should take our goodbyes whenever we can."

SOME THINGS WORTH NOTICING

A Game of You is the game of identity. No one is who she seems; and one of the tale's morals is that, ultimately, no one gets to define who you are but you. It's a story about people, and the fate of one relatively obscure fantasy land among thousands (in the words of the Sandman, a "distant islet in the shoals of dream"); and most of its action takes place in a young woman's head. As a result, it's a more intimate tale than *Season of Mists*, with the potential of hitting closer to home.

One of the key identity games played involves names, which various characters use to define themselves (Barbie married a man named Ken), reinvent themselves (Alvin Mann became Wanda, and Donna Cavanagh became Foxglove) or hide behind (Gwas-Y-Gog called himself George so he'd seem like a normal guy; and Thessaly never reveals her real name, probably because it would make her more vulnerable to magic-casting enemies).

Names are also often used to label others. For example, Wanda calls the homeless woman she snubbed the "I-don't-like-dogs" lady, while Barbie attends the funeral of Maisie Hill and thinks of her as the woman who saved her life. Further, the emotional climax of the story is Barbie asserting her best friend's right to define her gender, and her very identity, by crossing out "Alvin" on a tombstone and writing "Wanda."

It's also notable that after Foxglove yells at Hazel for getting pregnant, Fox lets her lover know she forgives her by saying, "Do you know how much a baby's going to cost us? For a start, we have to buy one of those dumb books full of names."

Wilkinson's parents clearly didn't go to that expense. As he explains, "I was one of 17 children. We were all named Wilkinson. I suppose it was roughest on the girls, but we all got used to it in the end. I blame the parents, really. . . . Lovely people. It was just when they found a name they liked, they stuck with it."

In contrast, the Cuckoo never had parents and gets by without a name; she's known only by the word describing her species. Similarly, Dream was created by the universe and has no real name, just a description of his function. Even Dream's former lover Alianora is hard to pin down—in chapter 2 of *Brief Lives* she's referred to as Eleanora, and in part 12 of *The Kindly Ones* as Alianore; i.e., her name is spelled a little differently every time it appears.

In a nutshell, names are flexible and powerful tools in the game of identity, having the potential to turn the ordinary into the extraordinary. Nothing demonstrates this better than Barbie's comment while in Kansas: "I never knew that places around here had such beautiful names. I was watching the road signs from the bus . . . Cloverdale, Florissant, Mulberry Grove, Boonville, Salina, Aurora and Goodland—they sound like the names of magic kingdoms, don't they?"

Another game played is that of life imitating art, and particularly the art of classic fantasy tales such as *The Wizard of Oz*. Princess Barbie can be seen as Dorothy, and her friends Prinado, Wilkinson, and Luz as seeking a brain, a heart, and courage—with Martin Tenbones, of course, as Toto. There are also analogues in Barbie's waking world: Thessaly is a witch; Wanda is from Kansas; the hurricane that blows down Barbie's building is like the tornado in *The Wizard of Oz* gone horribly wrong; and our last image of Wanda shows her looking like Glinda, the beautiful good witch of Oz. Barbie even makes explicit references to Oz, such as when the forest path revealed by the Porpentine reminds her of following the Yellow Brick Road, and when the boon she asks of the Sandman is "the Dorothy option."

Ironically, the Cuckoo has the opposite goal throughout the story—all she wants to do is destroy her home so she can grow up and move on to more wondrous worlds. And, although she doesn't consciously wish it, that's ultimately what happens to Barbie as well. The building she lives in is destroyed and the friends she made there are effectively lost, but Barbie learns to finally grow up and move on— thanks to, again ironically, a defiant act she performs in Kansas, using lipstick the color of the Porpentine to rewrite the Hierogram inscribed on Wanda's tombstone.

The game of the Cuckoo pops up in other ways. Hazel has a one-night stand with a man and ends up pregnant, creating a human analogue to a mother bird having a cuckoo egg placed in her nest and then raising the cuckoo as her own.

In addition (as the Cuckoo herself points out), it's a common fantasy of little girls to imagine *themselves* to be cuckoos, by pretending their moms and dads are adoptive parents, and their blood kin royalty from a distant land: "And one day the king and queen, their real parents, will take them back to their land, and then they'll be happy for ever and ever." That's effectively what happens when Martin Tenbones appears and begs Barbie to return to her dreamworld; and why Princess Barbie exclaims (on page 12 of chapter 4), "I'm *really* happy. I can't remember ever being so happy before. Not when I was first dating Ken. Not even when I was a little bitty kid, having picnics with my toys. I'm just . . . *happy*." As events in the dreamworld grow increasingly dark, however, the story makes clear Barbie's rescue fantasy is ultimately a dangerous one. In this sense, *A Game of You* is an anti-fantasy story.

It would be a huge mistake to conclude the tale is against *all* fantasies, though. As Wanda demonstrates with flamboyance and courage, fantasies can be enormously enriching and nourishing; and as Thessaly demonstrates, the line between fantasy and reality isn't clear-cut, anyway. For that matter, Barbie's own dreamworld was terrific for her when she was growing up; but she's reached a point where she needs to move on from it.

What *A Game of You* is arguing against are fantasies we cling to that keep us from growing and connecting to others.

To properly play *A Game of You* is to use your fantasies, not let them use you. And to recognize that if you look closely enough at any person, you'll find secret worlds that are surprising, frightening, and wondrous.

THE LEAST POPULAR STORY

HB: I've heard you refer to various collections as "male" or "female." Could you talk a bit about that?

NG: *Sandman* was always designed to move from male stories to female stories. *Preludes & Nocturnes* is a guy's tale—it has a male hero, the Sandman, who triumphs over various difficult challenges. The next book, *The Doll's House*, is fundamentally Rose Walker's tale, and it deals with women, relationships, and the tearing down of walls. The following book, *Season of Mists*, is again a Sandman story, in which Dream uses his courage and wits to deal with a problem of diplomacy. And then there's *A Game of You*, which is about women, fantasy, and identity.

HB: That pendulum swing helps explain why *Sandman* has, by all accounts, nearly as many female readers as males. The only other major comics series I know of able to make that claim is Jaime and Gilbert Hernandez's *Love and Rockets*.

You didn't only alternate between male and female stories, though—you also alternated between stories that you knew conventional comics readers would like, and stories that you knew would go against the grain of most of your audience. This is epitomized by *A Game of You*, which is all about women—and is easily the least liked collection in the series.

NG: Which didn't surprise me. A story like *Season of Mists* tickles readers in the places where they like to be tickled, but I knew *A Game of You* would *not* do that; it would say things that most readers didn't want to hear. But I expected everyone to like the next major storyline, *Brief Lives*; and everyone did. The key thing to me was to keep that balance, where I wasn't pandering to readers, but I wasn't making them perpetually miserable either.

HB: You've said that *A Game of You* may be your favorite story in the series. Why?

NG: I like the people and the themes. It's a tale that, bizarrely, hadn't been told before—a sort of antifan story about the nature of fandom and why people seek out fantasy. It also deals with girl versus boy fantasies, and the idea of gender versus the reality of gender. It went off in all these cool directions, many of them unexpected for me, and I'm happy with where they led—Wilkinson, and the Cuckoo, and the weird bittersweetness at the end when Barbie puts on her makeup in the ladies' room. I love the way that it's funny and sad at the same time.

I guess the main reason it may be my favorite, though, is that I had this thing in my head that I wanted to do, and at the end I'd done it.

HB: Isn't that true of every story in *Sandman*?

NG: Oh God, no. Normally I start with a kind of Platonic ideal of a story, without details—something glistening, perfect, and brilliant—and then I look at what appears in print and see whether it's a stone's throw or a car drive away from what I had in mind. But *A Game of You* turned out to be almost precisely what I'd hoped for. Ironically, that's also true of *Sandman* 50, "Ramadan," which is probably the most popular issue of the series.

SHAWN MCMANUS

I COULD NOT FIND IT IN MY HEART TO BLAME HER: I, TOO, HAD BEEN ONE OF THE SERVANTS OF THE CUCKOO, FELT THE OVERPOWERING NEED TO PROTECT AND NURTURE HER; TO DO ANYTHING THAT WOULD MAKE HER HAPPY.

Luz, another servant of the cuckoo, is returned to life by Morpheus.

THE SANDMAN COMPANION

HB: A good share of the credit for making your vision come true has to go to the principal artist of the collection, Shawn McManus. How did he get the assignment?

NG: One of my favorite comics ever is *Swamp Thing* 32, "Pog," which was written by Alan Moore and illustrated by Shawn. That story demanded an artist who could draw both cute fantasy and realistic horror, and mix them seamlessly; and so did *A Game of You*, for which Shawn's range of talents was perfect. Artists Colleen Doran and Bryan Talbot came in later to help out, simply because Shawn had too much to draw in too little time. I was very happy with all of their work.

HB: Another irony is that you almost didn't do this story at all . . . not due to concerns about audience reaction but over a reluctance to cover the same ground as another writer.

NG: True. My original plan for *The Doll's House* was to have Rose Walker live in a relatively mundane world by day and a fantasy questlike world at night. Before I began the actual writing, though, I happened across the 1988 novel *Bones of the Moon* by Jonathan Carroll; and although I greatly enjoyed it as a reader, my reaction as a writer was, "Oh fuck. Here's somebody who's just used the same structure I was planning." So I pretty much threw my idea away. The only remnant of it appeared in issue 15, which shows the amazing dreams of Rose's fellow tenants—especially the dream of Barbie, who in the waking world seemed shallow and irritating, but who turned out to have a rich, wonderful fantasy life. Barbie's dream also featured my tip of the hat to Jonathan's novel—which, if memory serves, includes a big, hairy doglike character with five bones—via her huge, hairy canine named Martin Tenbones.

HB: You stuck in another nod to Jonathan Carroll on page 17 of issue 16, where one of the books piled up in Rose's room is *Sleeping in Flame*, his novel about fairy tales.

NG: Yes, sitting below Kathy Acker's book *Empire of the Senseless*.

I couldn't shake my original idea, though. I did Barbie's dream as a one-off thing, but I found it haunting me; I kept having an image in my head of Martin Tenbones getting killed in real New York.

Still, that would've been the end of it . . . except, by a wild coincidence, a short time later I received a postcard from Jonathan Carroll. He wrote that he'd been following my graphic novel *Signal to Noise*—which was being serialized in *The Face* magazine at the time—and he was finding a number of very scary similarities between my story and his as yet unpublished novel, *A Child Across the Sky*. He concluded, "We're like two radio sets tuned to the same goofy channel."

I wrote back and said, "I think you're right. What's more, I abandoned a whole storyline after reading *Bones of the Moon*, but I keep thinking I ought to return to it." Jonathan then sent me a wonderful letter with this advice: "Go to it, man. Ezra Pound said that every story has already been written. The purpose of a good writer is to write it new. I would very much like to see a Gaiman approach to that kind of story." With that encouragement, I began creating *A Game of You*.

THE GAME OF TITLES

HB: How did *A Game of You* get its name?

NG: Through a series of title changes. I originally wanted to call it *Inside of Your Heart*, which is a lyric from an old Velvet Underground song, but Karen felt that sounded too surgical. Then I wanted to call it *The Bimbos of Night*, which I liked for its irony, because one of the main points of the story is that *nobody* is a bimbo; but Karen didn't care for that either. I came up with several other possibilities, such as *Immaterial Girls*, but none of them worked out.

Finally, the ghost of a 1965 spy novel titled *The Game of X* by Robert Sheckley fought its way up to my consciousness—helped, no doubt, by the fact that *Sandman*'s assistant editor at the time, Alisa Kwitney, is the daughter of Robert Sheckley—and I named the storyline "The Game of You." Then Dave McKean rang me to say that the title had too many letters to fit easily across the cover, and asked if I could change it to something a bit shorter; and so the title ended up as *A Game of You.*

HB: Although you abandoned your original idea of titling the entire collection after a song lyric, you named each of the individual chapters after a song.

NG: Right. The names of the first two chapters, "Slaughter on Fifth Avenue" and "Lullabies of Broadway," are slightly altered versions of the musical theater staples "Slaughter on Tenth Avenue" from *On Your Toes* and "Lullaby of Broadway" from *42nd Street*. The names of the next two chapters, "Bad Moon Rising" and "Beginning to See the Light," are the titles of songs by, respectively, Creedence Clearwater Revival and Lou Reed. Chapter 5's "Over the Sea to Sky," is a line from the old Skye Boat Song about the flight of Bonnie Prince Charles to the island of Skye. And the final chapter's title, "I Woke Up and One of Us Was Crying," comes from a line in an Elvis Costello song called "I Want You."

HB: Is there some thematic link between music and this story?

NG: Not really; I just liked the idea of catchy titles for the chapters that were some-how connected to each other, and the connection happened to be songs. It created a useful foundation for beginning each new chapter, a hook for hanging the next story on.

HB: Before we plunge into the story, one other thing I'd like to chat about is Samuel R. Delany's essay. It was one of the most thoughtful in the series, but I suspect there are some things in it with which you don't agree.

NG: Well, part of the fun of having someone else write an introduction is to see how their perspective differs from your own. I thought Chip wrote a very insightful essay; but sure, there are some points of disagreement.

For example, I was surprised Chip couldn't find a definition for the word *tantoblin*. It's listed in my version of the OED as "a tart or round piece of pastry" or as "excrement"—in other words, a word that means either cake or a lump of shit. I always tended to base the names in *Sandman* on real words, or on historical or mythological names.

I also disagreed with Chip's saying that in the story, "the dominant ideology is not socially constructed but is rather enforced by the transcendental order of nature"— as in the moon caring whether or not you have a Y chromosome. I was actually always with Wanda on that score. Yes, the gods have their points of view; but in *Sandman*, those have no more validity than the point of view of anyone else, even that of the humblest character.

HB: I know that you greatly respect Delany's introduction, though, so let me also ask what you like about it.

NG: Chip's essay makes some very sharp points regarding the nature of fiction in general and comics in particular. For example, I enormously liked what he said about ironies and subtleties, and about the nature of cuteness. But most of all, I appreciated the seriousness with which he took the comic, and how well he thought about it and discussed it.

THE GAME OF BARBIE

HB: What are some of the highlights for you in the first few chapters?

NG: The main joy was simply wandering around and meeting the different characters. On page 6, for example, Thessaly asks if the soy milk she's got will do for Barbie, and Wanda answers, "I don't think she'd be satisfied with anything that wasn't squirted from the udder of a real cow." That foreshadows some of the themes to follow.

HB: Barbie debuted in *Sandman* 11 as little more than a human doll; you even gave her a boyfriend named Ken.

NG: It goes further than that. On page 17 of chapter 1, Barbie reveals that Ken left her for a woman named Sindy, which is an insider U.K. joke: "Sindy" was the name of the English knockoff version of the Barbie doll.

HB: So what prompted you to bring such a seemingly vacuous character back as a protagonist for this story?

NG: Just that, actually. A lot of the fun of Barbie was taking this person who's such a cliché and then showing that she really isn't; that even someone so apparently shallow has incredibly rich worlds inside her.

HB: And not because of some trauma, either. You had the opportunity to supply Barbie with a dark, buried past when she meets the Cuckoo in chapter 5; but you took the opposite tack.

NG: There was a spate of stories at the time about a character who suddenly discovers, to her shock, that she was abused as a child, and that was the hidden secret that had fueled the events of the story. That's why, on page 4, I have Barbie say, "What is this? Some kind of moment of revelation? ... Is this where I find out I was abused as a child and I've been blocking it all these years?" And the Cuckoo answers,

"You weren't abused as a child, Barbara. Your childhood was dull, quiet and boring. You had two dull parents, and a dull house. And an overactive imagination." I liked the fact that Barbie's fantasy world came about simply because she was bored.

HB: You do show us some of the sources for that imagination, though. On page 5 of chapter 5, the Cuckoo points out Barbie's old toys, including a 1967 Barbie doll wearing her princess dress and high heels, and a little paper crown. And on her childhood nightstand are the books *The Wizard of Oz* by Frank Baum, *The Lord of the Rings* by J. R. R. Tolkien, a book titled *Witches*, and *The Magician's Nephew* and another volume from *The Chronicles of Narnia* series by C. S. Lewis.

NG: In fact, that whole sequence where the land dies was inspired by C. S. Lewis's *The Last Battle*. But it's important to understand that those toys and books explain only why Barbie had the particular fantasy she did. She would've enjoyed some kind of amazing dream life even if she didn't have any toys or books. One of the key points of *A Game of You* is that nobody is a stereotype, and nobody is what he or she seems on the surface, once you get to know the person. Every single one of us has glorious, weird, majestic, stupid, magical worlds inside us.

HB: You gave us a glimpse of other characters' inner worlds—albeit twisted by the Cuckoo—in chapter 2. Particularly striking is Hazel's dream.

NG: That's actually one of the few instances in the series where I used a dream of my own. I'd dreamt I found a terribly old, dead baby in a box and took it out, and then watched it crawl around and eat other babies.

HB: In Hazel's case, the dream is prompted by her learning that she's pregnant—something she first reveals in a conversation with Barbie.

NG: Chip criticizes that scene in his introduction, by the way, arguing Hazel's questions about getting pregnant represented implausible ignorance for a resident of a Lower East Side tenement. The truth is that I lifted that scene from life—I was asked those same questions by a lesbian friend of mine who was living in the heart of metropolitan London at the time. But, as I often tell young writers, just because something really happened doesn't necessarily make it credible fiction. It's not unusual for the most incredible bits of a story to be the parts that are true.

HB: In that same conversation, Hazel mentions someone named Scarlett, who's "out of town." We never learn anything else about her outside of chapter 6, where Barbie mentions that Scarlett owned the now demolished building and was fond of Wanda. What's her story?

NG: Scarlett was a very short, very fat drag queen who used to sing in shows with Hal—who, in turn, was Barbie's landlord in *The Doll's House*. I'd intended to include her at some point, but she just never fit in, so she ended up staying with friends in Maine for the duration of the story.

HB: I guess sometimes you have to plant seeds and then see which of them take root. An example of one that blossomed is Foxglove, who was first mentioned in

Sandman 6 as Donna, Judy's lesbian lover. That issue also features the first mention of Rose Walker, who is the straight friend Judy talks to over the phone about the fight she and Donna had the night before. Judy is in the midst of writing an apologetic letter to Donna when John Dee arrives to turn everyone mad . . . and to persuade Judy to plunge an ice pick and a skewer into her eyes.

NG: Which is why, when Judy returns in Foxglove's dream, her eyes are hidden by shadows; and Judy interrupts their conversation by saying, "Hold on. I got something in my eye."

HB: Despite that trauma, though, Foxglove seems to be a pretty together person. And she and Hazel seem to have one of the most solid, loving relationships in the series.

NG: It's a very sweet relationship. I especially like the scene in chapter 5 where Fox learns about the pregnancy. After yelling at Hazel and making her cry, Fox plunges her hands deep into the pockets of her ratty bathrobe, looks straight ahead, and says, "Oh. . . . Shit. Do you know how much a baby's going to *cost* us?" A greatly relieved

George, also known as Gwas-Y-Gog, servant of the cuckoo, releases the psychic birds that create nightmares for the characters of *A Game of You.*

Hazel responds, "Fox, I *do* love you." And Foxglove says, "Damn straight you do. *Jerk.*" It's the nearest to a romantic moment in all of *Sandman*.

HB: You obviously had a lot of affection for the characters, because you brought them back in the second Death miniseries, *The Time of Your Life*—for which you received an award from GLAAD, the Gay and Lesbian Alliance Against Defamation, for "positive portrayals of gay and lesbian characters."

NG: I remember receiving that award very well, because it was the only time a room of people cheered simply for the correct pronunciation of my name. [*Laughter.*]

I wasn't pursuing an agenda with Hazel and Fox, though. I just wanted *Sandman* to reflect some of the people I knew in real life. That was really the progressive thing— to represent *any* sort of woman, regardless of sexual orientation, as nice, cool, and sensible, when the tradition in comics was to portray a woman as either a damsel in distress or a man with tits. To my mind, Rose Walker and Barbie broke the rules every bit as much as Hal, Fox, Hazel, or Wanda.

THE GAME OF WANDA

HB: I've read that Wanda, the preoperative transsexual, is your favorite character in *A Game of You*. Was there a real person you had in mind when creating her?

NG: Yes. One of the scenes was planted by meeting, briefly, a friend of a friend in London, and one of the most beautiful women I've ever met . . . who just happened to have been born with a penis. And she was terrified of surgery, and so was never going to allow any part of her to be cut off. I was very taken by the contradiction in that, and the level on which gender can become elective.

HB: Is that the person you refer to in the afterword: "The late Don Melia and his unnamed just-as-late roommate, who planted a seed that became Wanda"?

NG: No, but thanks for reminding me about that. Don was a very nice guy who used to be the publicist of Titan Books. When I visited him during his final days in a hospice, he told me that his roommate there had gotten AIDS during a blood transfusion . . . for a sex change operation. So the roommate successfully changed sex from male to female, but simultaneously became infected with a then fatal disease. I never learned the roommate's name, but Don told me the last thing she read before dying was *The Doll's House*. I found all that haunting; and so I had that roommate in mind as well when creating Wanda.

I find fascinating the different ways people react to Wanda, by the way. For example, Chip's introduction criticizes her dream sequence in chapter 2 because he felt I was saying Wanda is confused about her sexual identity. The truth is, I meant the dream to indicate that—like the friend-of-a-friend she's based on—Wanda's terrified of the surgical operation that would be needed to remove her penis.

Also, I very much wanted to do a dream sequence using Bizarro logic.

HB: Now that you mention it, I was wondering why the characters in the dream are called "Weirdzos," when they're clearly meant to be the Bizarros from old *Action* and *Superman* comics.

NG: They *were* Bizarros in my script, but some of DC's Superman people caught sight of the story and wouldn't green-light it. Therefore, I simply changed a few names around: Superman became Hyperman, Lois Lane became Lila Lake, and Bizarros became Weirdzos.

HB: Were there any other alterations you recall having to make for this storyline?

NG: A couple. On page 5 of chapter 2, Barbie's line "Guys think with their dicks" was changed by Karen to "Guys think with their dorks." [*Laughter.*] And on page 7 of chapter 3, Hazel sees the bulge in Wanda's panties and, pointing at it with her cigarette, remarks, "You've got a dick"—and Karen had me change that to "You've got a thingie." To which Wanda replies with dignity, "Hazel, didn't anyone ever tell you that it's not polite to draw attention to a lady's shortcomings?" [*Laughter.*] I consider those changes to be benchmarks for how far DC's Vertigo line has come since 1991.

HB: Getting back to Wanda: what are some of the other reactions to her you've encountered?

NG: In a nutshell, my older friends tend to find her offensive, while my younger friends seem to find her inspirational. That clearly came across in a sort of "dueling essays" piece I did years ago with my fellow DC comics writers Rachel Pollack and Caitlín R. Kiernan, in which we each expressed a different point of view.

HB: I know what you're referring to; the text is posted on a World Wide Web site titled "Crossing the Frames" at Web address home.wxs.nl/~tuinstra/crossing.htm. I have the essays in my notes, so let me briefly summarize their positions.

Rachel Pollack, who I guess you'd characterize as representing the old guard, has two basic complaints. First, she objects to page 19 of chapter 4, in which George— i.e., the face nailed to the wall—tells Wanda that he, Thessaly, and the moon all consider Wanda to be a man. Pollack points out that no answer is ever provided to explicitly counter this viewpoint; instead, she writes, "Neil tacitly supports it by having Wanda realize that she's unable to cope with things the 'real' women take in stride." Second, Pollack objects to Wanda being killed because, she writes, "When you see a story that seems sympathetic to a minority character, and then that character is the only one that dies, you have a clue that the writer cannot really accept the minority figure as a person . . . as a reality."

Caitlín R. Kiernan writes, "It hurt a lot, when she wasn't allowed to go with Foxglove and Hazel and Thessaly, because of the genetic thing. And I was devastated when she was killed. But that last part of the story, with Barbie going to the funeral in Kansas, was so perfect that there was no way, ultimately, to be angry with Neil for having written the story he wrote." Kiernan also says that Wanda was "the most positive transsexual character I'd ever encountered. And it was someone like me, someone I actually identified with."

NG: Yep; and those are the two basic perspectives I've run across regarding Wanda. Regarding the contentious page 19, where George comments that neither Thess nor the moon believe gender to be elective, lots of readers assumed that that was my position too, because who could argue with an opinion shared by an ancient witch and a lunar god? In fact, my feeling was always that that's an opinion the gods can take up their sacred recta. I feel the story makes clear that Wanda considers herself a woman; and that, at the end, Death does too. To my mind, that's all that matters.

As for Wanda's death, do you have my own essay in your notes?

HB: I do. The first paragraph reads as follows: "I think—and this is applying some kind of after-the-fact pondering to the affair—I killed Wanda because she was the only person whose death made the story a tragedy. I certainly didn't plan who would live and who would die when I began the story, everyone was up for grabs. As the story progresses, and Wanda became the only character who was doing noble and valiant and brave and good things, it also became fairly obvious that she was going to be killed when the house collapsed in the hurricane. Which meant that I was going to be able to do her funeral, and give Barbie a chance to show what she'd learnt."

NG: That basically says it. I'll just add that when chapter 1 was published, we received mail from lots of readers saying, "Who is this horrible, creepy Wanda character? How dare you put somebody like this into our nice comic?" And I really enjoyed the fact that many of those same readers wrote back six issues later to say, "They cut off her hair!" "They didn't even let her be buried under her name!" I found that immensely satisfying.

HB: Did you base the things done to Wanda on a real-life funeral?

NG: No, it's something I simply made up. Over the years, however, a number of people have come up to me to say they witnessed precisely those things happen to transsexual and drag queen friends of theirs. So it's one of those unsettling cases of art accidentally mirroring life.

HB: Wanda wasn't the only one who died when the building collapses; perishing with her was the "I-don't-like-dogs" lady. Do you have anything to say about her?

NG: I actually met her. She was a young woman on the subway in England who spotted a couple carrying a tiny puppy with them, and she reacted to the dog by having a complete psychotic breakdown. I instantly decided she was going into *Sandman*; and so she did.

It's also worth noting that on page 24 of chapter 5, she reveals that her grandson Billy was a preoperative transsexual, and that Billy was murdered before being able to get the operation. You can assume that the killer was the Connoisseur, who discusses his obsession with transsexuals on pages 23 and 24 of issue 14, "Collectors."

THE GAME OF THESSALY

HB: Another fascinating character who debuts in *A Game of You* is Thessaly, the bookish-looking witch with the big glasses and the even bigger knife. What led you to create her?

NG: I'd noticed a movement in some neopagan circles to reinterpret historical witchcraft, making it into some completely bloodless, sweet religion about female empowerment. The truth is the ancient Greeks and Romans were terrified of the witches of Thessaly, so I thought it would be interesting to show one of those women in contemporary times, and have her still behave in a bloody and lethal manner. And not by flying around on a broomstick with a black cat, either, but by following a Greek code of values going back three thousand years.

HB: So is Thessaly three thousand years old?

NG: At least that. She could also be something like twenty thousand years old. When Hazel asks about her age, Thess answers, "I was born in the day of greatest darkness, in the year the bear totem was shattered." That's not a reference to any particular mythology, but to my mind it could date her to Neolithic times.

HB: What about her name? Does Thessaly even have one?

NG: I'm sure she did once, a long time ago. At this point, though, she's most comfortable using the names of places where she used to live. The next time she appears, she calls herself Larissa, which is a town in Thessaly.

HB: What historical sources did you use for the Thessalian material?

NG: *The Golden Ass* by Lucius Apuleius, and stories by Lucan, which contain lots of lovely creepy stuff about the ancient witches. For example, the scene where Thess brings back George's face is derived partly from a scene by Lucan, and partly from a tale in *The Golden Ass* where a man who's guarding a corpse falls asleep and, in his dreams, tries to stop the witches from stealing the corpse's face. When the man wakes up, he finds that he was successful . . . but he no longer has a nose.

Thess's calling down of the moon was also based on these tales—although I never encountered any mention of repercussions regarding the weather, which is an omission I decided to rectify. I also got a kick out of Thess performing the moon ceremony and then having Wanda call her "a frigging lunatic" and "a goddamn loony-tunes."

HB: They're fun puns. Wanda's got a point, though; Thessaly is absolutely obsessed with taking revenge on anyone who attacks her.

NG: Oh, I think Thess would simply say she's acting out of self-preservation. To her mind, giving at least as good as she gets is the main reason she's remained alive so long; and so her taking revenge is just intense pragmatism.

For example, when she's asleep and a cuckoo bird lands nearby, she calmly grabs it, smashes it against the wall, and burns it. And then she puts on her bathrobe and her fluffy bunny slippers, locates her knife, and moves to deal with the people responsible. At no point does she appear upset or angry; she's behaving out of practicality.

HB: I like the way you describe her in your scripts. For example, in the scene where Thessaly's about to go into the bathroom to cut off George's face, you wrote: "She's holding up the knife at about neck level, and she's looking at us coolly, crisply. There's nothing scary about her, which, with luck, is going to make her very scary indeed. I want to try to stress the dichotomy here between this nice, in control young woman, and her actions. She's from a different culture: older and darker and bloodier."

NG: Yep. Her basic attitude is, "You attempted to harm me, your life is mine." When she finds the creature who she thinks is the cuckoo, Thessaly immediately picks her up and breaks her neck; and when Hazel asks why, Thess answers, "She needed to be taught a lesson." The lesson is, don't fuck with Thessaly. [*Laughter.*]

THE GAME OF MURPHY

HB: We've chatted so far about the characters rooted in the waking world. Can you talk a little about Barbie's dreamworld?

NG: Well, I wanted it to feel like a magical fantasy novel, with the Citadel and the Hierogram and the Brightly Shining Sea ... and yet feel very real. In other words, I wanted it to be a parody, but at the same time to be the very thing it was parodying.

The latter, by the way, came from my staying in a hotel room in Wilmington, North Carolina, that looked out on the ocean. There would be a point every morning when the water would go silver—the sun would rise past the clouds and turn the sea into liquid diamonds. The Brightly Shining Sea was my attempt to capture that little moment of magic.

HOW TO DRAW WANDA AND THESSALY

Artist Colleen Doran on illustrating chapter 3:

I enjoyed drawing Wanda. Neil told me some artists have trouble doing a guy dressed in women's clothing because they're not sure how masculine to make them, so they get the rib cage wrong, and they understate the little package in the pink panties. But I knew some transsexuals, so I understood how to make Wanda look feminine without losing sight of the fact that she's got the body of a man.

The character I got the biggest kick out of, though, was Thessaly. I gave her a lot of my features, like my eyebrows—which you can see if you compare a panel of Thess from chapter 3 with my picture in the back of the book. I also gave her a lot of my expressions—for example, the last panel on page 5 is my "uh-oh, don't mess with Colleen" look. Neil told me that one of the tips he gave Marc Hempel on illustrating *The Kindly Ones* was to "make Thessaly look like Colleen with her makeup off."

Wanda, the preoperative transsexual born Alvin Mann, from *A Game of You*.

HB: Cool. What else sticks in your memory about Barbie's world?

NG: Lots of little things. I like that the snow isn't drawn, it's just open areas on the page, with spatterings of black on white. I like the Cuckoo jumping around and going "lally lally lally" after destroying the Hierogram, which I stole from my daughter Holly, who was six at the time, and used to dance around and sing like that when she was happy. And I like the Room Patrol on page 5 of chapter 4—a group of creatures who carry a room around with them, and when you walk into it, you end up somewhere else.

Something else I enjoyed writing was Wilkinson's dialogue. On page 11 of chapter 4, he says, "Wish in one hand, shit in the other, see which fills up first," which is actually an old European proverb. And I loved his rant about his name.

HB: Where did Wilkinson spring from?

NG: When I was fourteen, I used to do drawings of a character called Jimmy the Shrew, who walked around in a trench coat and hat, and always described himself as "the world's greatest shrew detective." When pushed, he would admit that he was the world's *only* shrew detective. [*Laughter.*] A lot of Wilkinson came from that.

HB: Where did the description of a cuckoo on page 7 of chapter 4 come from?

NG: I lifted it whole from a 1920s reference book titled *The Birds of the British Isles and Migrations.* So everything there is true—including the part about the voice of the young cuckoo having a "commanding, almost hypnotic power." I got a lot of use out of that bird book. I'd previously lent it to Alan Moore for his material about owls in *Watchmen* 4; and I later used it again for issue 40's "The Parliament of Rooks."

HB: Finally, can you walk us through the events following the destruction of the Hierogram?

NG: Well, it triggers the appearance of "Murphy." Most readers assume I made up that name as a word-play substitute for Morpheus, but I actually took it from the OED.

HB: You mentioned that to me earlier, so I looked it up. Murphy is listed as an "il-literate perversion of Morpheus." I also found this usage example from 1890: "It's the nightmare I'll be having as soon as I'm in the arms of Murphy."

NG: There you go. And as Dream uncreates the land, we get to meet his former lover Alianora, with whom he made the compact. I ought to tell her story some-time; it's a very pretty, very sad tale.

Following that is one of my favorite puns in the series. Near the beginning of chap-ter 6, Barbie and Foxglove are standing on a strip of dirt, which is all that's left of the skerry. The Sandman mentions that Barbie's friend Rose Walker played a part in tying the Cuckoo to the dream, and Fox says, "Rose Walker? I knew a Rose Walker. She was Judy's token straight friend. Multicolored hair?" Barbie responds, "Yeah." And Fox, standing on this little island in the middle of nowhere and nothing, says, "Hmm. Small world." [*Laughter.*]

Once Barbie returns home, she finds Wanda and Maisie (the "I don't like dogs" lady) dead. And at that point we know more about the story than Barbie does. She doesn't know why George was in the bath, or why Fox and Hazel are avoiding her, or why she was in George's room. She doesn't even know who the "I-don't-like-dogs" lady was ... and she ends up going to her funeral!

Still, Barbie behaves with instinctive grace. I loved her drawing the veil on her face, which in a comic book is indistinguishable from her really wearing a veil.

HB: Barbie also places on Wanda's casket an eighty-page *Hyperman Giant* featuring "Weirdzo" stories, and in the process offers a scathing description of the comic shop where she bought it. Did the latter draw any reader reaction?

NG: Oh, yes; I received letters from a number of young men telling me how there are no comics stores like that in the whole world. But I've also gotten women read-ers coming up to me ever since saying, "How did you *know?*" [*Laughter.*]

fables and reflections

8

**The most merciful thing in the world . . . is the inability
of the human mind to correlate all its contents.**

—H. P. LOVECRAFT

Comedian Steven Wright once observed, "You know how when you're sitting in a chair, you start pushing against the floor and tipping the chair backward on its rear legs? And you keep pushing until, if you tipped the chair back just another fraction of an inch, you'd fall over? I feel that way *all the time*."

So do many of the characters in the short story collection *Fables and Reflections*. Some, like Marco Polo, tumble briefly into the unknown but land on their feet; others, like Orpheus, fall hard and never recover; and a few, like Emperor Norton, spend their lives precariously balanced on the edge of reality.

The collection begins with a ten-page story titled "Fear of Falling," which is about a young writer/director named Todd Faber who's on the verge of canceling his first play because he's afraid of both failure and success. After watching Alfred Hitchcock's 1958 classic film *Vertigo* on TV, Todd falls asleep and dreams about climbing a rocky outcrop—despite the fact that, like Jimmy Stewart's character, he's terrified of heights.

When Todd reaches the top, he meets the Sandman; and Todd explains his fears stem from a dream he had as a child about being in a house with three witches. In this dream-within-a-dream, the young Todd escapes to the top of the house, but the roof suddenly tilts and throws him off, and he begins plummeting to the ground. The boy manages to exit from the falling dream but can't wake himself up, which leaves him aware but immobile. When the young Todd finally awakes, "I was soaked in sweat, and I started crying, partly because I hadn't died and partly because I was alive."

The Sandman responds that when you dream that you're falling, "sometimes you wake, and sometimes, yes, you die. But there is a third alternative." A lightning bolt then strikes the rock on which the adult Todd stands, causing him to fall . . . and to discover that the third alternative is *to fly*. When Todd wakes up, he resumes work on his play with a new assurance; and he closes the story by saying, "Okay, everybody! Let's take it from the top."

Following this introductory fable are eight full-length stories, which are described in the next three sections.

Forming the heart of *Fables and Reflections* are four historical tales about emperors. They're titled after the names of months: "Thermidor," "August," "Three Septembers and a January," and "Ramadan." These four issues were collectively labeled *Distant Mirrors*, a title that reflects both their coverage of our past and their relevance to our present.

"August" is about the Roman emperor the month is actually named after, Augustus Caesar . . . who was born Caius Octavius, but changed his name upon taking office "from piety, trusting that my reign would *augur* well for Rome." The story begins with Augustus and a dwarf actor named Lycius disguising themselves as beggars so they can spend a day sitting incognito in the Roman marketplace. We learn through their conversation and flashbacks that Julius Caesar was Caius's uncle, and more: "He was the greatest man in the world. He was my hero." But he was also a pitiless conqueror. When Caius, at age sixteen, joined his uncle during a campaign in Spain, Caesar visited the young man's tent every night and brutally sodomized him while promising, "Do what I say, and I will adopt you as my son. Do what I say, and you will rule when I am gone. Do what I say, and the world will be yours."

Caesar's promises come true, and Augustus eventually becomes a strong and effective ruler . . . but one who's forced by the nature of Rome to exercise brutality as well. When Lycius asks about the early days of the empire, Augustus tells him, "It was chaos, held at bay by a handful of men: Cicero, for example . . . A fine mind, and an honorable man. The last of the giants." "Cicero," Lycius innocently inquires, "whatever happened to him?" Augustus responds, "I had him killed."

Augustus justifies his actions as necessary: "I have done many evil things, but they were all to preserve Rome." But he's clearly dissatisfied with that pat explanation. After studying his kingdom's volumes of prophecy, Augustus determines there are two possible paths for the world: "In one future, the Romans sputter and flare like Greek fire, last a few hundred years and then are gone—eaten from outside by barbarians, from inside by strange gods. In the other future, the whole world becomes a province of our empire: the eagle standard will be carried through lands we have barely dreamed of . . . and that empire will last for ten thousand years, or more." Augustus is sick of Roman brutality and its perpetual need for conquest, but he fears the wrath of the gods; and so, based on advice the Sandman gives him in a dream, the emperor becomes a beggar one day each year, so the gods don't notice him as he works out plans to make the *first* prophecy come true. Augustus accepts the responsibility of making this choice because he sees that as his job: "Humanity. They follow leaders—queens or kings, chiefs or emperors. We tell them what to do, and they do it. We know no more than they, but still, they follow us . . . [and] we follow our dreams." And so it's dreams that rule the world.

A very different kind of emperor appears in "Thermidor": Maximilien

THE SANDMAN COMPANION

Robespierre, the head of the 1794 French Revolution. While Augustus publicly supported imperial rule but secretly acted to destroy it, Robespierre publicly condemns the ancient concept of kings but acts like a bloodthirsty tyrant. This story is titled after a month from the ill-fated Revolutionary calendar Robespierre commissions to obliterate any remnant of what he considers the decadent past's myths; *Thermidor* replaces *July*, which is named after the emperor/god Julius Caesar. Similarly, Robespierre seeks to destroy the immortal head of Orpheus, who is both a Greek myth and the Sandman's only son (and whose own story appears later in *Fables and Reflections*). Lady Johanna Constantine, who previously met the Sandman in issue 13, is hired by Dream to help get his son to safety, but through bad luck she's captured by Revolutionary forces. When questioned by Robespierre, she responds to his claims that he acts for the people by observing, "You will save France, if you have to kill every child, woman, and man in the country to do it." Robespierre and his cronies eventually discover that Johanna Constantine hid Orpheus in plain sight amidst a pile of heads chopped off by the guillotine. Before they can act, however, the head of Orpheus begins a soul-searing song about senselessly spilt blood, and about freedom, liberty, and love . . . and the other heads around Orpheus take up the singing, forming a chorus of the dead. The song turns Robespierre and his followers into broken men, allowing Lady Constantine to escape with Orpheus; and mere days later, Robespierre's political might collapses and the former ruler is himself led to the guillotine.

Following these tales that take place in July and August is "Three Septembers and a January," a (mostly) historically accurate account of Joshua Abraham Norton, who was a respected entrepreneur until a business decision went wrong and wiped him out. The story begins with Norton, in a San Francisco flat during September 1859, contemplating suicide. Despair of the Endless detects a hidden potential in the man, however, and so issues a challenge to the Sandman from her, Desire, and Delirium: "Life has hurt him. What can you do, with your little dreams, to redeem him? . . . Keep him from my realm—from all our realms—before our oldest sister comes for him." After some needling, the Sandman meets the challenge with a waking dream that persuades Norton to crown himself the first emperor of the United States.

Norton publishes a proclamation in a local newspaper declaring his royal status, which tickles the fancy of a number of people, including Mark Twain. Norton is later arrested for lunacy, but the judge sets him free, saying, "Mister Norton has shed no blood, robbed no one, and despoiled no country, which is more than can be said for most fellows in the king line." Norton goes on to become a famous tourist attraction, wearing an emperor's uniform donated by the city council, and deriving an income by selling his own currency (which becomes as accepted as standard money by many San Francisco restaurants). Delirium visits Dream and observes, "He's not mine, is he? His madness . . . his madness keeps him sane." The Sandman responds, "And do you think he is the only one, my sister?"

On January 6, 1880, Norton dies of a heart attack. When he meets Death, she not only acknowledges his office but also tells him the Jewish legend of the three dozen tzaddikim: "They say that the world rests on the backs of 36 living saints— 36 unselfish men and women. Because of them the world continues to exist. They are the secret kings and queens of this world . . . I've met a lot of kings, and emperors and heads of state in my time, Joshua. I've met them all. And you know something? I think I liked you best." The closing caption then informs us, "Joshua Norton was buried on Sunday, the 10th of January 1880. Ten thousand people filed past the body, as it lay in state; and his funeral cortege was over two miles long. His burial was marked by a total eclipse of the sun. He was the first and last emperor of the United States of America." The story is a powerful, mystical argument for the supremacy of dreams, and for the importance of ruling wisely, first and foremost, over one's own soul.

The fourth and final *Distant Mirrors* story, "Ramadan," is for many people the single most popular tale in the *Sandman* series. It describes how during the Islamic holy month of Ramadan, Caliph Haroun Al Raschid becomes obsessed with preserving his city of Baghdad, "the Heavenly City, the jewel of Arabia . . . a city of marvels, of wonders." And so he undertakes a lengthy journey within the depths of his castle, through a door of fire . . . to the globe of Sulaiman Ben Daoud, King of the Hebrews, who two thousand years ago imprisoned in the glass ball "nine thousand and nine ifrits, djinn, and demons [who] have sworn a mighty oath to wreak vengeance on the children of Adam our father, to destroy our work and our minds and our *dreams*." With the threat of these spirits being released, the Sandman comes; and the caliph indicates he has a unique bargain to put forward.

Haroun first gives the Sandman a tour of Baghdad on a flying carpet. The caliph then observes, "This is the greatest city that Allah . . . has seen fit with which to bless the world. And this age is the perfect age. [But] how long can it last? How long will people remember? . . . I propose to give you this city. My city. I submit that you purchase it from me. Take it into dreams." "And in exchange?" asks the Sandman. "In exchange," is the reply, "I want it never to die. To live forever."

The Sandman agrees; and when Haroun asks what must be done to seal the bargain, Morpheus echoes the previous words of Emperor Augustus: "All you need do is tell your people. They follow you, after all. And yours is the dream." Haroun therefore gets up on a magnificent fountain in the middle of the marketplace and proclaims that he has "given the Golden Age of Baghdad, of Araby, to this one who stands by my side. It is his forever providing that, as long as mankind lasts, our world is not forgotten."

The next morning, we see Haroun awakening in the marketplace on a tattered carpet; and his jewel-like city now appears rather muted and ordinary. As he staggers back to his palace, Haroun happens upon the Sandman—whom he no longer recognizes—carrying the most magical city to ever exist on earth, housed within a bottle. Dazzled, Haroun asks, "Did you construct it? Is it for sale?" Dream replies, "I did not construct it. It was given to me. And it is no longer for sale." Haroun stares at it and then, without consciously knowing why, leaves feeling utterly happy and fulfilled.

The story then abruptly shifts to the place in our time where Baghdad once proudly stood—only now the city is a bombed-out Middle Eastern hellhole. We learn the tale we've just experienced was told by a ragged storyteller, in exchange for a coin paid by a poor, hungry boy. The child asks, "But how did it work? The bargain? How could the city last?" The boy has no more coins, however, so the storyteller tells him to go home. The boy does so, "picking his way in a series of child's shortcuts across the bomb sites and the rubble of Baghdad. And, though his stomach hurts (for fasting is easy, this Ramadan; and food is hard to come by), his head is held high and his eyes are bright. And behind his eyes are towers and jewels and djinn, carpets and rings and wild afreets, kings and princes and cities of brass. And he prays as he walks (cursing his one weak leg the while), prays to Allah (who made all things) that somewhere, in the darkness of dreams, abides the other Baghdad (that can never die). . . . But Allah alone knows all." No other tale in *Sandman* so perfectly captures the transcendent magic of stories and dreams.

CONVERGENCE

In addition to its four superb tales of emperors, *Fables and Reflections* contains three stories titled "The Hunt," "Soft Places," and "The Parliament of Rooks" that originally appeared in issues 38, 39, and 40. These issues were cover-labeled *Convergence*, because they all involve characters of different ages, and from disparate times and places, coming together to spin fantastic yarns.

"The Hunt" is an amalgam of standard fairy tale plots . . . but with several twists. The hero is a naive young werewolf, not a man, and the old-fashioned fellow telling the story of young Vassily to his teenage granddaughter is relating a more-or-less true account of his own life. Finally, the hero/werewolf doesn't end up with the Princess, because he chooses instead to return to the old forest . . . and to a she-wolf who lives as freely as he does.

The second *Convergence* tale, "Soft Places," begins with a young Marco Polo who becomes lost in a sandstorm in the uncharted desert of Lop. After encountering music, objects, and people from disparate points in time, Polo realizes that he's meeting dreams; and it's eventually explained to him that until a location is defined by an explorer such as himself, it's potentially a "soft place" where dreams have as much force as physical reality.

This tale also makes explicit why one of Dream's titles is "the Sandman." On page 4, Polo remembers his mother telling him, "He throws the magic sand into your eyes, and that's what sends you off to dreamland. That's the sand you find in your eyes when you wake." In addition, on page 11, the story plants the seed for an important new plotline by having Gilbert casually mention the Sandman's new love interest: "The only reason I'm out here is because they keep coming for walks in me.

Long ones. Gazing into each other's eyes. Whispering sweet and (to be frank) rather embarrassing nothings. So I've taken an evening off." (Gilbert also gets the best line in the story, when he says wistfully, "I remember when I was just a young vicinity.")

The final *Convergence* tale, "The Parliament of Rooks," offers many fun moments, but also provides information about key characters in the series. Lyta Hall tells her eighteen-month-old baby Daniel (last seen in *Sandman* 22) a homogenized Goldilocks yarn and then puts him to bed.

Asleep, Daniel makes his way to the fringes of The Dreaming where stand the houses of Cain and Abel, the first murderer and first victim. Matthew the raven and Eve also happen by, so Abel decides to throw a tea party. The Sandman's new love interest is again referred to: "They've been pretty inseparable for the last few weeks," says Matthew. "Oh dear," responds Eve. "She's not really his type, is she?" With rat in beak, Matthew replies, "I didn't think he had a type."

Cain, Abel, and Eve then each tell a story for the benefit of their human visitor. Eve's story is about Adam's three wives: Lilith, whom Adam rejects for demanding equal treatment; an unnamed woman, whom Adam can't bear to touch because "he saw her full of secretions and blood" as she was constructed; and Eve, who was made from Adam's rib while he was asleep.

Abel's story goes back to the beginnings of Death and Dream, and of him and his brother Cain. Because his audience is a baby, Abel simplifies the events and makes the characters appear childlike. Abel concludes the tale with Dream inviting him and Cain, as the characters of one of the universe's first stories, to live in his realm. With a shout of "Hurrah!" says Abel, "the two brothers hugged each other joyfully. And they lived next door from that day to this, happily ever after." Cain's critique: "That was undoubtedly the most meretricious garbage I've ever heard." In the midst of the joking comes some important information, however. During the story, Cain comments, "They didn't even look remotely human. None of us did, back then." And Abel later adds, "Oh, this whuwasn't on Earth." From this, we can infer that the Cain and Abel in The Dreaming aren't the Cain and Abel of the Bible, but are recurring patterns of murderer and victim that surface throughout time and space; and they may be almost as old as the universe itself.

Finally, Cain tells a story for Matthew about the mysterious parliament of rooks, which gathers around one lone bird and may stare at him for hours. The bird, in turn, continually caws at his brethren until all the other rooks either suddenly take flight as one ... or just as suddenly peck the lone rook to death. As Eve, Daniel, and Matthew leave the party, Abel reveals the secret behind this ritual: the lone rook is telling the others a story. "And whuwhen it finishes," says Abel, "it finds out whether or not they, uh, liked the story it told." Cain (as he is wont to do) then murders Abel; and while he drags away the body, provides this writerly advice: "I keep telling you, it's the mystery that endures, not the explanation. . . . Nobody really cares who-done-it. They'll peck you to pieces if you tell them . . . [but] a good mystery can last forever."

Finally, *Fables and Reflections* contains one story titled "The Song of Orpheus" that was published outside of the series' numbering system as *The Sandman Special*; it was released between *Sandman* 31 ("Three Septembers and a January") and *Sandman* 32 (the first issue of *A Game of You*). The forty-eight-page tale recounts the classic Orpheus and Eurydice myth, but with the Endless playing key roles; and it reveals lots of information about the Endless that had been only hinted at previously.

The story begins three thousand years ago in Greece, with a distressing dream Orpheus has of his head floating in the sea. He's then joined in the dream by the Sandman, who is his father. Morpheus implies the dream is of a future event, but he refuses to say anything else about it.

Orpheus quickly forgets the unsettling incident because he has other things on his mind; it's his wedding day to the beautiful Eurydice. He's soon greeted by his mother, Calliope, who's an immortal Muse (and, as we've already seen in *Sandman* 17, is fated to be imprisoned during the twentieth century by writers Erasmus Fry and Rick Madoc). Also attending the ceremony are all seven members of the Endless family, using Greek names to represent their functions: Oneiros (Sandman/Dream/Morpheus), Teleute (Death), Potmos (Destiny), Aponoia (Despair), Epithumia (Desire), Mania (Delirium), and a new character referred to as Olethros.

There are hints that the joyous day will turn tragic, however. Orpheus walks past a field of red roses on his way to the ceremony, and Eurydice's hair sports a red rose . . . which is a symbol of death. Destiny fails to wish the couple well, saying, "I do not wish. I know. What must happen will happen." Death lingers after the ceremony, mysteriously explaining that she has "things to do" and then looking at Eurydice. The Sandman refuses to dance with his wife, as if he knows this will not be a happy occasion for long. And a disaster does indeed occur: Eurydice is bitten by a venomous snake, and dies.

Unwilling to accept what's happened, Orpheus asks his father to plead with Hades to get Eurydice returned from the Underworld. Morpheus's response is concise and cold: "You are talking foolishness, my son. I will hear no more of it." Thousands of years before his imprisonment in Roderick Burgess's basement, this is a Sandman who takes adherence to rules much more seriously than the feelings of others . . . including his only son. (To underscore this, Calliope notes later in the story that Dream could indeed have intervened on Orpheus's behalf, as the gods of the Underworld "respect him . . . Sometimes I think they even fear him.") The Sandman appears proud and regal, but distant; for example, he makes no move to hug or even touch his son, or to offer any words of comfort other than "She is dead. You are alive. So live." When Orpheus persists, Dream cuts him off with the words, "No more." A hurt but equally proud Orpheus responds, "Very well, then. No more. I am no longer your son."

Determined to be with his wife, Orpheus decides to kill himself by jumping off a cliff. Just before he does so, however, he's stopped by Olethros—a name that's Greek for devastation or destruction. Olethros/Destruction is the missing Endless alluded to in issue 10 (where he's referred to as The Prodigal), and in #16 and #21 (which reveal that he's abandoned his realm). This story takes place before Destruction left his job and his family, and it marks his first appearance in the series. He comes across as huge and powerful, but also as someone bursting with life and laughter.

When Orpheus explains his planned suicide, Destruction observes, "That's the stupidest thing I've heard in centuries . . . Orpheus, you're a strange child. I think you are more in love with the idea of your dead love than you ever were with the girl herself." He later adds, "You're a romantic fool, but that's no surprise. You get that from your father"—who, as we've seen in previous collections, is also prone to behave irrationally when it comes to women.

Destruction then suggests Orpheus get advice from "your aunt," meaning Death. That Destruction doesn't refer to her by name is significant. If you've been reading the series carefully, you may have noticed that none of the Endless call her "Death" and instead typically refer to her as "our sister." The reason is revealed here for the first time, when Destruction mentions that there are three ways to see his older sister. The first way is to die. Alternatively, says Destruction, "You could be born. But you people never remember that particular conversation with her. I don't know why not. You just don't." In other words, the Endless avoid calling their older sister "Death" because doing so would be too restrictive a way of describing her function. (Some of the implications of this are explored in subsequent collections.)

The third way to see his older sister, continues Destruction, is to "go to her house"; and that's where, with the best of intentions, he ends up sending Orpheus. Before the Endless does so, however, he smells a red rose . . . which has proved to be an ominous symbol in this story. And it's by definition perilous to follow a path set by Destruction.

Like Dream, Death tells Orpheus to abandon his quest, but more kindly. Orpheus stubbornly persists, prompting Death to repeat Destruction's observation: "Did anyone ever tell you you're a lot like your father in some ways?" Although she doesn't agree with her nephew, it's Death's practice to let a person choose his or her own course (as demonstrated, for example, in *Sandman* 20's "Facade"), and so she agrees to grant Orpheus his wish by promising to never take him (thereby making him immortal) and then telling him how to get to the Underworld, which is "where you people go" (meaning it's the afterlife for those who believe in Greek gods).

Orpheus is soon standing before the Underworld's rulers, Hades and Persephone. Because he's a balladeer—and, being the offspring of a Muse and the Prince of Stories, an extraordinarily talented one—Orpheus pleads his case by singing of his pain while playing a haunting melody on his lyre. His sad song brings the Underworld to a standstill, causing even the Furies to weep—regarding which

Persephone comments, "They will never forgive you for that." Hades finally agrees to let Eurydice go, but only on the condition that Orpheus doesn't turn back to look at her until she's left the Underworld. Orpheus agrees; but after hours of walking, and with daylight just ahead, he becomes convinced that Hades lied to him and swivels around. Eurydice is there as Hades promised; but she's quickly drawn back to the land of the dead.

Losing his wife a second time drives Orpheus temporarily insane; and so when Calliope urges him to flee from the savage Bacchante, who are sisters of the Furies, Orpheus simply bids his mother good-bye and stays put. The Bacchante soon arrive . . . and, in a sexual frenzy, they rip Orpheus apart. (One especially memorable image is of Orpheus's heart being torn out and consumed, which is a gruesome parody of the series' recurring image of a jeweled heart being handed from one person to another; see, for example, page 16 of "The Hunt.") When the Bacchante are done, all that's left of Orpheus is his immortal living head, which is thrown into the river. Echoing the dream that begins this tale, Orpheus then drifts helplessly in the water while calling out the name of his lost love.

The next morning, Orpheus's head washes ashore on an island. A snake similar to the one that killed Eurydice then appears and is about to strike . . . when it's crushed underfoot by the Sandman. His pride still stung, Dream behaves in a startlingly cold manner toward his son, saying, "I have come to say goodbye. It seemed the proper thing to do." He adds that he's arranged for Orpheus to be cared for by priests on the island, but "I will not see you again." Orpheus begins to protest, "But father—" Dream interrupts, "'Father'? Did you not say you were no longer my son?" When Orpheus pleads for death, his father replies, "Your life is your own, Orpheus. Your death, likewise. Always, and forever, your own. Farewell. We shall not meet again." And then Dream walks away . . . and, unlike Orpheus, "never even tried to look back."

As you might imagine, these events have consequences. One of them is the estrangement of Sandman and Calliope, who don't meet again until 1990. Other repercussions are explored in subsequent collections.

SOME THINGS WORTH NOTICING

Fables and Reflections is an anthology of miscellaneous tales, but there are nonetheless common elements that can be found throughout it.

For example, every single story involves characters telling stories. This is most obvious in "The Hunt" (with its grandfather narrator) and "The Parliament of Rooks" (with Cain, Abel, and Eve each spinning yarns); but it's also true of "Soft Places" (in which Marco Polo trades tales with Gilbert); "Ramadan" (which, we discover at the end, was told by a street beggar in exchange for a boy's coin); "Fear of Flying" (in which a dreaming Todd relates an earlier dream he had to the Sandman himself); "Thermidor" and "Orpheus" (which both feature Orpheus telling a story through song); and even "Three Septembers and a January" (in which Emperor Norton helps Mark Twain develop his first major story—not to mention Norton himself becoming virtually a living dream).

Another recurring theme is recognizing the distinct personality of a particular location. This concept is best expressed in "Soft Places" by Rustichello, who explains the adult Marco Polo's genius was "being able to describe cities. Not just the land, or the trade, but the *soul* of the city. What made it uniquely itself." Ironically, this notion is epitomized by the being sitting next to him named Gilbert, who's a plot of land in the guise of a person. But it's also expressed by Haroun Al Raschid's determination to immortalize his city of Baghdad; Vassily's love for the old forest, and the old values it represents; the terrors witnessed by Orpheus in Hades; the comfort found by Abel, Cain, and Eve in The Dreaming; the acceptance afforded to Emperor Norton in San Francisco; and the complex mix of love and hate felt by Emperor Augustus for Rome.

An element that repeats through not only *Fables and Reflections* but the entire series is that of the Fates, or the Three-Who-Are-One. In this collection, they can be seen in "Fear of Flying" as the three witches in young Todd's house who force him to the roof. They also pop up in "The Parliament of Rooks," within Eve's tale; page 16 portrays Adam's wives as maiden (the unnamed virgin), mother (Lilith), and old Eve (crone). Further, Eve concludes her story by saying, "This is true: Adam had three wives. . . . But some say Adam married only once, and they speak truly too."

In less obvious form, the Fates can also be spotted in "The Hunt," with the Princess as maiden, gypsy as mother, and Baba Yaga as crone. And a more savage aspect of them can be seen in "The Song of Orpheus," as the weeping Furies on page 35. The Furies are additionally referred to in "Three Septembers and a January" when Desire says of the Sandman, "I'll make him spill family blood; I'll bring the Kindly Ones down on his blasted head." In Greek mythology, the Kindly Ones is another name for the Furies. Desire's oath provides an explanation for its rape of Unity Kinkaid in *Sandman* 1.

One other key theme that recurs in *Fables and Reflections* is that of personal dreams versus other values, such as love and family. In "The Hunt," for example, Vassily abandons his dream of the Princess he has fought for throughout the story for the passionate love of a soul mate. His choice was apparently the right one, as grandfather Vassily appears to have lived a rich, full life. The old man, while gruff, is also down-to-earth and loving, with strong ties to family; and is someone who— as he says of his late wife—knows "the value of things."

In fact, this story can be seen as the flip side of issue 19's "A Midsummer Night's Dream," in which the wish the Sandman grants William Shakespeare costs Shakespeare his relationship with his family and, indirectly, the life of his young son, Hamnet. This connection is even referred to in "The Hunt" on page 21, where we learn the book Lucien sought to restore to his library of dreamed tales is *The Merrie Comedie of the Redemption of Doctor Faustus* by Christopher Marlowe. "Kit" Marlowe is the playwright who was with Shakespeare in the pub where the Sandman made his offer in issue 13, "Men of Good Fortune"; and Marlowe's real play *Doctor Faustus* is, of course, a tragedy about a man who gets his wishes granted but loses his soul.

It's also significant that the Sandman doesn't question Vassily's decision because "the Lord of Dreams knew that wishes are sometimes best left ungranted." Just how well acquainted the Sandman is with that lesson is spelled out in "The Song of Orpheus," in which Dream's son refuses to accept one of the basic rules of the universe: people die. Despite being repeatedly advised to let his deceased wife go and move on with his life, Orpheus doggedly pursues his desire to go to the Underworld and get Eurydice back. Unlike Vassily, however, Orpheus fails to pull back from his wish on the verge of its being granted . . . and the results are tragic.

But just as Orpheus falls because of his prideful refusal to accept fundamental rules, the Sandman pays a heavy price for just as pridefully refusing to even try to bend those rules. The story indicates that, thanks to Orpheus's oracular dream, the Sandman suspects something terrible will happen at the wedding, but he fails to warn his son or to protect Eurydice from the snake that kills her.

Further, following Eurydice's passing, Morpheus fails to properly comfort his son and instead just says of death: "It is the mortal way. You attend the funeral, you bid the dead farewell. You grieve. Then you continue with your life." The words are accurate, but they're presented without warmth or compassion. The Sandman's perspective seems to be that all humans die sooner or later, so it's pointless to get worked up over any individual's passing.

Similarly, when Orpheus asks his father to plead for the return of Eurydice from the Underworld, Dream's position is that rules are rules, and it's "foolishness" to not adhere to them. He may be thinking of a time when he ignored the rules himself for love: specifically, about seven thousand years earlier, when he pursued Nada in issue 9's "Tales in the Sand" despite a universal law that forbids a mortal from becoming romantically involved with a member of the Endless. On one level, Morpheus may be hoping to prevent Orpheus from making the same mistake he did. On another level, the Sandman may subconsciously feel guilty witnessing his son's resolve to rescue his lover from the Underworld . . . while Dream has condemned his *own* lover to eternal damnation in hell.

Whatever his thoughts, the Sandman's pride doesn't allow him to express them to his son. Instead, he just forbids Orpheus to say another word about the matter. And, demonstrating how much of his father is in him, Orpheus responds with equal pride: "Very well, then . . . I am no longer your son."

Calliope is furious over the Sandman's behavior. She tells her son: "He should have talked to the gods of the Underworld for you"; and because he didn't, "I walked out on him. I . . . think I have hurt his pride." Orpheus responds, "He is not one to forget a slight. Nor to forgive."

That proves to be an accurate assessment; when Orpheus asks for his father's help a second time—in this case, so he can achieve peace by dying—Dream reminds Orpheus of their argument and walks away, saying they'll never meet again. The Sandman leaves Orpheus in the care of priests on a remote island, which in a sense echoes his treatment of Nada; in both cases, Dream deals with a person who's been close to him and then rejects him by keeping that person imprisoned and far away. It's the ultimate act of control for someone uncomfortable with emotions.

And yet the Sandman isn't heartless. His brother Destruction, who in this story demonstrates a consistently keen eye for reading people, tells Orpheus, "He's a dark one, your father. He does care for you, though." Orpheus says, "He has a strange way of showing it." Destruction responds, "Aye. But that's his way. He's set in his ways."

Echoing that evaluation is Calliope, who explains to Orpheus that her leaving Dream has "been coming for a long time. He cannot share anything, any part of himself. I thought I could change him. But he does not change. He will not. Perhaps he cannot."

Actually, he can . . . but it takes three millennia, plus seven decades of imprisonment in a glass cage, for him to do so. When Sandman frees Calliope in issue 17, she observes, "You have changed, Oneiros. In the old days, you would have left me to rot forever, without turning a hair." She then asks, "Do you still hate me? For what I did?"—which, we now know, refers to her leaving him. Dream responds, "No. I no longer hate you, Calliope. I have learned much in recent times, and . . . no matter. I do not hate you, child."

Just how much the Sandman can change from the hardworking but prideful being in "The Song of Orpheus" who uses rules, responsibilities, and dreams as shields against personal contact is arguably the major question of the series. The surprising answer unfolds in coming storylines.

FEAR OF FLYING

HB: How did you come to name this collection *Fables and Reflections*?

NG: Actually, I didn't. What I wanted to call it is *Accounts and Reflections*, but nobody at DC would let me. My thinking was that the book contained a set of stories about different elements intersecting titled *Convergence*, and a set of historical tales titled *Distant Mirrors*, and "accounts" would represent both things being totaled up, or coming together; and ancient tales being recounted. But DC felt all that title would do is make readers think of chartered accountancy. [*Laughter.*]

HB: The collection kicks off with a ten-pager drawn by Kent Williams called "Fear of Falling." The title works as a pun because the story was originally written for *Vertigo Preview*, the comic that launched DC's Vertigo publishing imprint in January 1993 to encompass fantasy/horror series such as *Sandman*. Despite its promotional origins, though, I suspect your story's content hit close to home.

NG: Sure, because *Sandman* was marketed as Vertigo's flagship title. All of a sudden, I'd gone from writing a little comic book to being somebody whose work was

A sketch
that was
transformed
into a
commemorative
Sandman
statue.

being looked at by everyone. And I was learning that fear of success could be every bit as crippling as fear of failure, a notion that had never occurred to me before.

I also loved the metaphor of falling in dreams. People often ask me, "Do you use your dreams as material for *Sandman* stories?" And I normally say, "No, because dream logic isn't story logic." But young Todd's dream of witches and the tilting roof is a conflation of two dreams I actually had when I was six and eight. The second one was the worst: as I was falling, I saw the ground coming toward me in perfect detail, and I knew that if I'd hit the ground, I'd die. So I stopped the dream and refused to go back; but I couldn't wake myself up either, leaving me trapped in the darkness in my head. I tried to scream and yell to get someone to wake me up, but my body was fast asleep and wouldn't respond for the longest time. Finally, I woke myself up; and that experience stayed with me.

HB: "Fear of Falling" ends more optimistically, though. Todd decides, "Sometimes you wake up. Sometimes the fall kills you. And sometimes when you fall, you fly."

NG: True, because in his case optimism is the best solution.

The rhythm of that ending, by the way, is based on the old fable about the guy who boasts that he can make a horse talk. When the sultan hears of it, he orders the man to prove it or be killed. The man agrees, but demands a year in the luxury of the palace, getting the best of everything, while he works at the task. A friend of his later visits and protests, "What kind of deal is that!? Are you crazy?" The man responds, "Twelve months is a long time. Over the next year, maybe the sultan will die. Or maybe I will die. Or, who knows, maybe the horse will learn to talk."

RESEARCH AND REVOLUTIONS

HB: Did you have any problems doing the extensive research necessary for the historical *Distant Mirrors* stories?

NG: Not for the most part, because I'd already been reading about those subjects for my own pleasure. For example, the *Distant Mirrors* title for the four issues was taken from a Barbara Tuchman book I'd read a few years earlier called *A Distant Mirror: The Calamitous Fourteenth Century*.

The only story I got caught flat-footed on was "Thermidor." That's because DC was sending out information about its comics five months in advance to its distributors and retailers. That was fine when I'd written an issue five months in advance, but sometimes I hadn't. So one day Alisa Kwitney rings me up and says, "I'm writing the blurb for *Sandman* 29 now," and I say, "Oh. Yeah?" [*Laughter.*] And she says, "What happens in it?" and I say, "I have no idea. I'm in the middle of *Season of Mists.* How do I know what I'm going to do afterward?" And she says, "Well, I have to write something. Pick something!" So I say, "I know I want to do four stories dealing with the responsibilities of kings, about successful and unsuccessful emperors." And Alisa says, "Fine. Pick one!" [*Laughter.*]

HB: A natural-born editor.

NG: So I say, "Okay, I'll start with a story about Lady Johanna Constantine and the French Revolution." I don't know why I chose that, but it was the only time I ever went "Right. This is the story I will do," and then I had to go out and research it like a son of a bitch. I remember buying every book I could find on the subject, including Simon Schama's *Citizens: A Chronicle of the French Revolution* and John Paxton's *Companion to the French Revolution.*

I was reading Thomas Paine. I was reading the Marquis de Sade—who was in the same prison, only about four doors down from Paine—because I was sure he'd make it into the story, but that didn't pan out. I wound up mentioning him in *Brief Lives* just because I was disappointed that he'd never gotten onstage in "Thermidor."

HB: You're referring to chapter 3, page 2 of *Brief Lives*, when a character is remembering a horror movie he saw the night before: "One of the villains was the Marquis de Sade, depicted as an athletic, debonair psychopath—the embodiment of pure vicious evil. He's thinking about the Marquis he knew, a pale little asthmatic, terribly obese from his years in prison, who started at shadows and wrote obsessively about actions he dared not perform."

NG: Yes. I'd still like to do a story one day about Johanna Constantine meeting the real de Sade—this fat, sad little man.

As I continued reading, I was fascinated by how a counterrevolution sprung up and, in a period of about two days, the previous revolution just fell apart. I also remember the joy of leafing through my old *Encyclopedia Britannica*, the eleventh edition, and reading an article on the French revolution by someone who hated Robespierre; and then reading the biographical entry, which was written by someone who idealized Robespierre. I loved the cognitive dissonance.

After the story was published, one reader sent me his high school thesis pointing out how Robespierre was a great man and so on, and I couldn't understand why he bothered. I could have written something about how Robespierre was a great man too, but that wasn't the tale that I was telling; I needed a story in which he wasn't.

THE EMPEROR OF THE UNITED STATES

HB: How about "Three Septembers and a January"? That title has a familiar-sounding rhythm.

NG: That's because it was playing off of *Four Weddings and a Funeral.* Which was a neat trick, since the story came out three years before the movie did! What happened was my friend Richard Curtis called while I was working on the script and said, "I'm five pages into a screenplay I'm calling *Four Weddings and a Funeral*, and so far all anyone has said is 'fuck.' " [*Laughter.*] And I said, "That's a lovely title. I'm going to take a spin off that, as a small tribute." Neither of us had any idea at the time whether the picture would actually be produced. Little did we know it would turn out to be the most successful British film ever made—that is, until men started wiggling in *The Full Monty.* [*Laughter.*]

HB: Any comments on the Norton story itself?

NG: It was a roller-coaster ride. I was really enthusiastic about it during the planning stages, as I thoroughly enjoyed the reading it was based on: Catherine Caufield's wonderful *The Emperor of the United States of America and Other Magnificent British Eccentrics*, Herbert Asbury's *The Barbary Coast*, and William Drury's *Norton I, Emperor of the United States.*

I took a wrong turn when writing it, though, and had to back up and restart, which was a problem I hadn't encountered for over a year.

Then I was okay with it until the pages came in. The artwork by Shawn McManus was terrific, but when I read my story in its finished form, I was horrified—it struck me as cheap and obvious. I phoned Tom Peyer—the associate editor at the time—and said, "Tom, this story will get us laughed out of the country. It's awful. Let's just drop it and plunge straight into *A Game of You.*" And Tom laughed at me. Or maybe he just said no politely, I don't remember. But he declined.

These days, though, I look at it fondly and wonder why I had such a bad reaction to it.

HB: Perhaps it's because you're suspicious of sentiment?

Emperor Augustus Caesar and the dwarf Lycius, drawn in an Aubrey Beardsley fashion.

DAVE McKEAN

NG: Maybe. [*Laughter.*] Probably. Though I find I'm less resistant to sentiment as I get older.

All the historical details in the story are true, by the way—Emperor Norton, the King of Pain, the Cobweb Palace, Mark Twain as a newspaper journalist. The main inaccuracy is that, because I didn't get to see coloring jobs until after issues were printed, Twain's hair color came out wrong; Clemens was a redhead.

I experienced some odd coincidences while plotting the story. It occurred to me to give the Emperor an Oriental chamberlain—and while I continued reading about Norton, I came across a passage that said, "During this period, he had a gentleman named Ah How who would follow him around like a chamberlain." And I thought, "How strange." [*Laughter.*]

THE EMPEROR OF ROME

HB: Let's move from America's emperor to someone who helped define the word: Emperor Augustus of Rome, in the story "August."

NG: I loved everything about "August"—doing the reading, writing the characters, and working with my old U.K. friend Bryan Talbot for the first time.

As for the story, its basis was the Robert Graves translation of *The Twelve Caesars*. This tell-all book about Rome's first dozen emperors was written by Suetonius, who was born around A.D. 70 and served for several years as secretary to Emperor Hadrian. Virtually everything in "August" was taken, directly or indirectly, from Suetonius's accounts of Julius Caesar and Augustus. So people can ask me where Lycius came from, and I can point to a passage in Suetonius that says Augustus banned anyone of noble birth from the stage except for Lycius, who was a two-foot-high dwarf for whom acting was the only way to make a living.

About the only thing I let myself put in outside of Suetonius was the notion of Terminus, "he who walks the boundaries," which foreshadows troubles the Sandman himself will later encounter with boundaries. Oh, and the bit about making skin looking blistered and ulcerated by rubbing on lye soap and vinegar was actually a Victorian beggar trick—but I figured, what the hell, the materials were just as available to the Romans, so why not?

HB: Is there anything notable you recall about the artwork?

NG: Oh yes. One of the bits of business Bryan did that I love, and that no one is likely to notice unless it's pointed out, is that when Augustus and Lycius sit down, the shadows are off on the left; and as the hours, and the pages, go on, the shadows move from left to right, and change in length, responding to the movement of the sun. Similarly, we see them put on hoods to shield their heads from the heat at noon when the sun is directly overhead, and we see them remove the hoods as the sun passes. We also see the beautifully clean marketplace stairs they sat down on in the

VISUAL NUANCE IN "AUGUST"

Bryan Talbot is an award-winning artist who pencilled "August" and "The Song of Orpheus," as well as all the framing sequences for *Worlds' End*, and parts of issues 36 and 75. Talbot has also won awards for drawing and writing his own projects, including *The Adventures of Luther Arkwright* and *The Tale of One Bad Rat*.

Talbot's creation of the latter title came as no surprise to the comics community, where he's well-known as a lover of rats. In recognition of this, Neil Gaiman put a rat into every story he and Talbot did together. In *A Game of You*, on page 8 of chapter 5, there's a rat crawling around some garbage; and in the next panel, a radio talk show host announces she's "Barbara Wong late night on WRAT New York." And on page 39 of "The Song of Orpheus," rats sit amid the variety of animals who are gathered around Orpheus to hear him play his lyre.

"But the most prominent appearance of a rat," says Talbot, "is on page 16 of 'August,' when the emperor grabs and crushes one to demonstrate his speed and strength. The garbage that attracted the rat was a device I used to show time had passed; when Augustus and Lycius sat down in the morning, the steps were pristine."

Talbot employed other visual devices in "August." "To give the story a classical feeling," he says, "I composed images with a lot of horizontals and verticals to echo Roman architecture. You can see this, for example, in Augustus's room at the top of page 3; and the temple at the top of page 5; and the steps Augustus and Lycius sit on through most of the story. I also used long, wide panels whenever possible, so the page layout itself would be full of horizontals.

"In addition," continues Talbot, "I used a great deal of white in the story to echo Roman statues, costuming and, again, architecture. Augustus and Lycius are often walking on the white of the page, unbounded by panel borders; and while sitting on the steps, they rest their feet on the white of the page.

"Another feeling I wanted to convey was the aura of power about Augustus," concludes Talbot. "So whenever Augustus and Lycius are in the same panel, I tended to draw things from Lycius's eye level—that is, the eye level of the dwarf. It was a subtle way of making Augustus appear large and dominant."

morning, when everything had been swept away, slowly accumulate rubbish as the day goes on. None of this is commented on, but it adds enormously to the reality of the story, because without even knowing why, the reader can feel that time is passing. Bryan did a lovely job of subliminally making us hear the clock ticking.

DREAMS IN THE SAND

HB: John Watkiss was a great choice for pencilling and inking "Soft Places." How did you find him?

NG: I met John at the Society of Strip Illustrators in London. His influences are Edwardian and Victorian artists; and his style is to leave patches of things that are open and ill defined, which was perfect for what I was aiming for.

I really liked how John drew the Sandman, by the way; very cool and very strange. It's one of my favorite versions of Dream.

HB: Where did the idea for the story itself come from?

NG: In part, from my reading about the Desert of Lop—which is a place that still exists—in a travel guide to China. The guide said that the desert's name translates to "The Place You Go Into and Don't Come Out Of." That sounded to me like one of the strange, soft places in the universe where reality is open to suggestion.

The story also came from my reading *The Travels of Marco Polo*; and Italo Calvino's 1986 short story collection *Invisible Cities*, which is about Marco Polo's reports to Kublai Khan on the fabulous and imaginary cities in the Khan's empire.

For example, the flashback sequence on page 12 is taken straight from *The Travels of Marco Polo*, simply because I thought it was a cool story. "Go back to your pope and tell him to send me one hundred Christian

A near powerless Sandman encounters a wandering Marco Polo in the Desert of Lop.

THE SANDMAN COMPANION

miracle workers, who will show my priests that your Christ can work miracles as great as those of their Gautama Buddha." I'm afraid the bit about the elderly Dominican priest who did tricks with a cup and a ball came from me, though.

On the other hand, the comment about Saint Joseph of Copertino is taken from seventeenth-century history; he actually *could* fly. And he was a tremendous embarrassment to the Catholic church at the time because he was quite stupid; but he'd go into these ecstatic trances, float up into the air, and be found stuck at the top of church pillars or tall trees. The church responded by transferring him to increasingly out-of-the-way places. Joseph's flying was deemed miraculous after he died, so he was eventually sainted; but it was done with some reluctance. [*Laughter.*]

HB: Something else you do in the story is establish that time is fluid in dreams. The young Marco Polo becomes lost in the year 1273, but he meets Gilbert from the year 1992, and a man named Rustichello who knows Marco Polo as an adult; and the three of them encounter an army of riders who have wandered the soft places for thousands of years in search of "the true world ... the hard lands." Further, it's the Sandman who's just broken out of his glass cage in 1988 who eventually bumps into Marco Polo and helps return him to his father's caravan.

NG: That was very deliberate, because the "soft places" concept was one of the escape hatches I'd built into *Sandman*. If I'd decided down the line to back out of the events I'd always planned would end the series, I could've employed the notion that time works differently in dreams as a plot device.

HB: Can you say a little more about that?

NG: I'll just point to page 17, where Gilbert notes, "Time at the edge of the dreaming is softer than elsewhere, and here in the soft places it loops and whorls on itself. In the soft places where the border between dreams and reality is eroded, or has not yet formed ... in the soft places, where the geographies of dream intrude upon the real." But it's an escape hatch that I didn't end up using.

YOUNG WEREWOLVES IN LOVE

HB: What led to "The Hunt"?

NG: I liked the idea of a young hero going out on a quest who, instead of a prince, was a young werewolf. This allowed me, for example, to do the standard fairy tale murderous landlord scene, but conclude it with the hero *eating* the landlord.

I was also inspired by an encounter I had in real life. I was visiting Alan Moore, and while we were having dinner at a restaurant Alan started very graphically describing a scene from his Jack the Ripper series *From Hell* involving the cutting up and removal of the interior bits of a lady. There was a point where Alan went, "And he holds up her insides and says, 'Look, Nately! Lights!'"—and I felt that if I heard any more, I was going to be violently ill. So I said, "I'm sorry, Alan, I have to go outside and get a breath of fresh air now." And I sat down on the pavement outside of the restaurant, and this old lady came up and began talking to me under the impression that I was homeless. I explained that I wasn't; and then she started telling me her life story as a beautiful young dancer and the things that happened to her when she was young.

Then she decided that she had to tell my fortune. She linked my little finger with hers, made these weird circles, and started talking. She began quite calmly but became increasingly scared as she went on: "Oh, you've been very hurt, dear. You've been very hurt by a woman. Oh no, oh no, I can't tell you anything else. Oh dear!" And when Alan came out to see how I was, she scurried away, quite terrified.

It must have left a great impression on me, because I ended up using that finger scene via the gypsy woman in "The Hunt"; and I also used the bit about being mistaken for a homeless person to begin my novel *Neverwhere*.

HB: That's fascinating, because Alan Moore spontaneously told me the same story, albeit from his own perspective.

NG: Whatever Alan said is probably true. I'm actually okay looking at gruesome pictures or movie scenes; but I'm in trouble when someone describes something, which causes me to make up the pictures in my head. And Alan can describe things very, very effectively.

HB: Speaking of storytellers, what are your feelings about the old Vassily who's telling his life story to his granddaughter?

TRADING CARD ART BY BRYAN TALBOT

Orpheus, son of Morpheus, and inheritor of his father's unbending nature.

NG: I loved him as a storyteller: "He was of The People, and he could see in full darkness, because he hadn't ruined his eyes with television." [*Laughter.*] His granddaughter responds, "Grandpa. My eyes are fine." And he says, "Okay. Okay. So you can blame an old man for being concerned? So your eyes are good too. That's good. His eyes were better."

Some people complained that I didn't capture the rhythms of a New York Jewish immigrant, but that's not what I was aiming for. Vassily's speech patterns are based on my own grandparents, who are British Jews and have a somewhat different patter.

Anyway, the attitudes he expresses are pretty much the same for all grandparents. The important thing is that, as Vassily says, "You shouldn't trust the storyteller; only trust the story."

HB: The interplay between him and his granddaughter is lots of fun.

NG: My favorite part of the story is their discussion after Lucien appears in the fairy tale. The granddaughter says, "So, this thin man. Was he one of the People? Was he a fairy or something? I don't believe in fairies." Vassily replies, "Of course you don't believe in fairies. You're fifteen. You think *I* believed in fairies at fifteen? Took me until I was at least a hundred and forty. Hundred and fifty maybe. Anyway, he wasn't a fairy. He was a *librarian*. All right?" She responds, "Mm. It all sounds suspiciously postmodern to me, Grandpa. Are you sure this is really a story from the old country?" Vassily says, "Listen, blood of my blood. Although I'm a hard man to anger, and love you deeply, if you interrupt me again so help me I'll rip out your throat with my teeth."

HB: And the girl meekly replies, "Sorry, Grandfather." [*Laughter.*]

The young Vassily in the fairy tale makes a speech about teeth as well. Do you know the one I mean?

NG: Sure; it's on page 19. "I am of the People, Man. What I seek, I find. What I hunt, I take. I can hide in a shadow. My teeth are sharp enough to cut bone. I run on four legs as easily as two. I am kin to dwarrow and nightgaunt. I owe allegiance to none born and I fear nothing. I want the woman." There was definitely an echo in my head, as I was writing that, of the werewolf at the end of *Prince Caspian*. That werewolf wasn't any kind of hero, but C. S. Lewis gave him a magnificent speech about not eating for a thousand years, and his belly being distended with blood; and it's the best speech in the whole of *The Chronicles of Narnia*.

I also loved having him get to the Princess, wake her up . . . and then go away.

HB: The sex scene that follows between him and the she-wolf didn't come off, thought.

NG: That's true. Duncan Eagleson did a beautiful job with everything else, really capturing the fairy tale feeling I wanted. But near the end, I wanted some sort of blend between human and wolf sex, and Duncan apparently drew it as a naked man having sex with a wolf, doggie-style. Karen thought that looked too bestial, so it had to be redrawn; but the new art didn't really convey the sexuality.

HB: Any comments about the very end of the story?

NG: Well, the granddaughter thinks the fairy tale's about her and her boyfriend, but of course it's not at all; it's a true story about her grandfather, and about dreams better left unrealized. If "The Hunt" works, it will do that nice thing of having you get to the end and then want to start again at the beginning.

THE SON OF MORPHEUS

HB: For an introduction of a new edition of Samuel R. Delany's classic science fiction novel *The Einstein Intersection*, you wrote that your first reading of that book imparted a number of lessons: "I learned that writing could, in and of itself, be beautiful. I learned that sometimes what you do not understand, what remains beyond your grasp in a book, is as magical as what you can take from it. I learned that we have the right, or the obligation, to tell old stories in our own ways, because they are our stories, and they must be told."

You reworked a number of old stories in *Sandman*, but you usually did so by taking disparate bits from different sources and mixing them together in extremely clever ways. One myth that you told relatively straight, however, was that of Orpheus in *The Sandman Special*. Why did you opt for that simpler approach?

NG: You know, that issue won bundles of awards, but the truth is that it's one of the stories with which I'm the least satisfied. My original plan for *The Sandman Special* was to do the equivalent of a series of jazz riffs, all on Orphic themes, spinning off of stories precisely like *The Einstein Intersection*. The result would have been much weirder and more interesting than what I ended up writing.

HB: So what happened?

NG: I was traveling around on a signing tour at the time, and when people would ask me "What's coming up?" I'd respond, "I'm going to do a series of stories about Orpheus," and they'd tilt their heads and say, "Morpheus?" [*Laughter.*] And I'd say, "No, Orpheus," and they'd look puzzled and say, "Who's Orpheus?"

This same conversation occurred over and over, all across America. I was very resistant at first, but finally the information I was being provided sunk in: despite the fact that I was dealing with well-educated, sophisticated readers, they didn't know the story of Orpheus and Eurydice.

You can't do jazz riffs and variations on a theme when the audience isn't familiar with the theme itself. So *The Sandman Special* became a literal retelling of the Orpheus tale, interwoven with my overall *Sandman* story.

Still, I had fun with it. I gathered up four different translations of the story, told by Virgil and by Ovid, and employed everything I could remember of the Latin I learned in school, and then recast bits in my own words. For example, on page 33, I began the song Orpheus sings in the Underworld as follows: "I sing of only two things: love and time. I journeyed to this world below, to which all born as mortals must descend in time. . . . I was not strong enough to bear my grief. Love was too strong for me, and dragged me down. The power of love is strong in lands above. . . . I beg you, by these silent realms, to weave again the destiny of one who died too soon. For we the living will be yours one day, and all we hope and feel and touch and dream, all we hold dear, will wither and be gone."

DANIEL'S TEA PARTY

HB: What was the genesis of "The Parliament of Rooks"?

NG: Part of it was my wanting to provide a glimpse of domestic life in The Dreaming; and part of it was taking a month for me and Jill Thompson to get to know each other before we went off and did *Brief Lives*.

Also, I loved the idea of the "Li'l Endless," of doing Death and Dream as Sugar and Spike.

JILL THOMPSON

As Abel tells the infant Daniel of his pitiful existence, Dream and Death are reimagined in a surprisingly innocent fashion. Here, for the first time, is the complete "Li'l Endless," from an unpublished sketch.

LI'L DREAM AND LI'L DEATH

Artist Jill Thompson on creating two of the most beloved characters in *Sandman*:

Li'l Dream and Li'l Death are my biggest claim to fame to date; they're what I'm asked to draw the most at conventions and signings.

Neil asked for something along the lines of *Sugar and Spike—really cute*—to embody these powerful, scary Endless creatures. Well, I have a "Hello, Kitty" alarm clock, and it's the cutest thing on the planet; so I studied it to figure out why. I noticed that it has a huge head with big eyes, but its face is all the way down in the lower third of its head. I then realized that kittens and puppies, and human babies, all have their faces smashed down toward the bottom of their heads; and their faces grow up into their heads as they get older. So I made Dream and Death look like little Japanese manga figures, with enormous heads and large eyes, but tiny noses and mouths that appear close to their chins. It worked, because those "li'l" characters have been extremely popular ever since they appeared in 1991.

HB: I can see why; Sheldon Mayer's *Sugar and Spike* series—about a very young girl and boy who understand baby talk, but nothing that adults say—is the most charming thing I've ever seen in comics. And Jill's rendition of *Sandman* characters as talking babies on pages 18 through 20 is utterly delightful and hilarious. I can't help breaking into a grin whenever I look at the panel where the Sandman trips over his cape and Death tries to suppress her giggle. I'm sure I'm not the only one, either.

NG: Actually, the response was so positive, I think we could've started up a Li'l Endless comic the day after the issue appeared.

HB: Speaking of cute, the story begins with Lyta Hall caring for her son, Daniel. Did any of those scenes reflect your personal experience as a parent?

NG: Definitely. On page 2, Lyta admits to going "Look! Fire truck!" when she's in a store without her child, and how embarrassed she became when everyone stared at her; and that's happened to me more than once. And Lyta's anecdote about unthinkingly taking an adult's steak and chopping it into small pieces is something my wife did.

HB: I really liked the panel on page 3 where Daniel, asleep and en route to The Dreaming, follows the alphabet on his wall past the letter Z; and he sees a sequence of bizarre symbols that, presumably, are part of a richer language than our waking one.

NG: I love that moment of his walking into dreams, too. It didn't occur to me until a reader pointed it out, but I may have been inspired there by Dr. Seuss's book *On Beyond Zebra!*, which takes you on adventures beyond the end of the alphabet.

HB: Once the tea party commences, each of the three former DC mystery hosts tells a story. We've already discussed Abel's. Do you have anything to say about Cain's?

NG: Just that, as far as I know, his description of a parliament of rooks is accurate. I got the information out of an old natural history book.

HB: What about Eve's tale concerning Adam and his three wives?

NG: That's a story which has haunted me since age twelve, when Cantor Meir Lev taught it to me during my bar mitzvah lessons. The cantor happened to be an expert on Jewish Talmudic, Mishnaic, and Midrashic apocrypha, and I found it all fascinating and pumped him for information; so by the age of thirteen, I knew more arcane Jewish lore than most adults.

I especially remembered Adam's second wife, and the fact that she never got a name. Rabbinical scholars deduced her existence from God's putting Adam to sleep before taking his rib to create Eve, figuring God must have had a good reason to first put Adam to sleep. The rabbis decided there was a previous wife who had been created while Adam was awake, and seeing everything that went into constructing this woman, "full of secretions and blood," so horrified him that he couldn't bear to touch her.

HB: There's one other story that's only hinted at; early on, you have Eve and Matthew chatting about the Sandman's new lover.

NG: What I wanted to do is tackle the situation of someone coming home with a new girlfriend or boyfriend, and everybody going, "Hold on, how does *this* work? I don't get their chemistry at all."

HB: So why *does* a person get involved with someone who's entirely wrong for him?

NG: I think the answer, quite simply, is that you don't always get to decide to whom you give your heart.

BAGHDAD IN A BOTTLE

HB: Closing up the collection is "Ramadan." I adore this story—and I'm not alone. When "Ramadan" was originally published as *Sandman* 50, it sold over 250,000 copies, making it the most successful issue in the series.

NG: I like it enormously, too. One of the special things about "Ramadan" is that I didn't write a full script for it. Only one other *Sandman* tale shares that distinction—issue 74, the next to last one.

P. CRAIG RUSSELL

Sketch of the Sandman as he appeared in "Ramadan," which provided inspiration for the popular Arabian Nights statue.

As you know, my scripts normally go into great detail about how pages should be laid out and what happens in each panel, and I often write a story panel by panel. Because I was trying to capture the spirit of an Arabian Nights tale, however, I decided to first write out "Ramadan" as a prose short story, so I could concentrate on capturing the appropriate rhythms and poetry of the language.

I wrote it up to page 18, where the caliph throws the globe; and then I called up the wonderful artist we'd gotten, P. Craig Russell, and asked him what kinds of things he likes to do in storytelling, because I felt ready to break the first part of the tale down into panels.

Craig replied, "Well, what have you done so far?" So I read him the text I'd written to that point. And Craig said, "Neil, finish it as a prose story, and let me take it from there." In retrospect, that shouldn't have surprised me, because Craig loves adapting short stories. He's done beautiful adaptations of Rudyard Kipling tales. I knew he could handle the breakdowns, so I said okay and did as he asked.

The results were spectacular. Craig did things that I wouldn't have even attempted, like using that enormous word balloon on page 25: "Noble lords, do not listen to him! He is a thief and a liar, and a magician to boot. A month ago he sold me an ass . . . ," and so on, fitting something approaching a novel into that one panel.

HB: How long did it take to create "Ramadan"?

NG: One of the nice things about issue 50 is that it was done out of sequence, so neither Craig or I was rushed. I began the story about a year ahead of time, while I was scripting issue 41; and I finished it while I was scripting issue 44 or so. I then gave the story to Craig, who did the job he did on it.

ILLUSTRATING "RAMADAN"

P. Craig Russell has been called "an artist's artist" and is best known for adapting classic works—such as stories by Oscar Wilde, and operas by Wagner and Mozart—into comics form.

His deep passion for his craft is demonstrated in "Ramadan," which many readers consider the single best issue of *Sandman*. To create Baghdad visually, Russell referred to books such as *Mirror of the Invisible World: Tales from the Khamseh of Nizami* and *The King's Book of Kings: The Shah-Nameh of Shah Tahmasp*, which reprint Islamic art, costumes, and patterns from centuries ago. The results can be seen in Haroun's clothing, the doorways of the palace, the fabrics at the marketplace, and throughout the issue. Russell also used those patterns memorably on the story's first page, which he says "was designed to be geometric and formalized, yet have the feel of a bursting sun, to make it look like the eye of Allah."

Russell shunned references (such as models and photos) when drawing the story's characters, however, figuring that "whatever would be lost in terms of realism would be made up for by the range and emotion of their facial expressions." For example, no real eye looks like Haroun's at the bottom of pages 10 and 17; but that cartoony face has an emotional power that drives this fairy tale.

While the beauty of Russell's artwork is evident at a glance, his storytelling techniques are often subtle. At the bottom of page 22, Russell needed to convey the feeling of a carpet lifting off and descending: "I designed the panel so your line of sight first goes straight up the acute angle of the building on the left, then hits the carpet and goes in a giant curve back down into the empty space of the picture, so you get the feel of a roller coaster going over the crest and about to swoop down." Russell didn't end the "swooping" effect at the drawing stage, either: "I also asked Todd to pencil in the panel's lettering at a tilt to follow the curve of the carpet ride, which is the reason for that unusual round caption. And I asked Lovern to make the coloring a cool blue in the panel's upper-left corner and a warm, rosy sunrise in the lower right, so the warmness would draw your eye from the top to the bottom."

The two people just referred to, letterer Todd Klein and colorist Lovern Kindzierski, also made major contributions to the story. The always inventive Klein lettered the captions in a style he describes as "curved and curly, elaborate and ornate." When editor Karen Berger saw the amount of work Klein poured into this issue, she gave him a bonus.

Even more important was the wizardry of colorist/separator Lovern Kindzierski. Among Kindzierski's achievements was making the Phoenix on page 14 look like it's really on fire; using computer effects to make the sky at the top of page 16 appear hallucinatory and alive; and turning the Baghdad we see throughout the story

into a shining jewel. Russell calls Kindzierski's work "one of the most sensitive coloring jobs I've ever seen."

This colorful issue created a problem regarding Dream's clothing, however. As Russell explains, "The Sandman had to be dressed mostly in black to stay in character, but he had to look opulent and kinglike to fit the story." The answer was a long, flowing robe with an intricate black and white design, which not only gave Dream the perfect look but helped him stand out against the glittering scenery in the background.

While Russell's illustrations are often lavish, he was equally happy to do very little. For example, in the middle panels of page 22, Haroun is handling the magic carpet, and it's the carpet that's the key visual. Russell therefore drew only the top of Haroun's head, and then Haroun's hands, to allow the carpet to hold center stage. Similarly, at the top of page 24, the main visual is the marketplace, so he drew the Sandman and Haroun as tiny figures descending into it. "They're still easy to spot, though," Russell notes, "because I put them in the center of the composition, with the marketplace circled around them; and I placed them against a white background."

The latter is just one of many instances of Russell's use of contrast. A more involved example begins on page 27, in which Haroun voices his fears about Baghdad turning into a bleak desert littered with, in the words of the story, "remnants

P. CRAIG RUSSELL

There were paths through the palace that none but Haroun Al Raschid knew; and this was because those who had drawn up the plans, and those who had built the paths, had all long since gone to their final reward: for it is seldom healthy to know the secrets of a king.

Todd Klein's lettering was never more evocative than in issue 50's "Ramadan."

of cities and palaces and gods [from] another age of man, forgotten and unremembered." (The last three words, *forgotten and unremembered*, are cleverly lettered to resemble desert sand drifting away.) As Haroun speaks, he's represented by a picture of an eye that grows increasingly smaller, and increasingly closed; and the eye appears within panels that grow increasingly smaller, as if they're being diminished with each passing moment. Just as we're ready to drift away along with the sand, though, we turn to page 28—and the story opens up again as Haroun proudly displays his Baghdad at the peak of its power and glory. This is a beautiful panel in any context, but its effectiveness is vastly enhanced by our memory of the dead city on the previous page—and by the contrast between those shrinking panels and this large, panoramic view.

Following this scene is the first of the story's, in the words of Russell, "false endings." At the end of page 29, the magic carpet stops hovering over the fountain and falls to the earth, concluding the bargain struck between the Sandman and Haroun. This really *is* the end of the story as far as Haroun is concerned, because when he wakes up on the next page, he no longer has a conscious memory of what happened. When he sees the Sandman's bottled city, however, the part of him that dreams understands that his wish has been granted.

The bottom of page 31, again, feels like the ending of the story—so much so that Russell felt it necessary to put a word balloon in the lower-right corner that trails off the right side, ensuring we turn the page to see who's speaking.

When we do so, we see the Arabian city as it appears in our time—and instead of a jeweled city, it looks like the terrible desert of page 27. But upon closer inspection, we see that Haroun's Baghdad lives on regardless—through the tales told by beggars, through the bright eyes of the young.

And through people like Gaiman, Russell, Kindzierski, and Klein.

Haroun Al Raschid shows the Prince of Stories his city, Baghdad, which he wished to have preserved forever.

brief lives

9

Life is what happens when you are making other plans.

—JOHN LENNON

rief Lives is the turning point of the *Sandman* series. A storyline that revolves around immortality and death (or, more broadly, *change*), it chronicles the Sandman taking a journey that will irrevocably alter him.

The tale begins with an Adriatic island that has two cliffs along the Greek coastline. On the left cliff is a mysterious villa of which we're initially provided only a glimpse. And on the right cliff is a small marble temple that's the home of the legendary bard Orpheus. Millennia after his immortal head was ripped from his body, Orpheus continues to live here under the care of guardians appointed by the Sandman, his father.

A caption notes that to his caretaker Andros, Orpheus is a miracle. Andros is steeped in ritual; every morning he climbs the cliff and every morning he places a flower on the grave of Lady Johanna Constantine (who rescued Orpheus in "Thermidor"). Despite his age, Andros performs his duties with vigor and joy. To him, every day is a beautiful day.

In contrast, Orpheus is thoroughly tired of life. At the top of page 4, his head is comically placed next to a similar-shaped Greek vase holding flowers. The vase is decorated with the image of a virile young man astride a chariot and admired by an attractive woman—the person Orpheus used to be. Both the vase and Orpheus are more than three thousand years old.

The last panel of page 5 is a study in contrasts: Andros, who is mortal and relishes every finite moment, holds up Orpheus, who is immortal and wishes only to die. As they move towards the garden, both of them are bathed by the eternal rays of the sun. This poignant image sums up many of the themes of *Brief Lives*.

The story then shifts from the sunny Greek island to a rainy London street, where a homeless woman is begging for change. Neil Gaiman loves wordplay; what's really being asked for isn't coins, but transformation. The woman is devastated because she's lost her son: "It's not fair when the young ones die before the old ones. I mean, they're all we've got to look forward to."

After receiving some small kindness from a passerby, the homeless woman nudges the figure next to her ... who turns out to be the youngest Endless, Delirium. Chatting with the old woman makes Del conclude, "I need a change." And with that, she decides to find her missing brother Destruction, who chose to abandon his realm and cut himself off from his family three hundred years ago.

Delirium first visits a nightclub, where she's clearly out of control—and very, very alone. Delirium screams out for the next youngest Endless. When Desire appears, Del explains that she wants to locate Destruction because "I miss him so badly. He was always so kind to me." This echoes the words of the homeless woman, who appreciated the kindness of a passerby even more than the change she received.

Del has actually already gone through a major change; as revealed in *Sandman* 21, Delirium began as Delight. More information about this is provided in chapter 2 of *Brief Lives*; page 20 shows a young Delight as innocent as a babe. Delirium remembers the transformation, "the moment she realized what was happening, that the universe was changing, that she was growing up or at least growing older." She also remembers turning for help to Destruction, who held and comforted her until she calmed down.

From these scenes, it can be inferred that Destruction was the only member of her family who showed Del extended kindness and understanding. (After all, who knows more about shattering, overpowering change?) We can also surmise that Destruction provided a stabilizing force that—given her habit of falling apart into butterflies—Delirium still desperately needs.

Delirium knows she's not up to finding Destruction by herself. Desire turns her down flat, however; and Desire's twin sister Despair also says no (albeit with reluctance, because she's known kindness from Destruction, too).

The youngest Endless after Destruction is Dream ... and so Delirium goes to the Sandman's castle next. Dream agrees to join Del's quest, not to help his sister, but in a rather sophomoric hope that he'll run into the woman who recently dumped him.

As they journey in the waking world, the dark, inflexible Dream and colorful, ever-changing Delirium make for a hilarious duo. But between such comic scenes as Delirium creating colored frogs and driving a car, we learn that people are dying.

Ruby DeLonge, a sharp young black woman acting as chauffeur for Del and Dream, falls asleep with a cigarette in her hotel bed and burns to death.

Bernie Capax, whose childhood memories include the smell of woolly mammoths, sees a wall about to fall on him and surprises himself with his plaintive last words: "Not yet ..." Standing over his corpse, Capax observes, "I did okay, didn't I? ... I lived a pretty long time." Death replies, "You lived what anybody gets, Bernie. You got a lifetime."

Ishtar, a former Babylonian goddess of love, sex, and war, makes a speech that clarifies concepts first presented in *Season of Mists*: "I know how gods begin, Roger. We start as dreams. Then we walk out of dreams into the land. We are worshipped and loved, and take power to ourselves. And then one day there's no one left to worship. And in the end, each little god and goddess takes its last journey back into dreams. And what comes after, not even *we* know." Shortly afterward, Ishtar unleashes the full power of her dance on the strip club she works in and blows both it and herself to smithereens.

Others narrowly escape a similar doom in the wake of Dream and Delirium's quest. Etain of the Second Look's apartment explodes scant seconds after she crashes out her window; and, taking the hint, she flees this plane of reality. The Alder Man, also sensing danger, turns himself into a bear and bites off his shadow, and instructs the shadow to take his place as a target.

The lives of ordinary people are turned upside down, as well. Highway patrolman Tom Flaherty makes the mistake of criticizing Delirium's driving, and is cursed with lifelong delusions of insects crawling on his skin. Ishtar's stripper friend Tiffany hits the talk show circuit to expound upon how she was saved from sin by an angel (who was actually Desire).

After observing the chaos he and his sister have been causing, the Sandman tells Delirium that he's calling off their search for Destruction. Feeling betrayed and hurt, Delirium responds by returning to her realm and sealing it off. Dream secretly continues to make inquiries on his own, however, by visiting Lady Bast, a cat-goddess who once claimed to know his brother's whereabouts (in chapter 5 of *Season of Mists*). Dream learns that Bast lied, but he nonetheless gets useful advice from her . . . which is to seek a family oracle.

Upon returning to his castle, Dream sees that Delirium's sigil has gone black and calls on his older sister for advice. But Death is angry and she tells him to straighten things out with Delirium; and so Dream visits Del's realm and—in a rare moment for the Sandman—apologizes. And he agrees to help her search for Destruction in earnest.

The duo first visit Destiny, who strongly advises the Sandman to "forget this foolishness. Drop it. Go home." When Dream persists, his older brother repeats what Lady Bast said: "You need an oracle." Dream protests, "There are no oracles who can tell of our family." Destiny replies, "There is, after all, an oracle who is *of* the family."

The Sandman finally allows this information to sink in . . . and falls apart. Concerned, Delirium asks Destiny what happened; but Destiny haughtily replies, "Surely that is his affair, not yours." A coldly angry Delirium responds, "There are things *not* in your book. There are paths *outside* this garden. You would do well to remember that . . . Coins have two sides. Destruction told us that, when he told us he was leaving. But I knew it already. You did too."

Demonstrating her own other side, Delirium calls on her wisdom and strength to help the Sandman pull himself together. Del then helps her brother do something he's been avoiding for the past three thousand years: visit his son, the oracle Orpheus. The Sandman and Orpheus have a short conversation, long enough for Orpheus to extract the promise of a boon in return for the information his father wants. Orpheus then reveals the location of Destruction . . . which is the villa just a few meters away, atop the cliff on the left.

After a brief rowboat ride, Sandman and Del finally reunite with their brother. Destruction invites them to dinner, and the Sandman shares news about their family. When he mentions his absent younger sister, Destruction comments, "Poor Despair. I remember when first she assumed the mantle of Despair; when first she became Desire's twin." Dream replies, "It was the only time one of the Endless had been destroyed, that another aspect of one of us had reassumed the position: we all had much to adjust to." This is the first time in the series that we learn a member of the Endless once died.

The Sandman then asks Destruction why he abandoned his realm three hundred years ago, in 1695. Part of the answer was actually revealed back in chapter 4: in a flashback sequence occurring around 1685, Destruction is shown to be uneasy about the path begun by Isaac Newton's study of "opticks"—because he realizes that Newton's question "Are not light and gross bodies intraconvertible?" will inevitably lead to the development of the atomic bomb. It's a scenario Destruction has seen many times before, on many worlds; but he's grown fond of Earth, and he appears reluctant to experience another cycle of "the flames, the big bang, the loud explosions."

Destruction points out that his realm is getting along fine without him: "People and things are still created; still exist; are still destroyed. They tear down and they build. Things still change. The only difference is that no one's running it anymore. . . . They can make their own destruction. It's not my responsibility. And it's not my *fault*."

Dream, whose life revolves around work and duty, presses his brother further. Destruction, who throughout the story has been engaging in acts of artistic creation (such as painting, poetry, sculpture, and cooking), echoes his sister in Destiny's garden: "Because there's no such thing as a one-sided coin. Because there are two sides to every sky."

Destruction then continues: "Destruction did not cease with my abandonment of my realm, no more than people would cease to dream should *you* abandon yours. Perhaps it's more uncontrolled, wilder. Perhaps not. But it's no longer anyone's responsibility. . . . As this universe came into being Destiny came with it, alone in the darkness. Before the first living thing came into existence, our sister was there, waiting."

Readers with excellent memories will recognize this comment as very similar to Death's own words in *Sandman* 20: "When the first living thing existed, I was there, waiting." But the subtle difference between the two statements —"before" versus "when"—is literally the difference between life and death. It's also no coincidence that Destruction was the first character to reveal his older sister's dual nature (on page 19 of "The Song of Orpheus"); and that *Sandman* 20 is about Rainie Blackwell, a person who refuses to let go of her old identity and, as a result, dies.

All this appears to be lost on Dream, however, who simply replies, "And when the first living thing awoke to life, I was also there. You tell me nothing new." Destruction responds, "I'm *trying,* my brother. It was getting you to listen to anything new that I always had problems with."

Destruction then walks out into the night and talks about the impermanence of everything: people, gods, worlds, stars, galaxies . . . and the Endless themselves. "Even our existences are brief and bounded," he says. "None of us will last longer than this version of the universe."

Destruction is indicating that, without exception, all must make way for change; or, as he puts it to the Sandman, "One cannot begin a new dream without abandoning the last, eh brother?" Like Death's advice to Rainie Blackwell in issue 20, these words can be interpreted in multiple ways. One can hear them as an exhortation for the Sandman to radically alter himself; or as an encouragement for Sandman to follow his brother's lead and abandon his realm; or as an invitation for Dream to commit suicide.

But what would death for someone like the Sandman mean, anyway? What are the Endless? "Merely patterns," says Destruction. "The Endless are ideas . . . wave functions . . . repeating motifs." And as far as people go, he continues, "we have no right to play with their lives, to order their dreams and their desires."

Although the Sandman doesn't appear to be taking in anything his brother is saying, Destruction suggests that, on a deeper level, Dream understands it all. Relating a long-ago conversation with his sister Death (set against jeweled waterfalls reminiscent of the Krypton depicted by artist Wayne Boring in 1950s and 1960s *Superman* comics), Destruction says, "She looked at me. *You* know her look. And she sighed. Then she told me everyone can know everything Destiny knows; and more than that. She said we all not only *could* know everything; we *do.* We just tell ourselves we don't to make it all bearable."

This discussion of omniscience and immortality hearkens back to the Biblical tale in "The Parliament of Rooks" (which was published directly before *Brief Lives*) about the Tree of Life and the Tree of Knowledge of Good and Evil. The Trees in the Garden of Eden are another example of two sides of the same coin. And given that the series posits life after death—Dream's older sister even states in issue 20 that oblivion "is not an option"—one might argue that not only do we all know everything, but that we all live forever, too.

Destruction says he enjoyed his time in the villa—"Life was comfortable and unchanging"—but having been found by his family, he now has to leave again. Delirium comments, "I could never leave *my* realm. It's got all my *things* in it"; and she tries to persuade her brother to join her: "Maybe you could come and stay in *my* realm. You can live there with me, and you can make me *laugh* and I'll do you little *dances.* And . . . And . . . You won't, will you?" Destruction says no, but he provides Delirium with a stabilizing force to help her get through what he refers to as "your next change": his wise and witty canine friend Barnabas.

As for the Sandman, Destruction says he has nothing to offer but this advice: "Remember what I did. Remember that I left. Remember how hard it was for me to leave; and that it was *not* your fault. . . . Remember." Dream responds, "I am not in the habit of forgetting things." Destruction astutely counters, "You forget nothing you have interest in; you forget, instantly, those things you do not care to know."

After placing his possessions, hobolike, in a spotted handkerchief tied to the end of a stick, Destruction shakes Dream's hand, hugs Delirium, and gives Barnabas a final pat. And declaring that he's headed "Out there, somewhere. Up. Out," Destruction ascends to the other side of the sky.

All that's left for the Sandman to do is grant the boon he promised Orpheus. Unfortunately, what the soul-weary Orpheus asked for was to finally attain death. And so the Sandman, violating the ancient rule against spilling family blood, thrusts his hand into Orpheus's head . . . and takes the life of his only son.

When Dream leaves his son's temple, the drops of blood that fall from his hand turn into red flowers (echoing issue 9, where Nada "spilt her virgin blood on the Earth; where the blood fell, red flowers grew"). The flowers are a breed that has never before existed, demonstrating Destruction's words about death leading to new life; but they're of no comfort whatsoever to the Sandman, who returns to his castle so changed by his experiences that his own guardians don't recognize him.

Dream arranges to fulfill his debts to those who have helped him in his quest. And then he retires to his private quarters to wash the blood from his hands . . . and to mourn.

Meanwhile, back at Orpheus's temple, Andros supervises the burial of his charge and hopes that the bard has finally found peace: "Perhaps his spirit is in Elysium, with his beloved Eurydice. And perhaps his spirit has returned to darkness, or to nothing.

"And perhaps he is at rest."

The repercussions of these events appear in subsequent collections.

SOME THINGS WORTH NOTICING

Brief Lives shows that all beings in the universe—ranging from ancient immortal to young child to talking dog—are connected to one another by some fundamental commonalities. Each has a life that's finite (and so may be thought of as brief). Each must learn to change and grow over time, or die. And each must struggle to create a life filled with rich experience and meaning.

Perhaps the best example of the latter is Orpheus's guardian Andros, who derives enormous pride and meaning from his job as the caretaker of a myth, but doesn't define himself by it. After Orpheus passes away, the old man deeply regrets the loss, but he wishes his charge happiness in the afterlife and mentally lets him go; and Andros ends the storyline as he began it: "It is going to be a beautiful day."

Dream's slaying of his son, Orpheus, is a momentous event, on a number of levels. Most obviously, it causes him to break a rule first revealed in issue 16, when

Destruction, the one member of the Endless who renounced his duties to humanity, from an unpublished sketch.

Desire tries to trick Dream into killing Rose Walker: "Was I to take the life of one of our blood," asks the Sandman, "with all that that would entail?" A hint of what it would entail appears in issue 31, "Three Septembers and a January," which shows the genesis of Desire's plan via the vow, "But I'll make him spill family blood; I'll bring the Kindly Ones down on his blasted head."

At least as important as the consequences of the Sandman's act, however, are the changes it indicates he's gone through. Three thousand years ago, Dream wouldn't consider violating even his professional protocol by speaking to Hades on Orpheus's behalf—or, for that matter, his personal protocol by hugging or otherwise comforting his son. But the Sandman's recent experiences have helped humanize him. So has his literally being driven among humanity in this storyline; his spending time with Delirium, who breaks through his stuffiness and forces him to confront his feelings; and his reunion with Destruction who, as the personification of change, is the Endless most aware of what we all have in common—and the Endless who demonstrates the most kindness.

Destruction even makes a sly *Wizard of Oz* reference to this when he says, "Well, it looks like neither of you is interested in the dinner I made. Is there anything else you were after? Brains? A heart? A ride in a balloon?" Delirium is, in fact, looking for mental stability, and she gets a fine brain in her new companion Barnabas. Destruction himself gets the balloon ride, when he ends up floating "up and out" into the sky. And Dream does finally get a heart.

The most famous father-son story in Western civilization is that of Abraham choosing to sacrifice what he loves most, his child Isaac, for the sake of the faith that rules his life. The Sandman's equivalent of faith is his reliance on ancient rules, and his determination to keep his word. In contrast to Abraham, Dream ultimately violates that faith—and thus his very identity—for the love of his son. It's this love that allows Dream to break a vow he made to himself to never again see Orpheus; and it's this love that leads him to break one of the oldest and most sacred rules of his kind to grant his son peace . . . by killing him.

The Sandman began his journey through the waking world in hopes of running into a lover who rejected him. He doesn't find her in this story, but given his melodramatic posing on a rainy balcony, it's questionable whether he really missed her or just the idea of love itself. In contrast, when he returns to his castle, Dream's genuine grief over his son is evident from how quietly he handles his mourning in his private quarters (a place shown only once before, in issue 24 . . . when the Sandman tries to recover from the shock of watching Lucifer abandon his realm of Hell, and the guilt Dream feels over the wrong he committed against another of his loved ones, Nada).

Also, for the first time, the Sandman spontaneously asks his castle guards, "Have I ever told you how much I appreciate your service? That I value you all most highly?" He runs into Nuala wearing his lover's pendant, and instead of flying into a rage simply says, "Ah, well. Keep it. . . . Do not trouble yourself, little one. Go in peace." And before retiring to his quarters, he makes a point of arranging for rewards or help to be given to those who have been affected by his quest.

In other words, by the end of this story, the Sandman learns how to perform an act of genuine love and sacrifice for his son. And that, in turn, teaches him something equally as fundamental when dealing with beings whose lives are brief . . . he learns to be kind.

EMPERORS AND PUMPKINHEADS

HB: In your script for issue 49, you say *Brief Lives* is about two things: "Change, and what change means to people. And life—its fragile, brief, impermanent nature . . . the way people come and go . . . the sheer wonderful teeming nature of human life."

NG: It's also a journey; and probably the most linear storyline in the series, tying up a lot of plot threads. *Brief Lives* provides information on how and why Destruction left; it tells of how Orpheus finally comes to die; it resolves Desire's goal of getting Dream to shed family blood, which goes back to the Emperor Norton story and *The Doll's House*; and it reveals a lot about Delirium . . . who's one of the few characters who comes out of it more or less unscathed. But most of all, it's the Sandman's story.

HB: When the Sandman first comes onstage, he's in a major funk as a result of yet another of his failed relationships. You never actually show us any moments from the romance, though. We don't even find out who the woman is until *The Kindly Ones*.

NG: Some people thought I was keeping the woman's identity secret just to be perverse. The truth is, my first stab at the script for chapter 2 began with a four-page scene between Dream and his lover in which she states what's wrong with their relationship and how she can't take it anymore, and walks out on him. But after I looked at what I'd written, it felt out of place to me, so I ended up throwing those pages away. Instead, I simply began with a line I remembered from a poem: "She has decided she no longer loves me."

A few panels later, I found the Sandman saying, "I would appreciate it if the palace staff would be so kind as to refrain from mentioning her in future, when in my presence." And I thought, "Oh, dear. We're not going to know who she is for a long time now." [*Laughter.*] I knew people would be irritated, but it's how the story happened to play out.

HB: You bring out the hilarious Mervyn Pumpkinhead, the smart-aleck pumpkin on a stick, who has appeared before, but only in brief nonspeaking roles; first as a bus driver on page 18 of issue 5, and then as a member of a crowd on page 7 of issue 22. Why did you plant images of Merv so early on if you weren't going to use him until *Brief Lives*?

NG: I like to build up texture. I figure it's fun for somebody rereading *Sandman* to look at issue 5 and suddenly go, "Oh my god, that's Mervyn."

And although I knew who he was all along—"the voice of the working man"—I simply didn't require Merv to speak until Dream was standing out on the balcony going, "My heart is broken, I want her rooms taken down and destroyed; and I'm just going to stand here feeling sorry for myself while I generate nonstop rain." At that point, I needed somebody to say, "Hey, you get to wallow in self-pity, but we're the ones who are getting wet." And so when Nuala expresses sympathy for the Sandman, Merv responds, "Nah, he enjoys it . . . He spends a coupla months hanging out with a new broad. Then one day the magic's worn off, and he goes back to work, and she takes a hike. . . . [And] he's gotta be the tragic figure standing out in the rain, mournin' the loss of his beloved. . . . In the meantime, everybody gets dreams fulla existential angst and wakes up feeling like hell."

Whenever I felt the Sandman was going overboard, I'd bring Merv on; he's the little voice in the back of my head that says, "Somebody really ought to tell Dream that he's acting like a flake."

HB: Dream occasionally gets to top him, though. In chapter 6, Merv tells Lucien, "He comes back and locks himself in his throne room. . . . Next thing you know, he's gonna be mooning around again—moon moon moon. . . . He oughtta hang out with guys like me. . . . Real everyday Joes, y'know? *We'd* set him straight. I mean look at *you*—you're a book-pusher. I mean, hey, nuthin' against books, but seems to me that these days you're practically running this place." And the Sandman appears and says, "When I was held captive, and the castle crumbled, Lucien stayed here, and did his duty as best he saw it, while the rest of you fled. Who else here can make that claim? You, Mervyn? What did you do, while I was imprisoned?" And Merv nervously replies, "I, uh. Bit a this. Bit a that. I drove a bus ..."

NG: I also like that scene for another reason. If you look carefully, the background action on page 16—which is never commented on—involves Merv with a roll of wallpaper walking into the Library of Dreams, which is filled with bookshelves except for one blank brick wall. Merv slaps some glue on the wall, and then unrolls and puts up the wallpaper, which turns out to be a picture of ... more bookshelves! Which works because everything on the page is a picture, so the wallpaper bookshelves are just as real as all the other bookshelves we see on the page. It's one of those lovely things that you ask someone with the skill of Jill Thompson to do, and she does it absolutely perfectly. And it's one of the places in *Sandman* where I just love the fact that a comic book is drawn.

RASPBERRY CREAM, RAINBOW FROGS, AND KANGAROOS

HB: As fun as Merv is, the real scene-stealer in *Brief Lives* is Delirium. When Delirium calls on Dream in the midst of his moping, his castle guards capture her, and the wyvern holds her in its mouth the way a cat would hold a kitten. Delirium goes "Wheeee ...," happily compares the experience to a ride at Disneyland, and kisses the wyvern on the snout when she's released. In other words, Del lives in the moment the way a child does; but she also exhibits the genuine class of a princess.

The two Endless then sit down for a memorable meal, in which Delirium requests a dish of chocolate people filled with raspberry cream. Sensing the Sandman's love problems, Delirium makes the chocolate people kiss and "squidge," which causes Dream to put his fingers to his forehead and wearily suggest they retire to his gallery. Following their departure, you provide an amazing caption: "Touched by her fingers, the two surviving chocolate people copulate desperately, losing themselves in a melting frenzy of lust, spending the last of their brief borrowed lives in a spasm of raspberry cream and fear." I love that.

NG: Frankly, so do I: it's probably my favorite caption in all of *Sandman*. In a way, it's the shortest of short stories, encapsulating the theme of *Brief Lives*. I also love the pun on *spending*, which means both "to use up" and "to come to orgasm, to ejaculate."

The phrase "copulate desperately," by the way, is an echo of a *Sandman* caption that appears on page 18 of issue 5, in the panel where Merv first appears: "I travel briefly by bus. In the back, the dreamer copulates desperately, not noticing his autonomous passenger. I sit at the front and talk to the driver."

HB: Given her unique perspective—seen through her mismatched blue and green eyes—a lot of readers were curious about what Delirium's realm looked like. You provided the answer when the Sandman enters it on page 21 of chapter 6; and it turned out to be a hodgepodge of colors and images and strange juxtapositions. What did you have in mind when constructing that place?

NG: I once was chatting with some friends online who argued that *Sandman* was surreal, and my reaction was "No, it's not. It's utterly real." So when Dream enters Delirium's world, I thought "Okay, *now* I'll do something that's surreal." That's what led me to write such captions as "A woman stands with doves on her shoulders, the doves are scorpions, the woman is a small pool of ice cream, melting on a sidewalk on a hot summer's day."

Delirium is a lot of fun, but she shouldn't be underestimated; she can also be very wise. As she tells Destiny, "There are things not in your book. There are paths outside this garden. You would do well to remember that."

GREAT DELIRIUM LINES

Like Stan Laurel or Gracie Allen, Delirium is a scene-stealer who gets the best lines. There are many examples of this in *Brief Lives*.

One is Delirium and Dream's visit to the travel agency (chapter 3, pages 7–8). The receptionist asks "Can I have your name?" and Delirium replies, "Don't you have one? You don't want *my* name. It would really mess you up." The exasperated receptionist asks Dream, "Is this person with you?" and Delirium says, "*I'm* not a person. Did you hear? She called me a *person*." Del then proceeds to demonstrate just how much she is *not* a person by making multicolored frogs.

Another memorable scene takes place when Delirium and Dream approach the home of Orpheus (chapter 7, pages 15–16). Del starts by asking the Sandman, "Have you ever spent *days* and *days* and *days* making up flavors of ice cream that no one's ever *eaten* before? Like chicken and telephone ice cream? . . . Green Mouse ice cream was the worst. I didn't like that at *all*." Andros's grandson holds Dream and Del at gunpoint and tells them to not make a false move. Delirium responds, "What's a *false* move? Is it *very* different from a real one?" The boy asks how they got up to the top of the cliff, pointing out, "You could not have walked here." Dream replies, "Nevertheless, we walked." And Delirium meekly adds, "But I'm a really *good* driver."

A few pages later, Delirium picks and eats some cherries, and then recites what's known as a cherry tree rhyme. This stems from the English tradition of giving a boy no more than eight cherries; after eating them, the boy counts the pits to see what he will be when he grows up. It goes, "Tinker, tailor, soldier, sailor, rich man, poor man, beggar man, thief." But Delirium picks herself some extra cherries, and so she carries on the rhyme: "Elf-lord, ivy, vinegar, toad, virgin, pilgrim, kangaroo."

A few pages after that, Delirium cheerfully scratches Barnabas under the chin and says, "Hullo, doggy. You're a very *nice* doggy, aren't you? Yes, you *are*. The cherry stones say I'm going to be a kangaroo when *I* grow up."

DESTRUCTION'S IMMORTAL FRIENDS

HB: *Brief Lives* is centered around the road trip taken by Dream and Delirium, but a number of people are affected along the way. There's Ruby DeLonge, the chauffeur who echoes Nada's fate as a young black woman perishing in flames; and Tom Flaherty, the cop who has the bad luck of noticing Delirium's driving and ends up in a psych ward battling imaginary insects.

In addition, there are the four ancient acquaintances of Destruction on Delirium's list: Etain of the Second Look, lawyer Bernie Capax, the Alder Man, and dancer-goddess Ishtar. Can you talk a bit about these immortals?

NG: I never got around to revealing much about Etain. There's something noteworthy about her appearance, though, which I'll mention when we discuss the artwork.

Bernie Capax originated from an anecdote Alan Moore told me. The rather dull father of a friend of his had died; and while going through the father's things, his friend found a blank passport and a load of Krugerrands. I simply expanded on that anecdote, adding pouches of heroin and cocaine; birth certificates and credit cards for multiple identities; guns and knives in the top drawer; and Picasso and Matisse paintings in the bottom drawer, along with what may be a da Vinci drawing.

HB: How about the Alder Man who, in a wonderful scene, turns himself into a bear?

NG: He was pulled together from a number of sources. Many of the details—the name Leib-olmai, the Lappish stuff about the Northern Lights—are based on genuine Finnish legend.

The idea of becoming an animal by taking off all your clothes, putting them in a heap, and pissing around them in a wide circle until they turn to stone is from Petronius's *The Satyricon*. If memory serves, a guy at the dinner party tells a story about taking his clothes off, pissing around them in a circle, and becoming a werewolf.

The concept of biting off your shadow—"neither easy nor painless"—came from, if anywhere, *Peter Pan*, in the sequence where Peter's shadow going out the window gets caught, and the children keep it; and Wendy later sews it back to his feet, which I've always assumed must have hurt a bit.

Finally, a couple of things came directly from me. The little leather traps to catch your death and your doom as it comes toward you are the result of my enjoying the notion of rainbow-hide cat's cradles that acted like dream catchers. And the final image comes from my simply liking the idea of a great bear convincing a shadow that it was now him as a man and should put on his clothes.

HB: That leaves Ishtar, the goddess with the show-stopping sequence that literally brings down the house.

NG: Ishtar's story was the only significant deviation from the linear progression of *Brief Lives*. In both *The Doll's House* and *Season of Mists*, I'd placed a tale in the center that thematically encapsulated the entire storyline. I didn't want to be predictable and so resisted doing that here; but Ishtar's sequence is the next closest thing.

I got the idea for it about eighteen months earlier, when I attended a friend's stag party. We all had dinner, and then we were herded onto a giant bus that took us to a strip club, which is something I'd never been to before. We went in at about 7:00 p.m., and I spent a fascinated fifteen minutes looking at the girls; and then an equally fascinated twenty minutes looking at all the customers. At that point it was 7:35 p.m., and I went to my friend and said, "What happens next?" And he said, "The bus comes at eleven o'clock to pick us up. Isn't that great?" And I thought, "I'm in hell." [*Laughter.*] I've got to sit here for another three and a half hours, and I've already seen everything there is to see: naked girl comes on, dances, writhes around a lot, stays in front of you as long as you give her dollar bills. Sad, upset-looking men stare at her.

The whole thing struck me as a shadow of genuine sensuality; a sort of falling away from something much deeper and more mysterious. So, with nothing else to do, I started wondering, "What would happen if the Sandman came in? Or if Delirium came in? What would happen if this place *blew up*?" And from that idle pondering, I came to realize that yes, this is what I was going to do; I was going to bring Dream and Delirium into this place and blow it to pieces.

About a year later, I was in Hawaii for a signing tour, and my hosts had promised to show me a good time; so I said, "Let's tour the strip clubs." They probably thought, "That Gaiman, what a libertine"; but they went along. We'd go to one club for twenty minutes, and I'd say, "Okay, good, now show me another one"; and we spent a couple of hours that way, strip club hopping.

Then I wanted to interview one of the girls. I asked how one does that and was told, "Give her money and you can talk to her." So I did, and asked her what she did outside of stripping; and she told me she was a computer programmer who was putting her boyfriend through college. [*Laughter.*] We had a long chat; and I walked away with enough information to write the story.

HB: Where did you find Tiffany's horrifying tale of shooting up drugs through the eyeballs?

NG: From a friend of mine who used to be both a supermodel and a heroin addict. I asked her, "How can you be an addict when you're going practically naked down catwalks and in front of cameras, with people scrutinizing your every pore?" She told me that to avoid visible needle tracks, she shot up between her toes. And she added that friends of hers, who had used up the veins in their feet, were shooting into the red stuff under their eyes. I found that memorable; and it also fit in with *Sandman's* "injury to the eye" motif, which pops up throughout the series.

HB: What can you say about Ishtar herself?

NG: I liked the idea of the Babylonian goddess of lust and sensuality being reduced to dancing in a strip club. I also love what she tells Tiffany about her relationship with Destruction: "In the end we split up. Fights about his family and his job. You know how it goes." [*Laughter.*]

And then the building blows, with just Tiffany left alive for Desire to stand over and say that lovely line from the Book of Job and, later, *Moby Dick*: "And I only am escaped alone to tell thee."

CATS, DOGS, AND DINNER

HB: Following Ishtar's demise, the Sandman goes to see the cat-goddess Lady Bast, who says to Dream, "Let me see. I suppose it is possible that today you thought to yourself: 'Why, it has been two years since last I saw Lady Bast ... It has been far too long since we sat beneath the summer moon together and talked of pleasant fripperies, of that and of this, and left others to speak sensible things of import and consequence. I shall rectify this on a moment,'—and suiting the thought to the deed, you sought me out." That's so charming and classy at the same time. Was there an inspiration for that passage?

NG: It's actually me doing my favorite fantasy writer, James Branch Cabell. He used that sort of dialogue in some of his historicals—a kind of poetic formality that people never really spoke but that sounds great—and I thought it would be perfect for Lady Bast.

Delirium persuades her older brother Dream to accompany her on the search for their missing sibling Destruction, in a sketch for retail poster art.

THE SANDMAN COMPANION

Another example is Bast saying, "Oh Dream. I do love you, you know. You make me laugh. Why weren't we ever lovers?" He replies, "Perhaps you know me too well, my lady." And she says, "See? You're so funny."

HB: Which is great, because most readers think Dream doesn't even *have* a sense of humor. Apparently it just takes a special kind of woman to dredge it out of him.

Following Bast's advice eventually moves the Sandman from feline to canine—specifically, to Destruction and his companion Barnabas. In a sense, Barnabas is to Destruction what Merv Pumpkinhead is to the Sandman; except Barnabas is wiser and wittier than Merv.

Your thoughts about creating Barnabas appear in chapter 13, "Secret Origins." The only thing I want to bring up here is a health issue; and you can probably guess what it is.

NG: Yes, I know that one should not actually give dogs chocolate.

HB: Did you have any compunctions about that?

NG: Absolutely none. Destruction didn't know; and Barnabas certainly wasn't going to tell him. [*Laughter.*]

JILL THOMPSON

HB: Jill Thompson's artwork in *Brief Lives* is stupendous. How did she come onto the project?

NG: When I was at the 1990 San Diego Comics Convention, someone asked me to sign a pencil sketch of Death in the nude, and I thought it was an amazing drawing. A half hour later, Jill happened to come by to introduce herself, and I said, "I just saw a sketch you did of Death, and it was beautiful. Do you want to draw *Sandman*?" She said, "Yes." And a year later . . . [*Laughter.*]

HB: The comics industry grinds slowly.

NG: Well, in all fairness, Jill was drawing *Wonder Woman* back then. Karen had to pull some strings to get Jill reassigned to us, and that process took time.

HB: Her people come off as very human visually; strong and vulnerable at the same time.

NG: I agree. A good example of that, by the way, is her handling of Etain of the Second Look—who *is* Jill Thompson, visually. If you turn to chapter 3, pages 13 through 16, that's pretty much what Jill looks like, and how she moves. I told Jill I needed a nice lady whose house blows up, and Jill asked if she could draw the things in her own house. I said sure, and added that she might as well draw herself as the lady while she was it at. Jill has a cool, unique face.

Jill also put a lot of herself into Delirium, in terms of body language, facial expressions, and so on. Jill was a terrific match for *Brief Lives*, and I think she did some of her very best work on it.

Jill Thompson's artwork is consistently intelligent, inventive, witty, and, above all, human. Her graceful juggling of fantasy and reality in *Brief Lives* brought characters such as Delirium, Destruction, Barnabas, Mervyn, and Ishtar to vibrant life and created an entirely credible and unforgettable visual journey.

Thompson credits much of the success of *Brief Lives* to the easy working relationship she had with Neil Gaiman. "Every time I received a script page from Neil, I was excited about pencilling it," she says. "I like drawing the human figure, and drawing expressions; and I like to emphasize visual storytelling, with the dialogue enhancing the art. Neil accommodated me.

"Neil and I would talk almost every day," says Thompson. "At the time he was doing signing tours around the world—Australia, New Zealand, Hawaii—so he'd fax me about a page of the script a day, and I'd pencil the page and fax it to him the next day. We got to a point where sometimes he'd forget to note in his script a certain effect he wanted, and he'd call me the next day to tell me that I'd put in exactly the effect he had in mind anyway."

Thompson confirms that, at Gaiman's suggestion, she drew herself as the fairy-woman Etain. Thompson adds that other characters were also based on real life: "For example, my brother appears as the bouncer at the dance place, Suffragette City. And the visual model for Barnabas was a sweet Australian herding dog who used to live in my neighborhood and was treated badly by his owners. One day they moved away and I feared his fate would not be a happy one, so I decided to immortalize that poor puppy dog by drawing him into *Brief Lives* . Many of the scenes I love best involve Barnabas—especially when he's critiquing Destruction's efforts at art."

The character Thompson feels closest to, however, is Delirium, who she says is "sprightly and fey; and kind of childlike, but not a child." After a while, the way Gaiman and Thompson interacted mimicked the way Dream interacts with Delirium. "Neil was always the straight man," recalls Thompson, "dressed in black and stoic, and expressing himself through succinct, eloquent sentences; while I surrounded myself with color, and tended to talk in roundabout ways, using lots of facial expressions and gesturing and visual descriptions instead of just saying something straight out."

Thompson is currently producing a comic titled *Scary Godmother*, mixing writing that's geared towards children with illustration that can be appreciated by anyone with a keen eye for witty cartooning. They can be ordered through Cosmic Therapy at 973-328-6606.

INEVITABLE ENDINGS

HB: In his introduction to *Brief Lives*, Peter Straub wrote, "Gaiman is preparing us for the end of the *Sandman* tales, perhaps even for the end of the *Sandman* mythos—for a kind of death."

NG: I agree, Peter's introduction is very perceptive. And *Brief Lives* is definitely preparing readers for some major events. You can actually go through the book and pinpoint the moment when the story becomes a tragedy.

HB: Which is ...?

Morpheus at last grants his son release from immortality; Orpheus's blood is transformed into the flowers of Desire.

NG: At the end of chapter 6, when the Sandman goes back to Delirium and says, "Okay, let's go and find our brother, for real."

HB: In other words, when the Sandman allows Death to talk him into going out and seeking Destruction.

NG: Well, if you want to put it that way … [*Laughter.*] Even past that point, though, Dream still could've changed course. When he goes to see Destiny for advice in chapter 7, his oldest sibling tells him flatly, "Drop it. Go home." When Dream says he can't, Destiny replies, "I know. And I am sorry. . . . I am your brother. If I could live your life for you, I would. But that is not within my power."

When the Sandman leaves Destiny's garden on page 12 to seek an oracle—that is, to see his son, Orpheus—the course of the rest of the series is set in stone. That's why, as Destiny's book flips and flutters between the past and future, we see on page 14 the very first appearance of a Dream dressed in white. That's a signal that there's no turning back from here. We're into the third act; the story is drawing to a close.

It was really strange writing *Sandman* from that point on, because part of me felt it was already over. Until then, I could've avoided the ending I'd planned; I'd actually built in several escape hatches, in case I changed my mind about the direction the series would take. But chapter 7 of *Brief Lives* is the point at which King Lear turns around and says, "Okay, which one of you girls loves me best?" I think that's what Peter was referring to in his introduction; that certain endings are inevitable.

—

brief lives

worlds' end

10

Sometimes too much to drink is barely enough.

—MARK TWAIN

Worlds' End is the third, and final, *Sandman* short story collection. Unlike *Dream Country* and *Fables and Reflections*, which never explicitly link their tales together, *Worlds' End* connects its stories via a framing technique dating back to fourteenth-century author Geoffrey Chaucer—travelers thrown together by circumstance maintaining one another's spirits by spinning yarns. Neil Gaiman explains that "I liked the idea of using one of the oldest storytelling devices in the English language. If you're going to steal, you might as well do so from a great source, and *Canterbury Tales* definitely qualifies."

In *Worlds' End*, the travelers arrive from all over time and space; they find shelter in a cosmic inn that exists between worlds; and the circumstance that throws them together is a "reality storm" generated by the death of someone of universal importance. Ultimately, however, Gaiman's goal is the same as Chaucer's: to tell stories that evoke awe and wonder.

The collection begins with two co-workers, Brant Tucker and Charlene Mooney, being driven off the road by "a huge, horned horse-thing, with a touch of panther." After dragging themselves from the wrecked car, they stumble across the Worlds' End inn, where they encounter a variety of unearthly characters who help them recover from their accident . . . and proceed to tell some unusual stories.

The first, titled "A Tale of Two Cities," is about a man named Robert who loves the city he lives in but tends to avoid the people in it (a clear parallel to the Sandman, who lives in dreams but tends to avoid the people doing the dreaming). One day Robert gets on a train he's never seen before, and he encounters the Sandman; but Dream simply stares at him. When Robert leaves the train, he finds himself in a city similar to his own . . . except that it's virtually devoid of people. After much wandering, Robert eventually meets an old man who surmises that both he and Robert have become trapped in the city's dreams. Shortly after that, the old man spots what he senses is an escape hatch from the dream—and disappears.

Robert continues exploring the dream-city, until one day he spots a beautiful woman, and behind her, a doorway that he senses is his own way out. Fleeing from the woman's touch, he plunges through the door—and emerges into the normal version of the city again. Since that time, Robert has lived in fear that something even worse may happen; that one day all the sleeping cities will wake up, and rise.

The second story is told by Cluracan, and it recounts how the Faerie ambassador brought down an evil religious leader by, basically, spreading malicious gossip about him. This tale of revenge doesn't really work (as Gaiman acknowledges later in this chapter); but it includes a notable scene in which the Sandman grudgingly saves Cluracan's life at the request of the fairy's sister, explaining that Nuala "serves me well and faithfully. I would not see her needlessly distressed. . . . She has a good heart, Cluracan."

The third story, "Hob's Leviathan," is an elegy for the days of tall ships and the romantic mystery of the sea. It's told by a girl who pretends to be a boy named Jim so she can live the life of a sailor. "The Sea Witch was its own little world. The sailors were from every land under the sun," says Jim, evoking comparisons with the inn itself. On the voyage Jim describes, the ship additionally carries two immortals: the Englishman Hob Gadling and a former Indian king who, many years ago, ate fruit from the Tree of Life.

The ocean is full of mysteries and secrets, and—as in The Dreaming—some of them are horrific. Its power and wonder can be summed up by an unforgettable image: a sea serpent that rises from the depths, and whose head and neck hint at a body so enormous as to stagger the imagination.

The fourth inn story told is "The Golden Boy," about an alternate Earth in which an earnest nineteen-year-old named Prez Rickard becomes president of the United States. Miracles and portents accompany Prez's election, and he ends up a savior who transforms America into a virtual paradise. This tale is packed with wonderfully surreal moments, such as an aging John Belushi explaining, "Prez showed me you didn't need to be fucked up to work at your peak." Prez consistently resists temptations from his world's god, Boss Smiley, to follow a darker path. After his two terms of office are over, Prez chooses to disappear from the spotlight. He eventually passes away in anonymity, but somehow everyone senses the loss: "Black armbands became commonplace, and, did you ask anyone to tell you who they wore them for they would say 'for Prez,' although no one could tell you for sure how they knew he was dead."

The fifth story, "Cerements," contains tales within tales within tales and creates an entire mythology around a city named the Necropolis Litharge that's devoted to the rites of death and burial. Among the story's highlights are a demonstration of an air burial and a visit to a mysterious room beneath the Necropolis that holds the cerements for Endless who have died.

All the stories just mentioned begin in the inn but then break out into other locations. The sixth story deviates from this formula by staying focused inside the inn. Told by Charlene Mooney—ironically, to prove that she doesn't have a story to tell—it describes the life of a modern woman who's terribly lonely, unhappy, and adrift. When she finishes, Charlene starts crying and runs away.

There are at least two other stories to be found in *Worlds' End*. One is the tale of the inn itself, which is threaded throughout the collection. For example, page 3 of the last issue shows the tavern as being almost infinitely large and yet utterly crowded. "When a world ends," says the Shiva-like host, "there's always something left over. A story, perhaps, or a vision, or a hope. This inn is a refuge, after the lights go out. For a while." And on page 8 of the same issue, the Centaur observes, "The tavern itself cannot be harmed. That is the way of things. It is being continually created; after all, worlds are ending all the time."

The other major story is that of the reality storm raging outside, which led many of the inn's current visitors to seek its shelter. The cause for the storm is hinted at on pages 12 through 19 of the last issue, which shows a covered casket and a solemn procession of mourners. At the front is Destiny, and at the back are Delirium and Death. We can also clearly see such familiar characters as Despair, Wilkinson, Luz, Queen Titania, Lady Bast, Odin, Thor, Emperor Norton, Gilbert, and Martin Tenbones. We also see an angel (possibly Duma), a raven (presumably Matthew), and shapes resembling such other characters as Nuala, Abel and Cain, and Mervyn. However, because the inn exists outside of normal time, and the storm further disrupts the shape of time and space, we can't be sure when or where this funeral is taking place . . . or who is being mourned.

On one level, *Worlds' End* can be seen as a return to the series' roots because, like *Preludes & Nocturnes*, it's an exploration of different popular genres, and of mostly idea-based rather than character-based tales. On another level, the collection can be seen as a sort of wake, since it involves people being brought together to drink and tell stories as a result of someone's death.

But most of all, *Worlds' End* is a tribute to the magic and power of stories. That's why it feels right when, at the end, Petrefax of the Necropolis Litharge chooses to leave his city to explore other worlds; and Charlene decides to abandon the "real" world to stay on at the inn. It's appropriate that the lives of these characters should be turned upside down after everything they've heard; transforming lives is what stories are for.

SOME THINGS WORTH NOTICING

Many of the scenes in *Worlds' End* foreshadow events that haven't yet happened in the series. The most notable example is the mammoth funeral procession.

Another echo of a future event is the train in the "A Tale of Two Cities" story; the same train appears on page 16, part 11, of *The Kindly Ones*. When you reach that scene in the next collection, you might imagine the Sandman encountering Robert just before getting off the train himself.

Worlds' End also serves to confirm or expand on information furnished earlier in the series. One example is Prez's encounter with Death in "The Golden Boy."

            THE SANDMAN COMPANION

On page 19, he says, "Hello. Have we met before?" She answers, "Once." This echoes Destruction's mentioning on page 19 of "The Song of Orpheus" that you see his sister not only when you die, but also when you're born.

Further, when Prez asks, "What happens now?" he's told, "Oh, different things to different people. It depends who you are. And you never get to learn what happens to anyone else." *Season of Mists* indicated that people reside in hell only if, on some level, they actually want to. The exchange with Prez can be read to mean *anything* that happens to you after death is dependent on the choices you make . . . and on what you can privately work out with Dream's older sister.

In addition to its internal *Sandman* references, of course, *Worlds' End* contains the usual slew of external references. A good example is the story "Hob's Leviathan," which was pencilled by Michael Zulli. The first Hob Gadling story, *Sandman* 13's "Men of Good Fortune," was also pencilled by Zulli, and it was named after a Lou Reed song. It's therefore no coincidence that elements of "Hob's Leviathan" echo another Lou Reed song, titled "Heroin," which contains such lines as, "I wish I was born a thousand years ago,/I wish that I'd sail the darkened seas/On a great big clipper ship." The lyrics also mention "all the Jim-Jim's in this town"; and near the end of her narrative, Jim says, "The sea is in my blood like a fever."

For additional pointers to *Worlds' End* references, see the "Origins of Character Names" section in chapter 13.

THE DREAMING CITY

HB: After completing *Brief Lives*, you could've directly followed up on the repercussions of that storyline by plunging into *The Kindly Ones*. Instead, you chose to first pull back a bit and write *Worlds' End*.

NG: Well, I love doing short stories because of the variety they provide, and I saw *Worlds' End* as my last chance to explore a bunch of different genres in *Sandman*. I'd previously found it arduous to begin every story from scratch, however, so this time I used an inn to provide framing sequences.

HB: What can you say about the first story, "A Tale of Two Cities"?

"THAT THE CITY SHOULD WAKE," SAID THE OLD MAN. "THAT IT SHOULD WAKE AND -- "

A distinctive drawing style highlighted the Lovecraftian story "A Tale of Two Cities."

NG: It's right in the H. P. Lovecraft vein—I even use the word *cyclopean* toward the end of it. I enlisted artist Alec Stevens because I'd previously seen a Lovecraft story that he'd adapted, and I really liked what he'd done. I also liked going from our relatively warm and reassuring inn framing sequence to a style that was all captions and panels and white space—no word balloons or borders—and very unsettling. I was thinking about cities at the time because I'd written an essay about them for the game Sim City 2000.

I think the single man, alone and lost, works well. The girl at the end shouldn't look so much like Death, though, and it's unfortunate that she does, because it adds overtones that don't belong to his almost instinctive decision to run from her touch.

BAD POPES AND SEA SERPENTS

NG: The next story, "Cluracan's Tale," was drawn by John Watkiss, and it's told by the elf-lord from Faerie whom we previously met in *Season of Mists*.

HB: In your script, you say, "The story comes from a number of places: A book on the early days of papal Rome; vague memories of reading *Metal Hurlant* strips by Druillet picturing huge, moldering cities with rotting towers; my fondness for the *Flashman* books, which center on a narrative hero who's a spineless, lying bastard; and my desire to bring Lord Cluracan of Faerie back into *Sandman*."

NG: All true. The book I referred to is *The Bad Popes* by E. R. Chamberlin, and it discusses the three or four occasions when the pope was also the duke of Rome. I was fascinated to see that every time a pope was made both a spiritual and a temporal ruler, things fell to pieces.

"Cluracan's Tale" turned out rather horribly, though. This issue taught me the humbling lesson that there are certain stories one just can't tell in twenty-four pages—or, in this case, twenty-two pages, after subtracting the three-page framing sequence, and getting special permission to add a page to this issue in the hope it would help.

One of my errors is that I was slow in making the adjustment from previous *Sandman* issues in which what happened in a story was never very important—what mattered was how what happened affected the story's characters. For *Worlds' End*, I thought it would be fun to turn that strategy on its head and concentrate on sheer storytelling. But that requires precise pacing and lots of story details, and on that level, "Cluracan's Tale" needed forty-eight or sixty-four pages to do it justice. As it is, I ended up trying to do a swashbuckler Errol Flynn movie in fifteen minutes, and fell flat.

HB: What about the next tale?

NG: "Hob's Leviathan" is me doing Kipling, more or less. The girl, "Jim," masquerades as a boy so she can be a sailor and spend her days on the sea—though she knows she'll soon look too much like a woman to continue the pretense and will have to begin a different life.

HB: The story also offers a nod to Melville's *Moby Dick* via your opening line, "Call me Jim." In your script, you say it's all about "secrets, and regret, and sea magic. Worlds keep ending in *Worlds' End*, and what's ending here is the world of the tall ships and the sea." Near the conclusion of the story, we're treated to a breathtakingly huge sea serpent, which Michael Zulli told me he based on "those old, strange nautical drawings of monsters from the depths, with a little oriental mythology and a dash of modern paleontology thrown in." The beast is showcased via one of the few double-page spreads ever used in *Sandman*.

NG: Right, because I reserved two-page spreads for scenes that demanded a sense of enormousness. Michael created a spectacular serpent.

HB: In the last issue of *Worlds' End*, on page 5, Charlene criticizes all the stories that have been told as "boys' fiction." When "Jim" protests that hers was a woman's story, Charlene snaps back this response: "Oh, please. Look, girl, the whole point of your story is that there wasn't a woman in it. Just a ship full of sailors, and a giant dick thrusting out of the ocean." That's a hilarious self-critique. Did you plan on that line from the start?

NG: Oh, sure. That was all done very knowingly. The first, Lovecraft-like story, for example, is about as alienating and antiromance as I can imagine. But there's nothing wrong with boys' stories. On the contrary, it was important to me to go that route, because I knew the next story arc was going to be *The Kindly Ones*, which revolves around women.

An unpublished sketch of the Sandman with Hob Gadling, who reappeared in the tale "Hob's Leviathan."

PRESIDENTIAL HISTORY AS SYNOPTIC GOSPEL

NG: Next is "The Golden Boy," my Horatio Alger story, of which I'm very fond.

HB: You're referring to your take on the hippie-type DC character from the early 1970s named Prez who, thanks to his moral character and diligence with clocks, became the first teenage president of the United States. In your script, you note that you had to throw away your first draft, which was unusual, as "the last time I threw something away was six months ago on *Sandman* 46, when I wrote a scene in which the Corinthian killed Ruby." You got on track when you acknowledged that you weren't very interested in politics, but in "the mythic aspect—young princes and powers, vanished kings and lost golden ages, journeys into the darkness and out the other side into legend—and the worlds that are lost."

NG: Well, during that period—the summer of 1993—I was still new to the U.S., and I was struck by how powerfully my friends reacted to Bill Clinton, who had become president about eight months earlier. They had been so happy when Clinton was elected, as if he was going to fix everything. And when some time had passed and he hadn't yet done the things they'd expected, they were genuinely heartbroken, as if something deeply religious had gone wrong. It seemed clear to me that they were yearning for a savior, someone to sort it all out for them. So I thought I'd do a story, in the form of synoptic gospel, in which I'd give my friends the kind of president they wanted.

HB: You clearly had fun with it.

NG: Oh, yes. I loved writing Richard Nixon, and his bit about "that dumb *expletive deleted* Jack Kennedy"; and the elderly John Belushi, who described meeting Prez as "the most inspiring experience of his life." I also loved the miracles that occur on election day: "A baby was born to a couple in New Haven, CT, with a birthmark in the shape of the USA on her back, lacking only Hawaii and Alaska; in Caesar's Palace, Las Vegas, every slot machine in the building bestowed its jackpot simultaneously; during a 42nd Street screening of *Hot Teenage Love Sluts*, the climactic sex scene was interrupted by the couple replacing their clothes and performing highlights from *Guys and Dolls* to an outraged audience."

HB: Michael Allred told me he enjoyed illustrating all the 1970s celebrities and pop icons because "they gave the story the feel of a rock and roll dream."

NG: You can tell Michael had fun; the artwork he produced is simply beautiful. And his version of Death is a standout.

HB: Agreed. What about reader reaction; did you get any flak for doing a story involving politics?

NG: Yes, which really surprised me, since it's so obviously a fairy tale. For example, the first panel of page 12 states, "That November, the Democrats fielded an 18-year-old football player, the Republicans, an aging movie actor. The election result surprised no one." I received snarky letters from Republicans saying, "Oh, so you're saying Prez is a Democrat." The whole point was, no, he was in his twenties by then, not eighteen, and he was running as an independent.

HB: I guess political passions don't inspire careful reading. What can you say about your handling of Prez's mysterious death?

NG: I really liked the strangeness of that; the idea that everyone knew that he was

Prez, America's youngest president and one of DC Comics' most short-lived characters, was revived for the story "Golden Boy," only to meet an early death.

dead, but no one knew how he died, or even how they knew it'd happened. As it says on page 19, "How he died meant little. What was beyond any manner of doubt is that the world knew he was gone. There was nothing about it in the newspapers, no word on television. Still, across America, the flags flew at half-mast, and people spoke in hushed tones. Prez Rickard was no longer spoken of in the present tense." It's a very R. A. Lafferty moment.

HB: Prez is spared a conventional death, however, so he can go help fix other versions of America on other worlds.

NG: It's also worth mentioning that Prez thanks the Sandman for his help by giving Dream his watch, which explains the watch we saw twenty-seven issues earlier—in *Season of Mists*, chapter 6, page 20—that was stored in the Sandman's treasure chest.

STORIES WITHIN STORIES

HB: The next story, titled "Cerements" and drawn by Shea Anton Pensa, is constructed a bit like an Escher painting. Please walk us through it.

NG: Well, you're in a story to begin with, just by virtue of reading *Sandman*. In this story, you're transported to an inn in which people are telling stories while a storm rages outside. In "Cerements," one of these visitors to the inn, an apprentice of the City of the Dead named Petrefax, tells a story in which he appears with three others named Mig, Scroyle, and Master Hermas, each of whom in turn tells a story.

Mig's tale is fairly straightforward. Scroyle's tale involves a meeting with Destruction, who is passing through the city. Within Scroyle's tale, Destruction relates how the Endless tried to bury the original Despair and how that led to the creation of the Necropolis Litharge—which is the place where Petrefax and his comrades happen to be telling their stories.

Next, Master Hermas provides a tale about Mistress Veltis, to whom he and Petrefax's master Klaproth were apprenticed. During this story, there is a storm one night, and Veltis comes down to comfort Hermas and Klaproth by telling them some stories. One of the tales she tells—at the top of page 20—is "about a coachful of prentices and a master, swept away from Litharge by dark magics, who took their refuge in a tavern, where the price of haven was a tale."

HB: In other words, at this furthest point in, there's a reference to the characters at the Worlds' End who are currently telling stories. Which means Veltis told the story of the people who are currently telling a story about her, turning time on its head, and making the storytelling process circular and endless.

NG: Yep. And then Veltis relates another tale, about a huge room she stumbled onto within the catacombs beneath the city. Finally, within the story that Petrefax is telling, it's Petrefax's own turn to tell a story. But he declines, saying that he hasn't traveled, hasn't seen or done anything extraordinary, and so has no stories to tell.

HB: That's quite a labyrinth of yarns spun. And over the course of it all, you manage to tell us a great deal about funeral customs.

NG: Practically everything I know, actually. [*Laughter.*] None of it was made up, either—it's all based on rituals in human history.

HB: Even the air burial, and the notion that after you grind up the deceased you should eat your lunch, because the bits of the corpse on your hands will make the lunch taste better?

NG: Yes; that came from Tibetan customs. The only flourish I added was calling the corpses "clients," which was a tip of the hat to Gene Wolfe's series *The Book of the New Sun,* in which the torturers refer to the people they inflict their skills upon as "clients."

HB: Aside from all the different ways you use Petrefax's tale to foreshadow future events in the series, this also works as a boy's story.

NG: Right, because it doesn't actually end with him about to spill the city's big secret and his master telling him—using lines from an old Masonic ritual—to "hush." It finishes when we're back in the inn, on page 21 of the last issue of *Worlds' End,* and Petrefax chooses to grow up by leaving the safety of the Necropolis Litharge and go off with the Centaur to explore other worlds.

HB: And that covers all the major characters at the inn, except for the two who led us there—Charlene and Brant.

NG: Well, Charlene complains that all she's heard are boy's stories, and says that she doesn't have a story of her own to tell—and, what I like best, then proceeds without realizing it to tell her tale, which is very much a woman's story. She says: "I've got a job I don't much like ... I've got an apartment that I loathe. I've got an ex-husband who comes over when he gets lonely and tries to talk me into having sex with him for old times' sake. And sometimes I even say yes. I joined a local theater group long enough to realize I'd never be an actor, and joined a writing circle long enough to realize that I don't have anything to say worth writing down. I come home from the office every night and fix myself nothing much interesting to eat or I send out for pizza, and I fall asleep in front of the TV."

HB: And Charlene is the one character who decides to stay on at Worlds' End.

As for Brant, he never actually tells a story in the Worlds' End inn. On the last two pages, however, we learn that *all* the tales we've experienced were told by Brant to a bartender.

Turning back to the artwork, I really liked the warm-hued reality of the inn created by penciller Bryan Talbot and colorist Danny Vozzo, which provided a solid foundation from which all the other stories could spring. Depicting a small room in which characters just sat and talked forced Bryan to rely heavily on body language and facial expressions. "I'd sit in front of a mirror speaking the dialogue," he told me, "so I could select the best mouth shape to express what each character was saying in each panel."

NG: Bryan also added all kinds of nice extra touches. For example, at the top of page 3 of the last story, he threw in an angel and a demon sitting together at a table, happily chatting. Also, at my request, Bryan occasionally placed some of my friends in the inn—such as my assistant Lorraine Garland, who's the leftmost person at the table on page 9 of the first issue, and Steven Brust, who's wearing a hat and holding a mug in the leftmost corner of the previous panel.

HB: One other artist I want to mention is Gary Amaro, who drew what are arguably the most memorable images in *Worlds' End*—the awesome procession of mourners. You said earlier that you reserved double-page spreads for events that demand a sense of enormity. This is the only place in *Sandman* where you use three double-page spreads in a row.

NG: Or even two in a row, for that matter. But this was a highly significant occasion.

HB: My absolute favorite part of *Worlds' End*, however, is your real-life reference to a world just beginning: your dedication of the book to your newborn daughter, Maddy.

NG: I was sitting in the hospital at 3:00 a.m., and the dedication was due in the next day. So I pulled out my little palm-top computer and typed precisely what appears on the page: "This book's for Maddy, pink and tiny, born one hour and ten minutes ago, who has spent most of the intervening time sucking vigorously on my fingers in the mistaken belief that they provide a viable source of nutrition. I give you all your tomorrows, and these small stories. With my love, Neil Gaiman."

—

the kindly ones

11

All around me darkness gathers,
Fading is the sun that shone;
We must speak of other matters:
You can be me when I'm gone.

—NEIL GAIMAN

ll the bad decisions we've watched the Sandman make culminate in *The Kindly Ones*, a tale of inexorable self-destruction. In this collection, characters and plot threads that have been planted throughout the series come to interact in increasingly complex ways—as indicated by the ever-weaving Fates in the framing sequence—until they collectively cause a death that rocks the universe.

The story begins with Lyta Hall, whose entire life revolves around caring for her son, Daniel. Her friend Carla persuades Lyta to finally take a night off and leave Daniel with a baby-sitter and go to a nightclub. Although she's gone for only a few hours, Lyta's worse fears are realized; Daniel is kidnapped.

Carla calls the police, but her call is magically diverted; and in place of genuine cops, Lyta is visited by two highly dangerous beings whose disguises indicate they've watched too many episodes of *Dragnet*: the trickster god Loki and the fairy Puck. After pretending to investigate the case, these phony detectives show Lyta a photograph of Daniel burned to a crisp; Lyta goes mad.

Lyta remembers the Sandman's comments about one day taking Daniel away from her (in #12), and his explanation that it was very rare to find a child who gestated in dreams (#22); and so she assumes the Sandman is responsible for Daniel's kidnapping and death. In a daze, Lyta simultaneously wanders the city streets and a world of myth, seeking a way to exact revenge.

She first stumbles across the gorgons Euryale and Stheno (the two immortal sisters of Medusa), which results in her growing snakes for hair. Lyta then finds the Furies, the revengers of the spilling of family blood, who are older than gods and more feared—and who prefer to be called the Eumenides, a Greek term that translates as "the Kindly Ones." Lyta volunteers to be the instrument of the Furies because they seek to punish Morpheus for killing his son Orpheus.

Meanwhile, Loki and Puck are having a grand old time as they keep Daniel in fire, which is a traditional method of gods for burning off a human's mortality. Puck's actions appear to have no more complex reason behind them than mischief making; but Loki's motive is to destroy Dream, who gave the fire god his freedom in return for a promise of a favor to come (in #28). When Lyta's friend Carla, a young black woman, asks too many questions about Daniel at her local police station, Loki incinerates her in her car; and over her smoking corpse, Loki refers to his agreement with Dream by darkly muttering, "I will be under an obligation to no one."

Meanwhile, other beings of power sense trouble coming. As a result, Queen Titania of Faerie dispatches Cluracan to retrieve his sister Nuala. Nuala is in love with Dream and expects him to refuse to let her go; but to her sorrow, he puts up no resistance at all. He does, however, enchant her pendant (which was a gift the Sandman gave his most recent lover, and his lover passed on to Nuala in *Brief Lives*), so that the fairy can call on him at any time and request one boon.

Dream senses trouble as well, and creates a new Corinthian (he "uncreated" the original in #14) that he dispatches, accompanied by the raven Matthew, to locate Daniel and bring him to the castle. After a heated fight with Loki, the Corinthian accomplishes just that—although Matthew disappears in the midst of the struggle, inexorably drawn back to The Dreaming by the slaughter that has begun because, as another of his kind explains, ravens have "a tendency to view a battle as a prelude to fine dining."

The Kindly Ones and their intermediary, Lyta Hall, are killing inhabitants of The Dreaming, and because the Sandman and The Dreaming are part of each other, each killing impacts Morpheus like a little death of his own.

The Sandman attempts to end the carnage by ending the life of Lyta Hall, who is powering this aspect of the Kindly Ones. When he travels to the waking world, however, he discovers that Lyta is protected by Thessaly (now calling herself Larissa), the millennia-old witch who was last seen in *A Game of You*—and, we finally learn, is the unnamed lover who dumped Dream in *Brief Lives*.

Thessaly has made a deal with the Three-Who-Are-One to clear some old scores and gain an extra couple thousand years of life in exchange for protecting Lyta Hall from harm. Thessaly does so with the same type of circle that kept the Sandman imprisoned in Burgess's basement. Dream could kill Lyta without breaking the circle, but not without breaking certain rules . . . which he refuses to do.

The Sandman is unsure of what to do next but remains comforted by the fact that as long as he remains in The Dreaming, no real harm can come to him. However, while searching for her dog Barnabas, Delirium bumps into Nuala and lets her know the Sandman is in trouble; and, out of concern and love, Nuala reacts by using her pendant to call on Dream for her boon. Dream has the option of simply ignoring his promise; but once again, he refuses to break the rules and so travels to Faerie. Morpheus explains that he is indeed in trouble: "I killed my son. I killed him twice. Once, long ago, when I would not help him; and once, more recently, when I did. . . . In my pride I abandoned him for several thousand years; and then, at the last, I killed him." Nuala astutely replies, "You *want* them to punish you, don't you?"

The Sandman returns to his castle, but in his absence it's been taken over by the Kindly Ones. They threaten to free his castle's prisoners and to shatter the stained glass windows "that hide your power and your madness." The Sandman decides that he has no other option but to confront the Furies and flies to a high peak with Matthew, who has been asking throughout the story what happens to ravens at the end of their service. Dream now answers that some of them, who've grown tired of life, are sent to his older sister; one was returned to his humanity; and a couple have stayed in The Dreaming in other forms. One of the latter is Lucien, who was the first raven . . . and, by implication, the first human.

The Kindly Ones arrive, and they make clear that they will rip The Dreaming apart until they achieve their goal. Feeling he's run out of options, the Sandman gives his helmet and pouch of sand to Matthew to take back to the castle, bids his friend good-bye, and then waits for his older sister, Death, to join him.

When she does, Dream asks her if she'd like to throw bread at him again, but she answers with resignation, "It's much too late for that." More angrily, she adds, "The only reason you've got yourself into this mess is because this is where you wanted to be. There's personal responsibility too, y'know? Not only the kind you're always talking about. . . . Destruction simply left . . . and took off into the forever. You could have done that." The Sandman replies, "No, I could not." His sister pauses, lays her head on his shoulder, and acknowledges, "No, you couldn't, could you?"

Dream then says, "I have made all the preparations necessary." "You've been making them for ages," his sister responds. "You just didn't let yourself know that was what you were doing." More gently, Death says to her brother, "Give me your hand." And a moment later, the Sandman passes on.

In the wake of death, however, is life.

And the child Daniel is transformed into the new Dream of the Endless.

SOME THINGS WORTH NOTICING

"When I came to write *The Kindly Ones*," says Neil Gaiman, "I pictured myself getting into a very, very big truck, aiming it at a wall and putting my foot on the gas." That's an appropriate metaphor, but Gaiman might have added that the "truck" didn't appear out of thin air; he built it with extraordinary meticulousness and patience.

It was back in *Sandman* 4, "A Hope in Hell," that Lucifer swore to destroy Dream and abandoned his realm. A bewildered Dream asked what Morningstar would do without his kingdom and received the reply, "I could lie on a beach, somewhere, perhaps? Listen to music? Build a house? Learn how to dance, or to play the piano?" And in the final pages of *Season of Mists*, Lucifer does indeed lie on a beach, as he admires a sunset in Australia.

Part 1 of *The Kindly Ones* gives us the other end of that answer, via a Lucifer in Los Angeles who's spending his time, as he puts it, "Playing a little piano, and running the best damned nightclub and restaurant in this whole city of the angels." And the final pages of *The Kindly Ones* completes the circle . . . when the Sandman is destroyed.

But Lucifer didn't kill Dream so much as hand him an opportunity. In *Season of Mists*, it was the Sandman's decision to take the key to hell; to accept a gift from Faerie; and, most significantly, to place Loki in his debt. (At the end of part 5, Loki provides this self-critique: "I am Loki Scar-Lip, Loki Skywalker, Loki Giant's Child, Loki Lie-Smith. I am Loki, who is fire and wit and hate." In other words, to deal with this trickster is to court disaster. In fact, Loki can be seen as the dark mirror of Lucifer . . . which makes utterly appropriate the battle he later has with the Corinthian, who's the dark mirror of Dream.)

The Sandman's fate wasn't determined solely by his choices in *Season of Mists*, however. It was also set up by his decision to tell a terrified Lyta Hall that he was going to steal her son; to care more about his job than his relationships, which resulted in alienating Thessaly; to seek out his brother Destruction, but not be open to hearing anything Destruction had to say; and on and on. What happens to Dream in *The Kindly Ones* is neither an accident nor an execution; it's a suicide.

Dream was so terrified of letting anyone get emotionally close enough to him that, over the course of the series, he consistently withdrew from women he has affairs with, such as Calliope and Thessaly. His only human friend, Hob Gadling, is someone he spoke to once every hundred years. And those he loved the most, he imprisoned.

Given that one of Dream's powers is to open doors, his consistent attempts to hide from, regulate, or close down relationships must have, on some level, weighed heavily on him; and that internal pressure was heightened enormously by the seventy-two years he spent as a prisoner in Roderick Burgess's basement. After that experience, Dream couldn't go back to the way he was, but couldn't move all the way forward, either. The Sandman's problem is summed up by Lucien in the next collection, *The Wake*: "Sometimes, I think, perhaps, one must change or die. And, in the end, there were, perhaps, limits to how much he could let himself change."

That said, one can argue that Dream did the next best thing. He could have kept fleeing the Kindly Ones from one plane of existence to another, or have followed Destruction's example by relinquishing his title and abandoning his realm. But taking such routes would have barred anyone else from assuming the Sandman's position as protector of The Dreaming—a situation that would have been intolerable to Morpheus.

Further, the Sandman may well have decided that his personal limitations kept him from being the Dream Lord his realm required and deserved. From this perspective, Dream's suicide was one of supreme sacrifice—an ultimate act of duty—because he felt Daniel could do a better job. This may explain why the Sandman's final romantic fling was with Thessaly, a woman who appears to value nothing over self-preservation. Without realizing it, the Sandman may have hoped that if he couldn't move forward, maybe Thessaly could help him move backward.

By the end, though, the Sandman couldn't move at all. In part 7, the Norse god Odin tells him, "You puzzle me, Dream-Weaver. Are you a spider, who's spun a web of cunning and deceit and now waits patiently for his prey to come to him; or are you a deer, frozen by the light of a hunter's flame, as disaster comes for you?" Ultimately, the Sandman was both.

PUSHING THE BOUNDARIES OF READER EXPECTATIONS

HB: When *The Kindly Ones* was first published, some readers demonstrated quite a bit of resistance to it. However, that resistance appears to have since gone away.

NG: There's a good reason. By the time that I was plotting *The Kindly Ones*, I knew the entire storyline would end up being collected in book form. I therefore chose to pace the story in a way that would work perfectly for a book—but that would *not* work very well for a monthly comic, as it would be too slow at the start and too fast at the end.

I also knew that in order to tell this story the way I wanted to, I'd have to abandon some of the gentle, comfortable techniques I'd employed for the earlier tales. For

The *Kindly Ones* was drawn in a graphic expressionistic style, as shown here in art from a promotional flyer.

MARC HEMPEL

The Kindly Ones

Beginning in December

Written By NEIL GAIMAN
Illustrated by MARC HEMPEL

SANDMAN

VERTIGO

Marc Hempel, the penciller of *The Kindly Ones*, employs a cartoony, emotionally expressive style that can be traced back to such comics giants as George Herriman (*Krazy Kat*), Steve Ditko (*The Amazing Spider-Man*), and Harvey Kurtzman (*Mad Magazine*). "My basic approach," says Hempel, "is to take a person and make him or her into shapes; and then use those shapes to convey emotion." Some illustrators like to create ornate, lush linework, but Hempel feels that less is more: "I try to keep the compositions and forms as simple as possible, because I believe everything that appears on the page should service the storytelling."

Hempel's admirers include P. Craig Russell, illustrator of *Sandman* 50 ("Ramadan"). "Marc Hempel is vastly superior to the sort of artist the fans typically idolize," says Russell. "His ability to nail a character in just two or three lines—the expression, the gesture, the mood—is amazing. Fans think that if you draw every leaf on a tree, you're god," adds Russell. "I don't knock that approach—I draw lots of details myself. But what really impresses me is being able to suggest every leaf on a tree with a single line."

example, if you look at the first two or three pages of most *Sandman* issues, you'll find someone describing to someone else where the story stands to date. Similarly, if a character reappears after being out of sight for a while, the character will in some way be reintroduced. All this is not accidental. I wanted to make sure that if a reader had missed an issue, or if a new reader was jumping into *Sandman* for the first time, he or she would get enough information to understand and enjoy what was about to happen.

For *The Kindly Ones*, though, I made no attempt to reorient the reader at the beginning of each issue or to periodically reintroduce various characters. This made it tough even for readers who never missed an issue, because you can forget a lot of plot development in a month, or forget the identity of a character introduced three months ago.

HB: Not to mention a year ago. *The Kindly Ones* was the longest story in the series, running for thirteen months.

NG: The audience remained loyal, but there were grumblings. Some monthly readers complained that they didn't feel the story was being done for them, that they were just being used to subsidize the book; and there's truth to that charge.

There were also some readers who said, "Well, I'm enjoying the story but I don't like all the digressions." I found that very weird, because there aren't any digressions; every panel in *The Kindly Ones* is plot, moving the story toward its inevitable ending. Then again, that may not have been apparent when it was being published in installments.

Another factor that was hard on regular readers was reorienting on a monthly basis to Marc Hempel's blocky, expressionistic artwork, which looks unlike virtually anything else in mainstream comics. If a reader plowed through a stack of other comics and then read an issue of *The Kindly Ones*, the visual contrast could be unsettling.

As a result of all that, a number of monthly readers sent in letters declaring *The Kindly Ones* to be the worst of the *Sandman* story arcs. After its issues were collected and published in a book, however, many people who read *The Kindly Ones* only as a full-length work said that it was the best storyline of the series.

HB: You mentioned Marc Hempel's unconventional art style. Why did you pick him to illustrate this story?

NG: *The Kindly Ones* is about shadows and shapes, form and fire. I therefore wanted someone with a simple, lucid style. I knew the cartoony quality of the art would alienate some readers; but I also knew that the next storyline, *The Wake*, would be illustrated by Michael Zulli, who'd draw everything so realistically that you'd think he was actually there sketching it all as it took place, which would make any readers grumpy about *The Kindly Ones* happy again. But the main thing is, Marc's art style was perfect for the story I wanted to tell. And I think it worked beautifully. There are things Marc and I pulled off visually that I'm astonishingly proud of.

HB: Could you give some examples?

NG: When Lyta goes mad, we keep switching between two views. One is of her journeying through a strange, mythic landscape in pursuit of vengeance, and the other is of her wandering dazedly through a modern city as if she was a homeless person living in the streets. Our challenge was to make it very clear, through visuals, that both of these things were happening at the same time—for example, that she's talking to a tall, thin cyclops at the same time that she's looking at a traffic light. Or that she's eating one of the Golden Apples of the Hesperides, and in the next panel we see her sitting behind a Dumpster eating a pale, rotting apple. In each case, these parallel events are happening simultaneously—both of the views being presented are *true*. By representing that idea visually, I thought we did something very special.

JACOBEAN TRAGEDIES AND TRIPLE ENTENDRES

HB: What can you tell us about the two quotes that start the collection?

NG: They're both from Jacobean dramas. The first reads, "The fool that willingly provokes a woman has made himself another evil angel, and a new hell to which all other torments are but pastime," which is from Beaumont and Fletcher's *Cupid's Revenge*.

The second reads, "What do the dead do, uncle? Do they eat, hear music, go a-hunting and be merry, as we that live?" "No, coz, they sleep." "Lord, lord, that I were dead. I have not slept these six nights." That's from *The White Devil* by John Webster.

Webster is especially significant, as he's best known for writing Jacobean revenge tragedies, such as *The White Devil* and *The Duchess of Malfi*—plays that are rich and cloying, contain lots of references to the Furies, and are filled with dark and twisted and inevitable events. Webster quotes therefore appear periodically in *The Kindly Ones*. Some examples are "Oh that I were a man, or that I had power to execute my

At the start of chapter 1 of *The Kindly Ones*, the three Fates appear to be knitting. The mother says, "Why, that's what I like about making things for people. You can start off in Birmingham and finish in, well, Tanganyika or somewhere. Every one we make's unique. Never seen before. Never seen again." The crone responds, "Hmmph. I don't know why *that's* exciting. It's not like anyone *notices* what we do. Not like anyone *cares*. And they're always com*plain*ing: they don't like the fit of it; too loose—too tight—too different—too much like everyone else's. It's never what they want, and if we give them what they think they want they like it less than ever. 'I never thought it would be like this.' 'Why can't it be like the one I had before?' I don't know why we bother."

The comments simultaneously work as a conversation about knitting; as a critique of the story to come; and as a description of someone's life.

The Fates then open a fortune cookie, and the maiden reads: "A king will forsake his kingdom; life and death will clash and fray; the oldest battle begins once more." Careful readers will recognize this as the prediction made by the Fates at the beginning of *Season of Mists*. Therefore, the maiden comments, "We've had that one before, haven't we?" And the mother answers, "It's definitely familiar, dearie."

Then the crone says, "Right. I think *that* one's gone on long enough." The mother replies, "Do you think so? I rather *like* this one. I thought maybe it could be a little longer . . ." But the crone says, "You're too *soft*. Both of you. Much too soft. All good things, eh? All good things. Got to finish sometime." And her scissors go "snip."

apprehended wishes—I would whip some with scorpions" at the end of part 3; "Now to the act of blood there is no fitter offering" and "oh, but the stars still shine," in part 9; and "the wolf and the raven are very pretty fools when they are young" in part 10.

Plus on page 12 of chapter 1, Matthew asks Lucien, "Whatcha reading?" and Lucien replies, "An unwritten play by John Webster. *A Banquet for the Wormes*." "Any good?" "Yes. Very good. 'Webster was much possessed by death and saw the skull beneath the skin.'" That's actually something T. S. Eliot said about Webster. Speaking of Eliot, another influence for this storyline was his poem *The Waste Land*—which brought the series back full circle, as *Sandman* was originally promoted with the Eliot line "I will show you fear in a handful of dust."

HB: Following the quotes is a ten-page prologue titled "The Castle." Did you and artist Kevin Nowlan create that specifically for this collection?

NG: Not quite. It was originally published as part of the first issue of *Vertigo Jam*, which is a smorgasbord title used to promote various series in DC's Vertigo imprint. However, I wrote it knowing that I'd probably use it as a prologue when *The Kindly Ones* was published in book form. It provides a nice recap of where the series stood at that point; and it reintroduces some of the key characters—such as Merv, who's not "afraid to call a spade a goddamn shovel," and Matthew, who for the first time wonders whatever happened to the ravens before him.

HB: You began the story proper with the three Fates, who have appeared throughout the series as maiden, mother, and crone—the Three-Who-Are-One. They're messing about with a ball of wool, and you play off that to create double and triple meanings.

NG: I loved doing multiple meanings in *The Kindly Ones*.

HB: That's evident from the opening "knitting" sequence. You didn't restrict the triple entendres to that first scene, either.

NG: Right; I made the first panel of each issue include a cord symbolizing the thread of the fate that was eventually going to be cut. And the cord was accompanied by text that commented on where we were in the storyline.

For example, the very first panel shows a ball of wool, along with the dialogue: "Is it ready yet? Are you done?" "Nearly. *There* we go."

In the first panel of part 2, there's a telephone cord, and the question, "Well? How long is it going to take?"

In the first panel of part 3, there's the silver cord tethering Daniel, and the line, "I think it's going to be bigger than I had planned."

HB: Which is true. You'd originally planned this collection to run for six issues, but it turned out to be thirteen issues long.

NG: Yes; but this late into the series, my feelings echoed the reply in the panel: "I don't mind. As big as it needs to be."

HB: That didn't keep you from indicating some ambivalence with the length—or with the fatal course the story was taking. Part 4 starts with a street construction "Men at Work" cord, and the line "I wish I could be certain that I was doing the right thing." And part 5 is a spider's web, and the comments, "It's happening very slowly, but it's happening." "It always takes longer than you think, doesn't it?"

And then the pattern breaks altogether with part 6.

NG: That's simply because part 6 returns us to *The Doll's House*, and I wanted to create an episode that very specifically mirrored Rose Walker's first trip to England in issue 10. For example, Rose originally debuted via a panel showing a passenger jet and the caption "Mom woke me up when we were coming in for a landing. My legs were cramped and I felt generally shitty." In part 6 of *The Kindly Ones*, we again start with a panel showing an airplane, and the Rose caption "Pressure in my ears woke me up when we were coming in for a landing. I woke up in pain, disoriented. I held my nostrils shut with my fingers, blew hard until my ears popped out and the pain started to go away."

Also, in both cases, there's an Englishman waiting for her at the airport holding a "Walker" sign, and who escorts her into his car. Only in *The Kindly Ones*, it's not Holdaway but his nephew Jack; and the car isn't a classic Bentley but a vintage Mini Minor. Further, when Rose returns to the nursing home, page 6 of part 6 echoes page 18 of issue 10, panel for panel—except in the latter, the broom closet stays a broom closet. Even the cover of part 6 was supposed to echo the cover of issue 10—but it actually echoes issue 11, because Dave misunderstood which cover I was telling him about. [*Laughter.*]

HB: And so the "thread of fate" pattern picks up again with part 7.

NG: Yes, with a telephone cord in the first panel, and the comments, "I never thought I would ever get to this place" and "Destinations are often a surprise to the destined."

Part 8 goes straight for the scissors poised over the cord of the Sandman's life, just to let readers know that we're getting there. The purpose of that issue was basically to give readers an idea of what the Sandman typically does, so they're reminded of why he's cool and why we like him. But I couldn't actually have a character speaking in the first panel, so I just put in the scissors.

Part 9 moves back to the Ladies for one panel, with the scissors still poised over the cord, but now with a hand visibly holding them; and the dialogue "Almost time." and "Nearly. Very nearly." And in part 10, we begin with the silver cord that was wrapped around Daniel being snapped, and the comment, "There."

Once the cord snaps, we more or less lose the metaphor; and so in part 11, we get Daniel coming towards the castle. And in part 12, having lost the cord, the comment is, "Still here, then?"

Finally, in part 13, we simply begin with the Sandman sitting silently, by himself. That's followed in the next panel by the question "What are you doing?" from Death; and Dream's reply, "Waiting for you."

So we get a progression of first panels throughout the story that comment on the action, on the overall story, and on the cord of the Sandman's life. Until we get to the end, where the Sandman is just sitting there with nothing left to say ... waiting for Death.

LYTA AND ROSE

HB: You mentioned earlier how much you enjoyed a particular Lyta Hall sequence. Are there any others that stick in your mind?

NG: I liked the scenes where she's going mad, and her amazingly flat tone as she moves beyond sanity: "He touches my neck and I don't want him touching my neck so I move his arm away and there's a crunching noise, and he starts saying I've broken his armbone and he winds up going off in an ambulance. The bones in the arm are called the ulna, the radius, and the humerus."

I also enjoyed her mythic journey in part 4. On page 16, Lyta meets two characters who look like the spider women duo from *The Doll's House*, but are actually the gorgons Euryale and Stheno. I always felt sorry for them, because everybody re-members the mortal gorgon Medusa, but no one recalls that when she was slain she left behind two immortal sisters. I love it when Lyta compliments them on their "sculptures"; "These are lovely statues. Did you carve them yourselves?" Stheno

Lyta Hall
with her infant
son Daniel,
who came
to prominence
during *The Kindly
Ones* as the new
Lord of Dreams.

Rose Walker,
who resurfaces
in *The Kindly Ones*
after an absence
of several years.

raises her hand and says, "Oh, please," the way a woman might who's been complimented on her dress—"oh, this old thing, I've had it for years" on the surface, but beneath it a sort of pride.

HB: What about Geryon?

NG: He was a three-headed creature slain by Hercules as part of the man-god's Twelve Labors. What Geryon says about Adam and Eve is true, by the way. If you ask someone why Adam and Eve were thrown out of the Garden of Eden, you'll typically be told, "Because they disobeyed." But what the Bible actually says is that God wanted to keep them from eating from the Tree of Life as well; that is, prevent them from becoming immortal.

HB: Yep. I looked it up: "So now, lest he send forth his hand and take also from the Tree of Life and eat and live throughout the ages . . . So God sent him away from the Garden of Eden."

NG: There you go. And after Lyta eats the apple, we get the marvelous slow appearance of the snakes on her head.

Then at the top of page 4, part 5, Rose gets to walk past Lyta on her way to visit Zelda—who *was* one of the spider women from *The Doll's House.* And we finally get to hear Zelda's reassuring moral homily, which Chantal mentioned in issue 15: "The story about the footsteps in the sand and there are two sets of footsteps together, because some of them are GGGGG—God's except there aren't always two of them. And the woman says to God, 'where were you when I was in trouble?' And He says, 'that was me carrying you.'"

Then she adds, "Chantal didn't bbb—believe in God. She loved spiders and skulls and graveyards for themselves. I loved them because they showed ttttt—tt—tttransience."

HB: That's some stutter.

NG: I used to stammer as a little kid. After years of elocution lessons, I threw it off; but I still remember what it was like, the sheer effort needed to get words out. At the same time, I think saying words like "ttttt—tt—tttransience" is a great way to stutter.

As for the slight madness and incredible horniness of people in the last stages of AIDS, that's also something I wrote from experience, from friends I knew who had it.

HB: The sequence concludes with Zelda telling Rose to return to England so Rose's late grandmother Unity can give her back her heart. Rose does so in part 6, which we touched on previously. Do you have anything to add about that issue?

NG: The women Rose speaks to in the nursing home are, on one level, three little old ladies and, on another, the title characters. And on a further level, the woman named Helena is Lyta Hall's mysterious missing mother.

HB: Also, that Amelia Crupp is quite a storyteller. What was your thinking behind the 8-page short drawn by Charles Vess?

NG: It's a folk tale about what revenge is for, and what it does. The original version I ran across was in a bizarre dialect; I remember first looking at it and misreading *worm* for *woman*.

I also like the conversation that follows it: "A woman shouldn't have to sleep her life away. Women aren't about dreaming. We're about the real world. Women are about waking, Rose."

Then Rose encounters an owl on page 20, which is an echo of the owl on page 20 of issue 10; and she meets the sleeping Alex Burgess and gives him Unity's ring, putting it next to the original Piglet doll that Alex and Paul stole from A. A. Milne's house when they were kids.

HB: Lucifer later quotes Milne, when Mazikeen asks where he's going next: "Anywhere. Everywhere. I don't know."

As for Rose, she falls in love with an English lawyer named Jack Holdaway, only to discover he's already involved with someone else. She then runs into her "grandfather," Desire, who's waiting for her in the basement where Dream was imprisoned.

NG: And if you look carefully at page 6 of part 9, you'll discover a paperback copy of Stephen King's novel *It*, still laying where Dream's guard Barney left it on page 26 of issue 1.

HB: Why did you put Rose through her failed affair with Jack?

NG: I made all that happen because I wanted her to grow up, to be a much more substantial person than she was with Zelda in the hospice. And so I felt it was time to break Rose's heart.

HB: If nothing else, it should make her a better writer.

NG: A writer with a very individual voice. If you look at her letters in *The Doll's House* when she was about twenty-two and compare them with the ones she's writing at about twenty-five, you can see her literary style has matured a bit, but it's still recognizably hers.

I also like that she's writing a thesis on the images of the maiden, mother, and crone in popular TV sitcoms. In part 4, there are books stacked on top of Rose's TV about such shows as *Bewitched*, which has Tabitha, Samantha and Endora as the triple goddess; and playing on the TV itself is *Roseanne*, which has Darlene, Roseanne, and Bev as the Three-Who-Are-One.

HIGHLIGHTS AND ECHOES

HB: What are some of the other scenes that stick in your mind?

NG: Well, I love the Cluracan sequence, where he vomits up his Nemesis. That also includes one of the earliest appearances of Daniel, as he wanders off into the raw dream-stuff.

I also love the reactions of the different inhabitants of The Dreaming to what the Kindly Ones are doing—like Merv rallying the troops in part 10, where he finally names the bats who've been following him around during the series, wearing their Walt Kelly–ish bowler hats.

And I like Lucien's reaction to Merv's death. And Cain's reaction to Abel's: "They wouldn't hurt me. Nobody's allowed to hurt me. That was my punishment. Not being hurt."

HB: What scenes were the most fun to write?

NG: A lot of them revolved around Loki. There was his dirty old joke: "You're ugly, you're hairy, and you're covered in shit. But you're mine, and I love you!" And his speech about murder and theology: "There's a theory that for a human to be killed by a God is the best thing that could possibly happen to the human under discussion. It eliminates all questions of belief, while manifestly placing a human life at the service of a higher power." And his threat to the Corinthian in part 9—"They can kill you, but we can kill you worse"—which is an R. A. Lafferty line.

MARC HEMPEL / D'ISRAELI

Cluracan of Faerie strays from the path the Sandman set him on, resulting in the creation of a monstrous stag.

But my favorite Loki bit is in part 10, when he's trying to get Thor to kill him.

HB: Yes, I have that right here: "Psst! Your wife, Thor. The Lady Sif. She has a birth-mark, high on the inside of her thigh, in the shape of an anvil." "How do you know that?" "She let me lick it. She let me do far more than that. She went down on her knees and swore to be my slave. She let me whip her, with a whip of leather. She let me explore every crevice of her body. She let me do things she swore blind she had never let you do to her. And when I was sated, she begged me—she pleaded with me to come back to her and do it again . . ." [*Laughter.*]

You just mentioned the Corinthian—of whom Puck says in part 10, "I shall restrain myself from inquiring whether you take your name from the letters, the pillars, the leather, the place, or the mode of behavior." What thoughts went into his revival?

NG: Strangely enough, Duncan Idaho in Frank Herbert's *Dune Messiah*. Most peo-ple read *Dune* first and then feel let down by *Dune Messiah*; but luckily, I read the lat-ter first and really liked it . . . and then felt kind of let down by *Dune*, which by comparison is kind of big and clunky and obvious. I was especially struck by Duncan Idaho being brought back to life, or recreated, with some of his own mem-ories but not *all* of them, so that he had to live with knowing he wasn't necessarily the same person.

Similarly, one of the reasons the Sandman saved the Corinthian's skull in issue 14—which we later see stored in a treasure chest in issue 27—is that it retained a fragment of his essence; and that's what Dream used to create the Corinthian Mark II. I also thought it would be fun for readers to genuinely not know if the new Corinthian would end up being just as murderous, or even more so, than the last one.

Of course, bringing the Corinthian back also allowed me to foreshadow what hap-pens at the end with Daniel. Those are distinctly different events, though. There's some question as to whether the Corinthian lives again; but the Sandman has defi-nitely died.

HB: Which reminds me: in the midst of the gorgeous "horse-drawn carriage to train" sequence, you placed a memorable short poem. Where did that come from?

NG: The phrase "You can be me when I'm gone" was something I said years ago to author Geoff Ryman at a science fiction convention. I was leaving early, so I took off my name badge and said, "Here you go, Geoff. You can be me when I'm gone." And I found that line echoing in my head, so I decided to use it in *Sandman*. I wrote six or seven verses based around it, but only two made it into *The Kindly Ones*. The first is the one you mentioned, on page 16 of part 11, and the second appears on the final page of the storyline.

HB: A number of the *Sandman* collections jump back and forth between the wak-ing and dreaming worlds, which has the potential to be confusing. You created an interesting technique to deal with that in *The Kindly Ones*.

NG: Yes; we color-coded the spaces between the panels. For scenes taking place in the waking world, we left the spaces white; and for scenes in other realms such as The Dreaming, we colored the spaces gray. It's not something anyone's meant to consciously notice, but it works as a subliminal color cue to help the reader know where he or she is at all points. It also occasionally provided important plot information—like on pages 5 through 8 of part 9, where Desire is meeting with Rose, and the coloring between the panels is gray.

HB: You play around with colors in another way in that scene. On page 20, Delirium says to Nuala, "I wish I could give you a present. Do you need a word that means red and green at the same time?" That word is provided by Celia Cripps on page 22: *sinople*, which can represent either red or green.

NG: Yep. By the way, the aunt Celia Cripps refers to there is the late Ethel Cripps—that is, the former mistress of Burgess, and John Dee's mother, in *Preludes & Nocturnes*.

HB: Which is just one of many references in *The Kindly Ones* to prior collections. They aren't all verbal, either; you also echoed a number of previous images. Could you flip through the stack of *Sandman* books in front of us and point some out?

NG: Sure. In part 3 of *The Kindly Ones*, the scenes of the Sandman threatening to take Lyta's baby on pages 23 and 24 are fairly explicit copies of scenes on page 23 of issue 12 and page 13 of issue 22.

On page 21 of part 5, Lyta and her two reflections in a mirror—one of whom tells her to "Take a moment to reflect"—are a recap of the scene on page 9 of issue 12 in which Lyta sits in front of a mirror. And we see that again on page 17 of part 7.

There's a sort of double echo at the end of part 11: page 23 repeats the sequence where the Sandman puts on his "battle glove" on page 23 of issue 11; and page 24 gives us the same "Dream framed by an arch as he's about to go to war" image we previously saw on the last pages of both issue 11 and issue 22. In *The Kindly Ones*, though, Dream is framed by the Ladies; and he says, "Rules and responsibilities: these are the ties that bind us. We do what we do, because of who we are. If we did otherwise, we would not be ourselves. I will do what I have to do. And I will do what I must."

Part 12 is crammed with references to past issues. On page 1, Daniel is playing in the background with the Wilkinson, Luz and Martin Tenbones toys from *A Game of You*. On page 2, the Sandman talks about the Eagle Stone emerald, which was first mentioned back in issue 17—Richard Madoc's new best-selling novel was titled *Eagle Stones*. Pages 4 and 5 visually echo scenes in issues 22 and 23; page 12 captures the look of pages 8 and 17 of issue 12; and the mountain the Sandman flies to is similar to the mountain in the *Fables and Reflections* short story "Fear of Flying."

Also, the top of page 24 recalls Matthew's flight on pages 16 and 17 of issue 11. The middle of page 24, where the Sandman sheds his clothing, is a sort of reverse-echo of the scenes in *The Doll's House* and *Season of Mists* where he suited up for war. And page 22 of part 13 is, of course, the scene that was first hinted at on page 14 of issue 47, when Destiny was flipping through his book in *Brief Lives*.

HB: I was very amused when, in the last few issues, you even started echoing scenes that had occurred previously in *The Kindly Ones*.

NG: Right. For example, the scene in Hal's dressing room on page 11 of part 12 reprises the scene of Lucifer getting dressed on pages 3 and 4 of part 4.

I also really like that on page 21 of part 9, Dream tells Thessaly, "I did not intend to hurt you." Thess coldly replies, "And what if you did not? Intent and outcome are so rarely coincident." Then on page 7 of part 11, Nuala tells Dream, "I did not mean to harm you"; and he says, "I know that, Nuala. But, as has recently been pointed out to me, intent and outcome are rarely coincident." [*Laughter.*]

The point of all this visual and verbal repetition was, of course, to create resonance, and a sense of closure.

HB: That comes through in the final sequence, when we return to the Fates: "So. It's finished." "What did we make? What was it, in the end?" "What it always is. A handful of yarn; a little weaving and stitching; some embroidering perhaps. A few loose ends, but that's only to be expected ..." And then, as a cat is viciously playing with a mouse at her feet, the Mother says, "It's the same old story ... Whatever it turns into on the way, whatever it is you originally undertake to spin or knit or weave, keep it going long enough and, in the end, my lilies, it's always a winding sheet."

NG: Which goes back to *Sandman* 6 and the waitress in the all-night diner: "All Bette's stories have happy endings. That's because she knows where to stop. She's realized the real problem with stories—if you keep them going long enough, they always end in death."

HB: It also makes me think of Hob's dream in part 3.

NG: That was something that actually happened to me. I dreamt about a friend who'd died six months earlier, woke up completely upset that she'd died, and then realized I'd simply had a dream and felt enormously relieved ... and then I woke up all the way and remembered that she really had passed on.

—

the wake

12

What the caterpillar calls a tragedy, the Master calls a butterfly.

—RICHARD BACH

The climax of *Sandman* occurs in *The Kindly Ones*, when the title character dies. However, *The Wake* ties up loose ends, offers us some insights about the new Dream, gives us a chance to say good-bye to the series, and sheds some final light on the Sandman whose world we've lived in for two thousand pages.

The heart of this collection is its first three chapters, which play off the different meanings of *wake*. Chapter 1, "Which Occurs in the Wake of What Has Gone Before," deals with the aftermath of the Sandman's death; chapter 2, "In Which a Wake Is Held," is about the *Finnegan's Wake*-style gathering in which people drink too much and tell stories; and chapter 3, "In Which We Wake," ends the dream—and, in many ways, ends the series. Following these chapters is an epilogue, "Sunday Mourning," that allows us to spend some time with Hob Gadling at a Renaissance festival; a sequel to issue 39's "Soft Places" that features both the old and new Dream; and a sequel to issue 19's "A Midsummer Night's Dream" that concludes the deal the Sandman made with William Shakespeare.

The story begins with each of the five Endless being visited by a winged messenger who summons them to the Necropolis Litharge (last seen in *Worlds' End*) to obtain the cerements and the Book of Ritual for the Sandman's funeral. Just who sent the messenger is never specified, as "there are some powers that no one, even the Endless, seeks to inquire into too deeply."

Four of the Endless sculpt an envoy from mud; Death breathes life into the statue's mouth; and Delirium names him Eblis O'Shaughnessy. With a Lion's Mane jellyfish floating above his head to light his way, Eblis enters the catacombs beneath the city and locates the Hall of Cerements (last seen in #55), where a mysterious voice asks, "WHICH OF THEM IS DEAD?" and Eblis answers "Dream." The voice then directs Eblis to take a leather-covered book and a cerecloth embroidered with Dream's helmet.

Meanwhile, the Sandman's replacement, Daniel, is busy resurrecting inhabitants of The Dreaming who were killed by the Kindly Ones, including Abel and Mervyn Pumpkinhead. But when Daniel tries to restore Fiddler's Green, Gilbert objects by saying, "If you bring me back to life, my death will have no meaning. I had a fine existence. I was a good place.... I lived a good life, and it ended. Would you take that away from me?" And so Daniel lets Gilbert rest in peace.

Another resident of The Dreaming who hasn't recovered from recent events is Matthew, who feels guilty about still being alive when *his* friend is dead. Matthew directs his feelings of anger and resentment at Daniel, saying "I was *his* friend. I'm not *your* anything." The old Dream might have become furious at being spoken to in such a manner, but Daniel responds with simple honesty: "This is very new to me, Matthew. This place. This world. I have existed since the beginning of time. This is a true thing. I am older than worlds and suns and gods. But tomorrow I will meet my brother and sisters for the first time. And I am afraid." Over the course of the story, Matthew comes to respect Daniel's straightforwardness, gentleness, and kindness, and so learns to get past his grief and befriend the new Dream.

Daniel isn't allowed to attend the Sandman's wake, but virtually everyone else is, resulting in cameos from dozens of characters we've met over the course of the series. These include: the Corinthian (who first appeared in chapter 1: page 10), Eve (1:13), Nuala (1:15), Rose Walker (1:15), author Richard Madoc (1:15), Lyta Hall (1:18), Alex Burgess (1:18), Hob Gadling (1:18), Queen Titania (1:21), the silent angel Duma (1:21), Lady Bast (1:21), Chiron the Centaur (1:23), Lord Ruthven the vampire rabbit and his Marie Antoinette–like companion (2:3), Taramis the waiter (2:3), the Fashion Thing (2:3), Lucien (2:3), Calliope (2:5), Thessaly (2:5), the reincarnated Nada (2:5), Lyta Hall's onetime date Eric Needham (2:7), Mad Hettie (2:10), Cluracan (2:11), Cluracan's Nemesis (2:12), Merv Pumpkinhead's companion Abudah (2:13), the Guardians of the Gate (2:16), Jed Walker (2:17), the immortal Indian king "Bhartari Raja" (2:18), Clark Kent a.k.a. Superman (2:22), Batman (2:22), Martian Manhunter (2:22), John Constantine (2:22), The Phantom Stranger (2:22), Doctor Occult (2:22), Barnabas (2:23), Destruction (3:6), Emperor Norton (3:7), Wesley Dodds, DC's original Sandman (3:11), Lucifer (3:14), Mazikeen (3:14), the Alder Man as a bear (3:15), Odin (3:15), Shivering Jemmy of the Shallow Brigade (3:15), Pharamond (3:15), Alinanora/Eleanora/Alianore (3:15), Anubis (3:17), Thor and his hammer (3:17), Orpheus (3:18), John Dee a.k.a. Doctor Destiny (3:19), and Paul McGuire (3:22).

Also making cameos are characters who were never given names. These include the old man with a swan's arm who tended the castle's back stairs in issue 64 (1:17); the couple who served the visiting gods food in issue 26 (2:1); the lady with the eyepatch who helped Taramis serve a meal to Dream and Delirium in issue 42 (2:3); and the horned pantherlike creature who ran Brant Tucker off the road in issue 51 (3:2). In addition, various characters who never before appeared in the series are sprinkled throughout, such as DC's supervillain Darkseid (3:7) and the god Kronos, who fathered Zeus and has four wings (3:17). Even real-life people put in an appearance, such as the story's creators, Neil Gaiman and Michael Zulli (3:15), and you, the reader (3:24).

Between the casual chatter during the wake and the speeches for the funeral ceremony, a number of characters help shed light on both the Sandman and themselves. One particularly notable conversation takes place on page 4 of Chapter 2, between Lucien (who was revealed in *The Kindly Ones* to be the first raven, which can metaphorically be read as "first man"), Cain and Abel (who represent the first children), and Eblis O'Shaughnessy (the youngest character there, having just been created from mud). Eblis is confused after meeting Daniel: "The young lord in white—who was he?" "He is Dream of the Endless," replies Lucien. "So . . . who died?" asks Eblis. "Nobody died," says Cain. "How can you kill an idea? How can you kill the personification of an action?" "Then what died? Who are you mourning?" pursues Eblis. And Abel answers, "A puh-point of view."

In additional to such verbal exchanges, there are a number of visual clues and in-jokes. For example, Abel's comment is pictorially confirmed on page 4 of chapter 3, where it's shown that the Sandman's cerement doesn't cover an actual body because an idea doesn't have a body. Instead, the cerement itself takes on the shape of a body.

Another visual clue appears on page 19 of chapter 2, where Lucien enjoys a second family reunion—he sits drinking in Eve's cave with "Bhartari Raja," the former Indian king from #53 who became immortal by consuming a special fruit. From seeing the three of them grouped together, we can surmise that Eve and Lucien/Adam represent the couple who ate from the Garden of Eden's Tree of Knowledge (which helps explains why Lucien is such a good librarian); and that the fruit the Indian king ate from was the Tree of Life.

After the funeral, a couple of the attendees drift to the castle to see Daniel. Lyta Hall seeks to find her son in the new Dream, but is informed, "What was mortal of Daniel was burned away. What was immortal was transfigured. I am Dream of the Endless." Lyta then fears being punished for her part in killing the old Dream, but Daniel—in marked contrast to his predecessor—tells her that vengeance "is a road that has no ending." Kissing her forehead, he continues, "You have my mark on you, Lyta Hall. No one shall harm you. Put your life together once more. Go in peace."

Daniel's second visitor is Alex Burgess, who was very much a victim of the Sandman's vengeance. Once again, though, Daniel showers forgiveness on his guest, and sends those who attended the funeral "home," back to the waking world.

Finally, with Matthew perched on his shoulder softly proclaiming, "The king is dead, long live the king," Daniel walks into the dining hall to meet his family. And set between windows that let show through a twinkling night sky dominated by the Sandman's shining star, a final series of captions read: ". . . and then, fighting to stay asleep, wishing it would go on forever, sure that once the dream was over, it would never come back . . . you woke up."

Chapter 3 effectively ends the series, but some of the story threads left dangling are addressed in the subsequent three issues. The epilogue, "Sunday Mourning," lets us watch Hob Gadling and his new girlfriend Gwen at a Renaissance festival. While Hob sits alone drinking, Death comes to visit him to confirm that his friend the Sandman has indeed—as he dreamed some months back—passed away. To ease his sadness, Hob articulates his own theory of death: "I used to think it was a big, sudden thing, like a huge owl that would swoop down out of the night and carry you off. I don't anymore. I think it's a slow thing. Like a thief who comes to your house day after day, taking a little thing here and a little thing there, and one day you walk round your house and there's nothing there at all, nothing to keep you, nothing to make you want to stay. And then you lie down and shut up forever. Lots of little deaths until the last big one." "It's an idea I've heard before," says Death. "And?" asks Hob. But Death just smiles a smile that says, "No, I'm not going to tell you *that*."

Death then offers to let Hob find out for himself, but Gadling declines. He adds that it's possible he'll *never* want to die; but he definitely doesn't want to give up the ghost right now because if he did, "Gwen'd kill me."

A little later, Hob falls asleep and meets his old friend the Sandman, accompanied by a jolly Destruction (whom Hob describes as "a pavement artist I met"). Remembering his previous conversation, Hob asks Morpheus, "You're dead, aren't you? And this is just a dream?" As Hob later describes it to Gwen, "He nodded, and we started laughing. Well, me and the pavement artist were laughing, anyway. And the three of us went off together, into the sunset, into the end of the story. And then you woke me up." Gwen responds, "Sweet dream," and asks about how it ended. "Well," says Hob," there's only one way to end a story, really." "Don't tell me," says Gwen. *"They all lived happily ever after?"* "That's the one," says Hob. The couple then drive into the same sunset Hob dreamed about, while in the foreground we partially see a traffic sign that says One Way with an arrow pointing upward.

The next tale, "Exiles," is described in its script as "the only completely redundant episode of *Sandman*. Redundant in that it's being done purely for fun, and to see whether it works or not." A follow-up to "Soft Places" in *Fables and Reflections*, it's a poetic journey by a Chinese advisor to emperors who, about seven hundred years ago, was cast out after his son committed an act that offended the state. While traveling to his assigned place of exile, Master Li becomes lost in a desert that shows him fragments of the past and future. He first meets the ghost of his son, whose head was cut off as punishment for dabbling in White Lotus magic. "Had you been content with life's surfaces," says the father, "we would all have been happier. Nothing good came of your studies into the magical arts." The Sage next runs into the old Dream, with whom he has much in common: Dream's son, Orpheus, also had his head ripped off for digging beneath "life's surfaces," and it soon becomes clear that we're seeing the Sandman during the period shortly after he killed his son. Dream tells this tale: "There was once a sage who loved his only son as much as you loved yours. One day the son died, and yet the father shed no tears and made no mourning. When they asked why, he told them, I did not mourn him before he was born, and I will not mourn him now he is gone. What do you think of that?" Master Li replies, "I think that was foolishness. You mourn, for it is proper to mourn. But your grief serves you: you do not become a slave to grief. You bid the dead farewell, and you continue." The Sandman replies, "Indeed": but it's advice he apparently couldn't bring himself to follow.

The Sage next meets Daniel, who ties up a hanging plot thread by finally freeing the riders in #39 from their endless wandering, noting, "I have no liking for prisons." Daniel then demonstrates that he's learned from his predecessor's experiences by observing: "Sometimes I suspect that we build our traps ourselves, then we back into them, pretending amazement the while"—which is, of course, a concise description of what happened to the Sandman. Daniel adds, "But whether this is the case or no, it is still a worthy thing to open cages, it is still a virtuous act to free the imprisoned"; and in that spirit, he offers Master Li a job as his advisor. The old man again shows he has much in common with the old Sandman, however, by deciding he must honor his emperor and continue to the small town where he's been ordered to live out his remaining days.

Finally, issue 75 gives us an elderly William Shakespeare writing his last great play, *The Tempest*, for the Sandman.

As Shakespeare composes his play, we see how his daughter Judith might have been an inspiration for the character of Miranda, how her boyfriend Tom Quiney might have fueled the Bard's vision of Caliban, and how various other people, events, and passions in Shakespeare's life could have been transformed into material for his art. Along the way, we also get a sense of Shakespeare's relationships with Judith and his wife, Anne, and how they were affected by his devotion to his work.

After he finishes *The Tempest* and their bargain is done, Shakespeare asks the Sandman why he requested this particular play. Dream replies he wanted "a tale of graceful ends ... a play about a king who drowns his books, and breaks his staff, and leaves his kingdom. About a magician who becomes a man. About a man who turns his back on magic." In other words, while *A Midsummer Night's Dream* was for the Faerie folk, this play is for the Sandman himself.

Of course, *The Tempest* is also about Shakespeare, who never wrote another play by himself after completing it. And, in a larger sense, it's about all artists—including Neil Gaiman, who with this tale draws to a close his two-thousand-page epic tale of gods, myths and dreams.

SOME THINGS WORTH NOTICING

In chapter 3 of *The Wake*, Matthew says, "Funeral's over. Time to get on with our lives. Time to grow up." Ultimately, growing up is what *Sandman* is about. Like a caterpillar shedding a cocoon, Morpheus sheds his life to make way for a potentially wiser and more humane replacement; a better and brighter Dream.

There's no end to growing up, either. In "Exiles," Daniel comments, "Tools, of course, can be the subtlest of traps. One day, I know, I must smash the emerald . . . But that day can wait." On one level, Daniel is saying that he will eventually destroy the green dreamstone that stores a large portion of his power, just as (in issue 7) the Sandman needed his red ruby shattered and its power freed before he could feel whole. On another level, though, Daniel's comment can be read as meaning that one day he, too, must give up everything that ties him to a physical existence; that one day he, too, must smash his life, abandon his form, and move on. When that day comes, it won't be a tragedy; as the wandering Roman rider notes in the same story, *Omnia mutantur, nihil interit*; i.e., "Everything changes, but nothing is truly lost."

Which leaves the question, who was the Sandman?

On one level, we can see him as any workaholic who's utterly comfortable when doing his job, but falls flat when having to deal with people outside of that defined function.

We can also see him as a calcified adult who's forgotten the wonders of childhood, who's become so stuffy that he's lost his sense of play—in other words, who's the opposite of Delirium. As *Brief Lives* demonstrated, neither of the extremes represented by these two Endless is a practical way to live; but Delirium had the wisdom to reach out for a balancing influence, first via Destruction and then via Barnabas. Despite repeated chances to do the same, the Sandman consistently opted to stand alone . . . and so he died.

Then again, because The Dreaming was a part of him, the Sandman literally lived in his own mind—which makes him a metaphor for the artist. The dangers of spending so much time in your head is demonstrated by one of Sandman's analogues, William Shakespeare, who wrote plays that are destined to be immortal but was so obsessed with doing so that he sacrificed his relationships with his wife and children . . . and the life of his son, Hamnet.

On yet another level, the Sandman can be seen as representing our old conceptions of gods as rule bound, vengeful, and demanding worship from on high. Looked at this way, his relinquishing his role as Dream to a flesh-and-blood human being was an acknowledgment that his power stemmed from us, and that it had to remain connected to its source. Joseph Campbell used to tell a myth about a man who travels to the Underworld and consumes his gods, saying, "I and the father are one. I have the power to be born a second time; I am reincarnation. I am that source from which the gods arise." Campbell described this as the man's realization that his gods were projections of our own energies.

But all we can ultimately say is that the Sandman was a highly complex character who starred in a comics masterpiece created by Neil Gaiman and a small army of collaborators. Like a dream, the Sandman's identity and meaning depend on your own personal reading of him.

OBLIGING WORDS AND NAKED PENCILS

HB: *The Wake* is, of course, a wonderful multiple pun. When did the idea hit you?

NG: In 1991, while I was in the middle of *Season of Mists*. I was really happy when it did. It's rare that a word is so tremendously obliging.

HB: It's of a piece with how you bookended the whole series. The very first line of *Sandman*, at the top of page 1 in *Preludes & Nocturnes*, is: "Wake up, sir. We're here." Similarly, issue 72 closes the series down with "you woke up."

NG: Issue 72 can indeed be seen as the last *Sandman* tale, the end of the story proper. Issue 73 is the epilogue for *The Wake*; and issues 74 and 75 are epilogues, or codas, for the entire series.

HB: Daniel is quite a contrast to the late Sandman.

NG: Especially compared to the pre-imprisonment Sandman. If you read the series in chronological order—that is, start with "Tales in the Sand" in *The Doll's House*, then "The Song of Orpheus" in *Fables and Reflections*, and continue working your way up through time—just how stuffy and irritating the Sandman initially was becomes painfully clear. His seventy-two years of imprisonment changed him a great

TEDDY KRISTIANSEN

Sketches of Daniel, the new Sandman, for the Dreaming PVC figure set.

deal; more than he ever realized or understood. He was almost a different entity by the time he emerged from Burgess's glass cage.

HB: Along similar lines, your artistic approach to *The Wake* was markedly different from what had gone before. In your script for chapter 1, you wrote: "It should be, in many ways, the opposite of *The Kindly Ones*. Lots of sunlight, lots of outdoors stuff, a feeling of space. Lots of large panels. I like the idea of many of the panels having slightly rounded edges, like playing cards. Everything very, very realistic, not stylized."

NG: We used an iconographic art style for *The Kindly Ones*, so for *The Wake* I wanted to go entirely in the other direction, with a style that was as detailed and naturalistic as possible. I felt Michael Zulli was the best choice for that; we'd worked together since *Sandman* 13, and I knew he could bring a level of hyperrealism to the story that would perfectly match what I had in mind. The accuracy of that judgment can be seen in his first seven pages, with his wonderful illustrations of the different birds, and the Necropolis Litharge, and the Endless constructing Eblis. I wanted to go a step further on this final storyline, though, and so started lobbying for DC to publish directly from Michael's pencils.

HB: What was your objection to the traditional inking process?

NG: Michael used to send me his pencilled pages, and they'd be breathtaking; and then they'd come back after being inked, and there would inevitably be some loss of detail, which saddened me. Inking came about because it's easier to reproduce dark lines than feathery pencil work; but by 1995, I felt that technology was at a point where anything could be scanned in, even pencils.

DC was very doubtful, so Michael drew a test page of Death with an eagle. We scanned it in and colored it, and the page that resulted was absolutely gorgeous, with no loss of detail. Therefore, DC ultimately acceded to the idea and let Michael do issues 70 through 73 in pencils only, with no inker. I'd say it's the only time readers got a sense of what Michael Zulli really does, what his stuff actually looks like.

POETRY AND FLOWERS

HB: On the first page of the collection is a poem. Can you provide some information about it?

NG: It's titled "The Bridge of Fire" by James Elroy Flecker: "Gods on their bridge above whispering lies and love shall mock your passage down the sunless river which, rolling all its streams, shall take you, king of dreams—unthroned and unapproachable forever—to where the kings who dreamed of old whiten in habitations monumental cold." I came across it in a book of poetry four years before the end, and I just went, "There we go. There's *The Wake*."

Flecker died in 1915 and, sadly, his work is almost forgotten except for "The Golden Road to Samarkand." That poem reads, "What would ye ladies? It was ever thus. Men are unwise and curiously planned. They have their dreams and do not

Michael Zulli was enthusiastic about Neil Gaiman's brainstorm of printing *The Wake* directly from his pencils. "The practice of inking comes from comics' history as a cheap throwaway item—thick black lines reproduce really well on cheap paper and cheap presses," says Zulli. "But those kinds of compromises are no longer necessary with modern technology." In addition, Zulli prefers the soft, moody look of pencils, because "they give illustrations an organic human dimension." He also prefers the visually open quality of pencils. "I find the gray whisper of the graphite line on paper incredibly evocative," he says. "When you ink something, you get a black line on white paper, and it's irrevocable. But a pencil line slips between the cracks of perception; it can go somewhere else, it has possibilities. And *The Wake* is full of possibilities: interior, surreal stuff that you can't put your finger on, like mercury. That's the pleasure of it—you keep reaching for something and it slips away, leading you into places in your head that you'd never thought to go."

There were some technical challenges to overcome, though. "The lettering had to be laid over the artwork," Zulli explains, "and being black with 100 percent saturation—versus the 70 percent or so saturation of the pencils—the dialogue looked like it was floating above the drawings instead of being fully integrated with them." Zulli and letterer Todd Klein found two solutions. "Pencil lead can shoot as black if it's heavy enough," says Zulli, "and I found that with the black borders and enough dark pencilling, the page automatically calmed itself right down. And in cases where we couldn't rely on that trick, we shot the page at 90 percent instead of 100 percent black, so it looked black but wasn't. Using those two techniques, we fooled the reader's eye to make the overlays gel with the rest of the work."

think of us. We take the Golden Road to Samarkand." I have the sailor-girl "Jim" misquote the poem in *Sandman* 53; and the play the poem appears in, Flecker's *Hassan*, was an important inspiration for *Sandman* 50, "Ramadan."

HB: Flecker isn't the only poet referenced in *The Wake*.

NG: True; there's also Arthur O'Shaughnessy, after whom I named Eblis O'Shaughnessy. Arthur is a late-nineteenth-century writer who's most famous for a poem titled "Ode," which is about what artists are for: "We, in the ages lying, in the buried past of the earth, built Nineveh with our sighing and Babel itself with our mirth; and o'erthrew them with prophesying, to the old of the new world's worth; for each age is a dream that is dying, or one that is coming to birth."

Much of the feel of *The Wake* comes from the romantic period of Flecker and O'Shaughnessy, around the turn of the last century. That's because Michael Zulli's art style is fundamentally Whistler and Astor—that is, art from the 1880s and 1890s.

HB: That fits with Michael telling me he used lots of Art Nouveau motifs. For example, the crypt Eblis enters was based on the Secession building in Vienna, which was designed around 1900.

Michael also said he leaned heavily on the work of the Symbolists, a group of turn-of-the-century painters who anticipated psychoanalysis by determining that certain objects often represented other things in a viewer's mind, and so deliberately selected images to evoke specific impressions or feelings. For example, Michael used a book that sprang from their theories, *The Language of Flowers*, when deciding to draw blue roses on the first page of chapter 3, and on the Sandman's bier, because "blue roses are the symbol of the subconscious and death."

NG: Michael also did a beautiful job with flowers during the speeches of the Endless in chapter 3. On page 5, Destiny has hydrangeas and foxgloves at his feet. On page 8, Desire is surrounded by red roses. On page 10, Despair stands amidst the same roses, which in her presence have wilted. And on page 12, we get Delirium's flowers ... which consist of yellow daisies, plastic pink flamingo and butterfly lawn ornaments, and an octopus. [*Laughter.*]

HB: There's one other subtle thing I noticed Michael did with flowers. On page 15 of chapter 1, Richard Madoc—the author who imprisoned Calliope in issue 17— is sitting in a deck chair in "the gray morning chill." He's wearing black leather gloves, presumably to hide the damage he did to his hands after the Sandman gave him more ideas than he could handle. And behind him is a virtual explosion of flowers, which doesn't make much sense, given that the scene appears to be taking place in January ... until you realize that the flowers are an indication that Richard is in the process of falling asleep and slipping into a dream.

NG: Yes. Which is why when we return to a waking Richard on page 23 of chapter 3, we see that the plant life around him is actually pretty nonexistent outside of some January plants, and a few recalcitrant dead leaves clinging to the tree above him. We received letters pointing this out as a continuity error, but it's not at all; it's just a reflection of the fact that he came into the story dreaming and left it wide awake.

OLD FRIENDS AND LOVERS

HB: I chatted with Samuel R. Delany about *The Wake*, and he praised it in musical terms, saying, "Its movement and rhythm created a stately and elegant conclusion." He added: "The way so many elements were slowed down and at the same time brought back, in a very musically satisfying way, established a note of unity that resonated back through all of the previous stories."

NG: Much of the joy of doing *The Wake* was bringing back characters we've met throughout the series. I felt that was part of the process of saying good-bye.

For example—leafing through the pages—on page 2 of chapter 2, I see a couple who was last seen serving dinner in chapter 5 of *Season of Mists*. I always meant to do a story about them trying to get together in the real world, and why it would've been impossible; but I never did.

The appearance of Cluracan and his Nemesis in chapter 2 was a fun scene to write, since the two of them have the same speech patterns, a kind of Irish brogue.

Rose Walker runs into Lyta Hall on page 17 of chapter 2, and when she asks who the party is for, Lyta answers, "A monster. They are celebrating the death of a monster." Rose then announces that she's pregnant, and Lyta's advice is, "Kill it, Rose Walker. Kill it before it breaks your heart."

On page 7 of chapter 3, Lady Bast steps up to say something I wouldn't mind on my own tombstone: "These things alone do I now regret: Things left unsaid." And in the panel directly below, we placed two emperors: DC Comics super villain Darkseid sitting over at the left, and Emperor Norton from *Sandman* 31 sitting on the right.

Page 15 of chapter 3 is an especially loaded one. In the bottom half, speeches are being given by Odin and Shivering Jemmy, who both first appeared in *Season of Mists*; Pharamond, the god who oversaw transportation in *Brief Lives*; and Alianora, a former lover of the Sandman who appeared in *A Game of You*, and is now dead but came back to say her little bit.

And in the top half of the page, we see a speech from the Alder Man of *Brief Lives*— who's still a bear. If you look closely at the crowd listening to him, you can find me and Michael Zulli in the upper right; and in the upper left, Alice Cooper, with whom Michael and I collaborated in 1994 to create a comic book adaptation of Alice's album *The Last Temptation*.

HB: In addition to real-life people, and the scores of characters you created over the course of the series, there are a number of DC Comics characters who make appearances. You just mentioned one of them, Darkseid. A bunch more appear on page 22 of chapter 2.

NG: Well, *Sandman* began as a comic whose stories took place only a short hop from the rest of the DC Universe, so I felt it appropriate for characters from every period of *Sandman* to appear at Dream's wake.

HB: And so you gave us DC's three top mystery men, John Constantine, Phantom Stranger, and Doctor Occult—each of whom almost always wears a trenchcoat. With a drink in hand, Constantine remarks, "Nice trenchcoat" and Occult replies, "Thanks" while the Stranger looks at his pocket watch. [*Laughter.*]

The first panel is lots of fun, too, featuring three of DC's top super heroes: Superman, in his guise as Clark Kent; Batman; and Martian Manhunter.

NG: Actually, the original panel was a much longer shot, further back. It showed Clark Kent with his Superman cape coming out from under his suit, and Clark looking around in an attempt to see it as he's talking. [*Laughter.*]

I thought having his costume accidentally exposed is precisely the kind of thing Superman would dream about; but DC's Superman editor said it "showed disrespect to the character" and made us redraw the panel. It's a double pity, because the close-up shot also cost us a full-body view of Batman ... which would have made it clear that Bruce Wayne's dream version of Batman isn't entirely human.

HB: It all works well anyway, thanks to the dialogue—though only old-time comics readers are likely to recognize Clark's comments about having an ant's head, turning into a gorilla, and perpetually moving forward through time as references to classic Superman stories from the 1950s and 1960s.

It's also fun when Clark complains, "The one I hate is where I'm just an actor on a strange television version of my life. Have you ever had that dream?" and Batman responds, "Doesn't everyone?" because both Superman and Batman have had bizarre live-action TV shows based on them that mostly missed the wonderful fantasy and noir elements of their comic book tales. And it's a nice punchline when Martian Manhunter responds to Batman's cheery "Doesn't everyone?" with a grim "I don't"—because no one's ever bothered to make a TV series about the Manhunter.

NG: But his time will come. [*Laughter.*]

HB: Moving from the absurd to the sublime . . . page 5 of chapter 2 reintroduces us to four of the Sandman's lovers: the Greek muse Calliope; Queen Titania of Faerie; the Greek witch Thessaly; and, in her reincarnated child's body, the African queen Nada. Nada doesn't get to say anything—and, for that matter, neither does Alianora, a fifth Sandman lover—but can you comment on the speeches of the other three women?

NG: Let me first note that I would've liked to hear what Alianora had to say; we simply ran out of space.

Calliope speaks first, and she does a pretty good job of dissecting her relationship with Morpheus. She also explains why someone would be attracted to the Sandman: "When I first met him, he was the most gallant of lovers. He knew so many things. He delighted in sharing his knowledge. He had a castle filled with treasures, and he took such pleasure in showing them, giving them to me. He was so gentle, and his skin felt like white silk against my skin. When we made love it was like a flame: I felt utterly engulfed, utterly loved. Treasured. I have been with many poets, many dreamers. But his love alone was ice and fire. His eyes were stars."

HB: Despite that love, Calliope left Dream because of what happened to their son Orpheus. She blames not only the Sandman, but also his siblings: "The boy was foolish. My love's family . . . encouraged Orpheus' foolishness."

NG: That ellipsis is meant to indicate a pause while Calliope searches for a tactful word. She could go a lot further but realizes it's unwise to say bad things about the Endless when they're just a short distance away from you.

And eight pages later, Titania gets to do her little remembrance—which basically consists of saying, "Fuck off and mind your own business."

HB: That's why the lady is a queen. [*Laughter.*] And six pages after that, Thessaly speaks.

NG: Yep. And although readers never got to see the fight scene that caused Thess to leave the Sandman, they at least get her side of the relationship summed up here.

HB: There's a certain symmetry: in "Tales of the Sand," you only get the male version of the Nada story; so here we only get Thessaly's version of the affair. Of course, she's lying when she says she never loved the Sandman.

NG: Of course; I think that's made explicit by the final panel, where she says, "I swore I would never shed another tear for him" while crying. But after he'd won her and then returned to his duties, he wasn't enough for her anymore. She wanted attention; and when she wasn't getting it, she said, "Right. We're done," and walked out on him.

I always wanted the relationship to be one of those strange things where two friends of yours get together, and you can't see it at all; and you know it's going to end in disaster, but you can't do anything about it. You can never quite get inside someone's head or follow the ways of the heart.

RESURRECTIONS AND GOOD-BYES

HB: We should also discuss the characters from The Dreaming—some of whom needed to be resurrected.

NG: Those scenes are some of my very favorites. I really enjoyed Daniel's construction of Merv Pumpkinhead on pages 15 and 16 of chapter 1. And I loved the resurrection of Fiddler's Green, two pages later, in which Gilbert refuses to come back from the dead.

HB: It made for a nice contrast with Matthew, who didn't die but initially wishes he had.

NG: Matthew played a very important role in *The Wake*. Daniel is actually much gentler and kinder than the Sandman we've followed throughout the series, but the fact remains that he's not *our* Sandman; and he'll never be. So we're simply not going to like Daniel right away.

Matthew therefore gets to be us. I wanted him to stand for every reader who was pissed off about the Sandman being dead, who missed the old Dream and felt he was irreplaceable.

I think that comes through on pages 13 and 14 of chapter 1, where Matthew is hurt and grieving and doesn't want to see anybody, least of all Daniel. But by page 9 of chapter 2, Matthew turns up at the castle and talks to Daniel, starting a process of bridge building. And by the end of chapter 3, Matthew has decided to accept Daniel and extend a hand—or claw—of friendship.

HB: You also use *The Wake* to make Matthew's past fairly explicit to knowledgeable comics readers. On page 19 of chapter 2, Matthew refuses a glass of wine, saying, "I don't drink. I stopped drinking the hard way."

NG: And Lucien responds, "The night can make a man more brave but not more sober." That's a quote from the Alan Moore–scripted issue of *Swamp Thing* 27, in which Matt Cable dies from drunk driving. That is, the first time he dies—Matt died a lot. [*Laughter.*]

HB: And as The Dreaming's librarian, of course, Lucien had read *Swamp Thing* and so can quote from it.

Mervyn Pumpkinhead, the "voice of the workingman," who serves as a counterpoint to Dream's somber nature.

Matthew the Raven, messenger and counselor to the Sandman.

NG: Lucien is definitely well-read. He's also quite perceptive; a couple of panels later, he pronounces what I'd say is a very charitable and accurate summary of what actually happened to the Sandman: "Sometimes, perhaps, one must change or die. And, in the end, there were, perhaps, limits to how much he could let himself change."

HB: One example of how much more the Sandman would've needed to change appears on page 6 of chapter 3—the scene with Daniel and the Guardians of the Gate.

NG: Yes, where Daniel just instinctively scratches the head of the gryphon and pats the winged horse, and the latter says, "In the thousands of years that I served him, he did not touch me. He fed me slices of apple, with his hands, though, from time to time." Through the whole series, we never see the Sandman touch anybody in affection; and it was fairly clear that he didn't like to *be* touched, either. He would indeed have still had a long way to go.

HB: Could you walk us through the rest of the other highlights in chapter 3?

NG: Sure. On the next page, Rose and her brother discuss her pregnancy. He says, "So I'll be Uncle Jed. Coooool. Families rock." Rose replies, "Aren't you the one that told me 'families suck'?" And Jed answers, "They do both. They rock *and* they suck." I really like that comment, because it sums up the way I tried to handle the Endless.

I also thought it appropriate that Jed's remark was immediately followed by Desire, who essentially says the same thing but takes a whole page instead of five words to do it.

And then we get to see Destruction pay a visit. Echoing his encounter with the Sandman in *Brief Lives*, he says, "You've never been inclined to listen to my advice in the past, but, well, things change, don't they?" Daniel, who knows this to be true, says, "Yes, they do." And Destruction says, "Wise lad." I love the kitchen range that Michael drew on page 9, by the way—all the beautiful little details, including the garlic hanging from the sink, and the big old stove.

I should also mention that the first two panels of page 13 are a visual pun—a pair of men crossing a bridge while two birds fly overhead is a famous image from a willow pattern plate, which is a Chinese pattern that appears on plates and crockery and was very popular during the Victorian era. I like what Destruction says after they cross: "Entropy and optimism: the twin forces that make the universe go around." I believe that.

the wake

HB: In between those Destruction scenes, we get a tender speech from Despair, and a silent "speech" from the angel Duma, who sheds a tear in which each member of the audience sees reflected "mercy, and miracles, and the knowledge that every thing that is, has a purpose, and the purpose, somehow, included every one of them on a deep and personal level." We also get Delirium's wonderful eulogy: "He was my big brother. He really was. I was always a bit scared of him. But I'm not scared of him anymore. I'm a bit sad of him instead. Okay. That's all."

And, to my amusement, there was a brief speech from Wesley Dodds, who was DC's original Sandman—a costumed crime fighter with a gas gun.

NG: Wes made it in mostly because he was still fresh on my mind; I'd recently coplotted and dialogued the *Sandman Midnight Theatre* graphic novel with Matt Wagner, in which Wesley stars.

Then the rest of the speakers come on, although the last one we actually get to hear is Matthew on page 14—accompanied by a lovely illustration of Lucifer and Mazikeen.

HB: Did the subsequent characters lack interesting things to say?

NG: Not at all; but I had to wrap everything up by the end of that twenty-four-page issue, and at that point I was running out of space. Therefore, Michael and I started sneaking in all the characters we could, even if they couldn't get speaking parts.

In fact, I'd planned to have Lucien give the final speech, which included his reading a poem by James Elroy Flecker that Flecker had never written, only dreamed; but there was no room for it.

I'd also written a speech for Death we couldn't fit in, but it's probably just as well. I ended up replacing it with two captions that simply describe her speech: "Now the girl in the red dress talks to you all, as the boat begins its passage down the slow stream. And her words make sense of everything. She gives you peace. She gives you meaning. And she bids her brother goodbye." That felt right to me; and it also served to emphasize that we were in a dream.

HB: You've just touched on the beginning of the barge sequence. As I recall, that was a problem in the original comic.

NG: Again, we were very tight on space at that point, and Michael had to squeeze it into two pages. That bothered us so much that DC permitted Michael to redo it for the collection, expanding the scene to four pages, which allowed him to create the proper pace and to put in more images.

I really like that whole sequence—the gods, angels, and others we first glimpsed in issue 55; Nada again, watching from the shore; and Orpheus with his lyre standing above the Waters of Night from issue 4. I also like that as Dream's body floats down the stream, the front of his boat transforms from a black swan to the Sandman's helm, and then to his head, and then to hands holding his red ruby. At that point, the boat flows toward a waterfall; and then it crashes past and over the waterfall into

MICHAEL ZULLI

A drawing of the new Sandman, Daniel, from an advertisement for the series' final story arc; the image harks back to the series' very first advertisement (see p. 18).

the night . . . where it turns into a star. We get to see that star burning through the rest of the issue, in every panel where the night sky is visible.

HB: You just mentioned visually echoing scenes from previous collections, and that's something you and Michael did quite a bit of in *The Wake*. A good example is the very next sequence, in which Daniel talks to Lyta Hall against a background that's clearly patterned after the scene in issue 1 where the Sandman confronts Alex Burgess.

NG: Yes, except that in issue 1 the background is very dark and gloomy, and the Sandman chooses to severely punish Burgess. In contrast, the background here is very white and light, and Daniel—who has much better cause for vengeance than the Sandman did—simply kisses Lyta on the forehead and says, "Go in peace."

Then we get a series of "And then he woke up." After Alex Burgess does so, he and Paul discuss the suicide of Jack the lawyer, for any reader who missed the newspaper headline on page 19 of the last issue of *The Kindly Ones*; and Paul says, "Silly, silly, silly boy. I suppose it must just've been one of those grand gestures that went horridly wrong."

Then we see Nuala in The Toad Stone inn, ready to head out now that the storm is over; and Richard Madoc, who we touched on previously, and who is now able to dream again and get ideas; and Lyta Hall, facing away from the mirror and with suitcase at hand, looking sane again.

So we have the three of them ready to get on with their lives; and then Hob Gadling, who's crying and blowing his nose into a handkerchief.

HB: And on the same page, as a kind of overlaid soundtrack, we get the conversation of the Endless.

NG: That's an instance where each Endless having an individual lettering style really came in handy. It allowed us to listen in without seeing them, and yet know who was saying what. And it leads us to the final page, where Daniel is headed to join his family. I love the body language Michael gave each of the Endless at the table, and the Sandman's star burning and glittering in the window behind them.

HB: I also like the painting hanging behind Destiny, which is by Giorgione, a Renaissance artist. Michael told me it was Lord Byron's favorite and is considered the first great psychological painting because of its attempt to depict the subconscious. It's titled *The Tempest*, and Michael said he included it as a nod to the upcoming last issue.

In your script for this scene, you wrote: "Last page of *The Wake*. Which is, more or less, the last page of the story that began in the first issue of *Sandman*. The last three issues are small codas. Scary. I never thought I'd make it this far."

NG: I didn't. I felt there were still a few things left to say, though, which is what I tried to cover over the next three issues.

THE RENAISSANCE FESTIVAL

HB: Hob Gadling at a Renaissance festival is pretty amusing, considering he actually lived through that period. In a 1993 interview with Sadie MacFarlane, you said, "I'm not a huge fan of Renaissance festivals, I think they're sort of lacking something . . . like, you know . . . plague . . . When people come up to you and say things like [*American accent*] 'Good day to thee, good sire!' you just want to kill them."

NG: Well, yes. [*Laughter.*] And I think that attitude came through in Hob's comments. He points out, "The first thing that's wrong is there's no shit. I mean that's the thing about the past people forget. All the shit. Animal shit. People shit. Cow shit. Horse shit. You waded through the stuff. You should spray 'em all with shit as they come through the gates." [*Laughter.*]

Hob continues, "No lice. No nits. No rotting face cancers. When was the last time you saw someone with a bloody great tumor hanging off their face?" That rant was at least partly inspired by my seeing the round Templar Temple in London, which includes a bunch of carvings of people from the twelfth century; half of them have cancer, and huge welts and boils, and so forth.

HB: You don't let Hob get away scot-free, though. On page 13, he complains to a waitress, "Those toilets are pretty bloody disgusting," and the waitress one-ups him by replying, "We strive for realism." [*Laughter.*]

Hob and Gwen have several memorable conversations. One involves the slave trade, on pages 6 through 8: "You only needed one voyage in three to make a profit. So you could afford to dump your cargo two out of three times, if the weather got too bad, or if you spotted a British man o' war. You throw the first few overboard. They were all chained together, so the rest of them followed. I have dreams about that, Gwen. The faces under the water." And Gwen responds, "Robbie? I've gotta be the first black woman you've dated. 'Cos if you'd pulled this shit on a sister before now she'd've killed you already. In self-defense."

NG: I especially like that scene because Gwen's talking about general responsibility, while Hob's talking about personal responsibility ... without her knowing it.

HB: Michael Zulli really likes Hob and Gwen as a couple; he told me "they're the sort of people you wish you knew." Michael additionally expressed great affection for Hob, whose physical appearance—hair color, body shape and so on—he based on rock singer Ian Anderson.

NG: Michael pencilled the first Hob Gadling story, as well as "Hob's Leviathan" in issue 53, so he has a long history with the character. I thought it right that Michael ended up drawing the last Hob tale. And I'm glad Michael likes Gwen. I wanted to show that the whole Nada thing was done, and Gwen seemed a nice way to do that.

HB: You're referring to the series' recurring image of a young black woman burning to death.

NG: Right. After the awful deaths of Nada, Ruby, and Carla, we have another young black woman in the person of Gwen—and nothing bad happens to her at all. That's important, because it shows that with the Sandman's passing, the pattern has been broken.

HB: Speaking of young women, I got a kick out of Michael slipping two real-life ones in the next-to-last panel of page 22: your assistant, Lorraine Garland, and her singing partner, Emma Bull, who together make up the musical group The Flash Girls.

NG: It was a reprise for Lorraine, who'd previously appeared in the first issue of *Worlds' End*; but it was nice to get in Lorraine and Emma together before the series ended.

HB: Following that scene, Hob dreams of meeting the Sandman and Destruction. Hob says to the Sandman, "You're dead, aren't you? And this is just a dream." Sandman nods; and Hob and Destruction laugh at the absurdity of the situation.

NG: That scene came about when it occurred to me that it's quite common to dream of dead people. And then I had the thought: if you can dream of the Sandman, is he truly dead?

JON J MUTH

A sketch
for a T-shirt
design,
based on
the Sandman
from "Exiles."

SOFT PLACES II

HB: Which brings us to "Exiles." You say in your script that the Sage isn't meant to be "a real man from a real time—he's more analogous to a knight in armor, someone from a place that never existed."

NG: That's so, but all the historical stuff the story mentions is nonetheless accurate. The story also includes a number of genuine Chinese folk tales, such as: "My wife once tortured a servant girl with wire whips. A gold ring was missing, and the girl the only suspect. My wife killed the girl before she could confess. Many years later we found the ring, fallen between two floorboards."

HB: What were some of the inspirations for "Exiles"?

NG: One was my realization that the time-bending concepts in issue 39's "Soft Places" gave me the opportunity to have the two versions of Dream—that is, both Morpheus and Daniel—in the same story.

Another factor was that artist Jon J Muth had done a poster for the *Sandman Gallery* of a slightly Asian-looking Sandman, and I loved it; so I wanted to do a story sparked by that.

I also wanted to continue our experimentations with form. In the previous four is-

THE SANDMAN COMPANION

sues, Michael Zulli illustrated using only pencils; so in this one, Jon skipped the pencilling process and did the story using only ink! Jon also handled the coloring himself, and again in an unconventional way—instead of using paint or watercolors, he glued down various swatches of fabric and different kinds of paper to create the colors and patterns.

Another thing that makes this issue special is that I didn't create my usual panel breakdowns for it. Instead, I just wrote brief descriptions of the action, followed by the text of the captions and dialogue, and let Jon break everything down into panels himself. The only other time I did a *Sandman* script that way was for issue 50, "Ramadan."

In addition, this is the only *Sandman* issue that includes a computerized font. Todd Klein created a delicate Oriental font specifically for this story and used it for the text of the Sage's letter that runs throughout the issue.

HB: What sort of effect were you aiming for with the language and rhythms in the story?

NG: I wanted to convey the feeling of Ezra Pound's Chinese-influenced poetry. Which is why I began, "When I was a child I lived amid the mulberry groves./In summer the mulberry trees would stain the green grass with crimson pulp./Birds of a thousand colors danced in the sky when I was a boy,/They brightened the day with their intricate songs." And I just went on like that, writing it very consciously as a poem. One of the lovely things about comics is that you can actually make people read poems who wouldn't otherwise. [*Laughter.*]

HB: In addition to the beauty of the language, you've got some pretty heartbreaking scenes between the Sage and his dead son. Page 11 offers this exchange: "Father? I am your son. That is only a kitten. Why do you abandon me to chase after it?" "When you were alive, you were all my joy. Now you are dead I see you only in dreams, and when I awake my pillow is wet with tears. The kitten is living, and it needs my help."

NG: And four pages later, we get the closest thing to introspection from the Sandman, when he talks about grieving for his own dead son. His words allow us to place at what point in the Sandman's life Master Li is seeing him.

HB: The old man then returns to the desert, where he encounters some utterly incongruous objects from an amusement park.

NG: That scene is one of the few places in the series where I used actual imagery from my dreams. I was writing the script for this issue, fell asleep, and dreamed of a weird laughing sailor in a box that I used to see as a boy outside of fun fairs in England—you put in a coin, and the sailor goes "aha ha ha ha" rather spookily while jogging back and forth. Then I dreamed that I needed to cross a bridge, and I came across another fun fair box that lets you grab for prizes with mechanical claws. And then I woke up, wrote down what I'd just experienced, and incorporated it into the issue.

HB: Following that, Master Li runs into Daniel, who we can identify from the emerald he wears around his neck. And he also meets the riders we last saw wandering the desert in "Soft Places."

NG: It seemed a nice way to tie up that hanging subplot. Then the kitten saves Master Li's life, by waking him up. And the tale ends with what seemed to me like a fitting epitaph for the whole series: "I place the kitten in my sleeve once more: I have saved his life, as he saved mine, and am responsible for him. We cannot evade our responsibilities. That which is dreamed can never be lost, can never be un-dreamed. . . . Only the phoenix arises and does not descend. And everything changes. And nothing is truly lost."

SHAKESPEARE AS MAN AND WRITER

HB: When we discussed *Dream Country*, you mentioned that at the point where the Sandman made his deal with Shakespeare in issue 13, you immediately knew what it was: the creation of two magical plays. Can you say a bit more about that now?

NG: I knew that the plays would be *A Midsummer Night's Dream* and *The Tempest*, because they're the only ones that are original, as opposed to being based on historical events or other people's stories; and because they're my favorites, which made the decision easy. They also worked well chronologically, as *A Midsummer Night's Dream* is arguably the first of Shakespeare's truly great plays, and *The Tempest* is his last play—or, at least, the last he wrote by himself.

HB: Did you know right away that you'd end the series with "The Tempest"?

NG: No; I'd originally planned on doing "The Tempest" about a year after "A Midsummer Night's Dream." But I later realized that because the play is all about stories and endings, it would be an appropriate subject for the last issue of the series.

It's the nearest I've ever come to try and answer, honestly and at length, the question "Where do artists get their ideas?" The story reveals details about Shakespeare's life, and it then proceeds to show that some of his writing is a reflection of that life; some of it is wish fulfillment, echoing things he'd like to take control of in his life; some of it stems from little observations he makes that bounce around his brain in strange angles and produce completely unexpected results; and some of it originates from places that are a total mystery.

HB: That leads to another question—how did you summon up the nerve to portray the life of a figure as esteemed as Shakespeare? Many writers would be too intimidated to even make the attempt, let alone pull it off.

NG: Let me begin to answer that in an indirect way. There's a school of thought that contends someone other than Shakespeare wrote his plays—the earl of Oxford, or the earl of Essex, or someone else famous and of the nobility. I think it's rubbish, but what pisses me off most is the underlying assumption that the plays had to be written by someone with property and a title, that they couldn't be the work of a "normal" person. The people who cling to this strange little snobbery ignore ten thousand years of recorded human history on who our writers are.

There were actually very few writers of the nobility who were any good. Rochester was a halfway decent poet—and also a flake, and a drunk; and Lord Dunsany was a good writer; but people such as Rochester and Dunsany are the exceptions rather than the rule.

NOTES ON "THE TEMPEST"

Here is the start of Neil Gaiman's script for *Sandman* 75:

"All things that are,/Are with more enjoyment chased than enjoyed."

Not to mention, "What win I, if I gain the thing I seek?/A dream, a breath, a froth of fleeting joy./Who buys a minute's mirth to wail a week?/Or sells eternity to get a toy?"

And with that, we start *Sandman* 75. Late, of course, but there comes a time when one has to cease procrastinating and just get down to it. Both of the above quotes are by Mr. William Shaxper.

Who was he, then, when he wrote this? I think of him as someone putting on weight. A thin man going paunchy. In his late forties. Probably with a slight, or not-so, venereal disease, which by now would have become systemic. He drinks a little more than he used to, although a glass of wine for him is still a bottle for other people.

He escaped his wife to go to London, over twenty years ago. They were younger then—he married her because she was pregnant: the evidence suggests a shotgun wedding (and there's evidence that he had also just got engaged to a lass he loved from a nearby village when he was forced to get hitched to Anne Hathaway, eight years older than he was, and three months pregnant when they married). He went to London, held the horses, acted a little, had not much talent, and wrote a very bad play . . .

And then he made a deal. He was offered what he wanted most in the world—what he thought he wanted most, at any rate. Create great dreams to spur the minds of men . . . tales that would live on after his death. . . .

The terms of the deal were simple. The Sandman would give him the genius to retell the "great stories"; and in return he would give the Sandman two original plays, one near the beginning of his career—a fresh and funny celebration of dreams; and one at the end, a darker tribute to the Dream King, and to the power and land of dreams.

And now he's come home from London to Stratford. He's living in this large house, New Place, with his wife, whom he loves, I think, to some extent, but does not like. His daughter Judith, half of the twins, is perhaps a disappointment to him: she's being romanced by Quiney, the young tavern-keeper-to-be, but is at present staying home, unmarried. She's been a little mad since Hamnet died—not crazy, but "touched" (this is my own invention, although the facts do not contradict it), and she's now twenty-six, which is oldish to be married. (Her mother, one can imagine, is telling her that, rather than die an old maid, she should do what the former Ms. Hathaway did: get knocked up and marry the knocker-upper.)

His other daughter, Susannah, is happily married to a local doctor. Shakespeare may have an illegitimate son, William Davenant, or he may not; it was the gossip, but there's always gossip.

So, now he's writing *The Tempest.*

HB: You remind me of an anecdote my father used to tell about a group of dignitaries who had traveled a long way to call on the great Russian writer Leo Tolstoy. Tolstoy was working some land at the time and so was dressed in farmer's clothes. When the VIPs approached him, they asked where they could find Tolstoy, and he replied that he was Tolstoy; but they didn't believe him. Annoyed, Tolstoy asked, "What is a writer supposed to look like?"

NG: Yes; and that's my point. Shakespeare's plays were written by a person—and, for that matter, by a writer. I'm by no means as talented as Shakespeare, but you know what? I can write about people. And I can portray the process of writing, because I've been there. So it didn't scare me to do stories about Shakespeare, nor strike me as some sort of hubris, because my whole approach to him was, "This is a man. This is a writer."

For example, on the writer side, when Ben Jonson says, "I have met all sorts of people . . . from the lowest to the most high. Thus, I understand 'em," I got a kick out of Shakespeare replying, "I would have thought that all one needs to understand people is to be a person. And I have that honor."

And on the human side, I loved exploring Shakespeare's relationship with Anne Hathaway. Here's a woman eight years his senior whom he impregnated and then

---

ILLUSTRATING "THE TEMPEST"

Charles Vess on drawing *Sandman*'s final issue:

When Neil and I were holding up our World Fantasy awards for *Sandman* 19 and camera flashes were popping, Neil leaned over to me and said, "Puts a little pressure on the next one, doesn't it?"

The "next one," meaning "The Tempest," actually required more research than "A Midsummer Night's Dream." I collected lots of visual references on Shakespeare's Stratford, for example, although I stuck to books—while I was visiting England, Neil told me, "Don't go to Stratford, because it's too different now. I want you to only have a picture in your mind of the way it was back then." My favorite reference was *Shakespeare* by Anthony Burgess, because Burgess is a talented writer who understands how to entertain.

I couldn't find any pictures of Judith or Anne. And there are pictures of the older Shakespeare, of course, but not as many as you might think, and they're all fairly different. Shakepeare's famous features—round face, round nose, bald head, and little goatee—tend to remain the same. But in some drawings he's got a lot of throat, while in others he doesn't; he's fat in some pictures and thin in others; and so on. As a result, a lot of my drawings of the Shakespeare family had to be educated guesswork. I found references on Ben Jonson, though, so the way he looks is accurate.

Neil wrote a beautiful script, full of emotional resonances, but it came in several months late. To meet the release schedule, I had to get help on about half the issue's pencilling from Bryan Talbot, John Ridgway, and "the Mysterious Mister Zed," which was a cute pseudonym for Michael Zulli. I then did all the inking to keep the story's look consistent.

THE SANDMAN COMPANION

The Prince
of Stories
revisits
William
Shakespeare
in "The Tempest,"
the final
issue of
The Sandman,
from art used in an
advertisement.

married in what appears to have been a shotgun wedding, and from whom he then fled for long periods to put on plays in London. After many years, he's finally returned to settle in at home—and he and Anne have virtually nothing in common, nothing they can talk about. And yet they enjoy a strangely comfortable relationship.

HB: Can you mention an example?

NG: On page 27, Shakespeare enthusiastically relates to Anne a scene he's just written for *The Tempest*. He begins: "Now in the play Ferdinand—the young prince—and Miranda—the beauteous maiden—are given to each other, after some wood-chopping on Ferdinand's part." He then reads a bit about spirits reveling to celebrate, and then continues with his speech for Prospero: "'Our revels now are ended. These our actors, as I foretold you, were all spirits, and are melted into air, into thin air. And, like the baseless fabric of this vision, the cloud-capp'd towers, the gorgeous palaces, the solemn temples, the great globe itself, yea, all which it inherit, shall dissolve, and, like this insubstantial pageant faded, leave not a rack behind. We are such stuff as dreams are made on; and our little life is rounded with a sleep.' There. Is that not fine?"

And Anne responds, "I am pleased you mentioned wood-chopping, Will, for wood-chopping certainly needs doing, else we shall freeze in our beds this night." "And my speech?" asks Shakespeare. And Anne answers, "For how you expect me to cook for you without firewood I would not know. And you would be the first to complain, were there no roasted goose, nor no hot pudding." Shakespeare smiles, strangely pleased, and says, "Yes, my dear." It's a weirdly romantic moment.

HB: There's a more cantankerous side to the relationship, though. A good example is on page 20, where Shakespeare recites another beautiful passage from his play, and Anne responds: "You know the trouble with you, Will? You live in words, not in the real world. You think too much. You dream too much." Would you pick it up from there?

NG: Shakespeare disagrees, saying, "Whereas I consider myself a practical man." And Anne, flicking a hand through her hair, replies with an indulgent air, "Of course you do, my dear. Practical men always desert their wives and run away to make up pretty tales; and write pretty sonnets to pretty girls and pretty boys." And she then leaves him to vent his frustration at losing the argument by writing this dialogue for Caliban: "You taught me language, and my profit on't is, I know how to curse. The red plague rid you for learning me your language!"

I love the oddness of Shakespeare's relationship to Anne; and his relationship to his daughter, for that matter. The tenderness, and the weird gulfs. Thematically, that's what "The Tempest" is about, as well.

HB: How do you mean?

NG: The cost of getting what you want is having what once you wanted. Here Shakespeare sits, with all the writing talent and achievements he craved in *Sandman* 13, in spades. But he no longer has any idea if those are the things he wants, because he's no longer the boy who wanted them.

This is one of the main themes of *Sandman*, as well—and, for that matter, of life.

HB: What other highlights in the issue do you recall?

NG: One small thing I got a kick out of was the third panel of page 31. Many readers might overlook it, but in the foreground is the seventeenth-century version of Merv Pumpkinhead, whose name is Merrow Turniphead.

HB: In your script, you describe him as follows: "He has no cigar or cigarette, and instead of a pumpkin his head is carved, like a jack-o'-lantern, out of a turnip or a

SHAKESPEARE'S HANDWRITING

Todd Klein on lettering the script of the Bard:

The captions in "The Tempest" were my attempt to imitate what Shakespeare's handwriting would have looked like. I tracked down the only thing that historians are sure was written by him, which is his signature; and I also found documents such as his will, which showed me the handwriting style of the time. I had to adapt it somewhat, though, because some of the letter shapes used back then were pretty hard to read.

THE SANDMAN COMPANION

swede, with greenery at the top. There's a neckerchief around his stick neck. He looks like a scarecrow, and he's carrying a huge wooden pail of water in each hand. Will is walking past him . . . and staring back at him."

NG: At which point Will asks, "Sir? Do I dream?" [*Laughter.*]

But the big scene in the issue for me starts around page 35. We move in for a close-up of Will, standing in front of the stained glass window for Death, and he asks the Sandman the real question: "So why this play? . . . There is some of me in it. Some of Judith. Things I saw, things I thought. I stole a speech from one of Montaigne's essays. And closed with an unequivocally cheap and happy ending. Why did you not want a tragedy? Something lofty, something dark, a tale of a noble hero with a tragic flaw?"

And the Sandman replies, "I wanted a tale of graceful ends. I wanted a play about a king who drowns his books, and breaks his staff, and leaves his kingdom. About a magician who becomes a man. About a man who turns his back on his magic." Will asks, "You live on an island?" And the Sandman says, "I am . . . in my fashion . . . an island."

Will reaches out, as if he expects the Sandman to touch his hand; but Dream's body language stays directed inward. Shakespeare says, "But that can change. All men can change." The Sandman answers, "I am not a man. And I do not change. I asked you earlier if you saw yourself reflected in your tale. I do not. I may not. I am Prince of stories, Will; but I have no story of my own. Nor shall I ever."

And that's really the capstone to *Sandman*, because everything he says there is simply not true, and becomes more untrue as he goes along. I think he knows it even then; but it really becomes apparent following his escape from Burgess's glass prison.

HB: Following all the stories, there's an acknowledgments page on which you mention that one of your favorite writers, Roger Zelazny, died as you completed the first chapter of *The Wake*. That must have been a blow, especially considering how influential Zelazny's work was on *Sandman*.

NG: It was. It turned out he'd been ill with cancer for months but had been keeping it a secret. I flew down for the memorial, and spent a day with his friends and admirers sharing stories of Roger, trying to explain him to us. And that day definitely informed chapter 2. I'd planned to do a wake in issue 71 anyway, but attending Roger's memorial made the whole thing especially real to me.

HB: Finally, what led to doing the final biography section as a series of self-portraits?

NG: Desperation. [*Laughter.*] We'd pretty much already done every other idea in previous collections. Plus it just didn't feel right to make up more bio ministories. My writing for the series ended with issue 75.

The story had been told.

—

Evocative pencil from *The Books of Magic* miniseries.

backstory

PART THREE

secret origins

13

I think I did pretty well, considering I started out
with nothing but a bunch of blank paper.

—STEVE MARTIN

Every profession has its occupational hazards. For doctors, it's being hit on for free medical advice. For comedians, it's being expected to act funny twenty-four hours a day. And for writers, it's being asked the dreaded question, "Where do you get your ideas?"

The latter is thrown at writers so frequently that they've come up with stock responses. The most popular is "From a think tank service in Schenectady."

Behind that humor, there's a certain amount of defensiveness. There's a fable about a bird being asked which wing he lifts first when he's about to take off from the ground; and the bird, who's never given the process a thought, becomes so self-conscious that he loses the ability to fly. On some level, writers fear sharing that fate.

That being said, Neil Gaiman is an exceptionally thoughtful writer who's more than managed to stay creatively aloft. I therefore asked him to share the process he went through to come up with his most compelling ideas: his characters.

According to Gaiman, "Everyone regularly gets ideas. The only difference between writers and other people is that we take notes when it happens. But story ideas aren't the hard part. Creating believable people who do more or less what you tell them to is much harder."

That's especially true in *Sandman*, where it's the characters who really drive the series. If you examine a typical *Sandman* story, you'll find its emphasis isn't on what event takes place or on why it takes place, but on how that event affects the story's people. You'll also find a lot of two-way dialogue, because *Sandman* characters tend to define themselves by who they talk to and what they say.

As a result, what you're likeliest to remember about *Sandman* are the personalities who inhabit it. First and foremost, there's brooding, duty-bound Dream, who dominates the series as much by his inaction as by what he does.

There's also beautiful, sensible Death, who careful readers will note does more than just end lives; colorful, ever-changing Delirium, who is poetically flaky and uncommonly wise, and scores the best lines in the series; robust, thoughtful Destruction, who'd rather make omelets than Armageddon; sexy but frightening Desire, who lives under our skins; the enigmatic Despair, who does unspeakable things with rings; and blind Destiny, who reads a book impossibly filled with the past and future history of everything. Together, they make for one of the most memorable dysfunctional families in all of literature.

There are other characters too, of course; virtually an army of them. They include many strong and capable women, such as Eve, Nada, Calliope, Rose Walker, Unity Kinkaid, Queen Titania, Lady Bast, Nuala, Hazel and Foxglove, Thessaly, Johanna Constantine, Ruby DeLonge, Ishtar, and Lyta Hall. Tori Amos has said, "I relate to Neil's female characters because he doesn't put them on a pedestal, and he doesn't abuse them either. I think he gives women a fair reading."

Gaiman actually tends to give a fair reading to all his characters . . . even when they're not human. Among *Sandman*'s most popular residents are Matthew (a wide-eyed raven); Barnabas (a sarcastic dog); Gilbert (a kindhearted piece of real estate); and Mervyn Pumpkinhead (a wisecracking orange fruit on a stick). These creatures are so imbued with personality that we quickly learn to look past their forms and take them to our hearts as friends . . . which, in *Sandman*, is the whole point.

ORIGINS OF THE ENDLESS

HB: You kicked off the *Brief Lives* collection with this introduction for new readers: "There are seven beings that aren't gods. Who existed before humanity dreamed of gods and will exist after the last god is dead. They are called The Endless. They are embodiments of (in order of age) Destiny, Death, Dream, Destruction, Desire, Despair, and Delirium." How did you come to create the Endless?

NG: When DC gave me a monthly comic to write, one of the first things I had to deal with was knowing I don't have what it takes to do super-hero stories, even though that's what the vast majority of comics buyers like to read. People such as Alan Moore, Grant Morrison, and Kurt Busiek can write super heroes beautifully, but I'm just no good at it.

On the other hand, I *can* write science fiction, fantasy, and horror. So I decided to find a way to cheat my way through—that is, to come up with characters who look enough like super heroes to entice a comics reader into giving them a try, but who really aren't super heroes at all.

That made me think of *Lord of Light*, a 1967 novel by Roger Zelazny. The book struck me as a very interesting model, because it's about people who take on the attributes of Hindu gods, constituting, in effect, a heavenly Legion of Super-Heroes.

I liked that approach, but I decided to take it a step further—instead of writing about humans acting as gods, why not just write about gods?

This especially appealed to me because Superman had just been revamped to give him fewer abilities, the reasoning at the time being that one couldn't weave inter-

MICHAEL ALLRED

The Endless (clockwise from top): Destiny, Delirium, Dream, Desire, Death, Despair, and Destruction.

ALLRED M.D.

esting stories around a character who was "too powerful." That struck me as wrongheaded, so I thought, "Okay, I'll do a series that starts out with characters who are virtually all-powerful, and I'll see where I can go from there."

HB: In the initial notes you made for yourself about the series, you wrote that you wanted to include three brothers: "death, sleep and ?" "Death" soon changed from brother to sister; and "Sleep" became Dream, or Sandman. Who did the question mark turn into?

NG: Destiny.

HB: The only member of the Endless you didn't have to create from scratch, because he was an established DC character conceived by writer Marv Wolfman.

NG: Right, I nicked him. Destiny was so mysterious, however, that no one knew much about him other than he floated around with a big book that held knowledge of the future. That was perfect for my purposes.

HB: What about the other family members?

NG: Once I had Dream, Death, and Destiny, I went, "Oh! All their names begin with the letter *D*. Well, I'll continue that for each additional member of the family." I never made a big point of it, because it was fun to just drop the name of each new member of the Endless into the series and allow people to gradually notice.

HB: You gave hints from the beginning, though. The Sandman's toughest battle in the first story arc, *Preludes & Nocturnes*, is with a character named Doctor Dee. And the very first page of *Preludes & Nocturnes* displays the quote "D is for lots of things," which you attribute to being said by Doctor Dee on All Fool's Day.

By the end of the series, you were even doing self-parodies of your naming convention. Do you know the scene I'm thinking of from *The Wake*?

NG: Sure, when Matthew meets most of the Endless family for the first time—and Delirium is there with her canine companion Barnabas—and Matthew guesses at their names based on what they look like: "You must be . . . let's see: Desire. Despair. Destiny. And, uhm . . . Dog?" [*Laughter.*]

HB: How did you determine the respective ages of the Endless?

NG: Destiny had to be the oldest, because anything that happens is influenced by destiny. With the first organism came life and the possibility of death, so Death came next. When the first living thing woke up, the possibility of dreaming existed, so Dream came third.

By similar reasoning, Destruction followed—and, a while afterward, the twins Desire and Despair; and finally the youngest Endless, Delight, who later became Delirium.

ORIGINS OF THE SANDMAN

HB: You've explained previously how the Sandman came to be the star of the series. Can you talk about the chain of thoughts that led to his development as a character?

NG: A major defining factor was my wanting him to be part of the DC Universe. Because if someone as powerful as the Sandman was running all the dreams in the world, a natural question would be "Why haven't we heard about him by now?"

The answer I came up with was "He's been locked away." And that solution formed an image in my head of a naked man in a glass cell.

My next question was "How long had he been trapped there?" The movie *Awakenings* hadn't been made yet, but I'd read Oliver Sacks's book a few months earlier, so I knew about the encephalitis lethargica, or "sleepy sickness," that had swept Europe in 1916. Scientists to this day don't understand what caused it, and I loved the idea of blaming it on the Sandman's imprisonment, so I determined the length of his stay to be seventy-two years—ending in late 1988, when the series debuted.

And so on; each plot point just seemed to naturally lead to the next one.

HB: Where did the Sandman's "rock star" appearance come from?

NG: I wanted him to look like royalty. In the late 1980s, kings and queens were dressing and behaving like ordinary people, and I felt it was celebrities—and especially rock stars—who were our true royalty. I made some drawings with that in mind, and with the Sandman dressed in a black kimono I ran across in a book of Japanese design. I sent those off to Sam Kieth, who was the first issue's penciller, and Sam developed the Dream we see in issue 1. Then Mike Dringenberg, who was inking the first issue, said, "Hey, he looks like Peter Murphy from Bauhaus." Dave McKean and I got some Bauhaus videos and immediately saw that Mike was right; and Dave ended up making the central image on the cover of *Sandman* 1 a Peter Murphy–like face.

HB: Dave also did an early Sandman drawing based on Bono's appearance in the Clannad music video "In a Lifetime." The illustration is reproduced on the first page of the afterword to *Preludes & Nocturnes*.

NG: I should add that the Sandman's look also sprung from my wanting to convey a brooding, adolescent alienation, the kind you typically get when you're sixteen—the sort of attitude, for example, Dream displays in chapter 2 of *Brief Lives* when he's standing on a balcony getting rained on for days on end just because a girl dumped him.

HB: He doesn't have much success with women, does he?

NG: No, that's a big part of his problem; he's useless at relationships.

HB: Where did the Sandman's personality come from?

NG: I don't really know. I can tell you it wasn't planned; it pretty much appeared on the page as I wrote him. But his speech pattern was probably influenced by Len Wein's and Jim Aparo's Phantom Stranger; both characters speak in a formal, gnostic way.

HB: Some have suggested another influence was Michael Moorcock's Elric—a tall, thin albino prince who traffics in magic and dark forces, and has a soul-eating sword that behaves similarly to Dream's ruby after it was altered by Dr. Dee.

NG: It doesn't ring true for me. For example, Elric frequently agonizes over his past actions, while Dream is the least introspective character I've ever written. As for the ruby, it was normally a kind of computer that automated things for the Sandman; instead of having to figure out how to perform a certain task, Dream would just say, "Ruby, do this," and it was done.

And the Sandman's chalk white skin was, quite simply, a coloring mistake. In my script for issue 1, I described Dream as being pale and light-skinned—which is the way he appears in the Dave McKean portrait on the cover.

HB: Well then, let me throw out one other possible source of inspiration: Roger Zelazny's short story "He Who Shapes," which the author later expanded into a novel titled *The Dream Master*. It's about a psychiatrist who treats patients through dream therapy and, because of his own suicidal tendencies, becomes lost in a dream.

NG: That story *did* play a role. "He Who Shapes" literally translates into "Morpheus," which got me thinking. And so did a Samuel R. Delany comment in his book of critical essays *The Jewel-Hinged Jaw*, in which he notes all of Zelazny's heroes were either immortal or suicides.

ORIGINS OF DEATH

HB: You've created many memorable characters, but the most popular is Death. How was she born?

NG: Very quickly. After Karen called in October 1987 to tell me I was doing a monthly series about the Sandman, I sat down and started jotting down stream-of-consciousness ideas and phrases. The first thing I wrote was "Gates of Horn and Ivory," followed by "Brother to Death." I then wrote a bunch of other things, including a note about three brothers, two of whom were Death and Sleep. But the Death character nagged at me, so I made a revision: "Death should be his sister: Lady Death. Yes."

HB: Yes, indeed. Once you determined Death's gender, where did her look come from?

NG: Death is the only major character whose visuals didn't spring from me; that credit goes to Mike Dringenberg. In my original *Sandman* outline, I suggested Death look like rock star Nico in 1968, with the perfect cheekbones and perfect face she has on the cover of her *Chelsea Girl* album.

But Mike Dringenberg had his own ideas, so he sent me a drawing based on a woman he knew named Cinnamon—the drawing that was later printed in *Sandman*

Sketch of Dream and Death for DC's *Who's Who* series.

Character sketches of the ever sensible Death, older sister of Dream.

11—and I looked at it and had the immediate reaction of, "Wow. That's really cool."

Later that day, Dave McKean and I went to dinner in Chelsea at the My Old Dutch Pancake House and the waitress who served us was a kind of vision. She was American, had very long black hair, was dressed entirely in black—black jeans, T-shirt, etc.—and wore a big silver ankh on a silver necklace. And she looked exactly like Mike Dringenberg's drawing of Death.

Every time she'd come over to serve us and then go away, I'd whisper to Dave, "Should we show her the drawing?" And Dave kept responding, "Oh no, it's too embarrassing." So we never did. But I took that incident as an omen, and I silently replied to the powers that be, "Oh, okay. This is what Death looks like walking around. Cool. Thank you." [*Laughter.*]

HB: How did Death come to be so pleasant and sensible?

NG: If you look at the numerous anthropomorphic representations of Death over the years, you'll find that most of them are scary, humorless, implacable people who you really wouldn't want to spend time with.

However, I already had a lead character, the Sandman, who was pale, tall, brooding, dark, relatively humorless, and Byronic in a late adolescent kind of way—in other words, who had all the characteristics typically ascribed to Death. I knew that readers expected Death to be just like the Sandman, only more so—larger, darker, very male. So I thought it would be fun to turn expectations upside down, and to provide some contrast as well, by making Death small, funny, cool, and nice.

Death's personality also played into one of the main themes of the series, which concerned the nature of responsibility—for example, how the Sandman is able to change only so much, because he feels locked in by his duties and obligations. I wanted one character who had no problem at all with the concept of responsibility. Death simply does what she does. She's been at her job a long time, she's really skilled at it, and she performs it with charm and good humor.

In addition, I liked the idea of creating a Death who I personally wouldn't mind encountering when my time comes—who would come up to me one day and say pleasantly, "You know, you really should have had that mole checked out." Or, more probably, "Now next time, try and remember—it's left pedal to go faster, right pedal to stop." [*Laughter.*]

HB: As opposed to some skeletal creature who approaches with a scythe, an hourglass and a grimace, and makes you feel uncomfortable about being dead.

NG: Right, because that strikes me as silly. [*Laughter.*] After all, Death is the only certainty for any living organism. Reproduction may not happen, joy may not happen, even dreams may not happen; but it's definite that death will come. I figured that Death must be very good at what she does. And I saw no reason why she wouldn't be nice, as well.

MIKE DRINGENBERG AND THE WOMAN BEHIND DEATH

Artist Mike Dringenberg was on the team that created *Sandman*. He was originally hired to ink Sam Kieth's artwork. When Kieth opted to leave the series, however, Dringenberg took over his job and ended up pencilling issues 6–11, 14–16, 21, and 28.

Because he worked on so many of *Sandman's* early issues, Dringenberg designed many of the series' key characters, including Matthew, Gilbert, the Corinthian, Nada, Rose Walker, and Barbie. Even more notably, he designed four of Dream's siblings: Desire, Despair, Delirium . . . and Death.

Dringenberg credits the look of Death to a young woman named Cinnamon he befriended in Salt Lake City. "Cinnamon had real star quality in her presence and bearing," he recalls. "She was an ex-ballet dancer with an amazing body, a beautiful heart-shaped face, and a memorable haircut, and was prone to wandering around with a little black umbrella. I felt Cinnamon had the visual qualities we were looking for, so I drew Death to look pretty much like her."

Dringenberg adds that while Death's appearance was relatively stable, her real-life counterpart was prone to continual makeovers. "Cinnamon would draw spiderwebs on her face one week, adopt an Egyptian fashion the next week, and style her eyes like a raccoon's the following week."

When asked about the famous ankh Death wears around her neck, Dringenberg explains, "Part of that simply came out of the ankh being in vogue at the time. I also liked the irony, though, because the ankh is the Egyptian symbol for life; and in some other cultures it became a symbol for immortality."

HB: And more than nice. Wallace Stevens once wrote, "Death is the mother of beauty" and I've heard you tell a tale from the Jewish Cabala that centers around that idea.

NG: The Cabala says the Angel of Death is so beautiful that when you see her, you fall in love. And you love her so hard that your soul leaves your body, drawn out through your eyes. I always thought that was a lovely notion.

HB: Death was enormously popular with readers, right from her first appearance in *Sandman* 8. Did you know that she was going to be an instant star?

NG: Oddly, yes, I knew from the start; and I treated her accordingly. You don't see Death popping in and out all the time, or coming onstage whenever someone dies, because I wanted her to always leave readers craving more.

Whenever I considered using Death, I thought of Marlon Brando getting paid $4 million to appear in just ten minutes of *Superman: The Movie*. So I would bring Death on only when I really needed her, and I mentally paid her $4 million for each appearance—and made sure that she earned the money.

HB: I'd say that, to a lesser extent, you used the same strategy with Dream.

NG: Absolutely, because the same reasoning applied. Whenever there was a choice of bringing the Sandman on or not, I'd think, "All the other characters are working for Guild rate, but a member of the Endless gets paid a lot of money. If one turns up, he or she has to earn the fee, even it's for an appearance in a single panel."

HB: That's an unusual way to handle the title character of a series. The only other examples I can think of in comics that even come close are Steve Gerber's *Man-Thing* and Will Eisner's *The Spirit*.

NG: But both those series worked. In fact, Eisner's *Spirit* stories had a very strong influence on me. During the nine years I swore off reading comics, the one exception I allowed myself was *The Spirit*.

HB: One last item I want to bring up is a spin on Oscar Wilde's hilarious comment, "Biography lends to death a new terror." Based on some interviews you've done, I think you might amend that to "Cartoon obituaries lend to death a new terror."

NG: It's true; I find it a bit scary knowing that if people still remember *Sandman* by the time I die, there's certain to be a whole bunch of cartoons showing this guy in a black T-shirt, leather jacket and shades being led off by a cute-looking girl with an ankh. It's not a very dignified way to go. [*Laughter.*]

ORIGINS OF DELIRIUM

HB: You clearly have affection for all of your characters, but I'm guessing that you had the time of your life writing Delirium. Is that a fair statement?

NG: Yes, completely fair. She never felt like work.

HB: Where did Delirium come from? Was she knocking around in your head a long time before *Sandman* even began?

NG: No, she came on after I started the series. In fact, she was somebody who wrote herself on the page.

Delirium began when I found a photograph in a magazine of a very young girl, maybe thirteen or fourteen, who was much pierced, and was wearing ripped, tatty, very strangely sexy clothes. Everything was wrong about that picture, and the girl looked very angry. That was my visual model for Delirium.

Based on the photo, I thought Delirium would be belligerent, and I wrote about a page of her that way. But it felt wrong, as if I was trying to push her off in some direction she didn't want to go. Then I tried again by just shutting up and listening to discover what sorts of things she actually said. And that did it.

HB: Where did you get the idea of giving Delirium a past history as Delight?

NG: A lot of the credit for that belongs to my friend Brian Hibbs. After *Sandman* 10 appeared, Brian asked me who the rest of the Endless were. Shortly afterward, I decided on a strict "no tell" policy, and stuck to it; but at the time, I replied, "Delirium and Destruction."

Brian followed up by later sending me a drawing labeled "Delight" with a note saying, "She should be an Endless, too." I loved the drawing; and I decided Delight would make for a very appropriate past existence for Delirium, because she's a character I wanted in a state of flux—she's been one thing, she's become something else, and eventually she'll change into something else again.

HB: Is this state of flux unique to Delirium?

NG: Yes. It has to do with her being the youngest; she's practically a cosmic afterthought.

HB: That unstable state causes her some pain, but it also gives her special insight There's been some speculation that Delirium was based on a person you knew, such as the late novelist Kathy Acker or singer Tori Amos.

NG: There's also the brilliant Tanaqui C. Weaver, who I first met when she was a student at Oxford and I was giving a talk to the Oxford comics group. She told me that she experienced a period where she was able to see only colors, and I remembered that interesting comment when creating Delirium. I also remembered the way Tanaqui sometimes said things that were amazingly right and slightly nonsensical at the same time.

Kathy Acker was also a component, although there was really nothing of Delirium in her personality—Kathy was always terribly focused. But if you look at, say, the first story in *Season of Mists*, and you turn to page 7, panel 6 . . . that's Kathy Acker. It's weird, because Mike Dringenberg had never met her; but externally, that's perfectly Kathy.

Bits of Tori went into Delirium too, later on. There are panels in *Brief Lives* where Delirium has a very "Tori" look to her. Contrary to popular legend, however, I did not encounter Tori and then create Delirium as a consequence; Delirium existed years before Tori and I met.

Of course, there's also a lot of Jill Thompson in Delirium, because Jill drew her more than anyone else. Lots of Delirium's mannerisms, the way she holds her body and so on, are things that Jill does.

If you flip through *Brief Lives*, you'll see that Delirium's look is constantly changing, pretty much whenever the mood strikes her, so it's easy for Delirium to look like several different people.

But the real truth is, Delirium is me. Just me shutting up and listening. And that's what I liked best about her.

It would take me hours sometimes to get the Sandman's dialogue right. I'd write a line, and then I'd have to hone it, because I'd initially write the *kind* of thing he would say, but I needed to get to *exactly* what he would say.

With Delirium, I just took dictation. I could give her a straight line, and she'd come back with the perfect Gracie Allen/Zen response. And I'd just type it out and say, "Wow, that's lovely," and start giggling. [*Laughter.*]

ORIGINS OF DESTRUCTION

HB: From whence came Destruction?

NG: I've always thought of Destruction as Brian Blessed, the fine actor who played King Richard IV. A big, bearded, booming character who loved to laugh.

HB: I recall Blessed's King Richard on the first season of *Black Adder* with great affection. He also played Prince Vultan, the Wing-Man, in the 1980 remake of *Flash Gordon*. His hearty laughter is especially memorable.

NG: I once read an interview with Brian in which he said he works out with weights, which he always takes along on trips. He loves to arrive at his hotel and watch the bellboy come and try to pick up his luggage . . . which have these five-hundred-pound weights in them! [*Laughter.*] That image—a huge man seeking out a silly situation to amuse himself—is something I remembered and used for Destruction.

ORIGINS OF DESIRE

HB: Was there a visual inspiration for Desire?

NG: There were two, actually. First, the sexy, androgynous prints created by artist Patrick Nagel that seemed to be everywhere in the early 1980s. Second, rock star Annie Lennox, circa 1987, when she was half of the Eurythmics. When you saw a Lennox music video, you didn't care if Annie was a boy or a girl; Annie was just *cute*.

I had to make Desire both male and female, because Desire represents . . . well, everything one might desire. I also liked that doing so gave the Endless family a nice symmetry, with three males—Destiny, Dream, and Destruction; three females—Death, Despair, and Delirium; and Desire.

HB: Considering all the relationship problems in the series, and particularly the Sandman's awful track record with women, I think it's interesting that Desire comes off as the least likable member of the Endless—almost a bad guy.

NG: What should be kept in mind is that Desire really, really didn't like Dream; and Dream didn't like Desire at all, either. They had a massive personality clash.

So while appearing in a series centered around the Sandman, Desire did indeed come across as a bad guy; but she got shortchanged. If I were to write the same story from the perspective of *Desire Comics*, readers would see the extent to which Desire perceives the Sandman as unbearably stuffy and irritating; and Dream would start looking like the bad guy.

ORIGINS OF DESPAIR

HB: How was Despair born?

NG: Visually, she started out as an image I discovered in an obscure 1980s book of photographs called *Modern Primitives*.

HB: Do you mean the *RE/SEARCH* book edited by Vale?

NG: No, that's a different work with the same title. The book I'm referring to had a photograph in the back titled something like "Mandy from Mars." It showed a strange, fat, snaggle-toothed naked woman staring forward. I took one look and said, "That's Despair."

We don't learn a lot about Despair over the course of the series, but I'm pleased with the description of her that appears in *Season of Mists*. I didn't care for Despair when I made her up. But she grew on me. I came to like the way she did her job, and her world behind the mirrors, and what she did with her rings.

HB: She's also refreshingly different visually. Jill Thompson told me that after the highly idealized versions of people she had to draw for super-hero comics, Despair's bizarre short and squat physique was a welcome change. Jill added, "It was challenging to convey Despair's facial expressions, because her features are so skewed and exaggerated. It was tough to express her body language too, because she's so squat and round—from any angle but straight on, she turns into a little ball. Well, unless you draw her from above, in which case she's a ball with hair on top." [*Laughter.*]

NG: Jill's a treasure. And, much for the reasons Jill indicates, I ended up becoming very fond of Despair as the years went on.

HB: That's evident from the bittersweet scene you wrote between Despair and Destruction in chapter 1 of *Brief Lives*, in which he kisses her cheek before parting: "His beard was rough against her skin. No one ever kissed Despair, save her brother. But when she next saw him it was in Destiny's hall, thirty years on . . . for the last time." And she looks small, sad, vulnerable . . . and lonely.

Lastly, do you have anything to say about the first Despair dying? For example, will that ever be followed up on?

NG: It happened, and you don't learn nearly as much about it as you'd like; but I don't know that it will be followed up on.

ORIGINS OF CAIN, LUCIEN, EVE, AND MATTHEW

HB: Not every character in *Sandman* was created from scratch; you lifted a number of them from other DC Comics series and then made them your own. The Three Witches, for example, were the hosts of a successful horror title during the 1970s called *The Witching Hour*. And Cain and Abel were respectively hosts of two highly popular titles during the same period, *The House of Mystery* and *The House of Secrets*.

NG: I was interested in using those characters because I loved their odd comics when I was younger. But I knew for certain that I had to include Cain when, while researching him in the Bible, I read Genesis 4:16: "And Cain went out from the presence of the Lord and dwelt in the land of Nod." [*Laughter.*] It was during such moments of discovery that I felt like the series was writing itself.

HB: Not all the horror hosts you resurrected were well-known, though. For example, Lucien was a very obscure spooky librarian created in 1975 by writer Paul Levitz—now the executive vice president and publisher of DC—and artist Joe Orlando. The series Lucien hosted lasted only three issues.

NG: Right, a DC comic with the silly title *Tales of Ghost Castle*. But it occurred to me that Ghost Castle was really the Sandman's castle during the period when Dream was imprisoned and his castle was becoming nebulous; and I really liked that idea.

As a result, I went into the DC offices while I writing *Sandman* 2 and asked if anyone had a picture of Lucien and information on his background; but no one remembered much about him. Finally, Tom Peyer, who was Karen's assistant editor at the time, spent half a day digging around the DC archives to get me what I needed.

Tom's research further unearthed another obscure 1975 series, *Dark Mansion of Forbidden Love*, that was hosted by a beautiful unnamed woman with a raven. That made me remember a mad crone named Eve who had a raven, and who appeared in

ORIGINS OF LETTERING STYLES

In a typical prose book (such as this one), the letters on a page are little more than tools to form words and convey content. In a comic book, however, the lettering is an integral part of the imagery. The styling and placement of series logos, story titles, word balloons, captions, sound effects, street signs, newspaper headlines, and everything else involving letters is a delicate art. When done right, lettering can be as important to setting the tone of a comic as music is to film.

Todd Klein is easily one of the most respected and award-winning letterers in comics. Klein's designed hundreds of logos, and he handles the lettering of most of DC Comics' covers. He's also one of the few people—along with writer Neil Gaiman, cover artist Dave McKean and editor Karen Berger—who's worked on *The Sandman* for its entire seven-year run.

Sandman required more of Klein than most comics, because Neil Gaiman asked him to design, and then maintain, a unique lettering style for almost every major character. "For example," says Klein, "the border of a Sandman word balloon has a blottiness that conveys Morpheus's shifting nature. Also, the letters are upper- and lowercase, and reversed—that is, white letters on black. The latter effect was created by DC's production department, which made negatives of my lettering and then pasted it over each original."

Delirium was a different challenge. "Her lettering constantly changes in size, shape, and slant, wobbling in and out, to indicate that she's always on the verge of madness," Klein says. "Her balloons also contain a variety of rainbow colors, which was my idea but executed by colorist Danny Vozzo."

In contrast, "Destiny speaks in all italics, which helps convey the emotionless quality of his voice," says Klein. "And Desire's lettering is in the style of Art Nouveau posters and ads, to make him-her look like a Patrick Nagel painting."

For other Endless, a plainer style was more appropriate. "Destruction simply has heavy lettering, surrounded by a heavy black border," continues Klein, "to give the impression that he speaks very loudly and forcefully. Despair has normal lettering but a very ragged border. And Death speaks in standard word balloons to express her down-to-earth personality, that she acts like she's just another person."

Klein created special styles for the series' talking animals, as well. "Barnabas the dog had upper- and lowercase lettering with a rounded quality," Klein says, "and his balloon shapes were kind of loose. And Matthew the raven's word balloon is made up of lines that overlap and have pieces sticking out, as if I'd laid down a pile of sticks to make it, which is meant to convey the quirky, scratchy sound of a raven's voice."

By the end of the series, Klein had created over thirty unique styles for *Sandman* characters.

---

several other short-lived DC titles, such as *Secrets of Sinister House, Secrets of Haunted House* and *Plop!* It occurred to me that the beautiful woman with a raven and the crazy crone with a raven were aspects of the same character, who was named Eve.

I also liked the idea of a woman who alternated, from panel to panel, between being old and being young, because it was an effect that was uniquely suited to comics; such back-and-forth visual switching doesn't work well in prose or film.

HB: Speaking of visuals, Lucien and Cain look a bit similar. Is there any significance to that in *Sandman*?

Original character sketch of Lucien as he first appeared in the short-lived 1970 series *Tales of Ghost Castle.*

NG: Nope, other than the fact both characters were designed by the same artist, Joe Orlando. We simply took 'em as we found 'em.

HB: And the similarity of Lucien's name to Lucifer's is also just a historical coincidence?

NG: Correct; I didn't even know Paul had originally intended to call him Lucifer until Paul happened to mention it to me years later.

But that's not the only direction from which Lucien came. I was also thinking of George MacDonald's book *Lilith,* which describes a tall man in a frock coat who turns into a raven, and who is actually Adam, the first man. That image always stuck in my mind, and it definitely informed my handling of Lucien, who's dressed in a frock coat and—as is revealed in part 12 of *The Kindly Ones*—began as the first raven.

HB: What about Matthew, the other raven in the series? He was originally a man named Matt Cable who appeared periodically in *Swamp Thing,* and who writer Rick Veitch killed in *Swamp Thing* 84.

NG: That's right. Shortly after *Sandman* began, Rick—who's a friend of mine—called and asked me if I'd mind his having Matt die in The Dreaming. Rather than mind, I saw it as an opportunity, because I'd been wanting to introduce a character for whom everything in The Dreaming would be strange and new. When Matthew flies around wide-eyed and asks, "What's going on?" characters explain aspects of The Dreaming to him—and so explain them to the reader.

THE SANDMAN COMPANION

HB: I assume it was Matt's dying in The Dreaming that opened the door to the Sandman giving him the choice of staying there.

NG: Yes, but that was never explicitly stated in either *Swamp Thing* or *Sandman*. Rick and I left it to readers of both series to draw the connection for themselves.

ORIGINS OF HOB GADLING

HB: One character in the waking world who appears almost as regularly as the Endless is Hob Gadling—the man who's granted eternal life in *Sandman* 13, "Men of Good Fortune," and who then pops up periodically through *Sandman* 73. How did you create him?

NG: Hob Gadling began life in my head as Bob Hoskins. That simple. Just keep in mind Hoskins's speech patterns from a film like *The Long Good Friday*—or from any taped interview, because that's the way he really talks—and read Hob's initial dialogue on page 3: "There you go, proves my point. All I'm saying is this: Nobody has to die. The only reason people die, is because everyone does it. You all just go along with it. It's rubbish, death. It's stupid. I don't want nothing to do with it." I thoroughly heard Bob Hoskins saying those words.

By the time I got to page 7, however, Bob Hoskins was long gone, and it was exclusively Hob Gadling talking. And it's been Hob Gadling's voice that's lived in my head ever since.

ORIGINS OF CHARACTER NAMES

HB: You've just said that Hob Gadling started as a voice in your head. Has a character ever started simply as a name?

NG: Oh, yes. One example is the Necropolis's Petrefax, as in turning to stone, whose story we learn in *Sandman* 55. It was only years later that I realized what I was actually thinking of was putrefaction, so he really should've been named Putrefax. [*Laughter.*] But Putrefax sounds silly, and Petrefax sounds like a name.

HB: Can you also explain how you performed the more common task, which is naming a character whom you've already created? For example, since you just mentioned Petrefax, how about discussing some other characters from *Worlds' End*?

NG: Okay. The first name we encounter in *Worlds' End* is Charlene Mooney. "Charlene" isn't particularly important, but I wanted a "moon" name because of the connection between women and the moon, to help me set up the male-female dichotomy that appears later in the book.

Charlene's car is being driven by a man she doesn't know very well. He's "Brant" because it's the name of a wild goose, and I liked the idea of him being a wild thing migrating across America. Also, it's one of those strange, monosyllabic American names.

HB: How about the name of the inn they arrive at, which is also the title of the entire book?

NG: "Worlds' End" is the actual name of a pub I used to see in the Chelsea area of London. I always loved the idea of "What if it was? What if you could go into this pub and be at the world's end?" I tackled that idea more head-on in a short story titled "When We Went to See the End of the World," which is in my prose book *Smoke and Mirrors*. But for *Sandman* 51, I liked the idea of an inn that was the end of many worlds, which is why the sign at the bottom of page 6, and the name of the entire story arc, has that damn annoying apostrophe—"Worlds'." [*Laughter.*]

As for "a free house," in England this phrase refers to a pub that isn't run by a particular brewery and so is free to serve any kind of beer. I extended the notion in *Sandman* to make "free house" refer to a house that had no ties to *anything*; that is, a house unbound by any time or dominion.

HB: How did you happen to name the folks we meet at the Worlds' End inn?

NG: The first inn character we encounter is "Menton," an elf who's friends with Cluracan. He's named after musician Todd Menton, who is a *Sandman* fan and a friend of mine, and who wanted to be in a *Sandman* story.

HB: Okay. [*Laughter.*]

NG: I should point out, however, that most of the character names in *Sandman* have genuine significance. In *Brief Lives*, for example, if someone is named "Ruby," or if a lawyer is named "Bernie Capax," it's no accident. You usually can't go wrong by looking up a *Sandman* character's name in a reference work such as *Brewer's Dictionary of Phrase and Fable*, or even a standard dictionary.

Let's go back to *Worlds' End*. The Centaur, who we first see at the top of page 7, is straight from mythology.

As for the lady who runs the inn, we never learn her name, but there are some indications in the last issue of *Worlds' End* that she's the Indian goddess Kali. For example, she makes certain Kali-like arm movements on page 2, panel 2; and the shadows behind her on page 22, panel 4, imply that she has more than one set of arms.

HB: So sometimes a character's name springs from mythology, sometimes it's a favorite pub, and sometimes a name is only hinted at by shadows.

NG: The real world is just as capricious. Once while I was on a tour, I signed a copy of *Sandman* for a young lady named Larissa. "It's a Greek shrine," she said. "It's a town in Thessaly," I told her. "When we meet Thess again, she'll be calling herself Larissa. But I thought I'd made it up as a name. How did you get it?" "Oh, my dad's named Larry, and my mom's called Clarissa." [*Laughter.*]

HB: That's actually a fine segue to the last two pages of *Worlds' End*, where we abruptly discover that the whole story arc we've just read was told by Brant in a low-lit American bar, to a female bartender—who bears a definite resemblance to Thessaly! However, there's no mention of who the woman is in the story, and there's not even a hint of it in your script for the issue. Any comment?

NG: No, I'll leave that determination up to the reader. Sometimes a character is best left unnamed.

ORIGINS OF BARNABAS . . . AND EVERYONE ELSE

HB: You've talked about creating characters inspired by photographs you've seen, voices you've heard, and names you've liked. What other "hooks" have been useful?

NG: Barnabas the dog in *Brief Lives* is one of the series' most beloved figures. How did he turn up? Quite simply, I had Destruction off on an island, and I wanted him to be able to talk to somebody.

Also, I loved the idea of Destruction creating paintings that weren't very good, writing poems that weren't very good, sculpting statues that weren't very good, all with complete enthusiasm. It's the act of creation, not the quality of creation, as far as he's concerned. And I needed someone to say, "You know, what you just did, that's really not very good at all."

I couldn't give him a human companion, such as a lover, because that would throw the story off in odd directions and give me complications I didn't need. So how about a talking dog?

Destruction is someone who I thought would like a dog; I've always thought of him as being dog-related, in the same kind of way that the Sandman is cat-related. I'd played with cat imagery in issue 18, "Dream of a Thousand Cats."

HB: And while *Sandman* had featured lots of cats and birds to that point, there was a huge dog vacuum.

NG: Right, lots of cats, lots of birds . . . so here we go, a dog.

HB: Where did Barnabas's name come from?

NG: Partly from the saint. And mostly from the comic strip *Barnaby* by Crockett Johnson. *Barnaby* is about a boy with a fairy godfather who only he can see, à la *Calvin and Hobbes*. It was done in the 1940s, and its characters got caught up in long and involved adventures such as "Mr. O'Malley, the Wizard of Wall Street," in which the fairy godfather takes over the financial world.

HB: One other thing I want to ask about is the large cast you created for *Sandman*. Was this because your mind was teeming with so many ideas and people that they just naturally flowed out onto the page?

NG: I think it was more that I wanted to create the feel of a populated world. Also, it was necessary for the stories. If you're going to do a tale about a serial killers' convention, for example, you've got to create thirty or so serial killers. My script for *Sandman* 14, "Collectors," actually contains a lot more information than appears in the story; and for a lot of the killers, I had much more background in mind than even made it into the script.

I like the feeling that the story I'm telling is in some way an iceberg. There should always be more that's untold.

—

music, poetry, and patterns

14

We are the music-makers,
And we are the dreamers of dreams,
Wandering by lone sea breakers,
And sitting by desolate streams.
World-losers and world-forsakers,
On whom the pale moon gleams:
Yet we are the movers and shakers
Of the world forever, it seems.

—ARTHUR O'SHAUGHNESSY

Writing a comic book has been compared to creating a screenplay, because in both cases the author is working with words and images. Writing a comic has also been compared to doing a radio play, because comics provide everything but sound and radio provides nothing but sound.

Neil Gaiman wouldn't argue against either of those comparisons, but he prefers to think of comics writing as a form of poetry. "You have this relentless economy," says Gaiman, "since you can comfortably fit only a few word balloons in a panel and only a few sentences in a balloon. Because I have to pack a lot of information into a relatively small space, I try to take the poetic approach of making words and sentences say more than one thing at a time."

Gaiman also carefully selects the imagery in the panels, and the arrangement of the panels themselves, to set up a rhythm that's appropriate for each scene. Between the beat of its panels and the poetry of its words, an issue of *Sandman* can be seen as a kind of soundless song.

WORDS VERSUS PICTURES

HB: When you create a scene, what comes first: the words or the images?

NG: Sometimes I construct a scene as the reader ultimately sees it, panel by panel. Sometimes I write out the entire conversation that takes place in a scene, and then go back and break the dialogue down into pictures and panels. And sometimes I just don't know what's going to happen in a scene, so I first work it out intuitively by drawing panels with little stick figures, and then turn those initial breakdowns into fully developed descriptions and dialogue.

PAGE 2 PANEL 1

SAME GRID, SAME PLACE, SAME SCENE. IT'S ALL VERY DOMESTIC, MARC. ALL VERY
SWEET AND REASSURING. THREE LADIES IN A LITTLE COTTAGE, HAVING A DISCUSSION
THAT COULD, QUITE POSSIBLY, BE ABOUT MAKING WOOLLY GARMENTS FOR PEOPLE. THE
MOTHER, SITTING IN HER CHAIR. SHE'S GOT ABOUT AN INCH OF KNITTING ON HER
NEEDLES NOW. BALL OF YARN IN HER LAP (AND THE END OF THAT YARN STILL GOING
OFF-PANEL). A HUGE BLACK CAT WITH GREEN EYES IS TWINING BETWEEN HER LEGS.

Mother: Now then, you mustn't say things like that. You know you don't mean
them.

        purl one, plain one, purl two together...

Mother: Why, that's what I like about making things for people. You can
start off in Birmingham and finish in, well, Tangyanika or somewhere.

PAGE 2 PANEL 2

IN THE KITCHEN. THE OLD HAG (WELL, LET'S NOT MINCE WORDS, THAT'S WHAT SHE
IS). SHE HAS AN ENORMOUS TEA POT, AND IS SPOONING TEA LEAVES INTO IT. THE
KETTLE IS STEAMING.

Mother (off):   That's not messy, my cherub. That's exciting.

Crone: Exciting my aunt banana!

        What's so exciting about it?

Mother (off):   Well, every one we make's unique. Never seen before. Never
seen again.

PAGE 2 PANEL 3

THE CRONE, BUT IN CLOSE-UP. SHE'S POURING BOILING WATER FROM THE KETTLE
INTO THE TEA-POT. LOTS OF STEAM. WE'RE LOOKING AT THE WATER AND THE KETTLE
AND THE POT, MAINLY.

CRONE: HMMPH. I DON'T KNOW WHY THAT'S EXCITING. IT'S NOT LIKE ANYONE
NOTICES WHAT WE DO. NOT LIKE ANYONE CARES.

Crone: And they're always complaining: they don't like the fit of it; too
loose -- too tight -- too different -- too much like everyone else's.

PAGE 2 PANEL 4

THE CRONE. SHE'S RAISED HER ARMS HIGH, IS WIGGLING HER FINGERS AROUND,
PRETENDING TO BE SOMEONE COMPLAINING. HER RAGGEDY SKIRTS ARE FLAPPING.
SHE'S TALKING, WHITE HAIR BLOWING AROUND HER HEAD.

Crone: It's never what they want, and if we give them what they think they
want they like it less than ever.

Crone: "I never thought it would be like this." "Why can't it be like the
one I had before?"

        I don't know why we bother.

4

A page from an original Neil Gaiman script for *The Sandman*.

The way I think of it is that sometimes it's easier to film a silent movie and then lay down a matching soundtrack, and sometimes it's easier to record a radio play and then synch it with the appropriate images.

HB: Do you feel especially strong at handling a particular aspect of comics?

NG: I definitely feel competent at coming up with the right images, and at telling a story smoothly by creating the right image-to-image transitions. I say that because my storytelling is recognizably *mine* from artist to artist. In other words, you can pretty much identify a story I've done from its selection of images and shots, regardless of whether it's been drawn by a realistic artist like Michael Zulli or an abstract artist like Marc Hempel.

And I like my dialogue—but I would, wouldn't I? [*Laughter.*]

HB: Do you ever find the words and pictures fighting one another?

NG: Only to the extent that whenever I'm in trouble, I fall back on words. If you read *Sandman* and run across a really pretty caption—a caption that makes you go, "my, how beautifully written"—that means you've reached a point where I was floundering and had no idea how to properly illustrate the panel. That's always my solution to such problems—pretty words.

HB: You're reminding me of what Goethe once said: "It is just when ideas are lacking that a phrase is most welcome."

NG: Exactly.

THE RHYTHM OF PANELS

HB: Can you talk a bit about how you used different panel layouts to tell stories effectively in *Sandman*?

NG: I often think of comics as songs. You're looking at the beat. And one of the things you get in comics that you never get in prose—or almost never, for it's much harder to do in prose—is the rhythm of a sequence of panels.

Look at, for example, part 8 of *The Kindly Ones*. On page 23, we jump into this nine-panel grid in which Rose is reviewing her past love life, or lack of same, which causes her to make a phone call to pursue her new romantic interest, and the dialogue goes bop, bop, bop, bop. In the last panel, the man she's just slept with tells her that he's already involved with someone else. We then move to the top of page 24, which is a three-panel grid of Rose, arms folded, sitting alone on her bed. The first two panels are completely silent—beat, beat—and then the third panel has Rose uttering one word—a little "fuck."

And the effect works completely. The panels control the timing, and they help us see how events are taking place in time. I don't know how you could do a comparable thing in prose and achieve that impact.

And it's not something you could do in film, either, because film also lacks that "beat, beat" effect—you can't cut into the same image in a movie.

So that's one of the special cool things you can do in comics. One of the main reasons I like comics is that things exist in time, and there are many ways you can play around with time using sequential panels.

HB: How about another example?

NG: Well, chapter 2 of *Brief Lives* started off with the Sandman being moody and distant, so I used the three, three grid for the first two pages, then ran three panels by themselves across the middle of page 3.

For pages 4 through 7, however, I went to a single large panel across the top that's centered on a silent, brooding Sandman. Below that panel, I framed a six-grid layout that portrays characters in The Dreaming talking about the Sandman's unexpressed feelings. The overall effect on the page is of the Sandman practically being the panel border itself, with all the emotional exposition below occurring within him.

HB: Which is quite appropriate, since he and The Dreaming are part of each other. Are there any other rituals you used to create *Sandman* scripts?

NG: I constructed a minicomic of each issue of *Sandman* I was about to write. Specifically, I took eight sheets of paper and folded them over to create twenty-four minipages. I sketched a little *Sandman* cover on the first page, ignored the next page, and numbered the subsequent pages 1, 2, 3, and so on, marking out where the ads are. And then I'd write, more or less, what I wanted to have happen on each page.

Cover doodle by Neil Gaiman himself, for the minicomic of "Hob's Leviathan."

THE CHALLENGES OF SERIAL WRITING

HB: One key aspect of doing a comics series as opposed to, say, a novel or a movie script, is that you have to publish an installment of your story every month. This sort of serial writing was common in the days of Charles Dickens, but it's rare now outside of comics and episodic television. What impact did writing *Sandman* in installments have on the way you worked?

NG: It forced me to produce a story every month, no matter what; and it allowed me to gauge audience reactions as a storyline progressed.

But it also robbed me of the freedom to go back and change something earlier in the story—because that installment had already been printed.

One of the things I love about writing novels is that if I'm on page 130 and I suddenly realize that I need a gun in a desk drawer on page 20, I can flip back and insert the gun—and when the book is published, readers will assume that that gun was always in the drawer on page 20. The same is true if I suddenly realize my tall, masculine protagonist should really be blond and curvy, or live in Quebec rather than Alabama—or that the entire story took a wrong turn on page 78.

But if I decide in issue 40 of a comics series than I needed a gun in a drawer in issue 20, I'm screwed. So I had to write *Sandman* in a sneaky way that attempted to mitigate such problems. In fact, when I read Dickens, I recognize him doing the same kind of thing.

HB: Can you give some examples?

NG: Sometimes, for the sake of pacing a story properly—say, to create a pause for breath between two major events—I'd devote a page to an event outside the main story. I'd generally create a new character for such a "filler" page, without any intention of using that character again. In the back of my mind, though, I knew that I was also creating insurance for myself, because the character might come in handy several issues later in ways that I couldn't possibly anticipate. Creating throwaway characters—and, similarly, throwaway scenes, and throwaway images—were things I did to help ensure I didn't eventually write myself into a corner.

I thought of it like juggling. I'd toss a story element into the air, knowing that I might catch it and set it down in a scene that occurs, say, twelve issues later. Or I might never catch it and just leave it floating up in the ether.

HB: Even so, were there times when you found yourself on an unexpected path with no elegant way to move forward?

NG: Oh yes. [*Laughter.*] One example that comes to mind is the blood on the Sandman's throne, which first appears in *Brief Lives* [*pointing to chapter 7, page 14, panel 4*]. This is where we first see, in a vision of the future, the Sandman's replacement—or his back, anyway. He's facing Dream's white throne, which has a small pool of blood on it. The caption reads, "There is blood on the throne of the Dream King. The Corinthian stands behind it, trembling—red, wet tears dribbling from his mouths. The Dream King looks up, slowly, and speaks to him. He is dressed entirely in white."

When I wrote that caption, the blood was meant to be Matthew's; I'd planned for the Corinthian to kill him in the last issue of *The Kindly Ones*. When I got to that point, however, Assistant Editor Alisa Kwitney got very, very upset about Matthew dying. Whether it had anything to do with her recently newborn son being named Matthew, I don't know; but Alisa convinced me the story would be better if we spared our favorite raven's life. So, I had the Corinthian kill an utterly unimportant and repulsive spider-creature instead—a creature we'd never seen before, and whose sole purpose was to have its blood spilled in place of Matthew's. I felt I'd cheated my way out of the problem, so I refer to the incident on page 55 of *The Wake*, in which Daniel tells Matthew flat out, "It should have been your blood spilled on the throne of the Dream King. The Corinthian was to have killed you." Matthew asks, "So why didn't he?", and Daniel responds, "Because I did not wish it. I summoned the Nybbas; I changed the Corinthian's mind." But actually, it was *Alisa* who changed *my* mind. This scene is one of the few places in the series where Dream is speaking directly for me as author.

REPEATING PATTERNS

HB: Another technique worth noting is your poetic use of both visual and thematic repetition. For example, *Sandman* is full of images that appear over and over, including birds, cats, books, doors, houses, food, rubies, fire beings, stained glass, broken glass, hearts—what else?

NG: There's a lot of eye imagery.

HB: Oh, sure, and eyes that take a lot of abuse. Near the end of part 9 of *The Kindly Ones*, ravens chat with Matthew as they peck out a dead Gilbert's eyes. And just one page later, there's a close-up of two empty sockets in Loki's face after the Corinthian has, off camera, plucked out and devoured the old god's eyes. At the beginning of your script for the issue, you refer to this mayhem in your typically understated way, writing that the story's events include "fighting and burning and banging and so forth—not to mention the injury to the eye motif, which has always been a part of *Sandman* . . . thank you, Dr. Wertham." [*Laughter.*] That's a reference to Fredric Wertham, the author of the infamous 1953 book *Seduction of the Innocent* that argued violence in comic books causes juvenile delinquency.

NG: We do what we can. [*Laughter.*] Actually, given that comics is an entirely visual medium—that is, the content isn't conveyed by sound, or touch, or taste, just sight—I think it's perfectly natural that an "injury to eye" theme would develop in horror comics.

HB: And it makes twice as much sense in a horror comic about dreams, which also tend to be primarily visual.

You also repeat certain events. One centers around young black women burning, which starts with Nada's city being consumed by a fireball on page 17 of *The Doll's House* story "Tales in the Sand." It continues with Ruby, who chauffeurs the Sandman and Delirium around in the waking world in *Brief Lives*; on pages 22 and 23 of chapter 4, Ruby dies in a hotel fire resulting from her smoking in bed. And it happens a third time in *The Kindly Ones* via Lyta Hall's friend Carla, who Loki incinerates in her car on page 24 of part 5.

NG: I even refer to that pattern in part 8 of *The Kindly Ones*, when the Corinthian consumes Ruby's dead eyes so he can find out who killed her. Matthew asks him what he sees, and the Corinthian replies, "I saw a hotel room burning. I saw fire engulf a city built of glass." Matthew asks, "You think those are clues?" And the Corinthian answers, "I think they're echoes, or ripples."

HB: Another recurring event is that of rulers giving up their kingdoms. For example, Lucifer leaves hell; Destruction abandons his realm; and, displaying more subtle methods of abdication, Augustus Caesar arranges for his kingdom to be destroyed, and the caliph of Baghdad relinquishes his kingdom so that it will live forever. And, of course, the series ends with the Sandman handing off his kingdom to a kindler, gentler Dream.

You also repeated certain storytelling techniques. Among the most notable—and least understood by readers—was your inserting into the middle of a storyline such as *The Doll's House* or *Season of Mists* a tale barely connected to the narrative. Each of these tales works to sum up and comment on the main themes of the storyline that it's "interrupting."

NG: Right. The first time I did this was in the *Preludes & Nocturnes* story "24 Hours." That tale contains an extended essay about the nature of storytelling, which is largely what *Preludes & Nocturnes* is about. The essay also provides considerable information about the entire series, including this line on page 4: "She's realized the real problem with stories—if you keep them going long enough, they always end in death."

Similarly, in the middle of *The Doll's House* I did issue 13, "Men of Good Fortune," which deals with the walls people build around themselves and the tearing down of those walls—in other words, most of what *The Doll's House* is about.

And in *Season of Mists*, I stopped in the middle and did issue 25, about the schoolboy who comments, "Hell's something you carry around with you," and his friend who replies, "I don't think I agree. I think maybe Hell is a place. But you don't have to stay anywhere forever." The two of them opt to walk away from it all; and thematically, that's *Season of Mists* in a nutshell.

Having followed this formula three times, I was concerned about being predictable, so I didn't use it at all in *A Game of You*; and I only halfway used it in chapter 5 of *Brief Lives*, via the tale of Ishtar the Dancer.

Finally, I returned to the technique in *The Kindly Ones* but tried to do it a different way. That's why, right in the middle of part 6, you see the fairy tale about winged children, dysfunctional families, and vengeance. In those eight pages is everything you need to know about the big story that's going on, told in miniature.

QUIET MOMENTS

HB: One last thing I want to ask about your storytelling concerns *Sandman* going against the grain of comic books, which have traditionally been loud and explosive. In a 1991 interview with the *Chicago Tribune*, you said, "It took a while for *Sandman* to click because it wasn't a formula comic. . . . It's about people. It's quiet." Up front I mentioned your use of silence, but I'd like to delve into the subject a bit deeper now. What did you mean by "It's quiet"?

NG: *Sandman* is very rarely about big things happening. My favorite scenes in the series are the little moments. Like Augustus and Lycius, from "August" in *Fables and Reflections,* sitting in the marketplace in the noonday sun. In *A Game of You*, Wanda goes upstairs to borrow milk and is forced to carry it downstairs using a cute frog mug as a container. To me, that's what *Sandman* is about—people carrying cute frog mugs.

I also really like the moment early in issue 19, "A Midsummer's Night's Dream," when Shakespeare's actors are waiting on the hill, before any of the action begins, and spend the time just readying themselves and trading banter. And in the following issue, "Facade," when poor Rainie is sitting alone in a room populated with empty face masks, and she's unable to get the person she wants on the phone.

HB: Please mention some more scenes.

NG: Well, I have a special fondness for the moment near the end of *Season of Mists* when the Sandman says good-bye to Nada.

And I'm very fond of the scene where the two schoolboys, Edwin and Charles, leave their school in episode 4 of *Season of Mists*.

Those for me are the high points, not the "big booms." *Sandman* was never about the big booms.

HB: Any other scenes you can think of?

NG: One other that comes to mind is chapter 3 of *Brief Lives*, when Dream and Delirium are flying on a plane. While Del is looking out the window at clouds, the Sandman overhears a conversation a little girl named Chloe is having with her mother. Chloe says, "I had a dream that I was looking for you and Daddy... and I was lost. And I was scared I'd be lost forever."

Her mother answers, "You're a silly mouse. You can't get lost in a dream," and then goes off to the rest room. The Sandman turns and says, "Child? Your mother was wrong. You can indeed become lost, in dreams. And you may not always find yourself when you wake up."

The two of them continue to chat off-panel. When the mother returns, she asks Chloe what the strange man was telling her, and Chloe responds, with a very thoughtful expression, "True things."

That whole sequence—including when, a few panels later, Chloe asks the Sandman about flying in dreams—is probably my favorite scene in all of *Brief Lives*.

HB: As opposed to, say, the climactic scene in the next issue, when Ruby dies engulfed in flames. Or the issue after, when Ishtar's unrestrained dancing blows a building to smithereens.

NG: Yes. The events you just mentioned were necessary to push the story forward, or to make a point. Given an equal choice in *Sandman* between a climax and an anticlimax, though, I'd always choose the anticlimax.

—

struggles and triumphs

15

Whenever I'm asked what kind of writing is the most lucrative, I have to say ransom notes.

—LITERARY AGENT H. N. SWANSON

The two hardest things to handle in life are failure and success.

—ANONYMOUS

Embarking on any creative endeavor requires taking several leaps of faith. Specifically, you need the belief that you have something worth saying; that you have the ability, courage and perseverance to say it; and that there will be a receptive audience for what you're creating.

Maintaining that belief can often be difficult . . . especially if your livelihood depends on something as ethereal as pulling characters from the air and making them come to life.

Ten years after its debut, *Sandman* is recognized worldwide as a critical and financial success; but this happy fate was far from assured at the start. As detailed in chapter 1 of this book, the young Gaiman had sold only a handful of comics (the forty-four-page *Violent Cases* and three issues of *Black Orchid*) when DC editor Karen Berger offered him a monthly series. Gaiman recollects that he was "not at all certain" he was up to the challenge and that "part of me was terrified at having to tell a story a month."

In this final interview, Gaiman recounts how he learned to listen to his audience and dealt with the dangers of success.

SANDMAN'S AUDIENCE

HB: Let's chat a little more about *Sandman's* audience. I'm not familiar with any of DC's marketing surveys, but I imagine you got a sense of who your readers were from your signing tours.

NG: Oh, sure. I can tell you that *Sandman* has many more female readers than a typical comic; possibly as much as half its audience is female. The people who came to signings initially were men, and girls, and tall guys with beards, and college students with knapsacks. As we got more readers, I started to see girls dressed as Death, and guys who looked kind of Sandman-ish.

HB: How influenced were you by feedback from your audience? For example, did you pay any attention to what people said to you at signings, or to what readers wrote in letters?

NG: Yes, but not in the way they thought. For example, when I began scripting *Sandman*, I already knew who Death was, and I knew that she would make her debut in issue 8. So I had the Sandman mention on page 37 of the first issue that he's Death's younger brother, knowing that the inherent sexism of language was on my side. And I was hugely gratified when letters started pouring in asking, "We've met Dream, the younger brother, but when are we going to meet Death, the older brother?" My reaction was, "Good. That's what I wanted." So I paid attention in that way—to make sure that seeds I'd planted were growing in the right directions.

HB: While we're on the subject of feedback, did the artists you collaborated with have an impact on the storyline?

NG: They did but, again, in indirect ways. I'd always try to tailor each script to the particular strengths and enthusiasms of the artist who was assigned to draw it, because the better the story looked, the better it would work. I'd also sometimes take things I'd see artists do in stories—including happy accidents—and make use of those elements in later stories. For example, if I especially liked the way an artist drew a certain character, I might decide to bring the character back.

HB: What about Dave McKean, who you refer to in the acknowledgments for *Brief Lives* as "my friend and collaborator and hardest critic"—did his opinions have an influence on *Sandman*?

NG: In some ways. For example, if I really didn't know what I was doing, I'd phone Dave and say, "At this point of the story, I can go in direction one, two, or three. What do you think?" And Dave would answer, "Choice one doesn't sound right, and choice two is kind of hokey. Why don't you do three?" But Dave's contributions to *Sandman*'s direction were mostly a matter of attitudes and intangibles.

HB: So what I'm hearing is that the primary audience you were writing for was you—your own tastes and judgments.

NG: Yes.

THE DOWNSIDE OF EXPERIENCE AND ACCLAIM

HB: Did coming up with interesting ways to tell stories become easier or harder as time went on?

NG: Definitely harder.

HB: That's not the intuitive answer; most people would assume the process got easier as you went along.

NG [*shaking head*]: When I started out and had almost no experience, everything that I did was new for me—every image, every panel transition. I'd sit there and go [*imitating a young, slightly giddy Neil*], "OK, on this page I'll have three panels along the top, three panels along the bottom . . . and one long panel in the middle!" Simply deciding something like that was fun and exciting; and such decisions flowed easily, because I didn't have to worry about repeating myself.

As I reached the halfway point on *Sandman*, however, my scripts began taking longer and longer to complete. I'd start to lay out a page and then say, "No, I already used that panel sequence in *The Doll's House*," or "I already exploited that image in *Season of Mists*."

HB: In your script for issue 71, you wrote, "God, I wish I were still a fast writer. I'm not slow, by any rational criterion, but I'm not fast anymore. Thinking takes longer—particularly on *Sandman*, where I've done it before. I've done it all before."

NG: Exactly. And I didn't want to go to places I'd already visited. As a result, I'd have to sweat out new ways to tell each story.

HB: This may be a stupid question, but—why?

NG: I'm not sure how to explain it other than to say I felt it was critical artistically to never stop—to keep moving forward, like a shark.

HB: Okay; but I'm guessing you also felt a certain amount of pressure to keep topping yourself. When you began on *Sandman*, no one knew who you were. By the midway point, you'd garnered praise from the likes of Norman Mailer, Stephen

---

SANDMAN'S AWARDS

The two major awards in comics are the Eisner—named after Will Eisner, whose groundbreaking work on *The Spirit* had a major influence on many comics creators, including Neil Gaiman; and the Harvey—named after Harvey Kurtzman, the brilliant artist, writer, and editor who cocreated *Mad Magazine*.

Gaiman won the Eisner for Best Writer four years in a row, in 1991, 1992, 1993, and 1994. In addition, *The Sandman* won for Best Continuing Series in 1991, 1992, and 1993; for Best Reprint Graphic Album in 1991; and for Best New Graphic Album in 1993.

Gaiman also won the Harvey for Best Writer in 1990 and 1991; and *The Sandman* won for Best Continuing Series in 1992.

Gaiman won numerous other awards as well, such as Diamond Distributors' Gem, which is voted on by comic retailers internationally to express appreciation for the creator they feel has helped the most to expand the comics market.

Perhaps most impressively, though, *Sandman* 19, "A Midsummer Night's Dream," won the 1991 World Fantasy Award for Best Short Story, making it the first monthly comic ever to win a literary award. In his introduction to *Fables and Reflections*, Gene Wolfe wrote, "It's almost incredible that a 'comic book' should be good enough to win—to force itself upon the judges . . . [that] some of the best writing of our time is appearing in a graphic medium in which writing traditionally comes second—and a long way second at that."

King, and Clive Barker. It must have been difficult continuing to turn out a story a month while feeling that the world's eyes were upon you.

NG: It definitely was. My favorite time on *Sandman* was when I felt no one was looking; not the comics intelligentsia and not the mainstream press. The early days when people were reading us, we had good word of mouth and nobody really cared what we did—that was great. G. K. Chesterton once said, "Angels fly because they take themselves lightly." I'd say there are spots in early issues of *Sandman* where it left the ground and elegantly floated into the air.

Then all of a sudden, around the time *A Game of You* began, we won every award in comics, and we became the standard by which other comics were judged.

HB: Snaring dozens of prestigious awards sounds wonderful on the surface. However, it can easily lead to a writer feeling self-conscious and pressured about continuing to perform his art.

NG: It was unquestionably a mixed blessing. After the first round of awards, I began freezing up, getting terrifying writer's blocks. I ultimately suffered five or six major writer's blocks over the course of doing *Sandman*.

HB: You refer to some of those periods in your scripts. By the time you've reached the script for *Sandman* 55, you appear to be feeling better, but you note, "I wish to God it got easier as you go along; I keep feeling that I've earned some kind of right not to sweat blood over each script. I mean, don't all these stupid awards and things mean anything? (Answer: No.) The beginning of each story is still a process of staring at a blank screen until blood beads up on my forehead."

Similarly, in your notes for *Sandman* 56, you say, "I was really worried that I had writer's block, but I just flipped screens on the computer and wrote the first three pages of a more or less pornographic short story, so [it looks like] I can still write. Sometimes I have my doubts."

How did you get over these writing blocks?

NG: The main thing that got me past any block on *Sandman* was the relentless monthly schedule, and the knowledge that people were depending on me.

I fell back on a couple of mental tricks too, though. Probably most important was the one you just referred to.

HB: Writing pornography?

NG: No, Hy. [*Laughter.*] Just writing something else for a while. The "more or less pornographic" work I referred to, by the way, became "Tastings" in my short story collection *Smoke and Mirrors*.

The point is, I almost never felt blocked from writing altogether. I would typically get stuck on a particular storyline—the characters in my head would stop talking, and stop moving, as if someone had pressed the "still" button on a VCR. But if I switched to an entirely different type of story, I'd find that I was still able to get characters to come to life and proceed through a tale—and that in turn restored my confidence in being able to write in general, which helped unclog my block. In fact, it's largely for this reason that I've developed the habit of always having at least two different writing projects going at the same time.

HB: You said you used a couple of tricks. What's the other one?

NG: It's not much of a trick, actually—I just sit down and write, regardless of how bad the stuff I'm producing is. I can do that because I know I'll wake up the next day, look at what I've done, and say, "Yes, that is indeed not very good; but it's mainly because this sentence here is entirely superfluous, the paragraph following it is clunky, and the scene in the middle should be moved to the top." In other words, when my writing facilities are on the blink for a little while, I can still rely on the editor part of my head to read what I've done objectively—that is, as if someone else wrote it—and fix the problems.

HB: I'll just add I find it oddly comforting that it was in the midst of your worst block, at the end of *Brief Lives*, that you wrote one of the most bittersweet and humane passages in the series: "We will put him to rest, thinks Andros Rhodocanakis, beneath the cherry tree. And perhaps his spirit is in Elysium, with his beloved Eurydice. And perhaps his spirit has returned to darkness, or to nothing.

"And perhaps he is at rest.

"Perhaps his spirit will move into the cherry tree, and in spring the new blossoms will be his, and in summer the cherries will taste of true poetry and song . . .

"No.

"Andros knows he will not live to see the tree blossom again.

"It is going to be a beautiful day."

—

THE SANDMAN COMPANION

appendixes

sandman credits

Give credit where credit is due.

—ANONYMOUS

Most readers are familiar with *The Sandman* via its ten book collections, but the series was originally published as a monthly comic book. The sequentially numbered series began with issue 1 in December 1988 and ended with issue 75 in March 1996. In addition, a key story titled "The Song of Orpheus" was published outside this numbering sequence as *The Sandman Special* in September 1991, so there are a total of 76 issues in the series. There were also two short-short tales, "Fear of Falling" and "The Castle," that appeared respectively in the anthology titles *Vertigo Preview* 1 and *Vertigo Jam* 1.

This appendix is a list of those issues. Each issue is represented by its number, the *Sandman* book collection it appears in, its title, and—most important—the names of the talented people who created it. An issue's story is twenty-four pages long unless otherwise noted.

1. *Preludes & Nocturnes—*
   Sleep of the Just   **40 pages**

Neil Gaiman	writer
Sam Kieth	penciller
Mike Dringenberg	inker
Robbie Busch	colorist
Todd Klein	letterer
Art Young	assistant editor
Karen Berger	editor

2. *Preludes & Nocturnes—***Imperfect Hosts**

Neil Gaiman	writer
Sam Kieth	penciller
Mike Dringenberg	inker
Robbie Busch	colorist
Todd Klein	letterer
Art Young	assistant editor
Karen Berger	editor

3. *Preludes & Nocturnes—*
   Dream a Little Dream of Me

Neil Gaiman	writer
Sam Kieth	penciller
Mike Dringenberg	inker
Robbie Busch	colorist
Todd Klein	letterer
Art Young	assistant editor
Karen Berger	editor

4. *Preludes & Nocturnes—***A Hope in Hell**
   Blurbed as "Going to Hell"

Neil Gaiman	writer
Sam Kieth	penciller
Mike Dringenberg	inker
Robbie Busch	colorist
Todd Klein	letterer
Art Young	assistant editor
Karen Berger	editor

5. *Preludes & Nocturnes—***Passengers**
   Blurbed as "Monsters & Miracles"

Neil Gaiman	writer
Sam Kieth	penciller
Malcolm Jones III	inker
Robbie Busch	colorist
Todd Klein	letterer
Art Young	assistant editor
Karen Berger	editor

6. *Preludes & Nocturnes—***24 Hours**
   Blurbed as "Waiting for the End
   of the World"

Neil Gaiman	writer
Mike Dringenberg	penciller
Malcolm Jones III	inker
(with special thanks to Don Carola)	
Robbie Busch	colorist
Todd Klein	letterer
Art Young	assistant editor
Karen Berger	editor

7. *Preludes & Nocturnes*—Sound and Fury

Blurbed as "Dream's End"

Neil Gaiman	writer
Mike Dringenberg	penciller
Malcolm Jones III	inker
Robbie Busch	colorist
Todd Klein	letterer
Art Young	associate editor
Karen Berger	editor

8. *Preludes & Nocturnes*—
The Sound of Her Wings

Blurbed as "A Death in the Family"

Neil Gaiman	writer
Mike Dringenberg	penciller
Malcolm Jones III	inker
Robbie Busch	colorist
Todd Klein	letterer
Art Young	associate editor
Karen Berger	editor

9. *The Doll's House*—Tales in the Sand

Neil Gaiman	writer
Mike Dringenberg	penciller
Malcolm Jones III	inker
Robbie Busch	colorist
Todd Klein	letterer
Art Young	associate editor
Karen Berger	editor

10. *The Doll's House*—The Doll's House

Neil Gaiman	writer
Mike Dringenberg	penciller
Malcolm Jones III	inker
Robbie Busch	colorist
Todd Klein	letterer
Art Young	associate editor
Karen Berger	editor

11. *The Doll's House*—Moving In

Neil Gaiman	writer
Mike Dringenberg	penciller
Malcolm Jones III	inker
Robbie Busch	colorist
John Costanza	letterer
Art Young	associate editor
Karen Berger	editor

12. *The Doll's House*—Playing House

Neil Gaiman	writer
Chris Bachalo	penciller
Malcolm Jones III	inker
Robbie Busch	colorist
John Costanza	letterer
Art Young	associate editor
Karen Berger	editor

13. *The Doll's House*—
Men of Good Fortune

Neil Gaiman	writer
Michael Zulli	penciller
Steve Parkhouse	inker
Robbie Busch	colorist
Todd Klein	letterer
Art Young	assistant editor
Karen Berger	editor

14. *The Doll's House*—Collectors   38 pages

Neil Gaiman	writer
Mike Dringenberg	penciller
Malcolm Jones III	inker
Robbie Busch	colorist
Todd Klein	letterer
Art Young	associate editor
Karen Berger	editor

15. *The Doll's House*—Into the Night

Neil Gaiman	writer
Mike Dringenberg	penciller
(with help from Sam Kieth)	
Malcolm Jones III	inker
Robbie Busch	colorist
Todd Klein	letterer
Art Young	associate editor
Karen Berger	editor

16. *The Doll's House*—Lost Hearts

Neil Gaiman	writer
Mike Dringenberg	penciller
Malcolm Jones III	inker
Robbie Busch	colorist
Todd Klein	letterer
Tom Peyer	assistant editor
Karen Berger	editor

17. *Dream Country*—Calliope

Neil Gaiman	writer
Kelley Jones	penciller
Malcolm Jones III	inker
Robbie Busch	colorist
Todd Klein	letterer
Tom Peyer	assistant editor
Karen Berger	editor

18. *Dream Country*—
A Dream of a Thousand Cats

Neil Gaiman	writer
Kelley Jones	penciller
Malcolm Jones III	inker
Robbie Busch	colorist
Todd Klein	letterer
Tom Peyer	assistant editor
Karen Berger	editor

19. *Dream Country*—
A Midsummer Night's Dream

Neil Gaiman	writer
(with additional material taken from the play by William Shakespeare)	
Charles Vess	penciller / inker
Steve Oliff	colorist
Todd Klein	letterer
Tom Peyer	assistant editor
Karen Berger	editor

20. *Dream Country*—**Facade**

Neil Gaiman	writer
Colleen Doran	penciller
Malcolm Jones III	inker
Steve Oliff	colorist
Todd Klein	letterer
Tom Peyer	assistant editor
Karen Berger	editor

21. *Season of Mists*—**Prologue**

Neil Gaiman	writer
Mike Dringenberg	penciller
Malcolm Jones III	inker
Steve Oliff	colorist
Todd Klein	letterer
Tom Peyer	assistant editor
Karen Berger	editor

22. *Season of Mists*—**Chapter 1**

Neil Gaiman	writer
Kelley Jones	penciller
Malcolm Jones III	inker
Steve Oliff	colorist
Todd Klein	letterer
Tom Peyer	assistant editor
Karen Berger	editor

23. *Season of Mists*—**Chapter 2**

Neil Gaiman	writer
Kelley Jones	penciller
Malcolm Jones III	inker
Daniel Vozzo	colorist
Todd Klein	letterer
Tom Peyer	assistant editor
Karen Berger	editor

24. *Season of Mists*—**Chapter 3**

Neil Gaiman	writer
Kelley Jones	penciller
P. Craig Russell	inker
Daniel Vozzo	colorist
Todd Klein	letterer
Tom Peyer	assistant editor
Karen Berger	editor

25. *Season of Mists*—**Chapter 4**

Neil Gaiman	writer
Matt Wagner	penciller
Malcolm Jones III	inker
Daniel Vozzo	colorist
Todd Klein	letterer
Tom Peyer	assistant editor
Karen Berger	editor

26. *Season of Mists*—**Chapter 5**

Neil Gaiman	writer
Kelley Jones	penciller
George Pratt	inker
Daniel Vozzo	colorist
Todd Klein	letterer
Alisa Kwitney	assistant editor
Karen Berger	editor

27. *Season of Mists*—**Chapter 6**

Neil Gaiman	writer
Kelley Jones	penciller
Dick Giordano	inker
Daniel Vozzo	colorist
Todd Klein	letterer
Alisa Kwitney	assistant editor
Karen Berger	editor

28. *Season of Mists*—**Epilogue**

Neil Gaiman	writer
Mike Dringenberg	penciller
George Pratt	inker
Daniel Vozzo	colorist
Todd Klein	letterer
Alisa Kwitney	assistant editor
Karen Berger	editor

29. *Fables and Reflections/*
Distant Mirrors—Thermidor

Neil Gaiman	writer
Stan Woch	penciller
Dick Giordano	inker
Daniel Vozzo	colorist
Todd Klein	letterer
Alisa Kwitney	assistant editor
Karen Berger	editor

30. *Fables and Reflections/*
Distant Mirrors—August

Neil Gaiman	writer
Bryan Talbot	penciller
Stan Woch	inker
Daniel Vozzo	colorist
Todd Klein	letterer
Alisa Kwitney	assistant editor
Karen Berger	editor

31. *Fables and Reflections*/Distant Mirrors—
Three Septembers and a January

Neil Gaiman	writer
Shawn McManus	penciller and inker
Daniel Vozzo	colorist
Todd Klein	letterer
Alisa Kwitney	assistant editor
Karen Berger	editor

32. *A Game of You*—Chapter 1,
Slaughter on Fifth Avenue   25 pages

Neil Gaiman	writer
Shawn McManus	penciller and inker
Daniel Vozzo	colorist
Todd Klein	letterer
Alisa Kwitney	assistant editor
Karen Berger	editor

33. *A Game of You*—Chapter 2,
Lullabies of Broadway   23 pages

Neil Gaiman	writer
Shawn McManus	penciller and inker
Daniel Vozzo	colorist
Todd Klein	letterer
Alisa Kwitney	assistant editor
Karen Berger	editor

34. *A Game of You*—Chapter 3,
Bad Moon Rising

Neil Gaiman	writer
Colleen Doran	penciller
George Pratt / Dick Giordano	inkers
Daniel Vozzo	colorist
Todd Klein	letterer
Alisa Kwitney	assistant editor
Karen Berger	editor

35. *A Game of You*—Chapter 4,
Beginning to See the Light

Neil Gaiman	writer
Shawn McManus	penciller and inker
Daniel Vozzo	colorist
Todd Klein	letterer
Alisa Kwitney	assistant editor
Karen Berger	editor

36. *A Game of You*—Chapter 5,
Over the Sea to Sky   39 pages

Neil Gaiman	writer
Shawn McManus / Bryan Talbot	pencillers
Shawn McManus / Stan Woch	inkers
Daniel Vozzo	colorist
Todd Klein	letterer
Alisa Kwitney	assistant editor
Karen Berger	editor

37. *A Game of You*—Chapter 6,
I Woke Up and One of Us Was Crying

Neil Gaiman	writer
Shawn McManus	penciller and inker
Daniel Vozzo	colorist
Todd Klein	letterer
Alisa Kwitney	assistant editor
Karen Berger	editor

38. *Fables and Reflections*/Convergence—
The Hunt

Neil Gaiman	writer
Duncan Eagleson	penciller
Vince Locke	inker
Daniel Vozzo	colorist
Todd Klein	letterer
Alisa Kwitney	assistant editor
Karen Berger	editor

39. *Fables and Reflections*/Convergence—
Soft Places

Neil Gaiman	writer
John Watkiss	penciller and inker
Daniel Vozzo	colorist
Todd Klein	letterer
Alisa Kwitney	assistant editor
Karen Berger	editor

40. *Fables and Reflections*/Convergence—The
Parliament of Rooks

Neil Gaiman	writer
Jill Thompson	penciller
Vince Locke	inker
Daniel Vozzo	colorist
Todd Klein	letterer
Alisa Kwitney	assistant editor
Karen Berger	editor

41. *Brief Lives*—Chapter 1

Neil Gaiman	writer
Jill Thompson	penciller
Vince Locke	inker
Daniel Vozzo	colorist
Todd Klein	letterer
Lisa Aufenanger	assistant editor
Karen Berger	editor

42. *Brief Lives*—Chapter 2

Neil Gaiman	writer
Jill Thompson	penciller
Vince Locke	inker
Daniel Vozzo	colorist
Todd Klein	letterer
Lisa Aufenanger	assistant editor
Karen Berger	editor

43. *Brief Lives*—Chapter 3

Neil Gaiman · writer
Jill Thompson · penciller
Vince Locke · inker
Daniel Vozzo · colorist
Todd Klein · letterer
Lisa Aufenanger · assistant editor
Karen Berger · editor

44. *Brief Lives*—Chapter 4

Neil Gaiman · writer
Jill Thompson · penciller
Vince Locke · inker
Daniel Vozzo · colorist
Todd Klein · letterer
Lisa Aufenanger · assistant editor
Karen Berger · editor

45. *Brief Lives*—Chapter 5

Neil Gaiman · writer
Jill Thompson · penciller
Vince Locke · inker
Daniel Vozzo · colorist
Todd Klein · letterer
Lisa Aufenanger · assistant editor
Karen Berger · editor

46. *Brief Lives*—Chapter 6

Neil Gaiman · writer
Jill Thompson · penciller
Vince Locke · inker
Daniel Vozzo · colorist
Todd Klein · letterer
Lisa Aufenanger · assistant editor
Karen Berger · editor

47. *Brief Lives*—Chapter 7

Neil Gaiman · writer
Jill Thompson · penciller
Vince Locke / Dick Giordano · inkers
Daniel Vozzo · colorist
Todd Klein · letterer
Karen Berger · editor

48. *Brief Lives*—Chapter 8

Neil Gaiman · writer
Jill Thompson · penciller
Vince Locke · inker
Daniel Vozzo · colorist
Todd Klein · letterer
Karen Berger · editor

49. *Brief Lives*—Chapter 9

Neil Gaiman · writer
Jill Thompson · penciller
Vince Locke · inker
Daniel Vozzo · colorist

Todd Klein · letterer
Karen Berger · editor

50. *Fables and Reflections/*
Distant Mirrors—Ramadan · **32 pages**

Neil Gaiman · writer
P. Craig Russell · penciller and inker
Lovern Kindzierski/ · colorist
Digital Chameleon
Todd Klein · letterer
Shelly Roeberg · assistant editor
Karen Berger · editor

51. *Worlds' End*—**A Tale of Two Cities**

Neil Gaiman · writer
Alec Stevens / Bryan Talbot · pencillers
Alec Stevens / Mark Buckingham · inkers
Daniel Vozzo · colorist
Todd Klein · letterer
Shelly Roeberg · assistant editor
Karen Berger · editor

52. *Worlds' End*—**Cluracan's Tale** · **25 pages**

Neil Gaiman · writer
John Watkiss / Bryan Talbot · pencillers
John Watkiss / Mark Buckingham · inkers
Daniel Vozzo · colorist
Todd Klein · letterer
Shelly Roeberg · assistant editor
Karen Berger · editor

53. *Worlds' End*—**Hob's Leviathan:**

Neil Gaiman · writer
Michael Zulli / Bryan Talbot · pencillers
Dick Giordano / Mark Buckingham · inkers
Daniel Vozzo · colorist
Todd Klein · letterer
Shelly Roeberg · assistant editor
Karen Berger · editor

54. *Worlds' End*—**The Golden Boy**

Neil Gaiman · writer
Michael Allred / Bryan Talbot · pencillers
Michael Allred / Mark Buckingham · inkers
Daniel Vozzo · colorist
Todd Klein · letterer
Shelly Roeberg · assistant editor
Karen Berger · editor

55. *Worlds' End*—**Cerements**

Neil Gaiman · writer
Shea Anton Pensa / Bryan Talbot · pencillers
Vince Locke / Mark Buckingham · inkers
Daniel Vozzo · colorist
Todd Klein · letterer
Shelly Roeberg · assistant editor
Karen Berger · editor

56. *Worlds' End*—Worlds' End

Neil Gaiman	writer
Gary Amaro / Bryan Talbot	pencillers
Dick Giordano / Steve Leialoha/	inkers
Tony Harris / Mark Buckingham	
Daniel Vozzo	colorist
Todd Klein	letterer
Shelly Roeberg	assistant editor
Karen Berger	editor

57. *The Kindly Ones*—1

Neil Gaiman	writer
Marc Hempel	penciller / inker
Daniel Vozzo	colorist
Todd Klein	letterer
Shelly Roeberg	assistant editor
Karen Berger	editor

58. *The Kindly Ones*—2

Neil Gaiman	writer
Marc Hempel	penciller
D'Israeli	inker
Daniel Vozzo	colorist
Todd Klein	letterer
Shelly Roeberg	assistant editor
Karen Berger	editor

59. *The Kindly Ones*—3

Neil Gaiman	writer
Marc Hempel	penciller
D'Israeli	inker
Daniel Vozzo	colorist
Todd Klein	letterer
Shelly Roeberg	assistant editor
Karen Berger	editor

60. *The Kindly Ones*—4

Neil Gaiman	writer
Marc Hempel	penciller
D'Israeli	inker
Daniel Vozzo	colorist
Todd Klein	letterer
Shelly Roeberg	assistant editor
Karen Berger	editor

61. *The Kindly Ones*—5

Neil Gaiman	writer
Marc Hempel	penciller
Marc Hempel / D'Israeli	inkers
Daniel Vozzo	colorist
Todd Klein	letterer
Shelly Roeberg	assistant editor
Karen Berger	editor

62. *The Kindly Ones*—6

Neil Gaiman	writer
Glyn Dillon / Charles Vess /	pencillers
Dean Ormston	
Glyn Dillon / Charles Vess / D'Israeli	inkers
Daniel Vozzo	colorist
Todd Klein	letterer
Shelly Roeberg	assistant editor
Karen Berger	editor

63. *The Kindly Ones*—7

Neil Gaiman	writer
Marc Hempel	penciller / inker,
Daniel Vozzo	colorist
Todd Klein	letterer
Shelly Roeberg	assistant editor
Karen Berger	editor

64. *The Kindly Ones*—8

Neil Gaiman	writer
Teddy Kristiansen	penciller / inker
Daniel Vozzo	colorist
Todd Klein	letterer
Shelly Roeberg	assistant editor
Karen Berger	editor

65. *The Kindly Ones*—9

Neil Gaiman	writer
Marc Hempel	penciller
Richard Case	inker
Daniel Vozzo	colorist
Todd Klein	letterer
Shelly Roeberg	assistant editor
Karen Berger	editor

66. *The Kindly Ones*—10

Neil Gaiman	writer
Marc Hempel	penciller
Richard Case	inker
Daniel Vozzo	colorist
Todd Klein	letterer
Shelly Roeberg	assistant editor
Karen Berger	editor

67. *The Kindly Ones*—11

Neil Gaiman	writer
Marc Hempel	penciller
Richard Case	inker
Daniel Vozzo	colorist
Todd Klein	letterer
Shelly Roeberg	assistant editor
Karen Berger	editor

68. *The Kindly Ones*—12

Neil Gaiman	writer
Marc Hempel / Richard Case	pencillers
Richard Case	inker

Daniel Vozzo   colorist
Todd Klein   letterer
Shelly Roeberg   assistant editor
Karen Berger   editor

69. *The Kindly Ones*—13

Neil Gaiman   writer
Marc Hempel   penciller / inker
Daniel Vozzo   colorist
Todd Klein   letterer
Shelly Roeberg   assistant editor
Karen Berger   editor

70. *The Wake*—Chapter 1, Which Occurs in the Wake of What Has Gone Before

Neil Gaiman   writer
Michael Zulli   penciller / inker
Daniel Vozzo   colorist
Todd Klein   letterer
Shelly Roeberg   assistant editor
Karen Berger   editor

71. *The Wake*—Chapter 2, In Which a Wake is Held

Neil Gaiman   writer
Michael Zulli   penciller / inker
Daniel Vozzo   colorist
Todd Klein   letterer
Shelly Roeberg   assistant editor
Karen Berger   editor

72. *The Wake*—Chapter 3, In Which We Wake

24 pages in the original comic,
26 pages in the collection (due to an expanded barge sequence)
Neil Gaiman   writer
Michael Zulli   penciller / inker
Daniel Vozzo   colorist
Todd Klein   letterer
Shelly Roeberg   assistant editor
Karen Berger   editor

73. *The Wake*—An Epilogue, Sunday Mourning

Neil Gaiman   writer
Michael Zulli   penciller / inker
Daniel Vozzo   colorist
Todd Klein   letterer
Shelly Roeberg   assistant editor
Karen Berger   editor

74. *The Wake*—Exiles

Neil Gaiman   writer
Jon J Muth   penciller / inker / colorist
Todd Klein   letterer
Shelly Roeberg   assistant editor
Karen Berger   editor

75. *The Wake*—The Tempest   38 pages

Neil Gaiman   writer
(with additional material taken from the play by William Shakespeare)
Charles Vess   penciller
(with help from Bryan Talbot, John Ridgway and Michael Zulli)
Charles Vess   inker
Daniel Vozzo   colorist
Todd Klein   letterer
Shelly Roeberg   assistant editor
Karen Berger   editor

The Sandman Special
1. *Fables and Reflections*— The Song of Orpheus   48 pages

Neil Gaiman   writer
Bryan Talbot   penciller
Mark Buckingham   inker
Daniel Vozzo   colorist
Todd Klein   letterer
Shelly Roeberg   assistant editor
Karen Berger   editor

Vertigo Preview 1. *Fables and Reflections*— Fear of Falling

Originally 7 pages, then expanded to 10 pages for inclusion in *Fables and Reflections*
Neil Gaiman   writer
Kent Williams   penciller / inker
Sherilyn van Valkenburgh   colorist
Todd Klein   letterer
Karen Berger   editor

Vertigo Jam 1. *The Kindly Ones*— The Castle   8 pages

Neil Gaiman   writer
Kevin Nowlan   penciller/inker/letterer
Daniel Vozzo   colorist
Shelly Roeberg   assistant editor
Karen Berger   editor

additional *sandman* tales

it ain't over till it's over.

—YOGI BERRA

The Sandman is a complete story with a definite ending. Over the course of its telling, however, Neil Gaiman created dozens of memorable characters about whom further stories could be spun. DC Comics has taken advantage of that by publishing several spin-offs from the original series.

The first appeared in 1993 and was done by Gaiman himself, in collaboration with penciller Chris Bachalo and inker Mark Buckingham. Titled *Death: The High Cost of Living*, it stars Gaiman's most popular character, focusing on the day in each century when Death chooses to become mortal. The first part of this three-issue miniseries outperformed even *Sandman* in sales. The issues have since been collected into book form along with a seven-page public service story (in which Death discusses using condoms to prevent AIDS) and an introduction by rock star Tori Amos.

Gaiman, Bachalo, and Buckingham, plus co-inker Mark Pennington, followed up in 1997 with a three-issue miniseries titled *Death: The Time of Your Life*; but Death plays only a supporting role in this tale, which revolves around the characters Hazel and Foxglove from *A Game of You*. These issues have been collected into a book with an introduction by actress Claire Danes.

In 1996, DC began publishing a monthly series called *The Dreaming* that tells tales of the Sandman's realm. Due to an informal agreement between Gaiman and DC, the writer of this title—who is currently Caitlín R. Kiernan—refrains from bringing on the Sandman or his family, but she's free to use any other characters from the series. Issues of *The Dreaming* have also been collected into books.

In 1997, DC began receiving proposals for a number of interesting *Sandman*-related tales that just didn't happen to fit in with the direction being charted for *The Dreaming*. Therefore, DC opted to publish the stories as miniseries under the umbrella title *Sandman Presents*. The first three of these *Sandman Presents* series are *Lucifer*, *Love Street*, and *Petrefax*.

Further, as I write this in 1999, Neil Gaiman himself is crafting a book titled *The Sandman: The Dream Hunters*, a lyrical prose fairy tale about Morpheus, a fox, and a monk that's being illustrated by acclaimed Japanese painter Yoshitaka Amano and will be released in fall 1999.

Additional *Sandman*-related projects are also in the works—and some will probably have already appeared by the time you read this.

The most famous is the *Sandman* movie, which has been "in development" for years. One of the main difficulties in getting this film off the ground is creating a screenplay that does justice to *Sandman*'s complexity and depth, and yet tells a story that's considered commercial by Hollywood standards. Here's how a somewhat frustrated Gaiman articulated the problem to interviewer David Carroll in 1997: "To make it film-shaped, it's like taking a baby and cutting off both of its arms and one of its legs and nose and trying to cram it in this little box, and filling the rest of the box up with meat. I don't think it works that way." Gaiman swore off involvement with this movie years ago, but he's gone on to write screenplays for a variety of other films; and (as this book goes to press, at least) there's talk of his both writing and directing a movie about Death.

for more information

Death ends a life but not a relationship.

—MORRIE SCHWARTZ

This appendix lists articles, books, CDs, Web sites, and other sources that contributed to this book and/or are likely to be enjoyed by *Sandman* readers. It also tells you where to send comments about either this book or the *Sandman* series.

Sources for This Book

The following publications were of great help in creating this book:

- "Lying Awake and Dreaming in a Storyteller's Field" by Thom Carnell. Article published in the #13/September 1998 issue of *Carpe Noctem*, a fine Goth magazine that often features interviews with genre writers and comics artists.

- "Refractions of *Empire*" by Samuel R. Delany. Article published in Delany's book *Silent Interviews* (Wesleyan University Press, 1994).

- "Tori Amos Interview" by Brian Hibbs. Article published in the October 1993 issue of *Magian Line*, edited by Sadie MacFarlane.

- "Dreamland" by Steve Erickson. Article published in the September 3, 1995, issue of the *Los Angeles Sunday Times Magazine*.

- "Aether/Ore: The Dreamworld Come Down to Earth" by Professor Alan Levitan. Paper presented at the seminar "Fictional Biographies of Shakespeare" during the 1996 World Shakespeare Congress in Los Angeles.

- *Magian Line*, edited by Sadie MacFarlane. Newsletter about Neil Gaiman that contains an interview with Gaiman in each issue; for subscription information, visit Web site sadieo.ucsf.edu/magian/magian.html, or write to Magian Line, P.O. Box 170712, San Francisco, CA 94117.

- *Understanding Comics: The Invisible Art* by Scott McCloud. Landmark book, done in comics form, that analyzes the medium (HarperPerennial, 1993).

- "Of Parents and Children and Dreams in Neil Gaiman's Mr. Punch and The Sandman" by Professor Joe Sanders. Article published in the #71/Autumn 1997 issue of *Foundation: The International Review of Science Fiction*, edited by Professor Edward James.

Other Work by Neil Gaiman

The following stories, graphic novels, and CDs mentioned in this book were written or cowritten by Neil Gaiman. All are highly recommended.

- *Ghastly Beyond Belief* by Neil Gaiman and Kim Newman. Fun 1985 book collection of SF and horror quotes (regrettably, out of print).

- *Violent Cases* by Neil Gaiman and Dave McKean. First Gaiman-McKean graphic novel, published in 1987 (out of print as I write this, but likely to be available again by the time you read it).

- *Black Orchid* by Neil Gaiman and Dave McKean. First Gaiman-McKean graphic novel for DC (1989, Vertigo/DC Comics).

- *Signal to Noise* by Neil Gaiman and Dave McKean. Haunting graphic novel about dying filmmaker, with text generation aided by Babble! software cocreated by Tracey M. Siesser (1989/1992, Dark Horse Comics).

- *Death: The High Cost of Living* by Neil Gaiman, Chris Bachalo, Mark Buckingham, and Dave McKean. First—and highly popular—*Sandman* spin-off starring Death (1993, Vertigo/DC Comics).

- *The Books of Magic* by Neil Gaiman, John Bolton, Scott Hampton, Charles Vess, and Paul Johnson. Fun tour of DC's magical realms that includes Death in a rare guest-starring role (1993 [collecting 1990–1991 four-issue miniseries], Vertigo/DC Comics).

- *Mr. Punch* by Neil Gaiman and Dave McKean. Semiautobiographical graphic novel and sort-of sequel to *Violent Cases* (1994, Vertigo/DC Comics).

- "One Life, Furnished in Early Moorcock" by Neil Gaiman. Semiautobiographical short story that appears in *Michael Moorcock's Elric: Tales of the White Wolf* (1994, White Wolf Inc.).

- *Sandman Midnight Theatre* by Neil Gaiman, Matt Wagner, and Teddy Kristiansen. Tale about DC's original gas-masked Sandman and a chance encounter with the imprisoned Morpheus in 1930s London (1995, Vertigo/DC Comics).

- *Maurice and I* by the Flash Girls. Terrific 1995 music CD by Lorraine Garland and Emma Bull that features two and a half songs written by Neil Gaiman, plus a song written by Alan Moore. To order, send $17 postpaid to Fabulous Records at Box 8980, Minneapolis, MN 55408. For more information, visit Web site www.player.org/pub/flash or send e-mail to FabRecords@aol.com.

- *Warning: Contains Language* by Neil Gaiman, with music by the Flash Girls and Dave McKean. Spoken-word CD on which Gaiman—who has a wonderfully expressive voice—reads aloud seven of his prose short stories (1995, DreamHaven Books).

- *The Sandman Book of Dreams* edited by Neil Gaiman and Ed Kramer. Anthology of *Sandman*-related prose short stories by various authors—though not Gaiman, who supplies only brief introductions—is far from great, but nonetheless offers an interesting look at *Sandman* in another medium (HarperPrism, 1996).

- *Death: The Time of Your Life* by Neil Gaiman, Chris Bachalo, Mark Buckingham, and Mark Pennington. Second *Sandman* spin-off featuring Death (1997, DC Comics).

- *Dustcovers: The Collected Sandman Covers, 1989-1997* by Dave McKean and Neil Gaiman. Big, beautiful art book reproducing McKean's work on glossy paper, with comments from both McKean and Gaiman (1997, Vertigo/DC Comics).

- *Smoke and Mirrors* by Neil Gaiman. Stunning collection of Gaiman's best prose short stories (Avon Books, 1998).

- *Neil Gaiman and Charles Vess' Stardust*. Prose fairy tale by Gaiman with color illustrations by Vess (1998, Vertigo/DC Comics).

- *Stardust* by Neil Gaiman. Best-selling text-only version of Gaiman's fairy tale (Avon Books, 1999).

- *The Sandman: The Dream Hunters* by Neil Gaiman and Yoshitaka Amano. Lyrical new tale of Dream told in prose form and accompanied by gorgeous Amano paintings (1999, Vertigo/DC Comics).

Sending Comments

If you have comments or suggestions about this book (especially kind ones), you can send them to me via e-mail address HyBender@aol.com. I can't respond to most messages because of time constraints, but I look at every note I receive and genuinely appreciate feedback from my readers.

If you want to reach anyone who worked on *Sandman*, you can write to the person care of DC Comics at 1700 Broadway, New York, NY 10019. Again, though, please be understanding if you don't receive a reply, as these are extremely busy people.

You can find *Sandman* on the Internet at www.dccomics.com/vertigo. Vertigo is the imprint of DC Comics that publishes such non-super-hero comics as *Sandman*, *The Dreaming*, and *Sandman Presents*. This site offers official information about current and upcoming *Sandman* projects. You can also send comments to DC/Vertigo at dcovemail@aol.com.

All the creators of *Sandman* I've spoken to are deeply grateful for the interest and support of their readers. Therefore, both for myself and on their behalf, thank you.

And sweet dreams.

I must down to the seas again,
to the vagrant gypsy life,

To the gull's way and the whale's way
where the wind's like a whetted knife;

And all I ask is a merry yarn from
a laughing fellow rover,

And quiet sleep and a sweet dream
when the long trick's over.

—JOHN MASEFIELD

To all, to each,
a fair goodnight,

And pleasing dreams,
and slumbers light.

—SIR WALTER SCOTT